PRAISE FOR

Thomas J. Cutler

AND

BROWN WATER, BLACK BERETS

"I WISH I HAD WRITTEN IT. . . . Brown-water moods, images, and sensations burst alive on these pages. Upbeat, unvarnished . . . Black Berets will stand taller."

—*Rear Admiral S. A. Swarztrauber, USN (Ret.),*
Commander Task Force Clearwater in Vietnam

"THE BEST WORK I HAVE SEEN ON THE NAVY IN VIETNAM FOR THE PERIOD I WAS THERE."

—*Admiral E. R. Zumwalt, Jr., USN (Ret.),*
Commander Naval Forces Vietnam

LT. KENNETH LOGAN MACLEOD III: In their converted, patched-up landing craft, "MacLeod's Navy" sailed into a maze of swamps and rivers—and took the battle to the VC in the "Forest of Assassins." . . .

LT. DICK GODBEHERE: He had been on several hundred patrols and more than sixty firefights, but one cool night in the Mekong Delta he would live through hell itself. . . .

A Dual Main Selection of the Military Book Club

(more . . .)

"Commander Cutler's book fulfills the highest purpose of written history by recording, forever, a forgotten corner of the Vietnam War. IT IS A VITAL REMINDER FOR ALL WHO THINK THAT NAVAL WARFARE IS FAR REMOVED FROM SHORE, THE ENEMY, AND THE THICK OF THINGS."

—*Paul Dean*, Los Angeles Times *reporter,*
Vietnam correspondent

"Cutler evokes memories of brave men in fighting boats. His account of Boatswain's Mate Williams's winning of the Medal of Honor is the best story I have read from the war."

—*Frank Uhlig, Jr., Naval War College,*
author of Vietnam: The Naval Story

BOATSWAIN'S MATE FIRST CLASS JAMES ELLIOT WILLIAMS: His stripped-down patrol boat slammed head on into a main force of the NVA. When the shooting stopped, Williams had earned the Medal of Honor. . . .

LT. COMMANDER CHARLES L. HOROWITZ: Operation Concordia I left 255 Viet Cong dead on the rivers, rice paddies and dikes. Horowitz directed fire from the top of his boat until he took a hit from an enemy AK-47. . . .

LT. DALE MEYERKORD: Senior advisor to River Assault Group 23, he was an aggressive, all-American golden boy, known for the Australian bush hat he wore into battle. In 1965, he became the first American Naval officer to die in Vietnam. . . .

BROWN WATER, BLACK BERETS

Coastal and Riverine Warfare in Vietnam

Lt. Cdr. Thomas J. Cutler, USN

POCKET BOOKS

New York   London   Toronto   Sydney   Tokyo

POCKET BOOKS, a division of Simon & Schuster Inc.
1230 Avenue of the Americas, New York, NY 10020

to Broad
typist, editor, critic, and loving wife

CONTENTS

CONTENTS

PREFACE

"When I was in Vietnam, a bunch of us de-
cided to—"
"Wait a minute. I must have misunderstood. I
thought you were in the *Navy.*"
"I am."
"Well, what were you doing in Vietnam?"

I have participated in conversations like this one many times
since returning from Vietnam, and other Navy veterans have
told me of similar experiences. Not many people realize that
the U.S. Navy and Coast Guard served in-country Vietnam
(as opposed to serving on ships off the coast) in coastal and
riverine warfare during America's involvement there. Few
books about the Vietnam War even mention this aspect; those
that do give scant coverage at best.

In proportion to the other services, the in-country participation of the U.S. Navy and Coast Guard was very small: a
peak strength of 38,000 Navy men compared with more than
half a million total American servicemen in Vietnam at the
height of the war. But those 38,000 grow to 1,842,000 when
stretched over the years of the war, and those Navy and Coast
Guard men who served do not deserve to be forgotten. My
own experiences in Vietnam were not heroic nor particularly
noteworthy, but there were thousands whose experiences are
worth telling for the benefit of future generations.

I have endeavored to record the facts and figures that tell
this unusual story, but more important, I have tried wherever possible to convey what it was like for the individuals
who participated: what they saw, what they thought, what

they felt, and, of course, what they did. To that end I interviewed veterans of the so-called "brown-water" experience and wrote chapters around those interviews. In every case, to ensure authenticity, I sent my chapter manuscripts for review by those individuals whose experiences were included. Therefore, I believe what is recorded accurately reflects the events and circumstances as those individuals saw them.

The examples rendered herein should in no way be construed as all-inclusive. Space limitations permit only the tiniest sample of the thousands of patrols, firefights, and personal experiences that go together to make up this complex story of men at war. Some readers will undoubtedly know of another individual who should have been singled out as I have done in the following pages or of an incident that would better have typified the story. But it would be impossible to record every individual's experiences or all the noteworthy incidents. I was forced to choose among many, and did so based upon their importance, as either typical or, in some cases, exceptional examples, and upon the availability of supporting documents and the individuals themselves.

The thrust of this work is primarily (and unashamedly) positive. Much has been written about the negative side of the Vietnam War, questioning the legality and morality of the U.S. intervention, or criticizing the strategy and tactics employed; it is not my intention to add to that. Conversely, I do not ignore certain negative aspects of the war where they are relevant to the account attempted here. In the course of my research I discovered (with no surprise) examples of men who lost their nerve in moments of crisis and even some who chose not to go on a particular patrol because of its high risk factor. I chose not to dwell on these few cases because I believe that if we are honest with ourselves, we can all empathize with such actions. The man who believes that he would never break under fire . . . has never been under fire.

The names given here are, in nearly every case, the real names of the individuals involved. In a few instances I have changed the names where the stories were controversial and I was unable to locate the individuals. I also changed the names of some of the Vietnamese to prevent reprisals against them by the Communist government now in power.

A total of 2,663 Navy and 7 Coast Guard men died in the war. Not all of them died on the rivers or coasts of Vietnam, but a large percentage did. For them, especially, this book had to be written.

ACKNOWLEDGMENTS

I must first acknowledge the contributions of my wife, Debby, to the writing of this book. The spouse of any writer endures certain peculiarities and hardships not associated with other habits; but in this case my wife not only endured, she contributed countless hours of work on a subject she had heretofore considered anathema. Her efforts and support were truly "above and beyond the call of duty."

In the interest of brevity I will not single out those whose names appear in the text. Their contributions should be evident. Each and every one was marvelously cooperative; I consider it an honor to have worked with people who contributed so much to their country. Many went far beyond professional assistance and have become my friends as well.

I owe a special debt to Louise Meyerkord for her willingness to share with me memories of her son. She and her former daughter-in-law, Jane Bonfanti, helped me to better understand the character of Dale Meyerkord, which would have been impossible without their willing cooperation. I acknowledge their assistance and admire their courage.

I am also indebted to Mr. Wilbur E. Garrett, editor of the *National Geographic*, who took time out of his busy schedule to review the portion of the book dealing with Dickey Chapelle.

In no particular order, I am indebted to the following people who are not mentioned in the text but who provided background information that helped me considerably: Jay Potter for helping me to understand the role of PGs; Martha Tilyard, Fred Joest, and Sea McGowen for providing much of the background on the development of the PBR; John Williams,

ACKNOWLEDGMENTS

Curt Lasley, Rod Thompson, Chuck White, John Mellin, Dave Capozzi, Gary Raymond, Joseph Heckendorn, Bill Moreo, Paul Bohn, James Walker, Bill Hedrick, and the other ''Gamewardens of Vietnam'' who talked with me about their PBR experiences; Tom Cruser and John Miller for giving me some insight into Sea Float; and Charles Gentile, who helped me better understand the Army.

At the various depositories of research material, I am particularly indebted to Ed Marolda of the Naval Historical Center in Washington, D.C.; Donna Hurley and Gloria Perdue of Nimitz Library at the U.S. Naval Academy in Annapolis, Maryland; Dennis Vetock of the United States Army Military History Institute at Carlisle Barracks in Pennsylvania; Harry Schreckengost of the Defense Technical Information Center in Alexandria, Virginia; Wilfred R. Morris, public affairs officer for the USS *Meyerkord;* and Paul Wilderson, Laurie Stearns, Paul Stillwell, Dick Hobbs, and Patty Maddocks of the U.S. Naval Institute.

Terry Charbonneau, Clarence G. Cooper, Fulton Wynn, Thomas Wooten, Stewart Harris, George Marthenze, Nguyen Pho, Alan R. Townsend, Dave Trostle, William J. Warren, Tom Rodriguez, Keith Nolan, Fritz Briggs, Charlotte Briggs, Jack Eggleston, Myra MacPherson, Cecil B. Smyth, James W. Hammond, and Garrett Cutler all contributed in miscellaneous but important ways.

Finally, there are many who offered to help, but space and time limitations prevented my accepting their kind offers. To these unsung individuals I extend a special thanks and a hope that each will be as generous when the next author comes asking for help.

BROWN WATER,
BLACK BERETS

PROLOGUE

On the night of 20 January 1969, five U.S. Navy riverine craft—one heavily armored "Tango" boat leading a column of four fiberglass river patrol boats (PBRs)—left the Mekong River and turned into the Kinh Dong Tien Canal. In the faint glow of starlight, Yeoman First Class G. H. Childress watched the barely visible wake of the boat ahead as he steered from the coxswain's flat of PBR-8137. The boats were proceeding slowly up the canal, fifty to seventy-five yards apart. Even at the slow speed, the twin diesels of the lumbering Tango boat, a converted landing-craft, growled much too loudly, promising little hope of surprising the Viet Cong.

As Childress watched the drooping fronds of nipa palm pass close aboard on the port side, the leaf tips almost within reach, a tremor of foreboding passed through him. This canal was exceptionally narrow, with many choke points so tight that even the highly maneuverable PBRs wouldn't be able to turn around. Normal operating procedure for the River Patrol Force had been to stay out on the main rivers where the PBRs could take advantage of their speed and maneuverability should they come under attack. But this was Operation Barrier Reef West, and old rules had been replaced by new tactics.

Flares popped off in the distance, signs of possible enemy activity up near the Cambodian border to the northwest. Childress, wanting to preserve his night vision for the darkness of the canal, forced himself not to look at the light just above the treetops. He glanced downward at the softly glowing dials on his instrument panel, then added several rpm to close the distance to the boat ahead by a few yards.

The night before, a similar patrol had been ambushed in this same canal; one boat had been lost and several men wounded. Childress wondered if he hadn't been a bit foolhardy in volunteering his boat for tonight's patrol. But somebody had to do it—might as well be him. At least this was an underway patrol. He hated those damn stationary am-

3

bushes in which the boats would moor to some strategic spot on a riverbank and wait for the enemy to come to them. The mosquitoes would always have a banquet, and the hours of silent waiting would wear on his nerves.

As the five boats crept along the Kinh Dong Tien Canal, no one aboard knew that farther ahead, along the banks, hands were reaching out of the tall stands of elephant grass and emptying pouches of rice-straw into the water. The ebbing tidal flow of the canal was slowly carrying the straw toward the approaching U.S. craft, where it would pass harmlessly through the churning propeller blades of the Tango boat and continue downstream to clog the jet-pump intakes of the PBRs following close behind. On the boats came, engines droning monotonously, their crewmen with eyes straining to function in the blackness and hands slippery with perspiration as they grasped the controls of boats and weapons.

Chief Quartermaster William J. Thompson, standing near Childress on PBR-8137, was the patrol officer in charge of both Childress's boat and the one just ahead. Through the "starlight scope," which amplified existing light 50,000 times to make even the coal-black banks of the canal visible in an eerie green glow, his experienced eyes carefully searched for any sign of the enemy. He particularly scrutinized breaks in the heavy vegetation where a crossing of the canal could be expeditiously made. The patrol's primary mission was to interdict any movement of enemy troops or supplies coming in from the Cambodian "sanctuary." Sometimes the enemy would move along the rivers and canals in sampans, but because the Kinh Dong Tien ran parallel to the Cambodian border, they would more likely attempt a crossing as they tried to penetrate deeper into the Mekong Delta.

Except for an occasional snake sliding into the water from the muddy bank, Chief Thompson could detect no movement. He switched off the scope and shut his eyes tightly for a moment, trying to squeeze out the remnants of green images that lingered, then opened them and peered at the faintly visible face of his watch. The time was 2157.

Another flare ignited far to the north; it was high, and some of its light briefly illuminated the canal. Childress could see that the space ahead was very narrow, and he felt the soft tickle of butterfly wings against the lining of his stomach.

All at once the night exploded into a frenzy of light and sound. The elephant grass along the starboard bank was strobing with muzzle-flashes as machine-gun and automatic-weapons fire slashed into the canal. Across the narrow waterway rockets sprayed their bright pyrotechnic trails. The sounds of heavy gunfire, furious explosions, and the disorganized shouting of angry and frightened men shattered the night. Almost immediately the PBRs and the Tango boat returned fire; illumination flares popped skyward to bathe the area in a cold white light. At the vertex of the hostile fire, bullets chewed at the fiberglass of the 8137 like piranha in a feeding frenzy. Amidst the cacophony Chief Thompson was screaming for Seawolf helicopter support.

The forward and after gunners of the 8137 poured fire into the canal banks in a continuous stream of hyphenated tracer rounds, and the boat's engineer emptied M-16 magazines at a frantic pace. Suddenly the 8137 lurched sideways as a rocket exploded in the starboard engine rea. Flames immediately emerged from the wound, and the abrupt list to starboard and the settling sensation told Childress that his boat was going down. He had hardly had time to assimilate this information when a second rocket crashed into the stricken craft, exploding against the armor-plate surrounding the coxswain's flat. Childress and Chief Thompson were thrown to the deck by this second explosion, both knocked unconscious by the impact.

When Childress regained consciousness, he became aware that his crew were still at their stations although the boat was slowly being swallowed by the canal. They seemed oblivious to the flames as well, and their weapons thundered on unabated.

Childress pulled himself to his feet and grabbed the throttles, jamming them ahead full in a desperate attempt to escape, but the rice-straw in his pumps would permit no response. Using what little way the 8137 still had on, Childress was able to drive the boat's bow into the muddy bank of the canal. He ordered the men off the boat in a rasping voice that was barely audible in the clamor. The five men scrambled across the mud bank and plunged into a drainage ditch that had been exposed by the ebbing tide, leaving the 8137 to die in the muddy waters of the Kinh Dong Tien.

The other boats had by now cleared the hostile-fire zone, and the firing had momentarily dwindled. Childress and the rest huddled in the ditch, trying to suppress their rapidly mounting terror. At that moment they had no way of knowing that the other boats were looking for a place wide enough to turn around so that they could come back to attempt a rescue. Childress tried desperately to think what he should do next, but all that came to mind was staying low in the ditch.

After a few harrowing moments, the firing picked up again, signaling the return of the other boats. Childress was elated to see PBR-770 approaching, but the situation was still not good. The enemy fire was so intense that the 770 seemed certain to meet the same fate as the 8137. As the craft neared the bank, Childress looked up and saw that tracers had turned the sky red.

At that same moment he saw, in the pallid glare from the flares, the squatting figure of Chief Boatswain's Mate Quincy Truett on the bow of the 770, returning the point-blank fire of an enemy machine gun with an M-16 rifle and calling to the stranded men in the ditch to come aboard. One of the 8137's crew clambered onto the 770; then it withdrew as the raking machine-gun fire threatened to tear the flimsy craft apart. Again the persistent PBR came in for the rescue, and again there was Chief Truett fully exposed on the bow, firing his M-16 relentlessly and calling words of encouragement to the men in the ditch. Bullets were cracking all about him, but Truett held his position, and in a moment a second man from the stranded crew was aboard. Again and again the 770 was driven off, only to return for another try. And every time Truett was on the bow, ignoring the bullets, firing and helping the man aboard.

Only Childress was left in the ditch when the 770 nosed up to the bank for the last time. While Truett provided covering fire, Childress scrambled up the scope of the ditch wall. His feet were slipping in the mud and it was all he could do to choke down his panic. As he grabbed on to the bow of the 770, Truett's reassuring hand grasped his shirt at the shoulder and helped to pull him aboard. Just as he got onto the bow, Truett's grip suddenly released. G. H.

Childress looked up in time to see an image he would never forget. Truett fell to the deck, hit in the throat by an AK-47 round.

It was cold on 3 February 1973 in Westwego, Louisiana. Some of the guests were stamping their feet as though trying to remove the cold as one would mud from encrusted shoes. The band had stopped playing, the speeches were over, and all eyes were on Geraldine Truett as she grasped the champagne bottle tightly and paused for a moment, looking up at the sharp prow towering above her.

Geri Truett had been more than ten thousand miles from her husband the night he lost his life on the Kinh Dong Tien Canal. She had no way of knowing that Chief Thompson had picked up Quincy Truett's M-16 and begun firing as Truett had, and that he too had been killed. She could not have known that the Seawolf helicopters had joined the battle as the patrol craft were withdrawing, and that one of the helos had been shot down. No one had told her that Chief Thompson had been awarded the Silver Star for his courage under fire, or that Petty Officer Childress and his crew had received Navy Commendation Medals for the way they had continued to fight when their craft was on fire and sinking. She didn't know that PBR-8137 had been resurrected from the Kinh Dong Tien by a salvage team and, unlike her husband and Chief Thompson, would fight again.

What Geri Truett did know as she looked up at the gray steel of the Navy's latest destroyer escort was that Quincy had been awarded the Navy Cross, second only to the Medal of Honor, for his bravery and selfless actions that night. She was very proud, yet so sad. She would wonder for the rest of her life what it was that drew her husband to Southeast Asia a second time, that caused him to leave her and their six children, saying, "That's where the war is; that's where I belong."

She swung the bottle hard, shattering it against the ship, and almost immediately the great gray mass began to move, seeking the sea for which it was meant. The newborn heeled over to a forty-five-degree angle as it entered the water, causing Geri to yell "Bring it back," for she had never seen a ship launched and feared that it was rolling over. The officers on the reviewing stand laughed, and Geri joined them when she saw the ship righting herself.

The band was playing again, the crowd was applauding, and for the moment the chill in the air was forgotten. Geri smiled at the Navy's newest ship, the USS *Truett* (DE-1095). Quincy would have been very proud, she thought.

1
GENESIS

The Early Advisors

A journey of a
thousand miles must
begin with a single
step.

—LAO-TZU, C. 500 B.C.

Mary Hardcastle

Mary Hardcastle stood at the door of 196 Yen Do and watched her oldest daughter, Susan, walk through the front yard toward the gate in the high wall that surrounded the house. From where she stood, Mary could see the bright morning sun glinting off the shards of glass embedded in the top of the wall to discourage any would-be intruders. The February sun was already hot, despite the early hour, and the notorious Saigon humidity was beginning to thicken the morning air. The Hardcastles' houseboy, Loc, was already at the gate waiting for Susan. He smiled as she approached, and they spoke as they waited for the bus.

What a strange and yet exciting life we lead, thought Mary, watching Susan talking with Loc. Mary found the Vietnamese to be fascinating people, and Saigon was an intriguing city bearing the embellishments and scars of a long and varied history. Chinese influence was everywhere, challenged primarily by the remnants of French colonialism and to a lesser extent by the detritus of the Japanese occupation.

Now the Americans were becoming part of Saigon's international panorama. With over 16,000 American advisors in country and a large percentage of them posted in Saigon, it was becoming uncommon not to see an American car or pedestrian, both gargantuan by Vietnamese standards, on the major streets downtown. Engineers, horticulturalists, architects, diplomats, journalists, and military men were all part of the American entourage, each playing a role in an unfolding drama that would rivet the attention of the world for a decade.

Mary and her family had landed at Saigon's Tan Son Nhut Airport more than a year before, in January 1964. Her husband, Bill, a Navy captain, had been assigned to head up the Naval Advisory Group, which was ardently struggling to assist the Vietnamese in building a potent navy of their own. Despite the growing military and political tensions at the time, the U.S. government had wanted the senior officers in the growing U.S. Military Assistance Command to bring their

11

families with them to Vietnam as a visible sign of confidence and commitment.

The Hardcastles were quartered in 196 Yen Do, about ten blocks from the center of the city. The two-story, three-bedroom house had once been the residence of one of Emperor Bao Dai's favored mistresses. Its two-foot-thick walls and the fortresslike wall surrounding the house and garden had provided both privacy and safety to the emperor during his frequent visits. Now this same protection had become a necessary part of the Hardcastles' lives.

Mary heard the government bus as it rattled down the street, and the shriek of the brakes as it stopped outside the gate. Although she couldn't see from where she stood, Mary knew that an American military policeman, armed with a sawed-off shotgun, would be leaving the bus and positioning himself to cover its front; a white-uniformed Vietnamese policeman toting a submachine gun would be covering its rear. Loc and Susan opened the gate and went outside. It had become part of the precautionary morning ritual for Loc to walk with Susan to the bus that would take her to the American dependents' high school out near Tan Son Nhut Airport. A moment later, Mary could hear the growl of the engine signaling the departure of the school bus. When it passed the open gate, she caught a glimpse of Susan looking out through the wire-mesh screens that had been placed over the windows as protection against terrorist grenades.

Mary turned and went into the house while Loc closed the outside gates. In the front hall she picked up the English-language newspaper and read the headline "PLEIKU AT-TACKED: EIGHT AMERICANS KILLED, MANY WOUNDED." The accompanying article told of a Viet Cong mortar barrage and infiltration of Camp Holloway and the nearby airstrip, which had left ten aircraft destroyed in addition to the personnel casualties at the Central Highlands base. She put down the paper and closed her eyes, exhaling wearily.

More violence, she thought. More deaths. Where was it all going? She remembered reading the accounts of the attack on Bien Hoa Airbase last October. Journalists had speculated that President Johnson would probably order U.S. planes from the Seventh Fleet to bomb North Vietnam in reprisal, as they had done following the Tonkin Gulf PT-boat attacks on U.S.

ships three months earlier, yet no bombing had been ordered. Conjecture in the press had pointed to the presidential election, just three days away, as the reason. But Mary also remembered the Christmas Eve bombing of the Brink Hotel in downtown Saigon, which housed those U.S. officers who did not have their families with them. Two had died then and fifty-eight others had been injured, but again no reprisals had been ordered. She vividly recalled the sound and concussion from the blast, more than a dozen blocks away. Previously there had also been the bombings of the movie theater, the bowling alley, and some athletic-field bleachers in the Saigon area.

The threat of violence was always present. Any significant gathering of Americans had to be considered a potential target. Several times Mary, as president of the Association of American Women, had been forced to cancel a meeting because the authorities had warned of a possible attack. Sometimes she had to cancel her trips to the station hospital in Cholon, the Chinese section of the city, where she worked as a Red Cross volunteer. Mary had learned that Saigon was no place for reckless behavior. Prudence had so far kept her and her family safe.

Not everything about Saigon was grim. Mary had sensed the excitement of the times, and she savored the kinds of experiences available only to those fortunate enough to live in a foreign country. She had grown to know the wives of Bill's high-ranking Vietnamese naval officer counterparts quite well. They had promised to teach her Vietnamese when she had first arrived, but after several weeks of valiant but less than successful efforts, they had suggested that perhaps they might teach her French instead.

The ringing of the telephone interrupted Mary's thoughts. From the slightest trace of tension in Bill's drawling voice, which only a wife would detect, she knew that something important was happening. "Mary, President Johnson is ordering all dependents to leave Vietnam," Bill said quietly; he quickly added, "It's not going to be an emergency evac. You'll have a few days to get organized."

They talked calmly about what would have to be done. Both had known that this might occur at any time. Bill had nearly a year left of his tour before he would be able to rejoin his family. Mary would have to establish a new home, put the children into new schools in the middle of a school year, and somehow find the patience and optimism to wait for her husband to return from a war zone.

Within a week Mary and the children would leave Saigon.

"Support Any Friend, Oppose Any Foe"

The formal involvement of U.S. military personnel in Vietnam had begun in August 1950, when the first contingent of the U.S. Military Assistance Advisory Group (MAAG) arrived in Saigon to set up shop. The MAAG consisted of a joint team of Army, Air Force, and Navy personnel; its purpose was to provide the military supplies necessary to prevent the expansion of communism in Indochina. Because the supplies were turned over directly to the French Expeditionary Corps, the MAAG members functioned in the early days primarily as a logistical accounting group with no real advisory role. The French adamantly refused to allow the Americans in the MAAG to provide any training assistance to either themselves or their protégé, the Vietnamese National Army. The Vietnamese Navy, such as it was, was under the direct command of a French officer, and by 1952 reports from American naval officers in the MAAG were taking a pessimistic view of French claims to have established a Vietnamese Navy that would someday be able to function independently. This "navy" consisted of approximately four hundred sailors serving under French officers and petty officers in the river forces, and a functioning training apparatus was nearly nonexistent.

American impotence in the advisory role continued throughout the next three and a half years, while the French and their Vietnamese allies fought against the determined forces of Ho Chi Minh and his Communist Viet Minh troops. Then on 8 May 1954 the Viet Minh overran the key French position at Dien Bien Phu after a spectacular set-piece siege that captured the attention of the world and proved the death knell for French military influence in Indochina.

According to the Geneva agreement, concluded after Dien

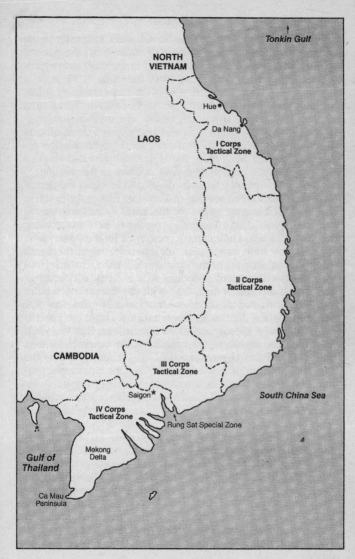

South Vietnam

Bien Phu on 20 July 1954, the French were to remain in the southern half of the now divided Vietnam until the general elections, to take place in July 1956. In an effort to synchronize American and French advisory functions in Vietnam, a Training Relations Instruction Mission was created on 3 December 1954 consisting of one Navy, one Air Force, and three Army officers from each nation. The mission grew rapidly (having thirty-three U.S. and seventy-six French officers three months later), but American naval representation remained low. By May 1955, the U.S. contingent had reached 155, yet there were only two naval officers in the mission.

During this period, tensions developed between the Americans and the French serving in Vietnam. Part of the problem lay in disagreements over how the advisory mission was to be accomplished, but these disagreements were exacerbated by President Ngo Dinh Diem's preference for the Americans. The French were humiliated, for example, when the South Vietnamese Army abruptly converted its uniforms from French-style to a more American type and began saluting as the Americans did, rather than with the French open-palm method. Too, American advisors apparently made no real effort to conceal their eagerness to take over from the French.

As July 1956 approached, it became evident that President Diem had no intention of conducting the general elections called for in the Geneva Accords. He recognized that the larger population of North Vietnam and the charismatic image of Ho Chi Minh as a nationalist hero in his struggles against the Japanese and French would probably have ensured a Communist victory. The United States indirectly supported his decision; surprisingly, China and the Soviet Union did not press for the elections. French presence in Vietnam was supposed to continue until the elections, but with that milestone removed, the question of a continued presence remained open. President Diem closed it on 26 February 1956 by asking the French to withdraw their forces completely.

Command of the Vietnamese Navy had been turned over to the Vietnamese in July 1955. The French command in Vietnam was disestablished on 26 April 1956, and two days later the Training Relations Instruction Mission was closed down.

With the departure of French military forces from Indochina, the United States stepped in to fill the void of anti-Communist, free-world strength, a role that the French had been playing simultaneously with that of stubborn colonialists. This duality of French objectives, opposing communism and yet preserving colonial interests, had long been a sore point for the Truman and Eisenhower administrations, who saw the former as so important that they, by association, were forced to support the latter. The departure of the French had left the United States able to assume the anti-Communist role without the embarrassment of colonial objectives. Secretary of State John Foster Dulles said in the fall of 1956: "We have a clean base there now, without a taint of colonialism. Dien Bien Phu was a blessing in disguise."

In the years immediately following the French departure, the American advisory commitment to Vietnam remained small. Despite the U.S. refusal to sign the Geneva Accords in 1954, official government policy restricted the number of advisors to the 342-man limit imposed by the accords. When the French were in the final stages of withdrawal in 1956, the South Vietnamese government requested increased U.S. support, arguing that replacing the departing French with American advisors would be in keeping with the spirit of Geneva. Still concerned about the image of adhering to the limit, however, the U.S. administration sent a 350-man increase to Vietnam not as an addition to the MAAG, but under the new auspices of a Temporary Equipment Recovery Mission. The purpose of this augmentation was to help the Vietnamese cope with the logistical nightmare of managing, maintaining, and reducing the huge inventory of American-supplied equipment that France was leaving behind in Indochina; it was argued that much of the equipment would be abandoned without the mission. The Geneva-created International Control Commission, composed of representatives from Canada, Poland, and India, approved the increase when assured that the overall effect would be to reduce the amount of military equipment in Vietnam. Instructions given to members of the mission by the U.S. State Department included provisions for training the Vietnamese in matters relating to the recovery and maintenance of the equipment, but this was supposed to be subordinate to the primary task of recovering designated quantities of the abandoned equipment. The chief of the

MAAG was, however, empowered to transfer men between the mission and the MAAG as he deemed necessary, and this made the dividing line obscure at best.

In the meantime, Communist insurgent activity was gradually gaining momentum. In June 1957, a MAAG report cited a "slight but notable increase" in the Communist-inspired violence in South Vietnam. In one month in the fall of that same year, six village chiefs were reported killed; more than twenty other local government officials had been killed, wounded, or kidnapped. Activity in the Mekong Delta in particular was stepped up. Curiously, a Viet Cong document captured years later by U.S. forces referred to 1957–58 as a period of low activity when full-time military units "became idle and . . . their main elements could not develop but deteriorated spiritually as well as organizationally."

By the end of 1958, the Communists had consolidated their power in North Vietnam and began diverting their attention to the South. New directions from Hanoi to insurgents in the South called for increases in armed activities, and infiltration routes into the South through Laos were improved. By the end of 1959 the monthly assassination rate had doubled; well over a hundred ambushes and attacks on government posts occurred in the last half of the year alone.

Performance of the South Vietnamese armed forces was less than spectacular during this period. In September a large South Vietnamese force traveling in sampans and launches through a flooded marshland in Kien Phong Province near the Cambodian border was attacked by an enemy contingent less than a quarter its size. Most of the government force jumped overboard in panic, and the resultant casualties were inordinately high considering the numbers involved. Two weeks later a forty-five-man government force surrendered to a much smaller Viet Cong group in the same province. Similar incidents elsewhere in the country reinforced a growing pessimism among American advisors.

In an attempt to counter the poor performance of the South Vietnamese troops, Lieutenant General Samuel T. Williams, then chief of the MAAG, had sent a letter to Admiral Harry D. Felt, Commander in Chief, Pacific (CINCPAC), requesting a revocation of the longstanding restriction against allowing U.S. advisors to accompany their Vietnamese counterparts on combat missions. General Williams believed that the South Vietnamese failures resulted from a lack of proper planning and aggressiveness, and he expected the presence of U.S. advisors to at least partially correct those problems. On 25 May 1959 Admiral Felt approved the request: American advisors were permitted to go along on operational missions provided that they themselves not actively participate in actual combat. This caveat of nonparticipation often proved unrealistic when advisors found themselves under fire, and there were increasing instances of active participation by the Americans from that time onward.

Despite this significant change in policy, the poor performance continued into the following year, and the situation deteriorated. An intelligence estimate issued in August 1960 stated that Viet Cong activities were becoming more widespread and intense, and that support for the insurgents among the general populace seemed to be increasing. Further, it stated that senior North Vietnamese cadres and military supplies were entering South Vietnam from infiltration trails through Laos and Cambodia and by junk along the eastern coastline.

It was against this backdrop of pessimism and alarm that John F. Kennedy stepped to the podium on the Capital steps and took the oath of office as president in January 1961. The ringing words of his inaugural address, though not specifically addressed to the situation in South Vietnam, marked a new level of commitment to the struggle there:

> Let every nation know, whether it wishes us well or ill, that we shall pay any price, bear any burden, meet any hardship, support any friend, oppose any foe, in order to assure the survival and the success of liberty. . . . To those new states whom we welcome to the ranks of the free, we pledge our words that one form of colonial control shall not have passed away merely to be replaced by a far greater iron tyranny. . . . To those peoples in the huts and villages across the globe struggling to break the bonds of mass misery, we pledge our best efforts to help them help themselves, for whatever period is required.

Almost immediately upon taking office, President Kennedy began grappling with the situation in Indochina. First Laos, then Vietnam became important considerations of his administration, although events in other parts of the world such as Cuba and Berlin continually competed for his attention. In May of the first year he sent his vice president, Lyndon Johnson, to Saigon, the capital city of South Vietnam, to confer with President Diem. The discussions between Johnson and Diem centered on the enlargement of the U.S. commitment to South Vietnam and included some specific talk about strengthening the Vietnamese coastal patrol force.

For quite some time the Communists had been suspected of bringing supplies into South Vietnam from the sea. The Vietnamese Navy had begun patrolling the coastal waters in junks, the traditional Oriental sailing vessels, and it was this Junk Force, as it was called, that would need considerable expansion if it were to have any significant success in interdicting the flow of Communist supplies. At a National Security Council meeting on 29 April 1961, President Kennedy approved the training of Vietnamese junk crews in Vietnam or at U.S. bases by U.S. Navy personnel.

Vice President Johnson's proposal to strengthen the Junk Force was endorsed and expanded, to include controlling the inland waterways as well, by General Maxwell Taylor, President Kennedy's personal military advisor, who had gone to Vietnam in October at the president's request to assess the military situation there. General Taylor sent a cablegram to the president proposing an extensive expansion of U.S. commitment, in which he said: "The U.S. Government will assist the GVN [Government of Vietnam] in effecting surveillance and control over the coastal waters and inland waterways, furnishing such advisors, operating personnel and small crafts as may be necessary for quick and effective operations."

On 11 November 1961, Secretary of State Dean Rusk and Secretary of Defense Robert McNamara sent a joint memorandum to the president outlining a series of recommendations and priorities for coping with the Vietnam situation. Among the specific proposals listed as immediate in nature was a call, similar in wording to General Taylor's message, for providing the small craft, "uniformed advisers and operating personnel'' as necessary to exercise control over the coastal waters and inland waterways.

In response to these recommendations from his top advisors, President Kennedy significantly enlarged the U.S. military effort in Vietnam. Although stopping short of sending combat troops, which had also been repeatedly recommended to him, he substantially increased the number of American advisors over the three years of his administration. By the end of 1961, the number had quadrupled to exceed 3,000; by mid-1962 there were 12,000; and by the end of 1963 the total passed 16,000. While most of these additional advisors were not naval personnel, President Kennedy, himself a naval officer in World War II, did not overlook the importance of a naval role in Vietnam. Lyndon Johnson wrote of the post-1961 period in his memoirs: "We increased assistance to the Vietnamese Navy to enable it to protect the coast against infiltration from the North and to patrol the inland waterways used extensively by the Viet Cong.''

With this increased support from the United States, the Vietnamese Navy (VNN) grew by leaps and bounds between 1961 and 1965. Three task-oriented forces had been established: the Sea Force, the River Force, and the Junk Force. The Sea Force, which consisted of the larger, more conventional coastal craft, grew from twenty-one to forty-eight ships during this period. The River Force, designed primarily for transporting troops along the waterways, increased its assets from five River Assault Groups consisting of approximately one hundred boats to seven RAGs with a total inventory in excess of 150 boats. The Junk Force grew to 644 craft by 1965. Total VNN personnel expanded from three thousand in 1961 to more than eight thousand in 1965.

The number of American naval advisors grew correspondingly from 53 in the MAAG in 1961 to 235 in the Naval Advisory Group component of MACV by the beginning of 1965. (MAAG was absorbed into the newly formed MACV—Military Assistance Command Vietnam—in May 1965.) As the number of advisors increased, more began to advise at the unit level. Increasingly, advisors appeared on Sea Force ships, with the River Assault Groups, and aboard junks. The die was cast: the American Navy had begun its coastal and riverine involvement in Vietnam.

CHNAVADVGRU

Captain William Hardcastle, USN, hung up the phone and leaned back in his chair facing the map of the two Vietnams on the wall to his left. He stared at the black letters on the blue part of the map that spelled "Gulf of Tonkin," knowing that a three-carrier task force was steaming in the vicinity of the "k," awaiting the return of nearly fifty strike aircraft that had been ordered to attack a North Vietnamese Army camp near Dong Hoi, sixty miles north of the seventeenth parallel. Operation Flaming Dart was under way by order of the president as a retaliation for the attack on Pleiku. It was 7 February 1965.

The captain was awed by how far things had come since his arrival in Vietnam. When he had received the orders to go to Vietnam as chief, Naval Advisory Group (CHNAVADVGRU), he had been less than pleased. It seemed at the time that Vietnam, while certainly in the news, was never going to amount to much in a military sense. Now, a little more than a year later, he was no longer seeing Vietnam as a mere outpost of the American military. It had become the focus of the U.S. effort to restrain the spread of communism. With each passing day he could see the American role becoming less and less advisory and more and more actively combative. The tempo had been increasing for some time. Prior to Captain Hardcastle's arrival in Vietnam, President Diem's nine-year rule had ended in a coup and his subsequent execution on 1 November 1963. Within three weeks, President Kennedy had died from an assassin's bullet. In the months that followed, South Vietnam was in near chaos as the generals who had engineered the coup struggled among themselves to consolidate their power. In 1964 the government changed seven times. The Hanoi Politburo seized upon the turmoil and stepped up its own efforts. An intelligence report locked in the captain's safe told of two North Vietnamese Army (NVA) divisions that had moved into South Vietnam in the autumn of 1964. Viet Cong raids and ambushes had increased markedly in the central highlands, the Mekong Delta, the provinces around Saigon, and Quang Nam province around the northern city of Da Nang. In the previous year, more than

1,500 South Vietnamese government officials had been killed or abducted. Nearly 10,000 other people, considered to contribute to the stability of the government, similarly fell victim to the Viet Cong.

But perhaps most telling of all, as far as Captain Hardcastle was concerned, was what he had witnessed while attending a meeting of the top brass with Secretary of Defense McNamara during one of the latter's visits to Vietnam. He had seated himself at the table in MACV headquarters and noted that he was the only officer there who was not of flag or general rank; he had looked about and counted twenty-six stars on the collars of the Army and Air Force generals in an impressive constellation of American power. His presence, with an eagle on his collar, symbolized the proportionately lesser involvement of the U.S. Navy at that time. Secretary McNamara had seated himself at the head of the table next to MACV commander General William C. Westmoreland, and in a dramatic gesture he removed his checkbook from his pocket and placed it on the table in front of the general. "Westy," Secretary McNamara had said, "tell me what you need to win this one."

Now the tempo was once again accelerating. There had been high-level talk about sending American combat troops to South Vietnam. Captain Phil Bucklew, after a fact-finding trip to Vietnam a year earlier, had recommended at that time that the Navy take an active part in the war by augmenting the coastal patrol efforts of the Vietnamese Navy and possibly by deploying forces into the waterways of the Mekong Delta to stop the Communist infiltration. Bombers were pounding the North. An American naval officer was a prisoner of war in Hanoi. And now American dependents had been ordered to evacuate.

His eyes moved down the map on the wall and traced the pattern of pins that protruded from South Vietnam. These symbolized his advisors, who were living side by side with their Vietnamese counterparts. Some were assigned to the ships of the VNN seagoing forces. Others were patrolling the rivers of the Mekong Delta in converted World War II landing craft as advisors to the River Assault Groups. Some lived at remote coastal bases in thatched huts with members of the Vietnamese Junk Force. Still others were helping to develop curricula at the naval schools at Nha Trang, and a substantial number were posted in Saigon to assist at the shipyard or at VNN headquarters.

The Navy's Bureau of Personnel had sent him top people in terms of abilities and motivation, but with the exception of the officers and men working at the shipyard and at the naval schools, few had experience to bring to their new roles as advisors. These men had come from a navy of global dimensions to give advice and motivation to a fledgling navy whose largest vessel would be considered a small craft in the United States. When America had first become involved in Southeast Asia, no coastal or riverine patrol craft had been in the Navy's inventory, no official doctrine existed for either kind of warfare, and even the unofficial literature appearing in Navy-oriented periodicals and journals reflected a paucity of interest in these operations. A study of American naval history would tell that there was certainly plenty of precedent—coastal and riverine warfare had played significant roles in the Revolution, the War of 1812, the Mexican War, the Seminole and Creek Wars in the Florida Everglades (1835–42), the Civil War, and the Yangtze River patrols in pre–World War II China—but the record was not a continuous one. "Brown-water warfare" had been used time and again, but on every occasion, once the necessity had passed, these capabilities were shelved and the Navy returned to "blue-water" operations. The only link between small-craft operations conducted in the past and these modern-day sailors was a history book.

Despite this limitation, Captain Hardcastle felt certain that his men were helping the Vietnamese. Their presence at the operational level, sharing the hard work and danger with the VNN officers and men, was tangible evidence of the U.S. commitment to South Vietnam. The Americans' inherent enthusiasm and impatience served as a counterbalance to the more leisurely behavior of the Vietnamese. And the Americans did have knowledge of mechanical devices, preventive maintenance, and administrative procedures that they could share with their predominantly agrarian counterparts.

They were making progress—never fast enough for the people in Washington who wanted a quick end to the war, but progress nonetheless. Few Vietnamese had held positions of responsibility during the years of French and Japanese domination, so it sometimes took a while for the advisors to get their message across. Captain Hardcastle had once told an unreceptive visitor from Washington, "We're capable of furnishing more advice and materials than the Vietnamese can really absorb." But by employing patience and taking care to get Vietnamese agreement on a goal before going ahead, it was often amazing what could be accomplished.

Some of these American advisors had to surmount personal obstacles. Those with a rural background had an easier time of it than those with an urban one, but all had come from an America technologically more advanced than this struggling Southeast Asian nation, and all therefore faced frustration when dealing with the majority of the Vietnamese. It was not uncommon for an American advisor to ask his Vietnamese counterpart about the status of a boat's engine and receive the reply "Engine number one, *Dai-uy,*" which translates to "The engine is running fine, Lieutenant." The next day the same advisor might ask the same question, only to find that the answer was "Engine number ten, *Dai-uy,*" meaning it was no longer working. The Vietnamese typically referred to everything as either "number one" or "number ten." Nothing was ever "number three" or "number seven"; it was either running or it wasn't. There was rarely an appreciation of the significance of a "knock" or a "ping," and the concept of preventive maintenance, as opposed to corrective maintenance, was difficult for the agrarian Vietnamese, predominantly rice farmers who worked the paddies with the help of water buffalo. Machines simply had not been a traditional part of their lives as they had for the Americans.

Not all of the problems encountered arose from cultural differences. The American advisors had to spend a significant portion of their short tours learning their job before they could do it. The Vietnamese found it difficult to take seriously the advisors who were constantly coming and going: some of the Vietnamese Navy men had been at their jobs for a decade, while the Americans were typically there to advise for only a year. The resulting pressures could be exacerbated by an advisor whose impatience to see tangible results caused resentment among the Vietnamese.

Captain Hardcastle believed that some of his naval advisors

were a bit too aggressive for their own good. He thought about Lieutenant Dale Meyerkord, down with one of the River Assault Groups in the Delta. Dale was an outstanding advisor who had been extremely effective in getting his VNN counterparts to go on the offensive, but his reputation for aggressiveness was a constant source of worry to the captain. And just a few weeks earlier, the captain had spoken with Lieutenant Jim Vincent, one of his Junk Force advisors, warning Jim to "stop acting like Robin Hood." Jim was supposed to be advising the Vietnamese in coastal patrol techniques, but he had been going on dangerous commandolike raids into Viet Cong strongholds ashore. Jim had explained that he wanted the junkmen and villagers to know that "the night no longer belonged to the VC [Viet Cong]"—not if there was a Junk Division nearby. He wanted the VC to come to the same conclusion.

The captain, himself a veteran of combat action in World War II and Korea, respected these young men, but he also worried that in their zeal, caution might be overlooked. He did not want to lose any of these fine officers. Because these dedicated men often neglected their health in their quest for achievement, they were all encouraged and occasionally ordered to go back to Saigon for a breather and for much-needed medical attention. The primitive living conditions with few of the conveniences that most Americans take for granted, such as running water and sewage disposal, resulted in cases of tapeworms, diarrhea, dengue fever, or other maladies. Many advisors suffered severe weight loss during their times in the field. Captain Hardcastle visited every location where he had advisors at least once a month to monitor the conditions, knowing that because of their conscientiousness, some of these men would keep putting off their recuperative trips to Saigon. There was always one more thing to do.

On his map, one pin stuck in an island off the coast near the Cambodian border represented Lieutenant Wes Hoch, one of the more colorful advisors. Wes had once obtained films from Walt Disney to show the Vietnamese people in the villages on Phu Quoc Island and the Ca Mau Peninsula, typically Viet Cong-held areas. In one of his reports back to Saigon, Wes wrote that the villagers enjoyed seeing the films projected on the white sheet that had been hung for a screen, and added that the Viet Cong also enjoyed watching the movies from the other side of the sheet. Captain Hardcastle had not doubted the latter statement.

On one of his trips to Saigon, Wes spent some time at the MACV dental clinic observing the dentists at work, asking a lot of questions and making a nuisance of himself. He returned to Phu Quoc with some dental equipment that he had managed to acquire and set up a clinic for the villagers. With the help of a local villager midwife and a Navy hospital corpsman, he filled and pulled teeth and provided basic medical care.

Phu Quoc Island's residents were a mixture of Catholics and Buddhists. In trying to get to know the people better, Wes learned from the Buddhist fishermen that they were envious of the bell that the Catholic mission had received from an American Catholic organization. Wes made another trip to Saigon, somehow came up with a 600-pound concrete statue of Buddha, and managed to get it flown down to Duong Dong Airport on Phu Quoc. From there, he loaded it on a VNN junk and delivered it to An Thoi on the southern tip of the island. Wes thus became something of a local hero to the Buddhist residents of the island.

Captain Hardcastle rose from his chair and walked over to his map. He reached out and touched one of the pins. Good people, he thought. I've got good people out there, and with the right amount of time we're going to help the South Vietnamese win this war.

His fingers traveled across the surface of the map, coming to rest on Pleiku, and he paused there for a moment, wondering just how much time was left.

Sat Cong

Georgette Louise Meyer Chapelle, or "Dickey," as she preferred to be called, removed the Australian bush hat with the two sets of paratrooper wings, revealing long blond hair that had been gathered into a bun. She blotted the perspiration from her forehead with the sleeve of her green and brown camouflage shirt and said loudly, "Well, Lieutenant, do you think we could maybe get the heat turned up in this place?"

Lieutenant James Monroe Vincent stared at her in fascination as she removed the camera straps from her shoulders, but he didn't answer.

The heat in the thatched-reed hut was stifling, yet cooler than in the sun outside. December was always hot in the tiny village of Tiem Ton, near the mouth of the Ham Luong River, sixty miles south of Saigon.

As Dicky continued to unpack her gear, Jim sat on the wooden-slat bed, still staring disbelievingly at her.

"I know," Dickey said, again in the too-loud voice. "You want to know what a woman is doing here in the Mekong Delta dressed like G.I. Joe." She pushed the plastic-framed glasses back up her nose with her index finger. "I'm a correspondent, and I don't believe you can write a good front-line story by reading official government handouts. They usually have about the same authenticity as a patent-medicine ad. I've got to eyeball my stories or I don't write them."

She went on to tell him that she was there to cover what the Navy was doing in Vietnam and that she expected the story to appear in *National Geographic* magazine. What she didn't tell him was that twenty years before, she had photographed the landings at Iwo Jima and Okinawa, and had since covered the various wars and crises in Korea, Cuba, Quemoy, India, Algeria, Lebanon, Laos, and the Dominican Republic. She had been captured, interrogated, and held in solitary confinement for six weeks while trying to smuggle penicillin to Hungarian freedom fighters. And she had earned those paratrooper wings on her bush hat by jumping into battle with U.S. and Vietnamese paratroopers. Her main interest had always been to cover what she termed "cutting-edge forces."

"So tell me what it is you do here, Lieutenant," Dickey said as she loaded film into one of her cameras.

Jim tucked his feet up so that he was sitting cross-legged on the bare wooden boards of the bed. He was ursine, with an engaging smile that made crescents of his eyes. "There are four of us Americans here, and we serve on roving duty as advisors to all eight junk divisions of the Third Coastal District. The Vietnamese coastline has been divided into four districts and we've got Third; basically, the Mekong Delta and about a hundred miles north.''

"The Vietnamese are actually using these sailing junks for military operations?'' Dickey asked.

"Absolutely. They may not seem too formidable, but they're not very conspicuous out there among all the fishing junks and they're able to get in close to the coast if they need to. Some of the junks in other coastal districts only have sails, but ours all have engines. The junk division's main job is to patrol the coastal waters and rivermouths checking traffic to be sure it's not serving the Viet Cong.''

"When I was in Saigon doing background work, I was told that the 'junkies' conducted raids on shore too. Is that true?''

"Sure, a lot of those stories are true. We have to make land raids for security reasons. A lot of the bases are what you might call 'behind enemy lines.' ''

Dickey looked out through the open doorway at the village huts so close to the junk-base perimeter and nodded sympathetically.

"There is a kind of Vietnamese commando group attached to the Junk Force called *Biet Hai* who specialize in raids ashore, to keep the local VC off balance,'' Jim continued. "But the main mission of the Junk Force is coastal patrol— stopping the flow of supplies from North Vietnam and interdicting the movement of VC cadre.''

Dickey pulled a notepad from an olive-drab bag. "I see you're wearing the black 'pajamas' I keep hearing about. Back in Saigon they call you all 'the black-pajama navy.' Is that the uniform of the Junk Force?''

"No, not really.'' Jim ran his hand against the grain of his crew-cut. "This organization is not really part of the Vietnamese armed forces—although there's a move on right now to assimilate it into the Navy. Because it started out as paramilitary, there were no uniforms, just black berets. These 'pajamas' are the typical peasant garb of Vietnam, so that's why you see a lot of the Junk Force sailors wearing them. They're both inexpensive and functional.''

Dickey scratched a few notes and then put the pad and pen down. "So when can we go on patrol?''

"Tomorrow, if you like.''

"Great.''

"How long are you planning to stay?"

"About a week to ten days."

Jim got to his feet. "It'll be dark before too long. I've got to go check the perimeter defenses. Want to go along?" He was startled when Dickey said yes.

They emerged from the straw-covered hut and set off across the compound. Clouds of mosquitoes hovered in aerial ambush along the way. Dickey noted that the six-foot-high mud walls, with their gun-ports, enclosed the compound in an equilateral triangle. Each of the three walls was less than two hundred feet long. Except for a wooden guard tower, the few buildings were all one-story, straw-covered huts.

They left the compound and moved cautiously through the barbed tanglefoot and concertina wire. Jim pointed out Claymore mine emplacements and tripwires attached to flares that would warn of approaching Viet Cong forces. He told Dickey that sometimes dogs would trip the wires, and that it was not uncommon in this climate for the wires to rust through and set themselves off. "Nonetheless," he concluded, "if you see any flares popping off in the middle of the night, assume it's 'Victor Charlie' first and we'll worry about canines and rust later." His tone was emphatic but not theatrical. Dickey had seen enough combat to know the difference between an accurate tactical assessment and the "blood and guts" talk of behind-the-lines glory-hunters.

They returned to the fortresslike compound, and after Jim inspected a mortar pit near its center, he paused for a moment. The squadrons of mosquitoes were no longer visible in the dusk, but they were audible as they maneuvered about their targets' heads. "I just want you to know," he said quietly, "that I'm impressed."

"By what?"

"By the fact that you seem to want to really understand what's going on here." He looked straight at her. "Too many of these so-called journalists want to come here, stay a few hours, grab a quick story, and get out. A lot of times I tell 'em, 'Stay around for a few days, get a feel for what's going on. Then you'll know what kind of questions to ask.' But they rarely do. They've usually got somewhere else to be. The truth of the matter is that they're leery of spending the night in a combat situation without the comfort of knowing the language and people. Then they rationalize their premature departure. But I believe you when you say you want to 'eyeball' a story before you write it. You're willing to stick around for a while, go out on patrol, walk the perimeter with me. I like that."

They started walking again, headed for an evening meal of fish and rice.

The next morning Dickey, Jim and *Trung-uy* (Lieutenant [j.g.]) Bong, the Junk Division's commanding officer, shared coffee prepared over a bed of charcoal in a small box lined with sand and then made their way down to the canal bank where the junks were beached. The mud sucked at their boots as they walked. Jim was clad in green jungle fatigues and a black beret with the silver Junk Force insignia pinned to it. His pockets bulged with hand grenades, and he wore a snub-nosed .38 at his hip; he carried a carbine that had once been an M-1 but had been converted to an automatic M-2 by an Army friend, which Jim had further modified with a folding stock.

They arrived just in time to see one of the junks sliding silently down the canal. It was long, low, and narrow with a low superstructure, no more than three feet high, projecting amidships. Two masts, the after one taller than the forward, supported ribbed sails the reddish-brown color of dried blood, Dickey thought. The sailors on deck were clad in a variety of clothing; some had black berets. None wore shoes.

The remaining junks along the beach were a mixture of the sailing variety she had just seen and another more modern type. The latter, called command junks or *chu lucs,* were black-hulled with a gray superstructure and no sailing masts, only a long whip antenna and a small cross-mast large enough to support a flag. Two things caught Dickey's eye: a .30-caliber machine gun was mounted prominently up forward; and on the highest part of the bow there was an area painted red to contrast with the black hull, and on each side a white oval with a black oval centered inside, looking very much like a pair of Oriental eyes.

"Why do the junks have those eyes painted on their bows?" Dickey asked as she fired her camera in their direction.

"To ward off demons," Jim replied matter-of-factly.

While they were loading their gear on board one of the *chu lucs,* Jim explained that the Junk Force, *Hai Thuyen* in Vietnamese, had been created in 1960 as a paramilitary force manned by civilian irregulars and led by the Vietnamese Navy. The original idea had been to buy the junks from local Vietnamese fishermen, but the fishermen balked, so the U.S. government contracted private South Vietnamese shipyards to build the vessels. Because of the rush job, however, a combination of unskilled labor and green sisao wood had produced inferior vessels. By the early part of 1964 nearly one third of them were laid up.

"Come on," Jim said abruptly, and led her along the canal bank to a junk that had been pulled completely out of the water. He pointed to the underside of the hull, which was riddled with holes, each about the size of a little finger. "Those holes," he said, "are the result of the wood-boring teredo worm. They drill their way into the junks until they make Swiss cheese out of the hull. We've probably lost more junks to that damn worm than we have to the VC!"

As they headed back, Jim explained to her how Captain Hardcastle, up in Saigon, had come up with a new kind of junk, called the *Yabuta* after a Japanese technician at the Saigon shipyard who had designed it. Lacking sails, these diesel-powered fifty-seven-foot-long vessels were functionally superior to the fishing hulls that had been used previously. Their greatest advantage was a fiberglass coating over the wooden hull that kept the teredo worms out. Taking particular pains to involve the Vietnamese in the planning and execution of the project, Captain Hardcastle had created an assembly-line method of manufacturing the junks at the rate of about one every ten days to two weeks, and more and more of them were joining the force all the time.

"If you don't have *Yabutas,*" Jim explained, "these other junks have to be pulled from the water every three months to have their hulls scraped. After scraping, we 'torch' the bottom to kill the worms, then plug the holes with bamboo slivers, and, finally, apply a coat of resin. Too often, though, the Vietnamese wait beyond the three-month interval and the damage becomes too severe."

An hour later they were leaving the mouth of the Ham Luong, and the deep blue of the South China Sea stretched before them. As they left the placid waters of the Mekong system and plunged into the open sea, the morning breeze freshened and blew with near-gale strength. Dickey drank in the breeze as if it were water on the desert—a welcome change from the oppressive heat and humidity they had left behind in Tiem Ton. She looked about and began to appreciate the magnitude of the Junk Force's task: there were vessels nearly everywhere she looked. Some were large, some small; some with the ribbed Oriental sails that reminded her of the huge fin on the back of a marlin, some sailless and coughing up clouds of bluish smoke as they pushed their way through the whitecaps; some carried fishermen tossing and hauling nets, while others were hauling sacks probably filled with rice. She moved forward a little unsteadily along the pitching deck and sat next to Jim. "How do you decide which ones to challenge?" she asked, sweeping one arm across the panorama of vessels.

"A lot of it's gut feeling," Jim replied. "But there are clues sometimes." He was nearly shouting to make his voice carry over the wind. "Take, for instance, those eyes painted on the bows. They're done differently in different areas. If we see a sampan or junk with eyes that are a different shape and color scheme from the local ones, then we know the boat is out of its home waters. May or may not mean anything, but it's worth a check." He nodded in the direction of a Vietnamese naval officer back on the fantail. *"Trung-uy* Bong there is good at spotting the differences and can even tell where they're from a lot of the time."

They watched a moderately large fishing junk pass close aboard, the eye on the port bow clearly visible. Dickey wondered if it could see any demons among the frothing whitecaps. "Local?" she asked.

Jim nodded.

A young boy struggling with a net on the junk's fantail stopped long enough to smile and wave in their direction. Jim returned the smile and the wave, and said, "One time we decided to search one of them because Bong saw a young man on board spit in our direction. I commented that maybe he just had to spit, but the Vietnamese put a lot of importance on symbolism, so we searched the boat."

"What did you find?"

"Nothing definite, but they were carrying an awful lot of

rice. Seemed possible they were making a delivery to the local VC battalion. And the spitter kept giving us such an ugly stare while we were searching, so we turned 'em in to the local police for more questioning and checking out."

Dickey flipped through her pad of notes. "According to what I was told in Saigon, during one six-month period the Junk Force checked over 122,000 junks and approximately a half million people. Something around 1,300 suspects were turned over to the South Vietnamese police and intelligence agencies for interrogation. Those are impressive statistics, but I can't seem to get much information on how much contraband has been recovered, or how many of those suspects turned out to be actual infiltrators from the North."

"I don't think many, actually." He wasn't looking at her as he spoke; his eyes were carefully scanning the sea ahead watching for any suspicious activity among the craft plying the turbulent waters. "There's some argument as to how much the North Vietnamese are using the coastal waters to infiltrate and send supplies. Some think a lot, others think very little, but few disagree that the Junk Force is a deterrent. I personally think that because of these junk patrols, the North Vietnamese are sending very little in this way. I think there's a lot coming in down through the jungles and across the Laotian and Cambodian borders, though."

A Vietnamese sailor squeezed past them to check the pedestal-mounted machine gun forward. He was shirtless, and as he passed, Dickey noted the words "SAT CONG," enclosed in a rectangle, tattooed on his chest. "What does that tattoo mean?" she asked.

"Kill Communists," Jim answered. "It's the force's way of showing their esprit de corps. Most of the Junk Force sailors have it. It was once explained to me that the original Junk Force sailors came from refugee camps near Da Nang, and they were the people who had fled North Vietnam after partitioning in 1954. Since they had left their homes in North Vietnam because of the Communists, they were pretty solidly anti-Communist, so they got the tattoos." He paused to look through binoculars at a small craft off the port bow, then turned and said something in Vietnamese to the VNN officer astern. "But I've also been told that the tattoo was mandatory for all members of the Junk Force, so I'm not so sure how much of a reflection of loyalty it actually is with some junkmen. Either way, it goes badly for them if they're ever captured by the VC. Some have had their tattoos carved off before they were killed. Nevertheless, it's our motto and we display it on some of our buildings. We even have a Junk Force flag with it, and we commonly use it as a toast when drinking."

Dickey stared at the sailor's tattoo until she realized that he was looking back at her, an embarrassed smile on his painfully thin face.

The junk began closing in on the small craft Jim had been watching before.

"Are we going alongside that one?" asked Dickey.

"Yes," Jim answered, his eyes never leaving the boat. "I don't like the looks of that tarpaulin on the deck there. From the shape of what's underneath, we could have some recoilless rifles marked 'special delivery' to the Viet Cong. Bong agrees." Jim peered through the binoculars again. "Besides, the eyes are not from our area."

Dickey readied her cameras as the crew members readied their submachine guns and rifles. Jim explained that it was important to keep the sampan between their junk and the nearest shore. In case of an ambush, the junkmen didn't want to be caught in a crossfire.

"Where should I station myself?" Dickey asked.

"Anywhere you like. There's no safe spot aboard, anyhow," came the reply.

As they came alongside, the rolling waves caused the two craft to rise and fall out of synchronization. First the junk's passengers would be looking down on the smaller craft; then the little sampan would suddenly swoop upward and pause momentarily above them.

An old man with skin like leather and a wispy white beard was holding the tiller, glancing nervously over at the junk and its heavily armed sailors. An old woman, her teeth blackened by years of chewing on hallucinogenic betel nuts, was chattering angrily from beneath the conical straw hat she wore to ward off the sun. *Trung-uy* Bong was shouting back and gesturing vehemently with his free hand; the other was clasped tightly to the top of the junk's superstructure to steady him against the leaps and dives of the struggling craft. He was unarmed, but at least a half dozen rifles and submachine guns were around him in the hands of the crew, and a man on the bow pointed the .30-caliber machine gun at the old couple.

At last the argument ended, and the old woman untied the tarpaulin, shooting hateful scowls at Bong as she worked. The old man at the tiller stared straight ahead while he steered, as though the junk and its armed occupants could cause him no harm if he did not look at them.

Dickey could see tension in the faces of Jim and the junk crew members as the moment of truth came: the old woman pulled back the tarp, to reveal the ends of long barkless logs. Simultaneously, the crewmen relaxed.

"Cay go," Jim said, turning to face Dickey for the first time. "It's a special wood they harvest down in the Nam Can district."

He moved toward *Trung-uy* Bong and they talked for several minutes while the two craft diverged. The old woman, busy refastening the tarp over her wood, was no longer firing angry looks.

Jim returned to Dickey and said, "The woman was apparently afraid we were going to steal her wood. Back in her village, the 'night visitors,' as she called them, told her that government soldiers would steal from her if they got the chance. *Cay go* is worth a fair amount of money to the Vietnamese. It's a very dense wood, so dense it usually sinks in water. They use it for construction and to make charcoal."

"By 'night visitors,' did she mean the Viet Cong?" Dickey asked.

"Most likely. There are still some antigovernment religious sects running around, but the odds are that her nocturnal 'friends' are VC."

Two hours later they were off the mouth of the Co Chien River, another branch of the Mekong, about nine miles south of the Ham Luong. As they neared the shore, the crew once again prepared their weapons.

"This area through here is a known Viet Cong stronghold," Jim said.

Dickey peered shoreward but saw nothing menacing. Mangrove trees seemed to be wading into the shallows on their great arcing roots, and an occasional stilt-legged bird cocked its head in their direction. Otherwise the scene, like so much of Vietnam, was a montage of greens punctuated in places by the browns and blacks of tree trunks and decay.

Around a point of land was a small inlet. Anchored close to the shore was an apparently empty sampan. *Trung-uy* Bong barked an order and the VNN junk came about to point its bow into the inlet. The Vietnamese officer said something to Jim in Vietnamese. Jim reached into the junk's wooden superstructure and withdrew an odd-looking weapon, shorter than a rifle and with a large-diameter barrel. He moved a lever and the weapon broke open like a shotgun. Jim inserted a fat-looking cartridge, closed the weapon, snapped on the safety, and glanced over at Dickey. Noting the puzzlement on her face, he said, "This is one of our newest weapons. It's called an M-79 grenade-launcher."

Dickey was scribbling notes as he spoke.

"This baby will heave these potent little pills a lot farther and more accurately than a rifle grenade, and they pack a hefty punch. Kind of a hand-carried artillery piece." He passed the M-79 to Bong, who pointed the weapon toward the anchored sampan. "We'll try a little 'recon by fire,' " Jim said. Without waiting to see if she would ask, he continued, "Reconnaissance by fire. Kind of like poking a hornet's nest to see if anybody's home."

There was a muffled thump, unlike the sharp crack of an M-16 rifle, and a moment later an explosion tore at the vegetation on the shore just beyond the sampan. "Takes a little getting used to," said Jim as Bong passed him the M-79. He broke open the weapon and inserted another round.

"How do you know that boat belongs to the VC?" Dickey asked.

"This is a designated 'free-fire zone.' Certain areas are known to be VC-controlled, so we don't need provocation to shoot. *Trung-uy* says he's certain that sampan is a VC supply boat." He squeezed the trigger. Another thump. This round fell short of the target.

"How many of these free-fire zones are there?" Dickey asked as another round hit just beyond the sampan.

"I don't know," Jim answered. "But Junk Division 37 here has fifty-one miles of coastline to patrol. Of that, approximately twelve miles are considered VC-controlled and are therefore free-fire areas.''

Bong's next shot scored a direct hit on the sampan. There was a sound like the one a large tree makes when it cracks in the wind. The sampan lurched and seemed to pull at its anchor cable for a second as a shower of shrapnel and splinters spattered the surface of the water nearby. Jim fired next, and this round hit at the sampan's waterline. When they pulled away, the sampan's gunwales were nearly immersed, and the stricken boat was settling into the murky water.

"Nice weapon," Dickey said quietly and bent over her notepad again.

Hours later, the junk left the turbulence of the South China Sea and reentered the Ham Luong River. The blue water became mottled with the brownish tint of Mekong silt farther upriver. Strangling heat began to envelop the boat as the wind faded. The hours of steadying themselves on the pitching deck had left the crew fatigued, and everyone was quiet—even Dickey Chapelle's nervous energy had run out.

Passing a small village nestled on the riverbank, Jim said in a monotone, "Some of the junks have received fire from that village. Not much—just a few rounds to make their sentiments known and maybe to draw some return fire."

"Why would they want to draw fire?" Dickey asked, her reporter's curiosity finding a cache of energy.

"Because if the VC can get us to fire into the village and do damage or kill someone, they can point to that as an example of how the government doesn't care about the villagers. 'Charlie' can get a lot of mileage out of something like that."

"Are the VC this close to your base?"

"Sure. In fact, within a day's walk there is a Viet Cong rest camp complete with a hospital and an officer training center." He removed a map from his pocket, unfolded it, and pointed to an area outlined in blue. "That's what our intel says, and every time we sail close to the beaches in that area, somebody shoots at us."

Dickey finished scribbling some notes, then looked up at Jim through the salt-encrusted lenses of her glasses. "Real soft duty you've got yourself here, Lieutenant Vincent!"

Three days later, the junk base came under attack from a Viet Cong force that had slipped into the neighboring village marketplace. Jim Vincent and Dickey Chapelle, carbine in one hand and camera in the other, counterattacked with the Junk Force sailors and local militiamen. The Viet Cong were repulsed; business went on as usual at Tiem Ton.

At the end of her stay a week later, Dickey Chapelle was awarded the silver, twin-sail insignia of the Junk Force by the "junkies" she had patrolled with. She declined, however, to have "SAT CONG" tattooed on her chest.

River Assault Groups

In the fall of 1945, French Army units attempted to take control of My Tho (the capital city of Dinh Tuong Province in the Mekong Delta). Viet Minh forces had sabotaged the only road, Route 4, and the French vehicles were bogging down in the less-than-solid ground of the muddy delta. To overcome this difficulty, French naval infantry were brought in by small craft and successfully seized My Tho. In the two subsequent sieges of Vinh Long and Can Tho (also Mekong Delta provincial capitals), the waterways again proved to be the only practicable way to transport the French troops.

These successes impressed the commander of French military forces in Indochina, General Philippe Leclerc. He ordered the establishment of a permanent flotilla of craft capable of transporting the naval infantry men where needed in the delta. This initial force was called the Naval Infantry River Flotilla, but as the concept was developed and more flotillas were created, the name was changed to *Divisions navales d'assaut* (naval assault divisions) and abbreviated to *Dinassauts*.

Using a mixture of modified U.S. and British landing craft, these *Dinassauts* evolved into effective battle elements that eventually saw service in the Red River Delta in North Vietnam (then known as Tonkin) as well as in the Mekong Delta. The *Dinassauts* varied in size and composition, but they averaged twelve vessels, with the largest having more than twenty. The typical *Dinassaut* had at least one LCI (Landing Craft, Infantry) or an LSSL (Landing Support Ship, Large) to provide fire support and serve as a command platform, a number of LCMs (Landing Craft, Mechanized) and LCVPs (Landing Craft, Vehicle or Personnel) for landing and support, and a harbor patrol boat to perform patrol and liaison. Some of the larger *Dinassauts* had LCTs (Landing Craft, Tank) for carrying armored vehicles and were supported by their own reconnaissance aircraft. All craft were modified for their new roles by adding armor and armament. A typical flotilla could transport and land a battalion-size force and all its associated equipment. As the war went on, the Viet Minh massed their forces, eventually a single flotilla with its one battalion was not large enough to engage the enemy, so the French organized river task forces by combining several flotillas and adding additional troop transports.

The *Dinassauts* played a key role in the Red River Delta battles of 1951 and 1952. In the spring of 1951, a *Dinassaut* reinforced a French garrison at Ninh Binh, one hundred miles south of Hanoi on the Day River. By providing fire support and inserting troops to cut enemy communications, the *Dinassaut* was able to help drive off the attacking Viet Minh.

In late 1951 one of the bloodiest battles of the French Indochina War was fought at a place named Hoa Binh, which ironically means "peace" in Vietnamese. Hoa Binh is located approximately thirty-seven miles west of Hanoi on the west bank of the Black River (Song Da). At dawn on 14 November, French paratroopers seized the city with hardly any resistance, but the Viet Minh almost immediately severed the only overland route into Hoa Binh, leaving the Black River as the sole remaining avenue of supply. The *Dinassauts* were called upon to keep this vital artery open. Running a gauntlet of ever-increasing firepower delivered from the Viet Minh-controlled riverbank, the river craft kept supplies flowing to the besieged city for nearly two months despite heavy casualties. Then, on 12 January, at a place on the river called Notre Dame Rock, despite gallant resistance, four patrol craft and one heavily armed LSSL were sunk by the murderous Viet Minh fire; most of the other craft were severely damaged, forcing them to turn back downriver, their vital mission aborted. Further attempts at resupply were abandoned, but the *Dinassauts* were not out of the fight yet. In an operation dubbed "Amaranth," the *Dinassauts* fought their way back upriver and were instrumental in the successful evacuation of Hoa Binh.

Despite the eventual defeat, the *Dinassauts* had done for two months what land forces acting alone could not. These and other battles had proven the effectiveness of this amphibious river warfare technique. In a region so dominated by waterways, the value of a river assault force had been recognized and exploited. The *Dinassaut* concept was a well-executed tactic in a war with few French successes, and its significance was not lost on the newly formed Vietnamese Navy or its American advisors.

Even before the French Indochina war had ended, the French had transferred control of some of the *Dinassauts* to the VNN. In the spring of 1953 two VNN *Dinassauts* were established at Can Tho and Vinh Long in the Mekong Delta. Two more were activated just before the end of the war in 1954. In the decade that followed, the number grew to seven and the name *Dinassaut* gradually yielded to River Assault Group, which the Americans quickly abbreviated to "RAG."

A River Assault Group typically consisted of nineteen craft, eleven of which were armored versions of LCVPs, and LCMs. Six were French STCAN/FOM patrol boats. Manned by a crew of eight, these 36-foot armored craft were capable of 10 knots and were armed with one .50- and three .30-caliber machine guns. (The acronym STCAN referred to the French government agency in charge of building naval craft—*Services Techniques des Constructions et Armes Navales*—and the FOM represented the term *France Outre Mer*, meaning "built overseas.") The remaining craft were a monitor and a *commandment*. Both of these were converted LCMs, the monitor designed for heavy fire-support and the *commandement* for enhanced communications capability.

River Assault Group 27, based at My Tho in the Delta, had a different array of craft: one monitor, one *commandement*, six armored LCMs, and ten RPCs (River Patrol Craft: 35-foot boats built as replacements for the aging STCAN/FOMs, capable of 14 knots, and mounting a varying array of .30- and .50-caliber machine guns).

Despite the stated primary mission of transporting and providing fire support for assault troops, the River Assault Groups were relegated to a logistic support role by the Vietnamese Army, which exercised control over their employment, in the late fifties and the early sixties. Because of an increasing reliance on American helicopters for transporting troops, the groups were mostly assigned to transport supplies. As a result, they engaged the enemy only when ambushed (which happened fairly frequently).

When more American naval advisors arrived in Vietnam in 1964, some of them were assigned (or volunteered) to accompany the River Assault Groups. An American advisory team normally consisted of three men: a lieutenant and two chief petty officers. The Americans became a catalyst for renewed emphasis on tactical employment of the groups. Their presence brought attention to the River Assault Groups, and this, combined with some interservice liaison among the American Navy and Army advisors, brought about a rejuvenation of their primary mission of assault support. Patrolling and minesweeping missions became more frequent as well.

And so it was that Lieutenant Dale Meyerkord came to be an advisor for River Assault Group 23 at Vinh Long in the Mekong Delta.

Hornblower

> He was never fearless, as some men are, but forgot his fears after battle was joined. He became a legend for saying no more than he needed to say but I knew him as he really was, a man of humility, of humour, of kindness and charm. It was not his fate to command in any general engagement but he will always be remembered in the . . . Navy as one of the finest officers of his day.
>
> —C. NORTHCOTE PARKINSON, *The Life and Times of Horatio Hornblower*

Harold Dale Meyerkord was a linebacker on the first football team ever formed at Riverview Gardens Senior High School in St. Louis, Missouri. He did not win his place on the team because he was big and powerful; in fact, at five feet nine and a half inches and 150 pounds, he wasn't big at all. But what he may have lacked in physique he more than made up for in aggressiveness. He had a way of meeting challenges head on that not only brought him success but would often capture the attention and admiration of others. At a party in his senior year of high school, one of his teammates told some friends, "When it was time to line up for attributes just before getting born, Dale spent so much time in the *aggressive* line that he didn't have much left for the *size* line." Years later, *Life* magazine's Loudon Wainwright would write: "The word 'aggressive,' in fact, is the one most often used by Meyerkord's colleagues in their efforts to describe him, and it is always offered as the highest form of compliment." Dale carried that aggressiveness with him to the University of Missouri, where he tried to continue playing football until finally the doctors who were putting him back together told him to "forget it, or the big boys are going to start using you as the football."

He graduated from the university in 1959 with a major in political science and then promptly joined the Navy, graduating from Officer Candidate School as an ensign in 1960. In January 1961 he and Jane Schmidt, whom he had met while both were students at the university, were married. His first tour of duty was on the cruiser USS *Los Angeles* (CA-135), followed by a destroyer tour in the USS *Duncan* (DD-874), whose home port was Yokosuka, Japan.

Dale's mother, Louise Meyerkord, visited her son in Japan in the summer of 1963. While she was there, the subject of Vietnam came up, and Dale told his mother, "A lot is going on there that will eventually change the world." So Louise was not surprised when Dale told her a few months later that he had volunteered to go to Vietnam as a naval advisor.

After six months of preparatory schooling, including Vietnamese language training (he finished first in his class), Dale left Jane and their two-year-old daughter, Lynne, for Vietnam. When he arrived, Captain Hardcastle assigned him to the post of senior advisor for River Assault Group 23, and after a few days of indoctrination briefings in Saigon, Dale was in a helicopter headed into the Mekong Delta.

River Assault Group 23's operating base was just outside the city of Vinh Long, sixty-five miles southwest of Saigon. The group was responsible for three of the thirteen provinces in the delta: Vinh Long, Vinh Binh, and Kien Hoa. This region was critically important to the Saigon government because of the concentration of people and the large quantities of rice produced there. The main road out of Saigon into the delta split at Vinh Long, one branch connecting with the Ca Mau region at the southern tip of South Vietnam and the other branch heading westward to Ha Tien at the Cambodian border. This made Vinh Long and the area around it a strategic terminus in the vital Mekong Delta.

With more than five million people living in the delta and with the bulk of the nation's rice crop being produced there, both the South Vietnamese government and the Viet Cong were intent upon controlling this "rice-bowl of Vietnam," as it was often called. In recognition of this, MACV had committed more than forty Americans to the Vinh Long area, including Army infantry advisors, helicopter pilots, supply and maintenance experts, and a three-man naval advisory team.

The Viet Cong no longer saw the Americans as insignificant background elements. Signs appeared at various places around the delta that were reminiscent of America's Old West: they offered rewards for the death or capture of certain key American figures. (Captain Hardcastle was at one time number three on the list.) Before the end of 1964, eighteen of forty-four Americans stationed at Vinh Long would be killed or wounded in the field.

It was into this milieu of extraordinary challenge that Dale Meyerkord's helicopter deposited him on a hot day in June 1964.

Chief Radioman Eugene Barney leaned back against the armor plating surrounding the *commandement*'s forward gun. He was sitting on a .50-caliber ammunition box, and feeling the heat from the olive-drab metal of the box, he wondered why the rounds inside didn't cook off. His eyes closed, he was teetering on the edge of an unwanted but compelling doze. The boat had only left home base at Vinh Long a few hours before, and as yet had made no enemy contact, but the delta sun had a way of draining the strength out of a man in a hurry, and he felt as though he had been out for a week.

He half-opened one eye against the glare of the afternoon sun and saw one of the LCVPs of River Assault Group 23 following fifty yards astern on the starboard quarter. Even through one eye he could make out the bright red scarves of the "Ruff Puffs" (Vietnamese militiamen whose name had been derived from the initials RF/PF, meaning "Regional Forces/Popular Forces"). Barney knew that the scarves were worn in lieu of uniforms, since the Ruff Puffs were seldom issued anything more than weapons or ammunition, but he thought the bright red color made them easy targets in a world that consisted of shades of green.

Barney was glad to be aboard the *commandement* rather than on one of the LCVPs or LCM-6s carrying the Ruff Puffs. It was always more crowded on the troop transports, and that made the heat even worse. He watched the heavily foliated banks of the Co Chien river slipping slowly by until the drone of the diesels began lulling him away.

He was startled awake by a loud laugh, followed by some words he couldn't quite make out. Looking aft, Barney could see only the back of a camouflage shirt and an Australian bush hat. From the exaggerated gestures and bursts of laughter, he knew it had to be the woman correspondent who was riding with them. She was quite a character; she dressed and even looked a little like a Marine "gunny" sergeant, and she had a rough voice like one too. Barney and Chief Gentile had been teasing their boss, Lieutenant Meyerkord, about "something going on between you and that lady reporter." This usually got a rise out of the lieutenant.

Barney closed his eyes again. A few minutes later he was aware of someone standing between him and the sun, and he reluctantly opened his eyes. Dickey Chapelle was looking down at him.

"Mind if I join you, Chief?" When Barney shrugged, she dropped to the deck next to him. "I'd like to ask you some questions about Lieutenant Meyerkord. What's he like to work for?"

Barney paused for a moment. "At the risk of sounding corny," he said slowly, "he's the kind of guy that you'd pick

45

if you knew you were going to be in a tight spot and you knew you could have only one person there to be with you."

Dickey smiled. "That's not corny, Chief," she said as she wrote in her notepad. "But what makes you say that?"

"Well, a lot of things, I guess. Lieutenant Meyerkord is what I'd call an 'all-American lieutenant.' He's totally self-confident. Cocky. Gung-ho. He just seems sure of what he's doing all the time." Barney wiped the droplets of sweat that had gathered on his upper lip. "I mean, he really believes in what we're doing here, and he goes after everything like it's the World Series."

They watched some children playing in the water near the left bank. A water buffalo stood stoically among them, shin-deep in the water, as the children climbed his legs and pulled his tail.

Barney turned back to Dickey. "Lieutenant Meyerkord isn't like a lot of young officers I've worked for out in the fleet. They work out okay as they get a little experience under their belts, but when they're new at a job, they mostly wait for somebody to tell 'em what to do. But this one's different. He goes out visiting the village councils and the hamlet chiefs. He tells them about the RAG and that we can provide heavy firepower and bring in troops against the Cong; that we can evacuate them if necessary and bring in medical supplies. Nobody told him to do that. He just does things like that on his own."

"How is he received by the villagers?"

"Most of them really like him. They think that blond hair of his is something else, and he speaks their language pretty well, so that usually impresses them. Some of them had some bad experiences with the French while they were here, and they aren't too receptive. And then some of them are just plain Cong sympathizers, or Cong themselves, so we don't get very far with them."

Dickey started to ask another question, but the chief was gathering momentum. "Another thing he does is go out on reconnaissance flights with the Army to learn the area and look for problems. He's real big on 'recon'—keeps a bunch of maps and is always marking on them. It's paid off, though. He knows his way around these waterways damn near like a native."

46

"What do you think about his counterpart?" Dickey asked.

"*Dai-uy* Hoa is the bravest man I ever met," Barney answered, looking straight into Dickey's eyes. "There couldn't be a better match than those two. Hoa and Meyerkord are like the Three Musketeers minus one. They're aggressive as hell; nothing scares them off. If they hear there's trouble brewing someplace, they're saddling up." He stood up and swept an arm panoramically. "Look at this outfit. The boats are all flying Jolly Rogers, the sailors call themselves 'River Rats.' This is a gung-ho group! They've got a lot of spirit and they fight well, because they've got good leadership. With those two lieutenants setting the example, it's bound to happen."

"How do they set the example?"

"They show a lot of spirit first off. They encourage things like Jolly Rogers and nicknames because they know that makes the sailors feel like they're part of an elite team." He laughed suddenly. "Hell, do you know what Lieutenant Meyerkord's radio call sign is?"

Dickey shook her head.

"He goes by 'Hornblower.' You know, the British naval hero in all those books."

"C. S. Forester."

"Yeah. I mean that's the type of guy he is. Gung-ho." He sat back down on his ammo box. "But more than that, he and Hoa have guts. They stand out in the open sometimes during firefights so they can see where to direct the fire. They maintain their cool no matter how bad things get. A few months back, in the middle of a firefight, a shell landed right on deck without exploding. Lieutenant Meyerkord looked down at it, kicked it over the side, and then went right on firing. I mean, he could've been swatting a fly for all the emotion he showed."

"I've heard some talk," Dickey said slowly, "that Dale is a little *too* brave; that he takes more risks than he really needs to or should. Do you agree?"

"I'll admit that there are times he scares me to death, when I wish he'd be a little more careful. In fact, one time Chief Gentile and I told him so. But he smiled and said, 'Those bullets just curve away when they start coming my way.' So we gave up." He looked back in Meyerkord's direction. Dale was talking with the Vietnamese boat coxswain and pointing downriver.

"But this is war," Barney continued, "and I guess it takes guys like him to lead people in situations like this. You don't get people to drive up rivers and canals looking for other people who are just waiting for the chance to kill you by being overly cautious yourself."

"I think you're probably right," Dickey said as she got to her feet and stretched. "Thanks, Chief. You've helped me a lot."

She walked aft along the deck, which had been painted green and brown for camouflage. Near the coxswain's flat she saw a spiral-bound notebook that lay open on the deck, its pages flapping in the hot wind. She stooped, picked it up, and flipped through it. It was a log that Meyerkord had apparently been keeping since his arrival in River Assault Group 23, summarizing the operations conducted by the group in colorless phrases. She skimmed through the pages, pausing occasionally to read:

13 AUG—Battle preparations are made. All guns are manned and loaded. Dai Huy puts on his helmet and flak vest. The river is very narrow and because our command post is on the open deck of the Monitor we are vulnerable to small arms fire. I don't wear a helmet or flak vest. My preparations consist of setting my carbine on auto and loading it with a clip of tracers. These I will use to direct fire.

22 SEP—I saw a VC battle flag planted in an open field on the south bank of the river. We deployed the two FOMs into a line abreast and beached in the vicinity of the flag. The expected sniper fire started as we beached and we raked the area with machine gun fire. I took a group of men ashore after the flag. It was not mined or booby-trapped. This is unusual. The VC normally leave a flag for bait and then set grenade traps around it. We looked carefully but could find no grenades or mines. The sniper fire ceased after we located the sniper positions and saturated them with machine gun fire. We returned to the boats with the flag. The flag I can use for

trade goods to obtain more weapons or other desired items.

Dickey put the log down and watched Meyerkord as he picked up a radio handset and spoke into it. She couldn't quite hear him over the diesels, but every now and then she thought she heard the word "Hornblower." In her notepad she started sketching with words: "Fatigues (jungle type), sleeves rolled, sunglasses, web-belt with large knife in sheath attached, revolver, Rolex watch, 'U.S. NAVY' stenciled above one pocket. . . ." She watched the young lieutenant for a moment as he moved about the boat talking with the Vietnamese sailors and then wrote in heavy capital letters with underlining: "a MAN!"

"Why can't I go?" Meyerkord persisted. "There are canals down there that I know better than anyone else."

Major Oscar Padgett, Jr., sat with his hands folded on his stomach and leaned back in the plastic upholstered chair. He was the Army's senior advisor to one of the Army of (South) Vietnam (ARVN) infantry regiments operating in the delta. "I told you, Dale. The ARVN didn't include any VNN on this operation."

"But the only way we're ever going to get them working together the way they should is to convince them to try it as often as we can. Eventually, they'll get used to it and put their damn politics aside." Meyerkord was sitting across from the Army major in a room of the Army's Military Advisory Group 52 billet in Vinh Long, better known as the "MAG House." The decor, if it could be called that, was stark by American standards, but by village standards it was a palace.

"All right, I'll see what I can do." Major Padgett rose to leave.

Meyerkord grabbed his bag from the chair next to him as he got up. Tied to the top of the bag, near the handle, was an Australian bush hat.

Major Padgett looked at the hat and scowled. "Why do you wear that damn thing?" he asked disapprovingly.

"That's my fighting hat." Meyerkord smiled broadly as he answered.

"I've seen you and Hoa with your 'fighting hats' from my helo," Padgett said. Hoa had a floppy hat that he often wore on patrol. "If I was shooting at your boats, I'd shoot at some-body with a hat like that." Meyerkord laughed. Leaving the MAG House, Major Padgett took one more shot: "You two look like a couple of sheepherders in those damn hats."

Two days later the "sheepherders" were proceeding up a narrow waterway twenty-three miles from Vinh Long. Hoa, Meyerkord, and Barney were in the same *commandement* in which Dickey Chapelle had ridden with them the month before. Their task was to set up a blocking force on the eastern flank of a suspected Viet Cong company while Major Pad-gett's ARVN infantry unit started a sweep from the west. If all went well, the VC would flee before the advancing ARVN units and run into the heavy firepower of the RAG boats. The flotilla, consisting of four STCAN/FOMs, the monitor, the *commandement,* four LCVPs, and three LCMs, stretched more than a quarter of a mile as they headed upriver in a column. Twenty minutes before, they had stopped at one of the hamlets along the riverbank and talked with the villagers. A gesticulating elder of the hamlet had confirmed that a unit of Viet Cong, perhaps company-strength, was operating nearby.

At 0800 the flotilla arrived at the planned debarkation point. The LCVPs and LCMs nudged into the bank and their bow doors dropped open, forming bridges to the shore for their human cargo. The troops moved off and were swallowed by the dense vegetation within minutes. The bow ramps were cranked back up, and the boats growled and coughed their way off the bank. They headed downstream about a half mile, then turned into a small canal no wider than a residential street in suburban America. The thirteen craft snarled along the narrow waterway for another half hour. A veil of blue smoke hanging motionless in the still air above the column's wake marked their passing.

Where the canal widened to almost double the previous width, Hoa signaled and the boats turned in to perch on the mud slopes of the bank to starboard. When all were in po-sition, the men shut the engines down and began their vigil.

Meyerkord pulled a pack of Pall Malls from his fatigue shirt pocket and offered one to the Vietnamese sailor sitting nearest him, who eagerly accepted. He lit both cigarettes using his Zippo decorated with the ship's crest of the USS *Duncan* and then inspected his AR-15 rifle. Hoa studied a chart.

Time passed slowly. No one spoke, and only the sounds of birds and monkeys in the trees broke the silence.

At last, at about 1100, one of the radios on the *commandement* crackled: "Hornblower, this is Battle-axe, over."

Meyerkord recognized the voice of Major Padgett. He lifted the handset with his left hand; his AR-15 was in his right. "Hornblower, roger, over," he said into the PRC-10 transceiver.

"This is Green Six. Chuck is headed your way, over."

"Hornblower, roger, out."

Meyerkord motioned to Hoa and gestured toward the jungle. Hoa nodded and picked up another handset to talk to the other boats. Both men donned their fighting hats.

A few minutes later, the chattering in the treetops ceased and a deadly quiet passed over the area. All eyes were staring into the dense undergrowth. Coxswains' hands were poised near the engines' starters; tense fingers coiled lightly around triggers; perspiration coursed over taut faces. At first the several shadows moving silently through the heavy growth were almost imperceptible, only their movement giving them away. They made no sound.

Hoa held the transmitter handset close to his lips. Meyerkord sighted the AR-15 on the shadows.

A moment later more shadows appeared farther down the bank. A metallic clink emanated from somewhere in the foliage. In a single second, Hoa spoke into the handset, firing erupted from dozens of weapons, engines coughed into throaty growls, and the chorus of cursing and shouting that usually accompanies men in combat rose in counterpoint to the staccato sound of automatic weapons fire.

The unmistakable bark of Communist AK-47s answered the flotilla's firing almost immediately from the opposite bank. Meyerkord was firing tracers into the vegetation where muzzle-flashes were visible from time to time. He could hear and feel the sharp clap of rounds passing close in response.

Some of the boats were under way now and moving in an attempt to become poorer targets. There wasn't much room to maneuver, but the coxswains did the best they could to keep the craft mobile. The *commandement,* too large to lumber about in the narrow canal, remained on the bank.

With a loud *whoosh,* a rocket erupted from the trees about thirty yards down the bank and crashed into the hull of one of the FOMs. The craft heeled over under the impact, nearly capsizing, and almost immediately ran aground on a mud bank near the shore. Several Vietnamese sailors were visible in the FOM, obviously wounded.

Meyerkord signaled the coxswain of a passing FOM to pull up close to the *commandement.* He jumped aboard and they headed for the lame FOM on the mud bank. When they got alongside, he jumped onto the stricken craft and administered first aid to the two most seriously injured sailors. The firing was intense all around him, but Meyerkord went about his task without hesitation. When he was finished, he reboarded the other FOM and returned, amid a hail of fire, to the *commandement.*

The firefight persisted for a few minutes more; then the firing from within the jungle dwindled and faded out. An order to cease firing was passed, and relative calm settled in as sailors went ashore to search for bodies and weapons. They returned dragging two dead Viet Cong, carrying one Russian carbine, and escorting three wounded VC soldiers. There was evidence in the undergrowth that other dead, dying, or wounded Viet Cong had been carried off by the fleeing force. The VC had apparently fled along the canal bank headed south at the blocking force's left flank.

First a radio call and then the identifying green smoke billowing out of the jungle signaled the approach of friendly units, and the previously debarked ARVN soldiers were soon reunited with their parent craft. Major Padgett's group continued in pursuit of the remaining VC force, to be recovered later in the day by the helicopters that had transported them in at dawn.

Chief Barney, like Lieutenant Meyerkord, had been keeping a log of their activities. Also like Meyerkord, he would never be accused of dramatizing the events he recorded. He pulled out his pocket-sized green notebook and wrote on the page for 13 January 1965:

1050—Boats made contact at coords 062 205. 2 VC KIA [Killed in Action], 3 WIA [Wounded in Action], 1 Russian carbine—2 friendly Navy WIA.

1120—Broke contact.

Three days later, Lieutenant Meyerkord and Chief Barney were embarked in the River Assault Group 23 monitor accompanying three LCMs, two LCVPs, two FOMs, and four more LCVPs belonging to the Civil Guard, another local militia force. They had left Vinh Long at 0945 and were en route to Tan Chau, near the Cambodian border. The morning had been uneventful, but at approximately 1400 the crew members on two tugs coming downstream waved frantically to the passing armada. Hoa had the monitor pull up to the nearer of the tugs and spoke with the master for several minutes, then moved aft in search of the two Americans.

Chief Barney and Lieutenant Meyerkord were amidships inspecting the 81-millimeter mortar. *Dai-uy* Hoa squatted on the deck above them and said, "Two tugs with tows. They say VC ambushed them two kilometers north of here."

Meyerkord looked up at Hoa through his gold-framed sunglasses. "What kind of tows?" he asked.

"Barges. Big ones. Mixed cargo," Hoa replied.

Meyerkord climbed out of the mortar pit. He looked at the tugs and their barges for a few seconds, and said, "Maybe we can get 'Charlie' to show his hand."

An hour later the two tugs were on their way back up the river, nearing the spot where they had been ambushed. This time, however, nestled out of sight between the barges were the two FOMs with Lieutenant Meyerkord and Chief Barney on one and *Dai-uy* Hoa aboard the other. As the strange little task force rounded a tight bend in the river, small arms fire burst from the bamboo thickets on the western bank, sending the tugs' crews diving for cover. The two FOMs throttled up and emerged from between the barges, opening fire as soon as they were clear. The fire from the bank hesitated as the VC registered their surprise; then it picked up again at a more rapid pace.

Meyerkord and Barney were firing into the thickets with their AR-15 and shotgun respectively. Suddenly a heavy burst of automatic weapons fire rattled toward them, causing them

53

both to drop to the deck behind the FOM's superstructure, their faces only inches apart. Meyerkord grinned at Barney as though they were sharing an inside joke and rose to one knee to peer over the superstructure. More automatic weapons fire gnawed at the tired old superstructure of the FOM, sending a shower of splinters up near Meyerkord's face. He dropped to the deck facing Barney again. The grin returned as he said, "What do you think, Chief? Is this worth sixty-five dollars?" Barney laughed as he realized that the lieutenant was referring to the extra monthly money they were getting from the Navy for "hostile fire pay."

The FOMs were pouring torrents of .30- and .50-caliber rounds into the bamboo, making shreds of leaves and stalks fly. After several minutes, the fire from the bank ceased and the FOMs ended theirs as well. The two craft cruised up and down past the hostile thickets, their guns bristling like the hair on a stalking cat's back. Finally Hoa's FOM nosed into the bank while the other covered it. Several sailors crashed off into the shattered bamboo and returned a few minutes later, dragging the body of an enemy soldier.

Barney sat down near the forward gun and removed an unexpended round from his shotgun. He watched as Lieutenant Meyerkord lit a cigarette and surveyed the scene of the firefight. Chief Barney smiled as he remembered the quip Meyerkord had made about the money right in the midst of the action. He sometimes wondered if Meyerkord was all right in the head, but he was awfully glad that their paths had crossed. It was hard to imagine what this strange job would be like if not for Lieutenant Meyerkord.

It was 16 March 1965. Chief Barney's pocket log-book contained the following entries:

0630—U/W from Vinh Long. Group consists of commandement, 3 LCMs, 2 LCVPs, 4 FOMs and 3 Civil Guard LCVPs. The 834, 274 and 853 companies embarked.

0910—Landing troops at coords ws 905 301.

0940—Wounded civ approached us in a sampan.

Claims he was shot south of us earlier. We administered
first aid.

1130—Picked up troops. Returning to outpost at coords
ws 883 308.

1200—Departed outpost. Enroute to Vinh Long.

The flotilla was cruising through the coffee-colored waters
of the Co Chien River; the wind caused by their 7-knot passage was the only relief in the otherwise still air. Chief Barney had a radio transceiver open on the wooden-slatted deck
of the *commandement*, troubleshooting a suspected transmis-
sion fault while a Vietnamese sailor squatted next to him,
watching eagerly. Lieutenant Meyerkord was nearby working
on a coconut he had taken from a wild grove near the last
troop pick-up point. A lanky Army captain, James Snooks
III, was perched on the deckhouse looking down at Meyerkord as he pried open the reluctant coconut shell with his
Kaybar knife. Snooks was a pacification officer for the Army
advisory group in Vinh Long. He had asked to go along on
the operation that day to observe.

"Hey, Dale," Snooks said, "I hear you just got back from
Hong Kong."

"Yeah. I was there last week." Meyerkord extracted a large
piece of gleaming white coconut meat and held it up, smiling;
he cut it in two and tossed half up to Snooks. "Jane came
over to meet me. I had trouble getting out of here because of
the latest coup, so we were cut short a bit. But we had three
days together."

The Vietnamese executive officer of the *commandement* was
passing by. Meyerkord proffered him a piece of coconut
skewered on the tip of his knife. Hoa smiled. "You Americans. Always thinking about your stomachs," he said reprov-
ingly. But he took the piece of coconut and popped it into
his mouth as he headed aft.

Snooks said, "You and your counterpart get along pretty
well, don't you?"

"That's affirmative. We see eye to eye on how to go about
winning this thing."

"Well, you're lucky to have it that way. Some of our advisors with the ARVN units don't get along with their counterparts, and it's pure hell for them. You never know for sure

whether it's the advisor's fault or the counterpart's, but it's a bad situation either way."

"I guess I'm doing okay with Hoa," Meyerkord said. "He's asked me to be godfather for his child."

"Lieutenant Meyerkord," Chief Barney called, "just got a call on the tactical net. Two ranger companies have contact with a good-size VC force just south of Duc Ton. The Army wants us to set up a block."

Meyerkord jumped to his feet.

"We can be there in less than an hour," Barney continued as he looked at a chart.

Within minutes the River Assault Group units had turned into a canal off the main river, their diesels straining toward their objective. A half mile into the canal, Meyerkord pointed toward the south bank, where a Viet Cong flag had been hoisted above the canopy of trees on a bamboo staff. "Looks like we're getting into 'Indian territory' now," he said to Snooks.

Twenty minutes later the bow ramps of the troop transports dropped onto muddy banks and the Vietnamese soldiers headed inland to the aid of the rangers. The smaller boats began patrolling up and down the narrow canal.

The next few hours were uneventful for the units. They maintained their position as requested by Major Padgett, the Army advisor who was running the operation from a helicopter. The FOMs patrolled while the *commandement* and the troop carriers remained against the bank. The canal was too narrow here to permit the LCMs to turn around, so they stayed put, angled into the bank.

At about 1615 the FOMs started exchanging fire with a squad of Viet Cong on the south bank three hundred yards up the canal from the beached troop transports. The firing continued for over an hour, but neither side appeared to inflict any significant damage. At 1730 the firing stopped.

The men in River Assault Group 23 did not know that the main Viet Cong force was farther up the canal, around a bend. The enemy troops were moving almost soundlessly through the web of vines near the waterways. They had to keep moving after their long battle with the ARVN rangers. More rangers had arrived and had flanked them, and the only way out was across the canal. They set up three machine-gun emplacements, two on one side of the waterway and one on the other, to cover the crossing.

Aboard the *commandement* Hoa gave the order for the LCMs and the *commandement* to back off of the banks and get under way. The big boats would have to go farther up the canal to find a spot wide enough in which to turn around. They lumbered off the banks and started toward the sharp bend nearly a half mile away.

Meyerkord stepped up to the raised forward section of the *commandement,* surveyed the scene ahead for a moment, and sat down on the port side to light a cigarette. Snooks and Barney were amidships near the starboard bulwark enjoying the little puffs of air that the boat's movement created. The whole crew was quiet; all were hot and tired, and the day seemed to be ending for them. The plan was to head back to Vinh Long. Lieutenant Meyerkord was already late for a planned awards ceremony in Saigon, where Captain Hardcastle was going to present him an Air Medal and a Purple Heart.

The *commandement* was leading the way around the bend in the canal. Ducks were paddling in the opposite direction. They scattered to the sides of the waterway as the huge craft bore down on them. Snooks laughed at their indignant quacking and turned to say something to Barney.

Like a thunderclap, the first rounds exploded from the riverbanks and rushed at the *commandement.* They struck with awesome power on both sides, sending shards of wood and metal flying. Men scrambled in every direction in search of weapons, cover, and cognition. Chief Barney grabbed his 12-gauge shotgun and threw a bench down to provide protection for Captain Snooks and himself. Lieutenant Meyerkord, still sitting on the raised deckhouse, pulled his pistol from its holster and returned fire on the port side. Barney and Snooks fired off the starboard side, as did most of the Vietnamese sailors. Bullets were coming from all directions; the din was deafening in the confined waterway.

Meyerkord called out, "I'm hit." Barney looked up to see his boss lying across the top of the deckhouse where he had been sitting. A dark stain was growing at his midsection. Meyerkord was still firing.

Barney, in a move that would later earn him the Bronze

Star, went to Meyerkord's aid. He moved over to the port side and pulled the lieutenant's legs, trying to get his boss down into the less exposed midships section, but he couldn't move Meyerkord and the latter seemed unable to help. Out of the corner of his eye Barney could see flashes in the nearby foliage on the left bank. In the confusion his mind registered that the *commandement* must be pouring high-explosive rounds into the jungle. That's good, he thought, that'll keep the bastards' heads down. He stood up and grabbed Meyerkord's armpits and started to lift him. It was then that he realized that those flashes were coming from the muzzle of an enemy gun firing at point-blank range. Before he could react, a round struck Meyerkord under the chin and another tore into Barney's back, exiting through his left arm. Both men sank to the deck as the *commandement*'s firepower came to bear on the enemy gun emplacements.

A few hours later, Major Padgett was standing on the pier at Vinh Long watching the *commandement* moor. Two Vietnamese sailors lifted a litter from the deck and carried it past him. They were not hurrying. On the litter, at the man's feet, was an Australian bush hat.

Captain Hardcastle picked up the "MACV Monthly Evaluation Report for the Month of March 1965" and read paragraph 2.b. for the third time:

> During an amphibious assault and destroy operation on 16 March, LT H. D. Meyerkord was killed by small arms fire. This was a great loss to the United States' advisory effort. LT Meyerkord was an outstanding and extremely aggressive advisor whose acts of bravery earned the respect of all who knew him.

He tossed the report onto his desk. The first American naval officer had now been killed in action in South Vietnam.

Postscripts

Bill Hardcastle has retired from the Navy and lives with Mary in Virginia Beach, Virginia, where they often see other retired service friends from the years in South Vietnam.

Jim Vincent works in real estate in California. When writing to old friends from his Vietnam days or to other veterans, he still appends the words *Sat Cong* to his signature.

Several months after Dickey Chapelle had left the Junk Force, *Trung-uy* Bong was killed when a Viet Cong force attacked the base at Tiem Ton.

After being wounded on the canal south of Duc Ton, Chief Barney was evacuated to Vinh Long by helicopter and then taken to the Third Field Hospital, near Saigon. He survived his wound and went on to retire from the Navy in 1978 as a master chief petty officer with twenty-six years of service. Today he is working for a defense contractor and lives in San Diego, California. He recently was contracted to do some work on the USS *Meyerkord* (FF-1058), and was made an honorary crew member.

On 16 October 1965, the homecoming game at Riverview Gardens High School in St. Louis was preceded by a dedication ceremony. A Navy color guard was present as the football field was renamed Dale Meyerkord Memorial Field. In the fall of 1965, Secretary of the Navy Paul H. Nitze presented the Navy Cross to Dale's widow. His mother and father were also present at the ceremony. In July 1967, Captain Hardcastle was the guest speaker at the christening of the destroyer escort USS *Meyerkord*. Later in the war, one of the officer billets in Saigon was officially renamed the Meyerkord. Dickey Chapelle's article "Water War in Vietnam" appeared in the February 1966 issue of *National Geographic* magazine. A picture of Dale Meyerkord, rifle in one hand, radio in the other, was captioned: " 'He was a *man,*' said Dickey Chapelle of Lieutenant Meyerkord. . . . It was her highest accolade. . . ."

Early on a bright November morning in 1965, a U.S. Marine patrol advanced on a Viet Cong–held village near Chu

Lai, on the second day of an operation called Black Ferret. Among the Marines was a woman clad in camouflage and armed with bandoliers of cameras and cans of film. She had spent the previous night in a foxhole she had dug herself, while rain and illumination flares had fallen from the sky. As the Marine patrol approached a cane field near the village, one of the Marines caught a tripwire with his boot and a VC booby-trap exploded, throwing shrapnel in a deadly arc that cut down seven of the patrol. One of them was Dickey Chapelle, the first American woman correspondent ever to die in action.

2

OPERATION MARKET TIME

The Coastal Surveillance Force (Task Force 115)

But as the Southern coast, from its extent and many inlets, might have been a source of strength, so from these very characteristics, it became a fruitful source of injury.

—Alfred Thayer Mahan, 1887

"On Missions in Distant Areas"

When Vietnam was divided at the close of the Indochina War in 1954, Article 14 of the Geneva Accords allowed a period of free passage during which "any civilians residing in a district controlled by one party who wish to go and live in the zone assigned to the other party shall be permitted and helped to do so by the authorities in that district." In the three hundred days that followed the signing of the accords, nearly a million people left the North, while only 40,000 left the South. The U.S. Navy participated in the evacuation from north to south in an operation dubbed "Passage to Freedom" by sea-lifting more than 300,000 people.

The partitioning of Vietnam was intended, according to the Geneva agreements, to be only temporary. But few took that intention seriously, as indicated by the fact that so many left their homes to go south and by the mad scrambles by both sides to accumulate equipment and supplies in their respective zones. Besides the thousands of people the U.S. Navy moved during the "Passage to Freedom," 68,757 tons of cargo and 8,135 vehicles were also removed from North Vietnam and turned over to the South.

Many of the refugees were Catholics who feared repression from the Communist government in the North. Most were people who saw a better chance for freedom in the South and were willing to "vote with their feet." Some, however, had less admirable motivations.

Ho Chi Minh, from his seat of power in North Vietnam, anticipated the need for troops in the South if he were to have any hope of reuniting Vietnam under his Communist regime. To accomplish that, some of his cadre remained in the South to build an insurgency against the South Vietnamese government; and some of those who moved south during the "Passage" came not in search of freedom but to subvert it.

By those means the seeds of insurgency in South Vietnam were planted. But such small forces alone could not hope to succeed. More men would be needed, and they would need supplies. The obvious answer was infiltration.

By the beginning of the 1960s, U.S. and South Vietnamese intelligence agencies were convinced that the Communists were infiltrating substantial quantities of men and matériel into South Vietnam. Even the Indian and Canadian members of the International Control Commission, created by the Geneva Accords, concluded in a report in 1962 "that armed and unarmed personnel, arms, munitions, and other supplies have been sent from the zone in the north to the south with the objective of supporting, organizing, and carrying on hostile activities, including armed attacks, directed against the Armed Forces and administration of the zone in the south." (Predictably, the ICC representative from Poland dissented.) Despite the general agreement that infiltration was taking place, there was considerable disagreement as to how it was being accomplished, with one school of thought holding that the infiltration was by sea, another that it was by land through the wilderness of Laos and Cambodia, and a third that it was a combination of the two.

In December 1961 attention was focused on the sea as U.S. Navy oceangoing minesweepers (MSOs) were ordered to join VNN ships in setting up a barrier patrol near the seventeenth parallel, which divided the two Vietnams. The MSOs themselves were not permitted to stop any ships, but using radar and visual surveillance they would locate suspicious vessels and then direct the VNN ships in to intercept them. Then, in February, similar patrols were added in the Gulf of Thailand using American destroyer escorts (DEs) to guard South Vietnam's southwestern flank against possible infiltration from Cambodia by sea. These patrols, not netting much of significance, cast doubt upon the sea theory. In May the DE patrols were suspended, and the MSOs followed suit in August.

But the controversy continued. For the most part, senior Army officers were convinced at this time that the infiltration was coming primarily, if not completely, from the sea. Captain Chung Tan Cang, Vietnamese Chief of Naval Operations, told his American counterpart, Captain Hardcastle, that he believed approximately 60 percent of the infiltration was by sea and the rest was coming by land. The U.S. Navy was undecided.

In early 1964 a decision was made to learn more about the problem. Admiral Harry D. Felt, CINCPAC, sent a nine-man team of naval officers, headed by Rear Admiral Paul Savidge, to Vietnam to explore the infiltration problem and to recommend remedial action. The team was to travel extensively by small plane, helicopter, junk, and patrol craft throughout the Mekong Delta and Rung Sat Special Zone, including the upper Mekong River complex, the coastline from Ha Tien to Vung Tau, and Phu Quoc Island. Just after the team began its survey, Admiral Savidge developed an illness serious enough to require him to return to the United States. Captain Phil Bucklew took over as head of the team.

Despite his anxiousness to get back to his new command (he had recently been assigned as prospective commanding officer of the Naval Operations Support Group in Coronado, California), Captain Bucklew attacked the Vietnam mission with characteristic energy. He and his team members covered thousands of miles and talked with local customs officials, members of the Civil Guard, Special Forces team members at remote posts, VNN officers on ships and junks, U.S. Navy advisors, staff members at South Vietnamese Army III and IV Corps headquarters, the naval attaché at the U.S. embassy, and General Paul Harkins (then chief of the U.S. MAAG). The team made many stops, scheduled and spontaneous, during its travels. Its members extended their journey well outside the delta region, traveling as far north as Da Nang, visiting remote offshore islands, and monitoring activity at the Cambodian border. They saw hamlets in the backwaters of the delta, located almost side by side, one flying the flag of South Vietnam and the other flying the flag of the Viet Cong. They observed Viet Cong craft in plain sight just across the Cambodian border. They visited a captured VC ammunition depot that stockpiled five tons of ammunition, 90 percent of which was Chinese Communist in origin. They read intelligence reports from the Central Highlands that told of elephants being used by the Viet Cong to move heavy weapons and supplies.

Captain Bucklew was not new to the Orient, and he knew that patience was one of the greatest weapons available to the Oriental when clashing with the West. From the evidence gathered, he concluded that the infiltration was coming from all fronts. It was the Oriental capability of moving and waiting, moving and waiting, perhaps even working in the fields as they went along, that made the infiltration so difficult to detect and, in the end, so effective. The Western mind sought efficient, economical ways of accomplishing a task. But the Viet Cong saw nothing wrong with using canoelike *klong* craft to move short distances each night through the myriad canals in the Mekong Delta. They didn't consider cost-effectiveness when they buried parts of a Communist Chinese 7.62-mm carbine in a sack of rice to be carried on the back of a "peasant." Their soldiers in the field did not consider it a hardship to assemble their ammunition from components smuggled in by sampan under a load of fish.

The report that came out of the team's fact-finding mission, dated 15 February 1964, became known as the "Bucklew Report." It provided a comprehensive assessment of the enemy's infiltration methods and the South Vietnamese counter-infiltration tactics. The report addressed the land and sea infiltration issues:

> It is believed that Viet Cong military personnel are infiltrated primarily over the land routes, while the Bassac and Mekong River complex provides a natural and easily penetrable waterway route for infiltration and movement of heavy material. . . . the use of seagoing junks and fishing boats as a means of infiltrating special Viet Cong agents by sea into the northern area of the Republic of Vietnam . . . [has] been proven by capture. There is evidence that limited amounts of supplies, including heavy machinery, and weapons have been infiltrated into northern and central Republic of Vietnam in the same way. . . . Capture on the island of Phu Quoc of material used for explosives, and reported movement of limited amounts of Viet Cong personnel to and from the island, reasonably indicate similar, though perhaps limited, activity in the Gulf of Siam.

The report was critical of the effectiveness of the Junk Force and the River Assault Groups in their ability to counter the infiltration. A long list of recommendations included a call for strengthening the coastal patrol to create a virtual blockade, augmenting the coastal patrol with U.S. Seventh Fleet ships and air reconnaissance patrols, increasing the number of U.S. Navy advisors to both the Junk and River forces, authorizing the use of U.S. Navy boat operators, and creating a viable means of controlling the rivers by implementing barricades, curfews, checkpoints, and patrols.

Although none of the Bucklew Report's recommendations were immediately acted upon, the report spawned a significant amount of debate, and it provided a documentary reference that would be relied upon time and again as new faces came to Vietnam to make new decisions and policies. Eventually, nearly every recommendation in the report would be carried out, but in early 1964, the time was not yet ripe for any major U.S. commitments in South Vietnam.

When South Vietnamese President Diem was overthrown and assassinated in November 1963, there began a series of coups and counter-coups lasting for nearly two years. This instability took its toll. The Viet Cong scored more victories against the demoralized South Vietnamese forces, and the potential for victory grew tauntingly closer for North Vietnam's military mastermind, General Vo Nguyen Giap. The architect of victory over the French at Dien Bien Phu ten years earlier, Giap decided it was time for a change. His strategy was based on a three-phase war, the third phase of which called for large-scale operations. Giap saw the precarious state of the South Vietnamese government as the signal for an escalation, and he decided to step up operations in the South by sending in units of the NVA and by employing the indigenous Viet Cong cadre in overt confrontations with the South Vietnamese government troops. Until this point, the Viet Cong had been carrying out the less intense phase one and two guerrilla operations using a motley collection of weapons that had been captured, or smuggled in; phase three would require more weapons and a lot more ammunition. Because supplying many different kinds of weapons with ammunition was a logistical nightmare, plans were made to standardize the Viet Cong weapons and make them compatible with those carried by the NVA units now coming south. This committed Hanoi to a significant expansion of its infiltration operation. NVA troops, weapons, and ammunition traveled down the Ho Chi Minh Trail through Laos, and seaborne infiltration efforts were stepped up. North Vietnamese Naval Transportation Group 125 was called into action.

On the morning of 3 March 1965, a UH-1B helicopter piloted by Lieutenant James S. Bowers, U.S. Army, lifted off the pad at Qui Nhon on the central coast of South Vietnam and flew south along the coast past the great green mountains of the Chaine Annamitique. This massive cordillera formed much of the border between Vietnam and its neighbors to the west, Laos and Cambodia; but here on the central coast, the mountains had reached across narrow Vietnam and crowded up to the shore, many of them with their feet immersed in the aquamarine waters of the South China Sea. Blanched-white beaches punctuated the irregular shoreline, and along some stretches large sand dunes looked like drifts of snow in contrast to the shadowy green of the surrounding slopes.

Just before 1030, Lieutenant Bowers passed the Cap Varella lighthouse and banked the helicopter slightly, rounding the promontory that embraced a small bay named Vung Ro. He looked down into the rather picturesque bay and for no conscious reason focused on a small tree-covered island. Almost immediately he realized something was not right. Helicopter pilots, because they sometimes fly in formation, rely on their ability to detect even the smallest amount of relative motion. Lieutenant Bowers's "pilot's eye" had sensed that the island was moving.

Taking a closer look, to his dismay he saw that the "island" was in fact a small ship and that many potted trees had been placed on the decks and superstructure as camouflage. Lieutenant Bowers immediately radioed the Second Coastal Zone senior advisor, Lieutenant Harvey P. Rodgers, USN. What was to be called the "Vung Ro Incident" was under way.

For the next several days air strikes and beach assaults were conducted. In the end, the "island" lay on her side, beached and broken. The captured vessel and surrounding land yielded the evidence that had long been sought. A preliminary survey revealed one million rounds of small-arms ammunition, more than 1,000 stick grenades, 500 pounds of TNT in prepared charges, 2,000 rounds of 82-mm mortar ammunition, 500 antitank grenades, 1,500 rounds of recoilless rifle ammunition, more than 3,600 rifles and submachine guns, and 500 pounds of medical supplies. Labels on the contraband revealed that the sources were Communist China, the Soviet Union, North Vietnam, Czechoslovakia, and East Germany. Aboard the vessel and in the possession of some of the dead crew members were a Haiphong (North Vietnam) newspaper dated 23 January 1965, North Vietnamese nautical charts, postcards and letters to addresses in North Vietnam, military health records of North Vietnamese soldiers, and a snapshot showing a group of men in NVA uniforms under a flag of the Hanoi government. On one of the bodies found at the site was a page from the dead man's Communist Party Record stating that he was a soldier of the NVA 338th Division; a notation stated that he had been "on missions in distant areas," Hanoi's euphemism for activity in South Vietnam. The vessel itself was a 130-foot, steel-hulled trawler, displacing approximately 100 tons. It had been built in Communist China, and documents on board indicated that it was unit K.35 of North Vietnamese Naval Transportation Group 125.

Members of the press and the International Control Commission were brought in to see the ship and its cargo. There was no longer any doubt that supplies were coming in from the sea. The controversy over proportions would continue throughout the war, but the evidence was at last incontrovertible that the North Vietnamese were shipping war supplies into South Vietnam by sea.

The day after the Vung Ro Incident ended, General Westmoreland requested CINCPAC and CINCPACFLT (Commander in Chief of the Pacific Fleet) to send representatives to Saigon to plan a counteroperation to the now-proven sea infiltration.

Nascent Market Time

The Vung Ro Incident had done more than prove that North Vietnam was infiltrating supplies by sea: it cast serious doubt about the South Vietnamese capability for countering that infiltration. Although the trawler had been disabled in early air strikes called in soon after Lieutenant Bowers had reported the ship to the Second Coastal Zone, nearly five days had passed before the ship was finally under friendly control. There were instances of bravery, but overall the American advisors perceived a reluctance among the Vietnamese to aggressively prosecute the incident. One advisor wrote a stinging postaction report that cited, among other things, Vietnamese inability to coordinate land and sea forces effectively, numerous instances of VNN vessels being driven off by enemy fire that the advisor did not see as heavy enough to warrant aborting the mission, and procrastination that "seemed to be based on a hope for cancellation of the operation rather than on any evidence of significant numbers of enemy troops." This same advisor concluded that "every decision of the Vietnamese Navy relative to landing troops was based on personal preference for avoiding contact with the Viet Cong and, in each case, completely ignored the assigned mission."

There is evidence that some of the alleged shortcomings were actually the result of misunderstandings between the Vietnamese and the Americans, and it is also possible that the Americans were being too aggressive under the circumstances. Whether the accusations were correct didn't matter; in any case, the result was that the Americans were disappointed in their ally's performance. At a time when U.S. forces were already beginning to assume new, more overt combat roles (U.S. aircraft had struck North Vietnamese barracks in Operation Flaming Dart nine days before Vung Ro and plans were already under way for landing two battalions of American Marines at Da Nang), this American vote of no confidence in the VNN naturally led to thoughts of American naval participation in the anticipated patrol effort. The stage was set when General Westmoreland convened his meeting with the representatives of CINCPAC, CINCPACFLT, and the Naval Advisory Group in March 1965.

The group met at MACV headquarters in downtown Saigon for about a week, with the discussion centering on the now-proven infiltration, the perceived poor performance of the South Vietnamese, and possible responses to the situation. Two kinds of sea infiltration would have to be countered: trawler traffic and seagoing junks. The steel-hulled trawlers were apparently coming down from North Vietnam well clear of the coast to avoid any patrolling forces, then making a perpendicular dash into the coastal point of debarkation, greatly reducing their chances of interception. The seagoing junks, because they were less obvious, could move closer to shore, paralleling the coast and mingling with the legitimate native traffic.

To interdict both kinds of traffic, a joint U.S./South Vietnamese patrol effort extending out as far as forty miles from shore was needed. Authorization from the South Vietnamese government was required to allow the U.S. units to "stop, board, search, and, if necessary, capture and/or destroy any hostile suspicious craft or vessel found within [its] territorial and contiguous zone waters." Coastal Serveillance Centers to coordinate the patrols were to be manned by Americans and Vietnamese at Da Nang, Qui Nhon, Nha Trang, Vung Tau, and An Thoi. Naval Advisory Group personnel would assume these new duties in addition to their regular duties until more personnel could be brought into Vietnam. The code name "Market Time," derived from the task of sifting infiltrators out of the many marketing vessels, was assigned to the operation.

The Vung Ro Incident had sparked a feeling of urgency. By 16 March the U.S. Navy destroyers USS *Black* (DD-666) and USS *Higbee* (DD-806), dispatched from Task Force 71, an element of the Seventh Fleet, were on patrol. Aircraft patrols were covered in the early stages by A-1 Skyraiders from aircraft carriers positioned at "Dixie Station" off the South Vietnamese coast and by P-3 Orion aircraft out of Sangley Point in the Philippines.

By the first week in April, twenty-eight U.S. Navy vessels were participating in Market Time patrols. But the draft of these ships (destroyers, destroyer escorts, and minesweepers) limited how close to shore they could go. The low confidence in the Junk Force and other VNN units expressed in the March meetings at MACV had resulted in the official conclusion that "the best tactic to interdict coastal traffic infiltration would be to assist and inspire the Vietnamese Navy to increase the quality and quantity of its searches." It was subsequently decided that the best way to assist and inspire was to introduce U.S. patrol craft that could join the search in the more shallow waters.

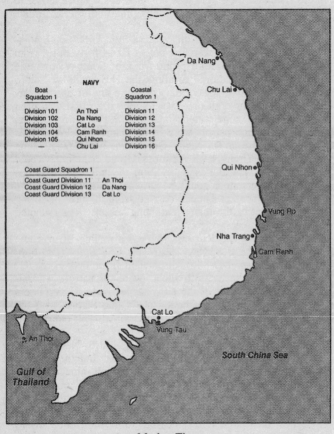

Market Time

Since no appropriate patrol craft existed in the U.S. Navy's inventory, two ways to obtain the craft were explored. The first was a priority study to find a suitable craft that could be obtained quickly, concentrating on finding an existing hull that could be easily modified because designing and building craft from the keel up would take too long. The second was to turn to the experts in coastal patrol, the United States Coast Guard. On 16 April 1965 Secretary of the Navy Paul Nitze asked Secretary of the Treasury Henry Fowler for Coast Guard help. Always prepared to respond in a crisis, the commandant of the Coast Guard informed the Navy Department that seventeen 82-foot WPB craft could be made available; planning was immediately begun to get them to Vietnam as quickly as possible.

Initially, the Market Time patrols were under the operational control of Commander Task Force 71 as a component of the Seventh Fleet, but on 30 April 1965 Secretary of Defense McNamara approved the transfer of control to the chief of the Naval Advisory Group as Commander Task Force 115 (designated as the Coastal Surveillance Force) to take place on 31 July. CHNAVADVGRU was upgraded to a rear admiral's billet, and Rear Admiral Norvell G. Ward, USN, was ordered in to relieve Captain Hardcastle. In April of the following year, CHNAVADVGRU donned the additional "hat" of Commander Naval Forces, Vietnam (COMNAVFORV), assuming command of all U.S. Navy operational forces in Vietnam.

On 11 May the South Vietnamese government granted formal approval for U.S. units to "stop, search, and seize vessels not clearly engaged in innocent passage." South Vietnamese territorial waters up to the three-mile limit were a "Defensive Sea Area" within which suspect vessels were subject to arrest; the contiguous zone extending out to twelve miles would be controlled "to the extent necessary to prevent infringement of their customs, fiscal, immigration, and sanitary regulations"; and vessels outside the twelve-mile contiguous zone could be searched if reasonably believed to be South Vietnamese, even if those vessels were flying a foreign flag or no flag at all.

So by mid-1965, the U.S. Navy (and the U.S. Coast Guard), like the U.S. Army, Air Force, and Marine Corps, had taken on an operational role in Vietnam in addition to an advisory one. The decision was not made without opposition, but those closest to the situation saw it as essential; and once the policy was decided, it would be aggressively prosecuted.

Hardware

President Kennedy, a renowned PT-boat skipper in World War II, did not live to know how prescient he had been in saying "the need for small fast armed vessels shall not wane." But neither Kennedy nor his successor, Johnson, had taken any steps to ensure the inclusion of shallow-water patrol craft in the U.S. Navy's inventory. As on other similar occasions in American naval history, the U.S. Navy found itself needing such craft but having none. In the words of Voltaire, "History does not repeat itself, but man always does."

Turning to the Coast Guard for help was an obvious remedy. Already in the Coast Guard's inventory were forty-four 82-foot cutters known as WPBs. These steel-hulled craft had aluminum superstructures and displaced approximately 65 tons, while having only slightly more than a 5½-foot draft. Twin-screwed and diesel-driven, they were capable of 18 knots and had a reputation for seaworthiness. Because engine speed was controlled by throttles on the bridge and main engine, and generator alarms were also located in the wheelhouse, a manned watch in the engine room was not required. This, coupled with a console centered about the wheel, containing controls for the navigation, radio, and radar equipment, enabled a single man to steer, control engine speed, talk on the radio, and watch the radar and fathometer, leaving the rest of the crew free to man weapons and conduct searches.

Weapons were an important consideration in the upcoming operations. The trawler that had been captured at Vung Ro was heavily armed, and even the junks and sampans to be searched could be expected to fight if carrying contraband and challenged by a search vessel. In preparation for these anticipated challenges, the single 20-mm gun on the forecastle was removed from the cutters and replaced by a "piggyback" arrangement of a .50-caliber machine gun on top of an 81-mm mortar. Four additional .50-caliber machine guns were installed on the main deck, aft of the wheelhouse, and ready-service ammunition boxes were also installed on deck. Crew members would be issued additional hand-held weapons as well. This combination of weapons was expected to provide the right mix of punch and flexibility to handle almost any situation. The machine guns would supply a high volume of fire that could suppress any close-aboard opposition, and the 81-mm mortar (unlike the 20-mm gun that was removed) was sufficiently powerful to inflict heavy damage on steel-hulled trawlers as well as to provide illumination fire and shore bombardment as necessary.

Other modifications for Vietnam service included the installation of additional bunks and refrigerators to increase on-station time. Another significant change involved the manning: normally WPBs were commanded by chief petty officers, but for Market Time two officers were assigned in addition to a nine-man enlisted crew.

Secretary Fowler had originally promised seventeen WPBs for us in Vietnam and nine more were authorized in September 1965. Of the original seventeen, nine were designated as Coast Guard Division 11, to operate in the Gulf of Thailand, and eight as Coast Guard Division 12, for service near the seventeenth parallel. In February 1966, the additional nine WPBs were dispatched to operate out of Cat Lo (near Vung Tau) as Coast Guard Division 13. These three divisions were components of Coast Guard Squadron 1, commissioned on 26 May 1965 at Alameda, California, under the command of Commander James A. Hodgman, USCG.

The original seventeen craft were removed from their stateside search-and-rescue duties and in May 1965 were loaded as deck cargo on Military Sea Transport Service ships in Seattle, San Francisco, Long Beach, Galveston, New Orleans, Norfolk, and New York. The crews of these craft were maintained as integral units, and they, with the added officers, reported for stateside predeployment training in communications, use of weapons, and survival procedures. Men and boats were reunited in Subic Bay, Philippines, where some last-minute modifications and repairs were effected. On 12 June Coast Guard Squadron 1 changed operational control to the Navy, and on 16 July the eight cutters of Division 12, under the command of Lieutenant Commander Richard Knapp, left Subic Bay with the LST *Snohomish County* for the trip across the South China Sea to Da Nang. The nine craft of Division 11 left for An Thoi, with the LST *Floyd County,* on 24 July. Commander Hodgman assumed command of this division as well as retaining overall command of Squadron 1. An Thoi was 1,100 miles from Subic, requiring the WPBs to refuel several times en route including underway refueling from the *Floyd County* in seas of 15 feet and winds of more than 35 knots.

Upon arrival at their respective bases, these units of Coast Guard Squadron 1 reported to Commander Task Force 71, but remained under his control only a short time. On 30 July 1965 the Coastal Surveillance Force was officially created as Task Force 115; all Market Time units thereafter reported to Commander Task Force 115.

One more modification to the WPBs was yet to come. On her first patrol, the USCGC *Point Orient* (WPB-82319) was fired on by mortars and machine guns from shore. On that moonlit night it quickly became clear that the characteristic white paint of Coast Guard vessels was not going to work in a combat environment. The very next day, work began on repainting the cutters a more practical deck gray.

The Navy's search for a suitable craft to augment the WPBs in shallow-water Market Time operations ended with the discovery of a fifty-foot, all-welded aluminum alloy boat that was being used in the Gulf of Mexico to transport crews to and from offshore drilling rigs. The builder, Sewart Seacraft of Burwick, Louisiana, readily agreed to do a combat version of the craft and soon was producing what became known as the PCF (Patrol Craft, Fast) or, more commonly, the "Swift boat." These snub-nosed little craft displaced 19 tons and had a draft of only 3½ feet; their twin screws were powered by two diesel engines, which gave them a maximum speed of 28 knots. Although the Navy's Bureau of Ships required more than fifty military modifications to the craft, Sewart was able to deliver the first four Swifts in a mere forty days. Among the most important modifications was the weapons configuration. A twin .50-caliber machine-gun mount was located in a gun tub on top of the pilothouse. The same piggyback arrangement (of an 81-mm mortar with a .50-caliber machine gun mounted over it) that had been mounted on the forecastle of the WPBs was placed on the fantail of the Swifts. Additional hand-held weapons would be included in the crew's arsenal.

The long trip to Vietnam started aboard railroad flatcars in Burwick, where the PCFs were taken to deepwater docks for loading aboard merchant ships. From two to eight were mounted on deck in skids for the transoceanic voyage to Subic Bay in the Philippines. At the Subic naval base they were transferred to the well deck of an LSD (Landing Ship, Dock) for the final leg to Vietnam. Several boats were sent to Coronado, and later moved to Mare Island, for training purposes.

Originally fifty-four Swifts had been planned for Market Time, but in a meeting convened in September 1965 at CHNAVADVGRU headquarters in Saigon, representatives from CINCPAC, CINCPACFLT, MACV, the office of the Chief of Naval Operations, and, of course, CHNAVADVGRU decided to increase the number to eighty-four for more thorough coverage.

The Navy organization for the PCFs had been set up somewhat differently from the Coast Guard's for the WPBs. Boat Squadron 1 was created to organize the anticipated eighty-four PCFs into five separate boat divisions: Division 101 operating out of An Thoi (in conjunction with Coast Guard Division 11); Division 102 out of Da Nang (with Coast Guard Division 12); Division 103 out of Cat Lo (where Coast Guard Division 13 would subsequently form up using the added nine WPBs in February 1966); Division 104, Cam Ranh Bay; and Division 105, Qui Nhon. A division was to be commanded by a lieutenant; and officers in charge of individual boats would be lieutenants (j.g.). A boat would be manned by one officer and an enlisted crew of five, with one and a half crews per boat to permit an adequate rotation schedule.

Commander Arthur Ismay, USN, who had been Admiral Ward's flag secretary, was given command of Boat Squadron 1. When informed of his coming command, Commander Ismay left Vietnam for a trip to Coronado to set up a training program there for the squadron. While in California he released a message on 1 October 1965 activating Boat Squadron 1. He alone was commander and staff, and his whole organization was at that time contained in a borrowed briefcase;

nonetheless, the squadron had been born and, like any healthy newborn, would grow quickly. Personnel, mostly volunteers, began rolling into Coronado faster than the training program could handle them. The first Swifts (PCF-3 and PCF-4) arrived at An Thoi on 30 October. Less than thirty hours after their arrival, they went on patrol with the WPBs *Point Comfort* and *Point Garnet,* firing on an unknown number of Viet Cong with their 81-mm mortars. Six more PCFs arrived at An Thoi on Christmas eve.

The buildup of PCFs continued until the programmed total of eighty-four was reached in November 1966. As new groups of craft arrived in Vietnam, they were allocated to the various divisions as deemed necessary. Of sixteen that arrived in July 1966, for example, five went to Division 102 (for a total of seventeen), three to 101 (total ten), five to 103 (total fifteen), three to 104 at Cam Ranh (total sixteen), and none to 105 at Qui Nhon (total ten).

On 1 January 1967 Boat Squadron 1 was redesignated Coastal Squadron 1, and Boat Divisions 101–105 became Coastal Divisions 11–15. An additional unit, Coastal Division 16, was activated at Chu Lai in June of that year.

While the WPBs and PCFs were the real workhorses of Task Force 115, making the most patrols and consequently accumulating the most impressive statistics, other craft also participated in the patrols.

Radar-picket destroyer escorts (DERs) patrolled the outermost barrier of Market Time. These 1700-ton, 306-foot-long vessels had been reconfigured from a simple destroyer escort design to a radar-picket version in the mid-1950s. They were designed to patrol the high latitudes of the Atlantic and Pacific oceans as part of the northern early-warning defense network set up by the U.S. and Canada to detect an incoming Soviet attack. By the inception of Market Time, these early-warning sea patrols had lost favor among strategists and the DERs were being decommissioned. About a dozen were retained in service for the new patrol requirements in Vietnam.

These little ships not only were well equipped with radar and communications equipment, they were powered by an economical diesel plant that required infrequent refueling; endurance was 11,500 miles at 11 knots. This factor, coupled with their sea-keeping ability, superior to that of the smaller

PCFs and WPBs, enabled the DERs to patrol with few interruptions; even when the monsoon winds had driven other patrol craft to safe haven, the DERs were more often than not still on station. Moreover, these ships were air-conditioned—no minor point in the heat of Southeast Asia.

In some areas, such as the Ca Mau Peninsula, the base was so far from the patrol sector that the PCFs and WPBs had to spend much of their time in transit, with a consequent reduction in their on-station time. The problem was solved by sending two crews to the area aboard the patrol craft and rotating them through a series of alternating twenty-four-hour patrols and rest periods aboard a nearby DER. With the DER functioning as a remote base, a shallow-water patrol craft could be kept on station for long periods at great distances from its parent base. Conveniently, the DERs' fuel and lubricating oil were compatible with those of the PCFs and WPBs.

The DERs' most important function was to watch for large infiltrators, such as the steel-hulled trawlers. Out in deep water, they encountered the very small craft typical of the coastal shallows only infrequently. Nonetheless, boarding and searching were common. A typical boarding inspection was accomplished by an armed boarding party in the ship's motor whaleboat. The coxswain, bowhook, and engineer were armed with rifles, while the actual boarders usually carried only sidearms so that their hands would be free to open compartments, move cargo, and aid in the precarious step (or jump) to and from the boarded vessel. The DERs had been augmented with several .50-caliber machine guns, and these were always manned as the ship hovered protectively near her motor whaleboat. Frequently a VNN liaison officer rode in the DER while she was on station and was normally included in the boarding party.

In addition to the DERs, minesweepers—both the MSO and the coastal minesweeper (MSC)—were frequent participants in the Market Time patrols. They provided radar coverage, sent boarding and inspection parties, and to a lesser degree served as parent ships to the WPBs and PCFs, though refueling from them was much slower than with the DERs. Typically, a minesweeper stopped in the Philippines on her way to Vietnam and received two .30-caliber machine guns to provide firepower. Because of the unusual nature of the operations, boarding parties had to be organized and integrated on a rotating basis so that the added burden could be adequately and equitably covered.

Because Market Time assets were stretched thin in early 1967, the Navy requested additional help from the Coast Guard. A squadron of five high-endurance cutters (WHECs) was formed at Pearl Harbor on 24 April 1967 and two days later sailed for Subic Bay, its permanent headquarters. This new squadron was christened Coast Guard Squadron 3. These World War II and pre-World War II WHECs were roughly similar in size and capability to the Navy DERs and performed many of the same functions. Like the DERs and MSOs (and unlike the PCFs and WPBs), the WHECs deployed from U.S. waters on a rotating basis averaging eight months per deployment. Coast Guard Squadron 3's assets were typically five WHECs at any one time.

Because of their shallow draft, the WHECs drew a lot of on-station time in the Gulf of Thailand, patrolling and parenting the WPBs and PCFs as the DERs did. There and elsewhere they provided gunfire support to units ashore, conducted antitrawler surveillance and intercept patrols, and provided frequent medical assistance to American and Vietnamese casualties. They used a helicopter flight deck to receive parts and supplies and to evacuate the seriously wounded. The WHECs remained in service in Vietnam through most of the war, until the USCGC *Cook Inlet* made the last cutter combat patrol in Vietnamese waters in December 1971.

The most unusual participant in the Market Time patrols was the Patrol Air Cushion Vehicle (PACV). The SRN-5-class PACV was a Bell Aerosystems version of a commercial craft developed in England by the Saunders-Roe Division of Westland Aircraft Limited; three were prepared as patrol craft for the U.S. Navy. They were capable of an amazing speed of 70 knots, had a hull-borne draft of only one foot, and skimmed across the water with a hull clearance of four feet when airborne. The 1,900-hp gas-turbine power plant drove an air screw for propulsion and a lift fan for airborne operations.

Three PACVs went to Vietnam for evaluation in several

roles. They participated in Market Time operations from 20 September to 17 October 1966 and were incorporated as part of Boat Squadron 1 under the administrative title of PACV Division 107 and the task designator of Commander Task Group 115.3. Operating out of Cat Lo near the mouths of the rivers leading to Saigon, these "dragon boats," as the Vietnamese fishermen often called them, conducted twenty-four patrols. Despite their innovative capabilities, the PACVs were not very well suited for Market Time. The nature of the patrols rarely required the phenomenal speed or zero-draft capabilities of the PACVs, and their range and endurance were considerably less than those of the conventional patrol craft. In addition, their high noise level and limited visibility hampered their effectiveness for surveillance, and anything more than a two-foot sea increased fuel consumption drastically, sometimes causing patrols to anchor or loiter in order to conserve fuel.

The PACVs moved on to participate in other aspects of the naval war after the Market Time evaluation.

On 30 April 1967, the USS *Gallup* (PG-85), one of the newly built *Asheville*-class patrol gunboats, sailed into Vietnamese waters. These 165-foot-long vessels were capable of 37 knots and were armed with a 3-inch/.50-caliber gun forward, a 40-mm gun aft, one 81-mm mortar, and two .50-caliber machine guns. Joined later by the hydrofoil patrol gunboats USS *Flagstaff* (PGH-1) and USS *Tucumcari* (PGH-2), these gunboats formed a new organization, Coastal Squadron 3, operating out of Cam Ranh. Coastal Squadrons 1 (PCFs) and 3 (PGs and PGHs) were then incorporated into a new command designated Coastal Flotilla 1.

The PGs at first suffered a number of mechanical difficulties, exacerbated by a repair parts supply problem, but eventually the setbacks were overcome and the PGs saw useful service in the Market Time scenario. The PGHs, on the other hand, proved too complex for the available repair facilities in the theater and were eventually withdrawn.

The most diminutive of all the Market Time craft was the "skimmer." Known to recreational and commercial boaters as the Boston Whaler, this 13-foot fiberglass craft found an unexpected but very useful niche in Market Time operations. Coast Guardsmen in the WPBs discovered that they were wasting a lot of time bringing the large WPBs alongside the smaller junks and sampans. They were also concerned about the loss of mobility while next to the Vietnamese craft, realizing that a quick response was impossible should an unsearched craft begin evasive or hostile action. So the skimmer was drafted into service to allow a boarding party to go alongside suspect vessels while leaving the WPB free to maneuver in the vicinity and able to pursue any would-be evaders or take defensive action if necessary. The skimmer's light weight and small size made it easy to handle and permitted convenient stowage on board. With the addition of a coat of gray paint, flak jackets to wrap around the gas tanks, signal flares, and a portable radio, the Boston Whaler of waterskiing fame became a wartime asset of the U.S. Coast Guard.

Naval aviation played an important role in Market Time as well. Various types of aircraft had been patrolling the waters off South Vietnam long before Market Time, but Market Time planners recognized their potential importance in giving early warning of inbound trawlers and spotting suspicious activities among junks or along the coast.

Through the years of Market Time a number of different aircraft from a large assortment of squadrons ran the tedious, inglorious patrols along the 1,200 miles of South Vietnamese coast. P-2 Neptunes, P-3 Orions, and P-5 Marlins from squadrons VP-4, VP-17, VP-40, VP-47, VP-48, VP-49, and VP-50 flew from Tan Son Nhut Airbase (just outside Saigon), Cam Ranh Bay, Sangley Point in the Philippines, and Utapao Airbase in Thailand. From May 1965 to April 1967, P-5 Marlin seaplanes operated from the seaplane tenders USS *Salisbury Sound* (AV-13), USS *Pine Island* (AV-12), and USS *Currituck* (AV-7) anchored as seadromes at Cam Ranh Bay, Condore Island, and Cham Island at various times.

The air patrols received little press coverage, were long and dull for the most part, and were involved in interceptions of infiltrators only a small percentage of the time. Yet their importance was apparent. Planes could cover large expanses of water in a very short time and, by a system of reporting to a central tracking center, could keep tabs on suspicious vessels lingering in international waters waiting to make their dash on the coast. The undesirable alternative was to commit DERs or WHECs to a full-time shadowing operation whenever suspects were loitering offshore.

The aircraft patrolled day and night, flying without lights during darkness to avoid being seen. Their altitudes were typically 400–800 feet, sometimes less. Besides being boring, their task was difficult: examining hundreds of vessels plying the waters with little to differentiate them. One pilot described the nighttime scene with so many vessels lit up by their running lights and cooking fires as "like a city at night."

The danger from hostile action while on patrol was slight, but flying at such low altitudes, particularly in total darkness, did not leave much of a margin for error to a weary or mesmerized pilot. A greater danger loomed when aircrews were off duty at the highly targetable air bases in Vietnam. At 0115 on 4 December 1966, for example, a Viet Cong unit attacked Tan Son Nhut. An airman guarding the perimeter heard the characteristic *thunk* presaging the incoming barrage of mortar rounds. Accompanied by a hail of small-arms fire, the rounds exploded among the five Market Time aircraft parked at the field. One plane, a P-2 Neptune, was mangled by a direct hit. Another received moderate damage from a near miss, two took only minor hits from the indiscriminate shrapnel, and one charmed aircraft escaped completely unharmed. Fortunately, no personnel were injured. One Market Time flight was missed as a result of the attack, but all aircraft except the one suffering the direct hit were back on line within forty-eight hours (and that one returned to service two weeks later). Such was the life for Americans in-country, Vietnam.

The Market Time aircraft carried out one important collateral mission. After meticulous planning under appropriate security precautions and the establishment of an extensive logistical pipeline, designated aircraft were loaded up with their specialized payloads, code-named "Gold Dust," and took off before dawn. Sometime later they rendezvoused with Market Time PCFs and WPBs on patrol and, after establishing communications, completed their mission by dropping that wartime essential to the patrol craft crews: magazines and newspapers from home.

Souvenirs

One of the certainties of war is that participants will bring home souvenirs. Perhaps for contemporary American sailors a legacy from the privateering part of our naval heritage drives them to seek these "spoils of war." More likely is the simple desire to have something tangible to show that "I was there"—something to hang on a wall or place on a mantel back home, so that visitors will ask the question that permits the veteran to indulge in one of his few rewards: the autobiographical account of his experiences (usually beginning, "I don't want you to think I was some kind of a hero, but . . .").

Another certainty of war is monotony, and monotony is an insidious enemy. It more often than not leads to complacency, which, above all else, causes casualties.

On St. Valentine's Day of 1966, these two certainties gathered forces and descended upon a Navy Swift boat on patrol in the Gulf of Thailand.

Market Time had been in operation for nearly a year by that time, and the pace had been less than stimulating. In July of the previous year, the USS *Buck* (DD-761) had captured some infiltrators during a routine boarding of a junk near the seventeenth parallel. Several of the WPBs had gotten into firefights with Viet Cong junks in the late summer. By close shadowing, the USS *Hissem* (DER-400) and USS *Ingraham* (DD-694) had caused a trawler to abort its New Year's infiltration mission and head back to Communist China. But for the most part, Market Time patrols were uneventful and monotonous.

Even the infrequent incidents of enemy contact were often unsatisfying. The January 1966 CHNAVADVGRU monthly historical summary recorded the details of an incident in which two WPBs, a PCF, and several VNN junks challenged four suspicious-looking junks as they left Bai Bung, on the eastern coast of Phu Quoc Island, presumably on a supply run to the mainland. When confronted by the Market Time units, the junks retreated to the island, where they beached and were abandoned. Heavy fire from the tree line prevented any investigation of the junks. Darkness fell and the opportunity was lost because the Viet Cong were able to remove their contraband before daylight returned. The summary ends with the following paragraph, probably expressing the thoughts of many Market Time personnel: "Incidents like this are apparently hindering intra-country transfer of arms and supplies. However, the inability to prosecute to a final conclusion makes the evaluation hypothetical, and when experienced often enough engenders a feeling of frustration."

PCF-4 had been on routine patrol for many hours on this Valentine's Day. So far the day had been like any other; the men were patrolling, boarding, searching, and patrolling again, scanning the blue waters and green shorelines with tired eyes that burned in the merciless sunlight, lulled into a stupor by the droning diesels. In the late afternoon the Swift was patrolling offshore in Rach Gia Bay, on the western coast of the Mekong Delta. In the distance loomed three small mountains, which the Americans called the Three Sisters, looking formidable in the surrounding alluvial plain. The rumor was that a Viet Cong ammunition factory was hidden in the bowels of one of the peaks. It was not a friendly neighborhood.

At a little past 1600, a crewman spotted an object in the water fairly close to shore. He reported it to the officer in charge, Lieutenant (j.g.) Charlie Bacon, USNR, who immediately ordered his coxswain to set a course to intercept it. Through binoculars, Bacon could see that the object appeared to be a small bamboo raft, empty except for a pole from which flew a Viet Cong flag.

That flag was a potential souvenir and, more important, represented a break in the tedium; Bacon decided to capture it. The young officer knew the risk, so he ordered his crew to battle stations and moved in cautiously, slowly circling the objective several times like a predator evaluating its prey. The flag appeared to be nothing more than an exhibition of defiance, an overt challenge of authority by the guerrillas in the area. But because Bacon's caution was still in control, he ordered one of the crewmen to toss some grenades at the raft. Several grenades exploded close to the little bamboo structure, causing the flagpole to wave frantically for a few seconds—then nothing; no secondary explosions. All was quiet except the rumble of the idling diesels of the Swift.

Charlie Bacon's caution had at last been seduced from him,

and he turned over his command to the fates. He ordered his craft to close in on the bamboo raft. With the ship handling skill characteristic of Swift boat sailors, the coxswain eased the craft directly alongside the raft so that the flag bobbed within arm's reach of the rail. A seaman reached out and grasped the pole. With his knife he began cutting the lashings while his officer in charge leaned out from the pilothouse to observe.

In the shadows of the mangrove trees on the nearby shore, a pair of eyes watched the great gray fish nibble at the bait. It was time to set the hook. Hands holding the wires of a crude but effective detonating circuit came together, allowing bare copper to touch bare copper in deadly union. An explosion erupted beneath the PCF-4, ripping into her underbelly. The main deck buckled upward, crushing and trapping the coxswain against the overhead of the pilothouse; the gunner above was hurled out of his gun-tub and into the water. The Swift, her hull torn open and her frame traumatized, plunged beneath the frothing water almost at once and soothed her wounds in the cool mud of the bay's floor.

Lieutenant Gil Dunn, USN, was sitting at the mess table eating his evening meal with several other Rach Gia advisors when the screen door crashed open. A young American sailor shouted, ''We're getting a 'Mayday' call from one of the VNN junks! They've got some Swift boat sailors on board and they're hurt pretty bad!'' Gil threw down his fork and ran outside to the radio shack in back of the mess hall. As he entered the small hut he heard the hiss and pop of the radio and a frantic voice calling ''Mayday, mayday. PCF-4 mined and sunk off Three Sisters. Need medical assistance immediately.''

Gil immediately called two Army aviators, Lieutenant Norm Svarrer and Captain Ed Lewis, and asked if they could help with the search and rescue operation. They were airborne within twenty minutes. Gil's counterpart, *Dai-uy* Dang, launched a fifteen-foot runabout, which normally served as a recreation boat, and fueled the 45-hp engine. Gil, an Army medic, and a Navy chief gunner's mate piled into the little boat with a first-aid kit, an M-60 machine gun, and a PRC-25 portable radio. They left Rach Gia and turned right, headed up the coast in search of the remnants of PCF-4. Fading daylight and mounting seas did not bode well for the tiny rescue party. The little boat soon gave up trying to climb the gathering swells and began instead to plunge through the aqueous hurdles, the resulting bursts of salt water soaking the occupants and threatening to swamp the outclassed craft. But Gil Dunn had been around small boats most of his life and knew their mettle. He said to the medic in his quiet drawl, "It's rougher'n a cob out here," but drove onward toward the Three Sisters, racing the retiring sun.

From the air, Captain Lewis spotted the broken hulk of PCF-4. As he swooped low, he saw that she was almost completely submerged, only the very top of the pilothouse still visible in the valleys of the swells and the radar mast protruding from the water as though the craft were snorkeling through it. A Vietnamese Navy junk was nearby with three figures lying on the deck. Captain Lewis called Gil on the radio and vectored him to the area. An Army "Dust-off" medical evacuation helicopter and PCF-3 were on their way as well.

Gil climbed aboard the VNN junk. First he reached a seaman lying quite still; Gil checked for his pulse but could find none. While the medic checked one of the others, Gil moved forward to the next figure and found Charlie Bacon. Gil had once ridden on PCF-4, and he and Charlie were friends.

Charlie's eyes registered recognition through the pain. "Gil," he said weakly, "how's my seaman? Is he all right?"

"He's doing fine," Gil lied.

The Vietnamese sailors on the junk had rigged a splint for Charlie's badly broken left leg using an M-14 rifle. He had no other serious wounds visible, but his weakened state worried Gil, who started to tell the medic to check him when the helicopter began hovering above them to take away the wounded.

The sea conditions had continued to deteriorate, and the junk was rising and falling dangerously now as the helicopter came closer. Only the wounded radioman was loaded onto the aircraft before the erratic pitching of the junk brought the helicopter's rotor blades much too close and the rescuers had to wave it off. They tried again, the pilot settling his skids right onto the top of the junk's aft cabin in an attempt to stabilize it, but again the seas were in control. The junk slipped out from beneath the skids and, moving sideways, nearly careened into the deadly rotor-arc once again. The risk too great, the mission was aborted. By radio Gil told the pilot that PCF-3, which had nearly arrived by this time, would take the seaman and the lieutenant on to Rach Gia, where there was a team of American surgeons and nurses. As the sound of the helicopter faded into the darkening sky, Gil looked down at Charlie and realized that he and the radioman were the only survivors of PCF-4's six-man crew.

Once aboard PCF-3, headed back to Rach Gia, Gil noticed that Charlie's other leg seemed swollen. He and the medic removed the elastic blousing strap from the lieutenant's ankle and found that the whole trouser leg had been filling with blood. Ripping open the material, the medic located a severed artery; he quickly applied a tourniquet. Gil sat down on the deck next to Charlie, who clasped his hand for the remainder of the trip. Gil did not yet know that the disaster had occurred because of a reckless souvenir hunt, so he was puzzled later when Charlie looked up at him from the operating table in Rach Gia and said, in a voice filled with remorse, ''I don't hurt in my legs, Gil, I hurt right here.'' He was pointing to his heart.

In the aftermath of the PCF-4 incident, the first loss of a Swift boat in the Vietnam War, Gil Dunn returned to the Three Sisters area with a 20-ton mobile crane loaded on an LCM-8 borrowed from RMK (Raymond, Morrison-Knudsen—a civilian company contracted to do Defense Department construction work in Vietnam). He and others from units in the area were able to recover the remaining bodies and attempted to salvage the sunken Swift. Hostile fire from the nearby shore greatly hampered the operation, but with the combined firepower of Army helicopters, WPBs, PCFs, and VNN junks suppressing the fire, the salvage team hooked onto the Swift and, after several unsuccessful attempts at raising her, dragged the stricken craft into deeper water, out of range of the Viet Cong weapons. The repair ship USS *Krishna* (ARL-38) then raised her. The craft was severely damaged and would never sail again, but the aluminum cadaver was shipped to Subic Bay, where it was carefully evaluated by engineers.

Their analysis of the damage led to improvements in the hull design that would reduce the craft's vulnerability to mine-inflicted damage in the future.

The wounded radioman recovered from his injuries and requested a return to Swift-boat duty. The last Gil ever heard of Charlie Bacon was word from a Saigon hospital that the leg with the severed artery had developed complications and there was considerable doubt that it could be saved.

Tedium and Terror

A market Time sailor's life was one of contrasts. He could spend weeks roasting in the Southeast Asian sun, then find himself battling the pounding seas and torrential rains of the monsoon seasons. He could slowly sink into boredom until nearly catatonic, only to find himself catapulted into a frenzied state of fear. He could encounter the shy but appreciative smiles of people who understood that he was trying to help them, or in a cargo hold he could find a venomous snake that was not there by accident.

And this Market Time life was a dilemma. The young sailor was in a distant land he had only recently heard of to help the Vietnamese people, yet he could never trust any of them. He was there to help them preserve their freedom, yet he had to intrude upon their private lives, rummaging through their possessions, violating their sanctum. The nature of the war and of his occupation dictated that he must review every Vietnamese as a potential friend and, at the same time, as a deadly enemy.

Even the routine was rarely routine for the Market Time sailor. Patrols came and went at different times to prevent the enemy from discerning a pattern. The time spent on patrol also varied depending upon weather conditions, availability of mother ships, and enemy contact. Market Time sailors were frequently called upon by friendly units ashore to provide fire support, often on short notice. Sometimes they were called in for search and rescue operations if a friendly aircraft or vessel went down in their vicinity. Later in the war they would be called upon to leave their coastal sectors and conduct operations in the confines of the rivers.

Market Timers had to deal with frustration. The big catches—the trawlers—were rare. It was not uncommon for them to realize when they had been discovered and abandon their mission before entering South Vietnamese waters. When they did make a run in, they were often countered by the DERs or WHECs on station before they got to shallower waters and the PCFs and WPBs. Consequently, the "small boys" had to deal almost exclusively with junk and sampan traffic. A typical small-craft tactic was to proceed along the coast near the surf line until ordered to come out for inspection by one of the Market Time craft and then run in to the beach, allowing the occupants to flee into the trees. The only thing left for the Market Time units to do was to destroy the beached craft by mortar fire. Such actions were playing an important role in the war: trawlers forced to abort their missions and junks destroyed on a beach without making their deliveries were certainly logistical setbacks for the enemy forces in the South. But these are not dramatic victories that young warriors can compare with the exploits of John Wayne, and Market Timers often found their role less than gratifying.

Their task was at times overwhelming. The coastline of South Vietnam is long, irregular, and dotted by hundreds of small islands, giving a would-be infiltrator an excellent environment for evasion. Different sources estimated the daily coastal traffic of South Vietnam during the war years between four thousand and sixty thousand vessels. (This discrepancy alone tells something of the difficulty of maintaining an effective barrier against infiltration.) Obviously, it was impossible to search every vessel, so the patrols had to rely on random boardings or educated selectivity in deciding which vessels to search. In Market Time argot, a "boarding" meant a search of the vessel by one or more crew members, and "inspecting" meant merely conducting a visual examination while alongside as well as checking identification and manifest papers. Once they sighted vessels, Market Timers had to decide which to board, inspect, or ignore altogether. Shortly after arriving in Vietnam the Coast Guardsmen on patrol devised a priority system for boarding. In order of highest to lowest priority, they would search the following vessels when encountered: vessels transiting the area; vessels fishing or operating in areas that had been designated as "restricted" by the South Vietnamese government; fishing vessels that were anchored but not working with their nets; and fishing vessels that were working nets.

Market Timers had to be careful not to create a pattern in their searching that the enemy could use to his advantage. If a particular patrol craft made a habit of searching the nearest junk in a detected group, infiltrators could exploit this by ensuring that an innocent vessel was between it and the Market Time unit. If a patrol craft curtailed its boarding near the end of its patrol, this information too could be used by an observant enemy.

Once a vessel had been singled out for boarding, a new set of challenges was at hand. The first one was the people on board. Besides the possibility of encountering the enemy, the boarding parties often had to contend with hostility from innocent people. Having their work interrupted, their belongings invaded, and foreigners questioning their right to be in the same waters that they and their ancestors had been working in for centuries would provoke anger in the most patient people. The boarding parties might find themselves confronted with anything from harmless but unsettling scowls to passive resistance or even outright defiance. Many of the Market Timers tried to counter these attitudes by giving the people candy, fresh fruit, C-rations, soap, medical attention, or anything they could come up with. One Market Time unit took instant photos of the junks and their crews and presented them as gifts. These things usually seemed to help, but sometimes they had an undesired side effect. As word spread among the local fishermen that rewards were given for having been searched, boats would flock around the patrol craft wanting to be searched, some again and again. Sailors on the USS *Vance* told of hailing two Vietnamese craft to come alongside and having five comply. This was counter to the objectives of Market Time and sometimes became a serious hindrance.

Another challenge confronting the boarding parties was how to ensure thoroughness. Some searchers used a six-foot-long rod to probe for contraband in a cargo of rice or fish. Others tried metal detectors, with some success. An angled mirror on the end of a rod was used for seeing around obstructions and into holds. Sometimes boarders pulled a line along the bottom of the hull from stem to stern to detect contraband suspended beneath the vessel. All of these methods helped, but nothing ever replaced a careful manual search as the most effective. This was not a pleasant job, however. Moving large amounts of cargo was grueling, particularly in the tropical conditions. Sifting through holds full of fish, sometimes having to reach in to the upper arms, was not envied duty. Many vessels were clean, but others were not. One veteran of many boardings said that he could tell from a distance whether there were any women on board a vessel simply by its cleanliness: the ones with men only were generally "the pits," but you could eat off the decks when women were present. This same veteran described crawling around below decks on one of the larger vessels he inspected:

> There were roaches *everywhere*. Big ones, the size of your thumb. I could *hear* them as well as see them. There was one part of the cargo hold that was way up forward and almost blocked off completely by large crates of brass faucets. I could see through an eighteen-inch crawl space and I knew there could be just about anything hidden up there and that I should go check it out. But there were several of those goddamned roaches running around right in the path where I'd have to crawl, and I could see more on the beams overhead that would be only an inch or so over my head as I crawled. So I didn't go up there and check it out. I felt guilty as hell about it for a long time. Still do. I always wonder if there were some weapons up there that I let get through to kill some Americans. But I just couldn't make myself crawl through there and let those things get on me.

When a cache of 7.62-mm ammunition was discovered under a load of rice, it was fairly clear that an infiltrator had been discovered. But at other times the call was much more difficult to make. For example, food and food preservatives were high on the Viet Cong's priority list, so how was one supposed to decide whether a cargo of rice was legitimate commerce or destined for enemy consumption? How much salt

could a junk be carrying before it was contraband? Cargo manifests helped sometimes, but in reality they were easily forged.

Inspecting papers was a simple process for Market Time units carrying VNN liaison officers, but for those without, the process was much more difficult. The South Vietnamese government provided sample papers, along with a list of known Viet Cong names, but an American was rarely able to discover a discrepancy in a vessel's paperwork.

Maintaining a level head in the face of danger was perhaps the greatest challenge of all. Every boarding or inspection was a potential enemy engagement; a lack of alertness could be fatal, yet the boarders could not be "trigger-happy." A Vietnamese might make a sudden move to prevent a sack of rice from spilling during a search: this called for split-second evaluation and great restraint on the part of a nervous young man with a powerful weapon and a will to survive.

Petty Officer Third Class Richard O'Mara, who grew up in the streets of the Bronx and served on Market Time as a Swift boat crew member in 1968–69, had many boardings to his credit. He had his own technique for spotting danger and protecting himself. If he saw something suspicious on board, he would first ask the crew members whose it was, carefully watching their eyes for signs of uneasiness; then he would instruct one of them to open it. He found that the innocent had no problem with his method, and the guilty often revealed themselves or at least cast sufficient suspicion upon themselves to warrant further questioning by the South Vietnamese authorities. His method also had the added benefit of keeping him from opening potentially booby-trapped objects, an important priority in his estimation.

There were other challenges as well. Commander (then Lieutenant) Daniel Bowler described one aspect of his experiences on Market Time while serving in the USS *Welch* (PG-93):

> Of course, anyone who sailed the coastal waters off Vietnam can tell you of "Sherwood Forest." That was a single name used to describe several fishing areas in which the Vietnamese fishermen would insert tall sticks in the water to hold their traps or nets in place. These

sticks would be stuck in the bottom and would extend 10–15 feet above water. They were easily avoided during the daytime. But at night, one really had to keep an eye out for "Sherwood Forest" or you would run right through it and almost certainly foul your screw. *Welch* ended up in dry dock in Subic Bay once because we had 20–30 feet of nylon fishing line wrapped around the shaft and stuck in the strut bearings. This caused excessive vibration on the shaft and was very noticeable when we were operating at high speeds with the gas turbine.

Life while not on patrol was no picnic either, particularly in the early days before the bases were fully developed. At some of the sites the sailors were berthed in barracks ships (APLs) until permanent barracks could be constructed. At Cam Ranh Bay, while waiting for the base to be built, the early Market Timers lived in two trailers and three tents. There were no bathing facilities and no latrines, so the sailors swam in the bay to keep clean and quickly learned why their Marine counterparts always carried shovels. The early arrivals at An Thoi set up tents in a clearing surrounded by dense jungle and lived there until APL-55 eventually arrived to provide a more civilized facility. The men at Cat Lo, much to the chagrin and good-natured taunting of their counterparts elsewhere, "roughed it" at a hotel in nearby Vung Tau City until their barracks were completed.

When the men were not actually on patrol they had little time for recreation, since they had to paint, repair, and re-provision their craft before each patrol. Most sites had few recreational facilities in any case. Good division commanders worked hard to rotate their units to permit crews periodically to unwind for a few days. The frequency varied, but a representative figure might be five days of rest and recreation every three months.

The threat of attack by enemy forces was a constant for Americans in Vietnam. They never knew when rockets or mortars would rain down, damaging or destroying facilities, fraying already sensitive nerves, and snuffing out lives in an instant. A sniper's bullet might come from across the perimeter at any time. Sappers frequently penetrated the barbed wire and mine-infested boundaries of the bases or came in under water to carry out acts of sabotage. Sometimes a saboteur walked through the front gate of the base in the guise of interpreter, laundry woman, or maintenance worker. And the threat of a frontal assault was always present. Intelligence reports, official and otherwise, frequently warned that "tonight's the night—they're coming through the wire." More often than not these reports or rumors were wrong, but on the occasions when they were not, the residents of a base might find themselves facing a harassment probe or a full-scale assault.

Even though the life of a Market Time sailor was one of hard work and frustration, it was not without reward. For those who wanted to be close to the war, Market Time was less frustrating than for men out on larger ships who fired round after round, day after day, in gunfire support missions but never saw their enemy or even their allies. For those who wanted to keep some distance between themselves and the war, Market Time could sometimes prove the lesser of evils: one Swift boat veteran of both the coastal patrols and the later incursions into the rivers said in his thick Brooklyn accent, "Hey, Market Time was no picnic, but we saw it as a gravy run compared to going up that damn river." There was the feeling of goodwill that came from seeing grateful smiles and hearing *"Cam on, ong,"* "thank you," after fixing an engine, providing medical attention, or sharing an understanding. And there was the autonomy. These young officers and men were entrusted with responsibility and authority rarely equaled elsewhere in the war. Hanson W. Baldwin, military editor of the New York *Times,* described the young officers in charge of PCFs on Market Time operations in a 1966 magazine article:

Coastal surveillance off Vietnam is a rugged duty but offers for the junior officer tremendous compensations of command, small craft experience and the exercise of responsibility and self-reliance. And the Swifts are one type of craft that cannot be reached readily by direct radio hook-up from Washington so a skipper can call his soul his own—at least for a time!

In a war that was characterized by complaints of too much high-level direction and interference, the autonomy of Market Time units was no small benefit.

Overall, life on Market Time was frustrating, boring, and dangerous. It required a man to be alert in mundane conditions. It subjected him to extremes of weather and poor living conditions. It made him do things he found unpleasant or even repugnant. Rarely, if ever, did his work receive any recognition from the people back home. And sometimes it cost him his life. Nevertheless, the U.S. Navy and Coast Guard sailors who joined forces as Market Timers carried on the longstanding traditions of both their services by accomplishing their mission as best they knew how, earning for themselves that coveted accolade of the sea services: Well done.

Fragments

Coast Guard Division 11 had been operating in the Gulf of Thailand as part of the newly formed Operation Market Time for about six weeks without seeing any evidence of infiltration. At about 0100 on 19 September 1965, that was about to change.

The USCGC *Point Glover,* a WPB, had been on patrol for several hours in the waters separating Phu Quoc Island from mainland South Vietnam. The night was dark, quiet, and sultry; the air seemed to cling in wet layers to the skin. Some of the crew on watch were fighting off sleep while those not on watch were finding sleep elusive in the humidity.

At seven minutes past the hour, a vessel appeared on radar off the cutter's port bow, headed in an easterly direction at fairly high speed, apparently bound for the mainland from Phu Quoc. The *Point Glover* closed in and challenged what appeared to be a twenty-foot junk, common in the area. No response came from the junk, which began to maneuver vigorously. The *Point Glover,* with battle stations manned, fired several warning shots across the bow of the junk. These too were ignored, and the junk's maneuvers became even more erratic. Suddenly the junk turned in toward the cutter and nearly rammed into her. The *Point Glover*'s commanding officer put the wheel hard over, throttled up, and ordered, "Commence firing." Fifty-caliber rounds shattered what calm had remained among the growls of straining engines. The junk returned fire briefly, but the cutter's machine gun quickly found its mark, gnawing its way into the engine compartment. Soon the junk was disabled and abandoned by her crew.

A few minutes later a boarding party from the *Point Glover* cautiously crept on board and searched the vessel. They found a sizable cache of Communist Chinese carbines along with nearly 500 rounds of ammunition. A search of the area yielded two dead Viet Cong, and no survivors. The *Point Glover* had suffered no casualties.

Late that evening, another WPB, the USCGC *Point Marone,* was on patrol in almost the same area, slightly closer to the mainland and near the Cambodian border. At a little before midnight Lieutenant David Markey, the cutter's commanding officer, saw a soft burst of phosphorescence on his radar scope. It was intermittent, weak, and faded quickly after each sweep of the radar, but it was consistent enough to convince Markey that he had a contact approximately two miles astern. As the *Point Marone* came about in a wide turn and approached the contact, a 35-to-40-foot junk became visible. Its after cabin and mast had apparently been removed; Lieutenant Markey suspected that this had been done to lessen the chances of radar detection. His suspicions aroused, he ordered his crew to commence challenge procedures and told the *Point Glover,* also on patrol in the area, what was happening.

When the junk ignored the challenges, the *Point Marone* fired two warning shots across the bow and continued to close in. Suddenly the crack of small arms fire erupted; someone on the cutter yelled, "Grenades!" The *Point Marone* veered sharply and opened fire with her bow-mounted machine gun. Several explosions joined the sound of firing, and a voice from the cutter's forecastle shouted that the junk was dropping mines into the water. Lieutenant Markey swept his cutter out in an arc about the junk while his weapons pounded at her.

A few minutes later, the *Point Glover* arrived on the scene. She shot several illumination rounds into the sky with her 81-

mm mortar and provided supporting fire with her machine gun and small arms. The fire from the junk, hopelessly outgunned, was soon snuffed out, along with the lives of eleven of the twelve Viet Cong crew members. The twelfth man, badly wounded, had made it ashore. Special Forces troops from a camp at the village of Ha Tien, near the Cambodian border, captured this lone survivor soon after he beached.

The junk was taken under tow by the *Point Glover,* but her hull had been "Swiss-cheesed," as one of the Coast Guardsmen aptly described it, and she soon settled and sank. The next day, divers from the *Krishna,* the Market Time support ship at An Thoi, raised the junk from the shallow gulf waters. The USCGC *Point Young* towed the junk back to An Thoi, where the *Krishna* lifted her clear of the water. On board were several rifles, several hundred rounds of Chinese Communist ammunition, a number of hand grenades, a large sum of money, and some documents indicating that one of the dead men had been a Viet Cong district chief.

Once again the Market Timers had sustained no casualties.

During March 1966, Coast Guard Division 13, operating out of Cat Lo, accounted for twenty-seven Viet Cong killed in action, seven captured, and large quantities of contraband confiscated. Part of this tally was contributed by the USCGC *Point White* on the night of 9 March while patrolling off the mouth of the Soi Rap River, twenty-five miles south of Saigon. This area was known to be controlled by the Viet Cong, but the cutter had been patrolling for several hours without incident. The *Point White*'s skipper, Lieutenant Eugene J. Hickey, decided to try a little deception: he steamed off out of sight of the rivermouth and then covertly returned after a while. As he had hoped, the VC took the bait; before long a 25-foot motorized junk emerged from the mangrove swamps of the Rung Sat Special Zone (also known as the "Forest of Assassins") and headed across the river. The cutter came within 150 yards of the junk, and then illuminated the area and hailed it. The junk replied with a burst of automatic and small-arms fire; this was answered by the *Point White*'s .50-caliber machine guns, which excavated chunks of the enemy's hull. Several VC fell, but the firing from the junk stubbornly continued. Lieutenant Hickey ordered the *Point White* to ram the junk amidships at full speed, throwing most of her occupants into the water. The men flailing in the dark river water had had all the fight knocked out of them, and Hickey would have recovered them except for a very determined Viet Cong still aboard the junk in the forward section. He continued firing until the junk sank out from under him, thereby preventing any rescue attempt until he finally went under. The result was only four crewmen rescued alive. One of these turned out to be a key leader in the Viet Cong's Rung Sat infrastructure.

One of the most tragic events in Market Time took place in the early morning hours of 11 August 1966. The USCGC *Point Welcome* was patrolling sector 1A1 directly adjacent to the Demilitarized Zone (DMZ) at eight knots when, at approximately 0340, a U.S. Air Force forward air controller dropped several flares, illuminating the cutter. Fearing the worst, the commanding officer immediately turned on the cutter's running lights, picked up an Aldis hand-held signal lamp, and used it to signal several aircraft heading at high speed directly toward the cutter. An American Air Force B-57 bomber and two F-4C fighters came screaming down on the cutter, strafing and bombing. Their first strike killed the commanding officer and wounded the executive officer and all the other bridge watch personnel. A senior chief petty officer came to the bridge to take command. At once he brought the cutter up to full speed and began maneuvering in an attempt to escape the illuminated area. All of the cutter's searchlights and communications equipment had been disabled in that first strike; just one message had been sent to Commander Task Group 115.1 before the equipment was destroyed. To the horror of those left standing on the *Point Welcome,* the aircraft circled around and came in for another pass. And another. And another. For a full hour the American planes rained death and destruction on their own, convinced they were attacking an enemy.

On board the *Point Welcome* was a free-lance photojournalist named Tim Page, who was to become one of the foremost action photographers of the war. In his book *Tim Page's Nam,* he described the scene:

I had never seen anything like it in my life. Here's two Phantoms and a B-57 strafing us with twin Vulcans blazing, giving us a stem-to-stern strafing. They hit some gas drums, which started cooking off, and I watched a guy get his hand blown off. . . . They made nine passes, and blasted the living hell out of the ship. Everybody on board was killed or wounded. I had pieces of commo wire coming out of my head like porcupine quills, a bone sticking out of my arm and countless shrapnel punctures.

Those not yet seriously wounded, convinced that the attacks would not cease until all were dead, at last paired up, wounded with able-bodied, and abandoned ship. While their craft continued to be pounded, the men swam toward the beach, wounded in tow. But in another stroke of fate, they came under mortar and automatic weapons fire from the beach, presumably this time from the enemy. They were trapped between the proverbial rock and hard place.

At last the aircraft broke off the attack, and the cutters *Point Orient* and *Point Caution* and some VNN junks from Coastal Group 11 came to the rescue.

The final toll was two killed and eleven wounded, many seriously. The *Point Welcome* had received extensive damage to her pilothouse and had nine large holes in her main deck. Tim Page had been wounded once before the *Point Welcome* incident and would be wounded again. On this occasion he had come out on patrol with the Coast Guard "to relax and have a swim."

Helicopters believed to be used by the North Vietnamese had been sighted along the coast just north of the DMZ and between the coast of North Vietnam and nearby Tiger Island. The use of helicopters by the North Vietnamese has never been proven nor disproven, but the reports seem to have set the stage for the tragedy that followed.

At approximately 0100 on 16 August, personnel aboard the USCGC *Point Dume* reported seeing two rockets fired from unidentified sources at PCF-19: one was a near miss, the other a direct hit. Within minutes the Swift boat went to the bottom, taking four U.S. Navy men and one Vietnamese petty officer with her. Salvage operations later revealed that the

PCF had been hit by three rockets, two in the cabin and one in the engine compartment. Even more confusing, the *Point Dume* and another Swift boat, PCF-12, were repeatedly attacked by unidentified aircraft for more than an hour. Neither was damaged. The heavy cruiser USS *Boston* and the Australian warship HMAS *Hobart* were also attacked in this same general area.

The evidence indicates that friendly aircraft had probably mounted the attacks: U.S. Navy and Air Force pilots reported attacking and shooting down North Vietnamese helicopters at that time, but no substantiating evidence was ever found. It is possible that the American pilots, having been primed for North Vietnamese helicopters by reported sightings in the weeks before, and finding difficulty in identifying targets at night from high-speed aircraft, attacked the friendly ships thinking that they were enemy helicopters. This theory is supported by the fact that no other incidents involving North Vietnamese helicopters occurred for the remainder of the war.

The fall of 1966 was not a good period for Market Time units. Three incidents proved that danger was never very far away for the Market Time sailor and not always lurking in the expected places.

On 18 October PCF-9 was delivering mortar gunfire in support of some U.S. Special Forces operations. Naval mortars, unlike their infantry counterparts, are not fired by dropping rounds into the tube, where they strike a firing pin and are immediately launched. The naval mortar round is inserted into the muzzle, as with the infantry version, but the gunner decides when to fire and does so with a conventional trigger. On this occasion the gun crew had just fired a white-phosphorus round and was loading a high-explosive round when it inexplicably exploded in the tube.

The mortar was destroyed; its piggy-back .50-caliber machine gun was thrown over the side. The fantail area of the Swift boat was extensively damaged; three men lay dead, and two others were seriously injured.

The second incident occurred eleven days later. Some Market Time assets had been shifted northward to operate out of the Hue River area to shorten the transit time to the northernmost patrol sectors and to provide gunfire support to allied operations in the area. In that region, that time of year is marked by bad weather and sea conditions. Such was the case when PCF-56 was leaving the mouth of the Hue River in the early afternoon of 29 October. A heavy surf surging into the funnel-shaped channel, causing confusion in the waters, buffeted the Swift about mercilessly and threw one of her crew over the side. A search and rescue effort was conducted with great difficulty by two PCFs and a number of aircraft, but to no avail. At 0730 on 31 October, a squad of South Vietnamese RF/PF troops discovered the missing man's body on the beach.

Two weeks later, the northeast monsoon had worsened the already bad sea conditions around the Hue River mouth. PCF-22 lost a man overboard while trying to cross the bar and enter Hue Harbor. PCF-77 was operating in the area and rushed to lend assistance in the search and rescue effort. The officer in charge, Lieutenant (j.g.) David G. Wilbourne, ordered all hands into lifejackets as a precaution against the angry seas. Large swells were gathering as the monsoon winds pushed the sea up against the shore. Within a few minutes, the crew of PCF-22 had saved the lost man. The men on PCF-77 barely had time to breathe a sigh of relief before their craft was assaulted by a thirty-foot wave that rose out of the sea like a moving mountain, dwarfing the waves around it. It lifted the stern of the diminutive craft and drove its bow down into the trough.

The effect was disastrous: PCF-77 was flipped end over end. The pilothouse filled with water almost instantly even though the doors and ports had been secured. Several of the crew managed to get out through the port bridge door, sprung by the force of the wave. As the boat filled rapidly, Lieutenant Wilbourne stayed behind long enough to rescue a crewman who was having difficulty getting out. Chief Machinery Repairman W. S. Baker, a qualified Navy diver, in an act of selflessness, forced his way into the after compartment to try to rescue Petty Officer B. A. Timmons. Less than a minute and a half after the wave hit, PCF-77 sank, keel up. Chief Baker, Petty Officer Timmons, and a third man, Petty Officer Harry B. Brock, were lost.

Later the bow section of the 77 washed ashore half a mile

north of the entrance to the Hue River. The rest of the craft broke up and was unsalvageable.

Storms at sea know no politics; the same monsoon that had treated the American Swift boats so violently late in 1966 chose to treat the Communist Chinese the same way. Twice great storms damaged Chinese fishing boats from Hai Nan Island and swept them along to the south until they at last were discovered off the coast of South Vietnam by Market Time patrols.

The law of the sea that requires able vessels to come to the aid of vessels in distress also knows no politics. PCF-54 rescued an 80-foot junk, containing thirty-six men and seven children, ten miles northeast of Nha Trang on 4 December. Four days later, the cutter *Point Ellis* came to the aid of a small nonmotorized craft with two very frightened men on board, twenty-eight miles northwest of Da Nang. In both cases, the people were returned to China through complex but effective diplomatic channels.

An American landing craft that had been ferrying ammunition was being unloaded at Duc Pho in June 1967 when it exploded. The explosion hurled some of the crew members into the water. Four PCFs (49, 51, 54, and 60) raced to the scene to find them. The explosion had started a fire, which spread to some nearby ammunition stockpiles onshore. Secondary explosions hurled shrapnel in vicious arcs as far as 1,500 yards from the beach. Heedless of the danger, the crews of the PCFs continued their work and succeeded in rescuing eleven men from the water. PCF-49 caught a blast of shrapnel at one point, which did minor hull damage and wounded two of her crew, one seriously. Had the Swifts not persisted in their efforts despite the danger, those rescued would have perished.

It was several minutes past midnight on 15 July 1967. A quarter moon had earlier slipped behind heavy clouds gathering in the west. This was fine for the crew of trawler number 459, off Cape Batangan; the darker it was, the less their chance of detection by American and South Vietnamese patrol units. The old steel-hulled vessel was laden with ninety tons of arms, ammunition, and supplies, enough to keep a regiment going for several months.

The USS *Wilhoite* (DER-397), a destroyer escort, had been lurking just beyond the horizon, keeping track of the North Vietnamese trawler by radar ever since a Navy P-2 aircraft had discovered her four days earlier. Because the trawler had no radar of her own, her master had no way of knowing that he was being stalked.

Trawler 459 had been moving up and down the South Vietnamese coast for days, awaiting the right moment to run in to the shore undetected. Her crew had placed fishing nets on her decks to disguise her real purpose and, to further confuse their enemies, had repainted the number on her hull to 441 during the night of the 13th.

As the trawler closed to within five miles of the coast, the Americans sprang their trap. The Coast Guard cutter *Point Orient*, the patrol gunboat USS *Gallup*, a Swift boat (PCF-79), and the *Wilhoite* closed in. At eleven minutes past midnight one of the American vessels broadcast a tape-recorded appeal for surrender: "You must stop and don't shoot because you are surrounded! We knew clearly that you were coming here and we have been waiting for you for three days. You must quickly wake up to that fact and surrender. The government will be merciful." Illumination flares dispelled the darkness as the appeal was repeated. But the trawler did not slow nor deviate from her course and continued her desperate attempt to reach the mouth of the Sa Ky River.

Two U.S. vessels opened fire from the trawler's flanks, sending lines of tracers across her bow. This message too was ignored, and the order was given for the American craft to engage the trawler. Six .50-caliber machine guns, two mortars, and a 3-inch/.50-caliber gun converged on the North Vietnamese vessel, spraying hot metal onto her decks and superstructure. Moments later, PCF-79 closed to within 200 yards and fired a white-phosphorus round into the trawler's pilothouse, causing her to lose control and run aground in the mouth of the Sa Ky.

Several of the American craft paused briefly to reload their weapons; this gave the trawler's crew an opportunity to man her 12.7-mm deck guns and to position a 57-mm recoilless rifle. The combatants exchanged fire for several minutes until the trawler's crew succumbed to the massive firepower of the American vessels and two helicopter gunships that had joined in. What had earlier been a seagoing vessel became a pyre, flames raging from stem to stern.

Shoals at the rivermouth and the inferno on board prevented the Americans from boarding the trawler during the night, so they continued to fire into the vanquished vessel, stoking the conflagration and making sure that no contraband could be removed by determined enemy forces.

At dawn several VNN junks joined the American units, and a detachment of South Korean Marines appeared on shore to assist them. The boarding parties who eventually searched the trawler found, to their amazement, several tons of ammunition intact in the hold. That afternoon the hulk was towed off the shoal and taken to Chu Lai, where she later sank at the pier.

In the article in the U.S. Naval Institute's *Proceedings* magazine in September 1968, Commander Charles R. Stephan, USN, who had been in command of the U.S. units involved in the Sa Ky River incident, gave well-deserved credit to the units that participated in the action, but recognizing the importance of maintaining the continuity of the Market Time barrier even (and perhaps especially) during the times of a major engagement, he added:

> But, a special word of praise is in order for the *Pledge* [an MSO on patrol nearby], and those Swift boats which patrolled within eye and earshot of the action, and, overcoming with exemplary discipline, an almost irrepressible urge to join the battle, maintained the integrity of their patrols. They also serve. . . .

Before dawn on 7 August 1967 an enemy force of about two battalions launched a frontal assault on Coastal Group 16's base, seventy miles southeast of Da Nang. It was one of a series of attacks on U.S. and Vietnamese installations throughout the month of August by the Viet Cong, who had suffered a growing number of setbacks during recent months and were apparently attempting to regain their credibility. The U.S. advisors at the base, Lieutenant William C. Fitzgerald, Lieutenant (j.g.) Anthony C. Williams, Chief Engineman Harold H. Guinn, and Boatswain's Mate First Class Leo E. Pearman, were swept into the fight as the situation became desperate. Lieutenant Fitzgerald radioed for help; PCF-20, patrolling nearby, intercepted the message, relayed it to other Market Time units, and headed for the base at flank speed. Arriving in less than twenty minutes, the Swift opened fire on enemy mortar and automatic-weapons sites that had been set up on the riverbank adjacent to the base.

Within minutes, the large enemy force was penetrating the northern minefield defenses of the base. Numerous Vietnamese Navy defenders were already dead, including the commander of the coastal group, Lieutenant (j.g.) Nguyen N. Thong, VNN. About three hundred enemy troops broke through and overran the central area of the base. The American advisors retreated to a bunker, where they continued firing on the advancing enemy.

PCF-75 soon arrived, and five minutes later the VNN PCE-10 joined the fray. All three craft delivered heavy fire, but they and the base defenders were unable to stop the enemy. Soon the base was under enemy control, and it appeared to Lieutenant Fitzgerald that his bunker was the last point of resistance. Ordering his men to escape to the river, he remained behind to provide covering fire. He also radioed a nearby U.S. artillery unit and called a strike in on his position. Once his men were clear, Lieutenant Fitzgerald tried to withdraw, but as he left the bunker a bullet struck him in the back of the head and killed him.

On the way to the river, Lieutenant (j.g.) Williams was hit in the face and chest by shrapnel and Guinn and Pearman received minor wounds, but all escaped.

In the meantime, the USS *Camp* (DER-251), USS *Gallup* (PG-85), PCFs 15 and 54, and a U.S. Air Force C-47 "Dragon Ship" had arrived and were saturating the enemy positions within the base with counterfire. The Swift boats evacuated approximately forty Vietnamese to the *Camp;* fifteen of them were subsequently flown by helicopter to the Vietnamese hospital at Quang Ngai. Thirty-two miles to the northwest, the USS *Widgeon* (MSC-208) served as a communications relay between the scene of the battle and First Naval Zone headquarters in Da Nang. For the next several hours, the ships and aircraft kept up a steady barrage until one U.S. and two ARVN infantry companies arrived and launched a counterattack against the Viet Cong forces. Within a half hour the base was again in friendly hands.

All but one of the base's buildings had been destroyed in the battle. Fourteen Vietnamese Navy men had been killed; thirty-five more were wounded. Twenty civilians were also killed or wounded. On the enemy side, eleven had been killed. Thirty-five VC suspects who were being detained at the base had been freed, and three others were killed.

Stable Door

Another task assigned to the U.S. Navy during the Vietnam war was harbor defense. Massive amounts of matériel came to Vietnam by ship and were unloaded at any of several major harbors in Vietnam. Ships waiting at anchor to unload were vulnerable to sapper attack. And because of the heavy traffic passing in and out of these harbors, infiltration of enemy supplies and men was a continual worry.

On 14 January 1966, MACV directed CHNAVADVGRU to create a plan for the defense of Vietnam's major harbors. In February representatives from CINCPACFLT, CHNA-VADVGRU, and COMIUWGRU1 (Commander Inshore Undersea Warfare Group 1—a San Diego–based command already in existence) traveled to Da Nang, Qui Nhon, Nha Trang, Cam Ranh, and Vung Tau. They found that Da Nang had already developed a good harbor defense system, but that the other ports needed some help. In Saigon the group decided that each harbor except Da Nang would need a Harbor Entrance Control Post, a tactical command center in the best location to see and control the harbor, equipped with enough radar and communications equipment to coordinate the operations of assigned patrol craft. COMIUWGRU1 would initially provide detachments to man the sites until permanent personnel could be gradually phased in. These units would fall under the operational control of Commander Task Force 115 as part of Market Time. In August 1966 they received their own name, Operation Stable Door, but remained a part of Task Force 115.

Assigned to these units were LCPLs (Landing Craft, Personnel, Large), 16-foot skimmer craft (Boston Whalers), and a specially designed 45-foot "picket boat" that began arriving in Vietnam after June 1967 and carried a crew of five men plus one officer. The other craft were assigned to all enlisted crews. The total Stable Door inventory would eventually reach a peak of sixteen LCPLs, twenty-five skimmers, and eight picket boaters.

In early 1968 another unit was established at Vung Ro Bay, bringing the total to five. They were designated by that time as Inshore Undersea Warfare Units: IUWU-1 at Vung Tau, IUWU-2 at Cam Ranh, IUWU-3 at Qui Nhon, IUWU-4 at Nha Trang, and IUWU-5 at Vung Ro. The total force consisted of more than 500 people at its peak.

A November 1968 COMNAVFORV press release described the Stable Door mission:

> STABLE DOOR units maintain 24 hour visual and radar surveillance of harbor approaches and anchorage areas. STABLE DOOR harbor patrol boats intercept and search local indigenous craft, maintain a vigilant watch for enemy swimmers or floating objects which could be mines, and carry Explosive Ordnance Disposal (EOD) diver personnel for inspection of ship's hulls and anchor chains.

These duties proved to be even more mundane than the average Market Time operation. Once the patrols began, the enemy moved their infiltration attempts from these harbors to the coastal areas where the chances of success were greater. Sabotage attempts on anchored ships continued throughout the war, but the men on Stable Door patrols were dealing with an unseen enemy. They conducted random sweeps of the harbor, dropping grenades into the water and watching for bubbles that might mark a sapper's approach. Occasionally bodies washed up on the beach as evidence of their success, or ships exploded as evidence of their failure, but very rarely did they find themselves in a direct confrontation with the enemy. Theirs was an important but intangible job. Not until January 1968 did a Stable Door unit make its first capture of an enemy swimmer.

Boatswain's Mate Second Class George W. Young, an

LCPL captain at Qui Nhon, in an interview conducted in September 1968, offered these thoughts on his Stable Door experiences:

> As many as ten ships can be counted at any time in the outer harbor while nine ships . . . are in the inner harbor at any one time. . . . We make sure none of the sampans or enemy swimmers get close enough to damage them when they're in the outer harbor unloading fuel, ammunition, or waiting for a pier berth. . . . While in the inner harbor, we have to watch out for floating debris which could easily conceal a command-detonated or contact mine. . . . Although there is a 2000 to 0500 curfew on the harbor, our hardest job is to keep the sampans out of the restricted area during the curfew. They know they aren't allowed in 'til 0500, but around 0300, they start drifting in. They wait to see if a patrol will stop them. When they see the boat approach, most of them turn around and go back out. But a few of them continue on in. A shotgun blast or a burst from an M-16 is usually effective in changing their minds.

Young described one junk captain who tried an inventive way of leaving the harbor before curfew had expired in order to get a jump on the other fishermen at Qui Nhon:

> On a particular dark night when we couldn't see anything, the harbor patrol radio circuit came alive saying a junk was seen entering the harbor. It was about 0300 and therefore the junk wasn't allowed in the area. I was sent to investigate. Our radar showed that he was actually leaving the harbor so we couldn't figure why the radio said he was entering. We sat for a while to see if there were two junks, one leaving and one coming in. Pretty soon we heard the junk's motor as it came into sight. It was leaving the harbor all right, but backing out! Usually we turn a boat around and send it back in the direction it came from. On hearing our boat, the junk stopped dead in the water and waited for the command to turn around. I sent him back into Qui Nhon amidst loud yell-

ing and flailing of arms by the captain. I don't think he'll try that trick again too soon.

Yankee ingenuity, ever present in the soldier or sailor looking for ways to improve his circumstances, shows in Young's elaboration of typical patrols:

The water at the base leaves something to be desired, so on our way out to the patrol area, we stop at a freighter, oiler or regular Navy ship in the harbor and bum water and ice off of them. . . . An engine that has been running for three or four hours gets awful hot. So we take cans of C-rations and place them on the engine heads, and after 30 minutes, our chow is hot, just as if it came off the serving line in the mess hall.

Young concluded the interview with:

I'm glad to be doing something for my country but I wish I was back in the fleet. There's nothing like sailing on a tin can in deep water out of sight of land.

"Bait a Trap and Clobber the Catch"

ENEMY LOSSES ARE NOW REPORTED AT ABOUT 44,000 KIA PLUS OVER 7,000 CAPTURED OR DETAINED ALL TO-GETHER EQUAL TO AT LEAST 100 VC/NVA BATTALIONS. ALTHOUGH CAPTURED DOCUMENTS AND PRISONERS IN-DICATE THE ENEMY PLANS TO CONTINUE ATTACKS AND HARRASSMENT HE OBVIOUSLY MUST BE HURTING CONSID-ERABLY. NOW IS THE TIME TO STRIKE HIM. NOW IS THE TIME RESORT AGAIN TO OUR BASIC PHILOSOPHY OF CON-CENTRATE AND CLOBBER. CONSIDER IT PREFERABLE TO ELIMINATE ONE ENEMY UNIT THAN TO TAKE SMALL AT-TRITION FROM SEVERAL. RECOMMEND WHERE POSSIBLE BAIT A TRAP AND CLOBBER THE CATCH. . . .

Despite the contrary image conveyed by the American press at home in late February 1968, the enemy's attempt at a nationwide popular uprising in South Vietnam, during the Lunar New Year celebration known as Tet, had been crushed by American and South Vietnamese forces. Initially caught shamefully off guard in the early hours of the holiday that had begun on 30 January, the Allied forces bounced back and in the weeks that followed decimated the Viet Cong, virtually eliminating the guerrilla force as a viable military entity and causing Hanoi to rely upon its own army for prosecuting the remainder of the war.

It was in this setting that Rear Admiral Kenneth L. Veth, COMNAVFORV, sent the above message to all forces under his command. For the Market Time units it meant business as usual. But the heightened combat activity throughout South Vietnam made infiltration attempts to replace North Vietnamese ammunition, medical supplies, and troops more probable, so U.S. Navy and Coast Guard personnel on the barriers watched their radar scopes and scanned the horizons with more fervor than usual.

The USCGC *Androscoggin* (WHEC-68) had been on station off the northern portion of the central coast since Valentine's Day. On 29 February, at approximately 1700, the high-endurance cutter rang up her maximum speed of 18 knots and left her assigned patrol area to intercept a suspicious trawler that had been detected off the coast of Quang Ngai Province by Market Time aircraft.

The *Androscoggin*'s crew accepted the new challenge with relish. They had been patrolling for two weeks without incident, and the men were beginning to develop that malady of the South China Sea known as "the Market Time stare." Day after day of routine operations would eventually take their toll on even the hardiest of sailors. Hour after hour of standing watches in the tropical humidity would drive a man's thirst to proportions approaching madness. When relieved of his duties, he would typically go to the mess decks or the wardroom and gulp down two glasses of iced tea in an attempt at slaking the powerful thirst. His stomach thus filled, he rarely had an appetite and would find his weight dropping considerably. The addition of boarding and support parties to the normal underway watches left few off-watch hours in which to do much more than sleep. There wasn't much to do anyway: write a letter home, perhaps, or read a book. The lethargy that inevitably accompanies such an existence would make a stimulating conversation or a rowdy card game impossible. Swim call was not an alluring alternative despite the heat: one did not have to peer into the clear Southeast Asian water for very long before spotting the undulating silhouette of a venomous sea-snake.

The men of the *Androscoggin* seemed to have regained the spring in their step as they prepared their ship for combat on the evening of 29 February. With the word that they were on their way to intercept a trawler, a wave of anticipation had swept away the boredom.

Battle orders came in the early evening as the cutter knifed her way through the gentle swells of the darkening sea. Commander Task Force 115 directed the *Androscoggin* to shadow the trawler until it crossed the twelve-mile limit, and then to take a position on the trawler's beam. When they came within six and a half miles of the South Vietnamese coast, the *Androscoggin* was to challenge the trawler and be prepared for surface action. The cutters *Point Welcome* (WPB-82329) and *Point Grey* (WPB-82324) and PCFs 18 and 20 were maintaining a barrier along the coast at the four-mile line. Two helicopter gunships and an Air Force flare ship had been placed in scramble status for the operation. The trap was set.

At 1947 Commander W. H. Stewart, USCG, commanding officer of the *Androscoggin* and officer in tactical command of the operation, was informed by his radar team that they had picked up Market Time air patrol 3011. The aircraft, which had the suspect trawler under surveillance, sent the cutter radar vectors and she moved in.

Nearly an hour passed as the glowing green arm of the surface-search radar scope went around and around, painting nothing on its face except the faint scatter of a mild sea-return. The minutes ticked by as anxious eyes peered into the cathode-ray tube. Then, at 2040, a soft burst of greenish-white light appeared at the edge of the radar screen. It pulsed and faded with each sweep of the glowing arm as the radar operator quickly turned the dials to place a range and bearing marker on the new contact, 15,600 yards off the *Androscoggin*'s starboard bow. Correlating by radio with 3011, the radarmen identified it as the trawler. To avoid being seen at this point, Commander Stewart ordered his officer of the deck to bring the ship hard left and take up a position eight miles astern of the contact, where they remained patiently for the next several hours.

Sometime before midnight an American LST, on a north-bound supply mission and unaware of the surveillance operation in progress, nearly sprang the trap prematurely when it challenged the trawler by flashing light as it passed through the area. Frantic radio messages called the signals off, and the LST cleared the area and left the trawler apparently undeterred.

At 0048 the trawler increased speed to 12.5 knots and appeared to be approaching the coast in earnest. Commander Stewart ordered his crew to battle stations. When the trawler crossed the twelve-mile limit, he ordered flank speed and began closing in on the trawler's beam to get into position for the challenge. As the ship raced along, the crew had moments of quiet anticipation. From past experiences with enemy trawlers, they knew that this one was more than likely armed. While no one doubted the outcome of an engagement, the possibility of injury or death was very real. Some crew members experienced that strange physical sensation—something akin to simultaneous titillation and nausea—that presages first combat. Others recalled images of the World War II movies they had been nurtured on. Some prayed quietly. All sensed that action was to come.

At about this same time other Market Time units were in similar circumstances. Fifty miles to the south, off the coast of Binh Dinh Province, U.S. Navy and Coast Guard units were shadowing another trawler believed to be on an infiltration mission. Another hundred miles to the south, off the coastal province of Khanh Hoa, U.S. Navy and Coast Guard and VNN units were closing in on yet another trawler. And finally, off An Xuyen, the southernmost province of South Vietnam, the USCGC *Winona* (WHEC-65) was covertly pursuing a fourth unidentified and highly suspicious trawler.

Those observing from Coastal Surveillance Force headquarters believed that a major coordinated infiltration effort was under way. Considering the attrition suffered by the Viet Cong and North Vietnamese Army units in the South during the Tet Offensive, now a month old, an intensified resupply effort was not unexpected. But this was the war's most significant attempt at infiltration by sea. There had been only nine known previous attempts at trawler infiltration since Market Time had begun in February 1965. Four trawler classes had been identified as potential infiltrators, and each was capable of transporting 100 tons of ammunition and supplies, enough to supply an entire battalion for significant activity. With this four-trawler attempt in progress, excitement was running high. This was what Market Time was all about!

At 0112 the *Androscoggin*, within 5,600 yards, challenged the trawler with her flashing light. Again and again she sent the International Code signal, which all mariners recognize as the call for identification. There was no response. At Commander Stewart's order for illumination, the 5-inch/.38-caliber gun mount on the forecastle raised its barrel skyward and sent starshells into the darkness. The third one, perfectly positioned, revealed a hundred-foot-long *Sa Ky*–class trawler. Almost immediately the trawler began maneuvering and belched out clouds of smoke to screen her movements. From the bright flashes visible through the pall, Commander Stewart knew his enemy had opened fire with deck guns. As the distance between the two antagonists closed, the twinkling light of heavy machine-gun fire could be seen coming from the Communist ship, and almost immediately a swarm of bullets raked the port side of the *Androscoggin*. The time had come to "clobber the catch."

The old cutter shuddered as her 5-inch/.38-caliber gun erupted in response. Like the breath of a dragon, bursts of flame roared from the barrel's mouth as the deadly projectiles sought their prey. Recoilless rifle rounds exploded in the water dead ahead of the *Androscoggin* and about 400 yards off her port bow. One round passed over the bridge before it exploded in the water just off the starboard quarter. Another found its mark and penetrated the hull about four feet above the waterline, several feet aft of the hawse. Machine-gun rounds peppered the cutter's port side, reaching as high as the flying bridge. For two minutes the vessels traded blows until a direct hit on the starboard quarter of the trawler caused her to turn rapidly about and make a desperate run for the beach.

At this moment, an innocent junk blundered into the line of fire between the *Androscoggin* and her adversary, forcing

Commander Stewart to stop the firing. He called in two helicopter gunships that had been circling nearby. "Shark 6" and "Shark 9" swooped in, their guns blazing and their rockets roaring downward, scoring many direct hits. When the flareship joined the action, dropping its wares into the night sky, the area was suddenly as bright as a night football game. The battered trawler was clearly visible but had moved in too close to shore for pursuit by the *Androscoggin,* so Commander Stewart ordered the WPBs and PCFs to take her under fire. The patrol boats moved in, relentlessly chewing at the trawler with their .50-calibers and mortars.

At 0210 the enemy ship beached. She was hit many times by the mortars, and by round after round of machine-gun fire. The *Androscoggin* also continued firing when her line of fire was clear. After nearly twenty minutes of this withering assault, an explosion came from the bow of the trawler. It appeared that she was trying to destroy herself, but the attempt fell short: the forward part of the vessel was mangled, yet she was still about 75 percent intact. The hammering continued until 0235, when there came a huge fireball that temporarily blinded those who saw it. Shrapnel sprayed the nearby patrol boats, injuring several men as the trawler disintegrated.

Elsewhere, Market Time units were ensuring that no Communist supplies would reach South Vietnam's shores that night.

The trawler off Binh Dinh, when shadowed by Navy and Coast Guard units, apparently thought better of trying to make delivery and reversed course, hightailing it back to Communist China.

The Khanh Hoa Province trawler was taken under fire by U.S. Navy, Coast Guard, and VNN units as she crossed into the twelve-mile contiguous zone. She beached at 0200 in the Hon Heo Secret Zone, eleven miles northeast of Nha Trang. The combined fire of Swift boats, Vietnamese junks, VNN Fleet Command ships, and an AC-47 aircraft set her ablaze. At 0230 an explosion on the vessel sent a giant ball of flame roaring 2,000 feet upward. The forward and amidship sections were destroyed, but salvage operations on the remainder later yielded seven 82-mm mortar tubes with 745 rounds of accompanying ammunition, 70 AK-47 rifles, 39 RPG-2 rocket launchers with 81 cases of rocket rounds, and 28 cases of 7.62-mm ammunition along with tons of other military supplies.

Market Time realized a clean sweep that night when the USCGC *Winona,* in a hail of 5-inch/.38-caliber and .50-caliber fire, sent the last of the four would-be infiltrators to the bottom of the sea seven miles off the coast of An Xuyen Province. Only a small amount of debris was recovered the following morning.

Commander Richard A. Baumann, who had been the inshore screen commander in charge of the four-boat force of PCFs and WPBs, boarded the *Androscoggin* to join Commander Stewart in conducting a post-mortem of the night's events. With a grin, he held a present for the commander: a piece of hatch board, approximately 6 inches wide by 36 inches long—the largest portion remaining of the trawler. They had indeed "clobbered their catch."

Postscripts

A final analysis of the effectiveness of Operation Market Time is difficult, for several reasons. A favorable analysis of any component of a lost war is automatically suspect and is subject to the counterargument that the ultimate loss of the war makes the success of a part of it doubtful. Nevertheless, the evidence at hand indicates that Market Time was, at best, extremely successful and, at worst, less successful than advertised but nowhere near a failure.

For an activity as clandestine as infiltration, the "captures" are the only known data for the most part, while the "misses" remain an unknown quantity. For example, an analysis by the Navy's Operations Evaluation Group stated that in the case of trawler infiltration, out of the twenty trawlers that attempted to penetrate the South Vietnamese coast after August 1969, nineteen had been countered while one had been successful. This encouraging information is more than likely accurate, but it is also possible that other trawlers went undetected and made their deliveries without the awareness of U.S. intelligence.

A press release issued by Commander Task Force 115 in November 1968 estimated that fewer ''than 200 medium-sized fishing junks could easily meet all of the Viet Cong's logistics requirements for one full day of combat operations south of the DMZ.'' And COMNAVFORV's Monthly Historical Summary for that same month presents the following statistics (it should be noted that in November sea traffic is inhibited by monsoons):

Junks and sampans detected	32,655
Junks and sampans inspected	14,386
Junks and sampans boarded	10,000

Several questions arise. How many of the 8,269 detected vessels that were neither inspected nor searched were infiltrators? How many more vessels were not even detected? Two hundred successful infiltrators could carry enough supplies to the enemy for a day's combat—a sobering thought. But it was unlikely that the 6,000 necessary to supply sustained operations throughout the month (relying entirely upon sea infiltration) could get through.

The COMNAVFORV statistics are impressive. In boardings alone (sighting and inspection figures are of course much higher but less significant) for the period from June 1966 to June 1968, the total exceeds 400,000. The overall average is 16,000 per month, although the figures actually range from highs of 29,000 to lows of 6,000 depending upon weather conditions. The overall daily average is a little more than 500 boardings.

An objective analysis requires consideration of the possibility that these figures may sometimes have been inflated, or at least liberally interpreted. The issue of inflated body counts during the war lends credibility to such a hypothesis, although by no means proving it. And even assuming that the data are accurate, there is no way of knowing how these figures fit into the total picture. As stated earlier, educated estimates of the daily coastal traffic of South Vietnam ranged from four thousand to sixty thousand vessels. With a disparity this large, it is impossible to come up with absolute conclusions.

The one sure way to get an accurate appraisal of Market Time's effectiveness would be to ask those it was directed against. This author attempted to do that by writing to the Vietnamese government now in power. Not surprisingly, they did not respond.

However, some indications of the effectiveness of Market Time do exist. For example, after the war, the Department of the Army commissioned the BDM Corporation to conduct a study with the goal of identifying lessons learned from the war. The nine-volume study that resulted said about the Coastal Surveillance Force:

> Operation Market Time has been judged to have produced significant results and is credited with forcing the enemy to change his logistic operations extensively. In early 1966, it was estimated that the enemy accomplished three-quarters of his resupply by infiltration from the sea. By the end of 1966 this was reduced to an estimated one-tenth of the total resupply.

More testimony favoring the effectiveness of Market Time came from MACV Commander General Westmoreland. In his book, *A Soldier Reports,* he backs up BDM's contention that Market Time forced the enemy to "change his logistic operations extensively":

> One of the basic reasons the enemy turned to Sihanoukville and Cambodia as his primary source of supplies for his forces in at least the southern half of South Vietnam was a project known as Market Time.

Furthermore, a November 1968 Commander Task Force 115 press release quoted General Westmoreland as saying:

> Market Time forces are a major element of my overall strategy, without which we would not succeed. Market Time forces have successfully blocked intrusions by sea, forcing the enemy to use the long, tortuous Ho Chi Minh

Trail, thus affecting significantly his ability to properly sustain his forces in the South.

General Westmoreland's deputy commander, General Bruce Palmer, Jr., echoes his superior's thoughts on Market Time in his book, *The 25-Year War:* "Our Navy and Coast Guard patrols offshore . . . had been highly successful in choking off enemy infiltration of supplies by sea."

Admiral Elmo R. Zumwalt, Jr., COMNAVFORV from 30 September 1968 to 14 May 1970, wrote in his memoirs, *On Watch:* "By the time I arrived on the scene, the interdiction mission had pretty much been accomplished as far as the coast [was] concerned."

Except for the BDM Corporation's analysis, these accolades do not come from unbiased sources (although whenever praise for the Navy is offered by the Army, an extra measure of credence is probably in order). Yet their consistency, and the fact that negative comments about Operation Market Time do not appear in the otherwise critical analyses of the war, indicates that the coastal surveillance mission was accomplished.

And even if it could be proved that the mission had not been accomplished, a large measure of credit would still be due to the men of the Coast Guard and the Navy who served as part of Market Time—men who searched everything from reed basket boats to steel-hulled trawlers; who endured the chill of operating near the DMZ in January and the heat of summer days near Ca Mau; who came in close contact with the Vietnamese people, sometimes making friends, sometimes killing; who faced the dangers of the sea and the violence of the enemy; who became intimately acquainted with boredom, fear, fatigue, and sometimes death.

3
OPERATION GAME WARDEN

The River Patrol Force (Task Force 116)

It had become a place of darkness. But there was in it one river especially, a mighty big river, that you could see on the map, resembling an immense snake uncoiled, with its head in the sea, its body at rest curving afar over a vast country, and its trail lost in the depths of the land.

—JOSEPH CONRAD, *Heart of Darkness*

Nine Dragons

In the Tibetan Plateau of Central Asia, melting snow sends rivulets coursing downward over ancient rocks in a relentless quest for the sea. These rivulets merge to become streams cascading through pathways defined by gravity, their adolescent voices gathering in chorus to penetrate the silence of the land, until at last they reach the stage of maturity that Western man calls a river. In Tibet the people call this river Dza-Chu, the Water of the Rocks.

Dza-Chu, the world's eleventh longest river, changes its name several times along the 2,600-mile journey to the sea. As it races through the forbidding gorges of China's Yunnan Province it becomes Lan-Ts'ang Chiang, or Turbulent River. Then it flows more placidly into the northern reaches of Indochina and continues southward, becoming Mae Nam Khong to the Thais, Me Nam Khong to the Laotians, and Mekongk to the Cambodians. As the great river flows past Phnom Penh, the capital city of Cambodia, it fans out; by the time it crosses into South Vietnam, it has created one of the largest river deltas in the world. Westerners refer to the entire river, from Tibet to Vietnam, as the Mekong, and this massive delta as the Mekong Delta.

The main river branches into four separate rivers as it crosses South Vietnam's foot: from north to south, the My Tho, Ham Luong, Co Chien, and Hau Giang. The Americans frequently called the southernmost of these by its French name: the Bassac River. The Vietnamese call the entire complex Cuu Long Giang—the River of Nine Dragons— symbolizing the many mouths that yawn into the South China Sea. In reality, there are only eight, but to the Vietnamese eight is an unlucky number, so they choose to count nine for good fortune.

The delta itself is an alluvial plain that constitutes about one-fourth of the total land area that was South Vietnam. It is an area rich in rice, and about half of the population of South Vietnam resided there. Little wonder that the Mekong Delta was vitally important to the South Vietnamese government and that the Viet Cong exerted some of their most intense efforts there. An embassy official said, "That's where the Viet Cong have their heart, their greatest strength, control, and influence."

In 1965 the delta had only one major hard-surface road, Route 4, running from Saigon to Ca Mau. Nearly all travel and commerce depended upon the network of rivers, streams, and canals that crisscrossed the area. In light of the growing commitment of American combat forces, U.S. strategists resurrected the Bucklew Report and took a serious look at introducing U.S. Navy patrol craft into the waterways of the delta to interdict the infiltration routes of Cambodia and to wrest some of the control away from the Viet Cong forces there. There were only two obstacles: the U.S. Navy had no river patrol craft to speak of, and no corporate knowledge of riverine warfare.

MacLeod's Navy

Two small boys sat across from one another on the cracked sidewalk, a cookie tin between them forming the arena. Each carefully lowered his matchbox into the tin while the other Vietnamese boys around them chattered excitedly. As the two slowly opened the boxes, long hairlike antennae emerged from each, waving in the oppressive Saigon air.

Lieutenant Kenneth Logan MacLeod III, USN, watched a large cricket emerge from each matchbox. They stood facing each other from opposite corners of the cookie tin, one black and the other a chocolate brown. MacLeod could hear chirps as he peered over the heads of the shouting and laughing boys into the miniature coliseum. One boy took a toothpick with bits of hair attached to the end and waved it in front of his cricket: an instant later the two insects were grappling in a fury of bites and kicks. The boys cheered wildly, and one of them jumped up so quickly his head nearly caught MacLeod on the chin.

In less than a minute the combat was over, with the brown cricket the victor. One of the boys turned to leave, but when he saw MacLeod hovering he stopped and grinned, revealing more spaces than teeth. "Hey, Joe," he said. "Black one VC, huh?"

"Let's hope so," MacLeod said and turned to continue down the tree-lined boulevard. He passed the Continental Palace Hotel, with its ever-present contingent of multinational reporters and various uniformed Americans scattered across the terrace. As he turned onto Duong Tu Do (Freedom Street—formerly the Rue Catinat in the days of French colonialism), he watched a young Vietnamese girl sail past on her Vespa motorscooter, the rear flap of her traditional *ao-dai* dress tied to the back fender to keep it from tangling in the cycle's machinery. The white flap billowed out behind like the mainsail on an ancient square-rigger, but the noisy engine coughed out a stream of blue smoke in adamant testimony to the twentieth century. Vespas, Lambrettas, and *xichlos* (bicycle-powered two-seater taxis) were everywhere. MacLeod smirked, remembering that he'd heard or read that the reason the Viet Cong had never taken Saigon was because they realized it would be impossible to fight their way through the traffic. He weaved in and out among the throngs of Vietnamese and foreigners that seemed to have been poured into Tu Do Street in equal numbers. In 1965 the many nightclubs that would later make Tu Do Street famous to American GIs had not yet emerged. There were many dressmaker's shops where the smart shopper could purchase a custom-made silk gown for about eight U.S. dollars.

Minutes later, MacLeod was in a small shop trying to adjust his eyes to the darkness. An old woman with the protruding cheekbones and coal-black teeth emerged from behind a curtain. When she saw him, she bowed slightly and vanished again behind the curtain, emerging a few seconds later with a bundle of brightly colored cloth draped over one arm. Shuffling over to MacLeod, she unfolded one of her creations for him to inspect. The diffused light from the street caught the colors of a beautifully tailored American flag.

"You like?" the woman said.

"I like," he said, and she smiled proudly, the blackened teeth glistening as she nodded.

MacLeod watched her carefully wrap the two flags and wondered how she could sew with such gnarled old hands. He paid her the previously agreed-on price and then handed her some extra piasters, which brought forth a torrent of thanks accentuated by deep bowing. MacLeod, embarrassed, quickly left the shop.

As he stood in the bright afternoon sunshine trying to decide on the best route back to his boats, he muttered, "Not exactly my idea of Betsy Ross."

The two thirty-six-foot-long LCPLs eased away from the Navy repair-facility dock at the foot of Saigon's Cuong De Street, the shark's teeth on their bows flashing menacingly in the fading evening sunlight. The American flags flapping from the masts of the boats moving down the river in tandem were already beginning to show the wear of several weeks' worth of nightly patrols.

The lead boat's coxswain, Boatswain's Mate Third Class Rick Chapman, looked back over his shoulder at the lieutenant standing near the starboard gunwale amidships. "Mr. MacLeod," he said.

The lieutenant turned toward Chapman, a Swisher Sweet cigar clenched between his teeth.

"Steinberger says we're the only boats on the rivers flying the U.S. flag. Is that right?" Chapman asked.

"Probably," MacLeod answered with a puff of smoke.

The boats droned along the Saigon waterfront. Red tiled roofs and lush green trees seemed to fill all the spaces between the multistoried white hotels and government buildings. Music drifted across the water from the Majestic Hotel.

MacLeod thought about what Chapman had asked. As far as he knew, they were the only boats on river patrol in Vietnam under the Stars and Stripes. U.S. craft had been patrolling the coastline for several months on Market Time, but MacLeod was certain that his two boats were the first on the rivers. Some weeks before, back in August, MacLeod, who had been conducting a feasibility study for using amphibious LCPLs as coastal patrol craft, had suddenly been assigned a new mission. Rear Admiral Ward, then CHNAVADVGRU, had directed that Market Time be expanded into the rivers of the Mekong Delta and the Rung Sat Special Zone, where the Viet Cong seemed particularly strong. MacLeod was told to start patrolling the river network south of Saigon with his LCPLs and to develop tactics for these patrols. Rumors were circulating that a new Navy patrol craft, specially designed for river patrol, would arrive in Vietnam by the beginning of next year.

MacLeod had been promised the best LCPLs that could be found in the Pacific Fleet. What arrived were four dilapidated relics, two of which had to be sent to Subic Bay for major overhaul, while the other two needed many hours of mechanical and hull repair by MacLeod's team of talented and enthusiastic sailors. They stripped off years of accumulated paint, reinforced rust-thinned areas, repaired the tired old diesels, and mounted a veritable arsenal of weapons. They got what they could through legitimate supply sources; the rest was obtained by "MacLeod's Midnight Marine Supply Company," as they liked to call themselves. Through patience and creativity they markedly reduced the engine noise by incorporating some discarded French mufflers into the LCPL exhaust system. They added searchlights by adapting a battery of tank headlights and some automobile spotlights. When they were finished, the LCPLs didn't look much like their former selves: pedestal-mounted .50-caliber machine guns stood prominently fore and aft, .30-calibers protruded amidships, a tall thin mast was mounted amidships with a circular white radome at its peak, and shark's teeth and eyes were painted on the bows.

MacLeod's sailors were a swashbuckling group of young warriors. The second-in-command, Lieutenant (j.g.) Hal Graber, USNR, had quit medical school in order to join the Navy. Petty Officer Chapman had served in the Junk Force as an advisor and found his subsequent stateside tour dull, so he terminated it early by volunteering to go back to Vietnam. They were all proud of their new role and were playing it to the hilt. They called themselves "MacLeod's Navy" in a reference to the then-popular *McHale's Navy* television series about a World War II PT-boat skipper and his unorthodox but always triumphant crew.

On this October evening, a war correspondent from the *Arizona Republic,* Paul Dean, had joined "MacLeod's Navy" for a patrol in hopes of getting a story. Tall and rugged, he quickly hit it off with the "River Rats" (another sobriquet adopted by the LCPL sailors).

As the two-boat patrol left Saigon behind, Dean followed

MacLeod into the tiny cabin just forward of the coxswain's flat. It was stifling down there, out of the breeze. MacLeod pulled out a chart and began walking a pair of dividers across the paper in a southerly direction.

"Where are we headed?" Dean asked.

"Into the Rung Sat," MacLeod answered.

"Is that the place they call 'Forest of Assassins'?"

"That's the one." MacLeod pulled off his green fatigue cap, revealing a closely cropped crew cut, and wiped the sweat off his forehead with his fingertips. "That place has always been a no-man's-land for anybody but pirates and out-laws. Now the Viet Cong have taken it over as a training and staging area. They've got a hospital and a munitions company somewhere in there and supply depots all over the place. Until we came along they had uncontested control of practically the whole area."

"What's it like in there? I mean what is there about the area that makes it such a great hideout?"

"It's a goddamned maze! Nothing but rivers and streams and canals all laced together through thick forests of man-grove. Half of it's swamp; the rest is islands, lots of them. There are no roads to speak of. The Vietnamese Army's got enough sense not even to think about going in there, so they turned it over to the VNN, but they haven't got the assets to set up any kind of meaningful deterrence."

Dean reflected for a moment and then asked, "So where do you and your LCPLs come in? What do you hope to ac-complish with only two boats?"

MacLeod picked up the chart from the table in front of him. "Our stated mission is basically experimental, to see if we can disrupt some of Charlie's movements in the area. If we're successful on a small scale, then the Navy will come in here and in the Mekong Delta in a big way and clean out this infestation." He rapped the backs of his fingers against the chart as he spoke. "In reality, I think we've upset Mr. Charles a lot more than was originally expected. He doesn't know when or where we're going to turn up. I never tell anybody where we're going each night so there's no chance of a leak. We just appear in different places at different times and give these bastards a big headache." He pointed to sev-eral places on the chart where grease pencils had left black crosses. "Here's where we've caught him with his pajamas down already." He pointed to several other marks on the chart. "And here's where he's tried to hit us. I have no doubt that we're high on his list of priorities."

"So you think there's a real need for the U.S. Navy to get involved in river patrol?" Dean asked.

"Definitely. The VC are in control of a lot of the Mekong Delta, and they use the rivers and canals there for infiltration of supplies from Cambodia. They practically own the Rung Sat. And the shipping channel into Saigon is along the Long Tau River, and that runs right through the Rung Sat! MACV is real worried that Charlie's going to be able to sink a large ship there and really screw up traffic. A lot of Vietnam's economy and the war effort depend upon keeping that channel open. I don't think there's any question that the Navy's coming in here. The need is obvious, and the coastal patrols have broken the ice for using Navy craft in an operational role. We're just the first in what I'm sure will be a major involvement."

Both men left the cabin and emerged on deck. Saigon was a soft glow of diffused light off their port quarter, and the palms along the riverbank to the west were silhouetted against the orange remnants of the sun.

"That's Nha Be just ahead," MacLeod said to Dean. "Last friendly outpost before the Rung Sat. Time to suit up."

All around the craft, crew members were donning helmets and flak jackets. There were nine men in the crew: MacLeod, a coxswain, an engineer, four gunners to man the machine guns, and two ammunition-handlers. Four of the crew were Vietnamese; the others were American.

A few minutes later they had left Nha Be behind. Ahead, the river looked black and forbidding. MacLeod turning on the radar. Crew members removed canvas covers from the machine guns, and the boat's running lights were extinguished. MacLeod spoke into the radio handset, and LCPL-2 began closing up the distance. Her running lights too blinked off.

Dean leaned close to MacLeod to be heard above the engines. "What now?" he asked.

"We head deeper into the forest and we watch for curfew violators," came the reply.

The boats continued. The glow from the west vanished, and soon they were swallowed completely by the darkness. An occasional flicker from the dense vegetation was the only light except for the dials on Chapman's instrument panel and the pale glow reaching out of the radar screen's hood whenever MacLeod's face was not pressed into it.

MacLeod's hoarse voice suddenly broke the silence that had set in when they entered the Rung Sat: "I think we've got a live one . . . dead ahead. Back it off, Chapman."

When the engines throttled back, the bow settled into the river. Dean sensed movement about him as crew members took up their stations. He could hear the metallic sounds of guns being loaded.

"Light 'em up," MacLeod said, and a searchlight that seemed brighter than the sun severed the darkness ahead.

A tiny sampan, no more than fifteen feet long, with a minute dinghy in tow was illuminated in the harsh white glare of the searchlight. Several figures that had apparently been sleeping on the low cabin roof jumped up and raised their hands high.

Chief Warrant Officer Tham, one of the VNN members of LCPL-1's crew, called out across the water, telling the sampan to come alongside for inspection. Its occupants didn't respond immediately, so Tham fired a .45-caliber round into the air from his pistol. The shot sounded like a thunderclap in the still air, and the sampan immediately began coming their way.

LCPL-2 hovered astern, careful to remain in the darkness behind the searchlights while LCPL-1's crew searched the sampan.

Dean noticed that the air exposed in the light of the searchlight beams was filling with flying insects that looked like snow in a blizzard. He dabbed quickly at a drop of perspiration tickling his cheek, not sure that it wasn't one of the flying creatures.

Because the search revealed only fishing lines and rusty bait cans, the sampan was released after its occupants received a lecture from Chief Warrant Officer Tham regarding curfews. Tham had also confiscated their identification papers and would turn them in for further investigation by local authorities.

During the next several hours the River Rats stopped about a dozen sampans without finding anything of interest. Each time, the crew's tension would build and then collapse as the danger came and went. The routine took its toll, and some of the crew dozed between confrontations.

Trying to ward off sleep, MacLeod, Chapman, and Dean took up the ritual of mid-watch sailors everywhere, swapping sea stories and tales of their lives. At one point they discovered that all three had been born in January. They wondered what the horoscope was for Capricorns that night.

The hours wore on. The boats reached the point where the Soi Rap River empties into the South China Sea, and they turned east briefly, then north into the Dong Tranh River. The radar showed the river gradually narrowing as they continued northward. MacLeod explained to Dean that the Dong Tranh eventually merged with the Long Tau, the main shipping channel, but got pretty tight before that point. He said that the banks of the Long Tau had been defoliated by chemicals to make it hard for the enemy to operate there; but their present stretch of river had not been defoliated, and they could be pretty certain that they would be "rubbing elbows" with Charlie as they got in deeper.

At 0515 it was still pitch dark when three moving contacts appeared on radar farther upriver. The engine sound climbed from a monotonous growl to a businesslike roar. Crew members awakened and moved to their stations, their anticipation climbing again.

As they closed in, MacLeod called to Gunner's Mate Second Class Ray Steinberger on the twin fifties up forward: "Get ready on the lights." A pair of spotlights had been mounted with the machine guns to permit easy training of the lights and illumination for the guns. "Okay, hit 'em with the lights," MacLeod said.

Steinberger complied, and a glare assaulted everyone's eyes. Dean could make out several startled faces aboard the three motorized sampans before them. Several seconds passed. Then, in a lightning-quick move, one of the men in the sampans whipped out a rifle and fired it without hesitation at the lights. The River Rats had their cue. Gunfire exploded from LCPL-1. Red and white tracers raced across the water, and answering bullets danced across the deck of the LCPL.

Dean watched as MacLeod, ignoring the rounds about him, calmly inserted a 40-mm round into his grenade launcher and fired it at the lead sampan. An instant later, the target disintegrated before their eyes, splinters raining into the river in every direction.

Out of the mangroves on the shore behind LCPL-1, automatic weapons fire announced the presence of more enemy as the remaining two sampans raced for cover. Lieutenant (j.g.) Graber's LCPL-2 opened up on the mangroves. One of the LCPL-1's crew nearly fired on LCPL-2 in the confusion, but MacLeod alertly averted his mistake, redirecting the fire to the shore position. Within seconds all enemy firing had been silenced. The two sampans, taking advantage of their shallower drafts, disappeared into the swamp.

MacLeod quickly assessed his damage. The boats had suffered no major casualties, and the only injuries to the crew consisted of a few skinned knuckles and Dean's brush with death as a tracer round passed so close that its heat burned his elbow.

The River Rats pounded one another's backs in exultation; all seemed to be talking at once. MacLeod went into the cabin and emerged a moment later to pass around a box of Dutch Masters, which he called his victory cigars.

Seven hours later, MacLeod's Navy arrived back at Saigon, tired but happy. They cleaned weapons, checked engine oil, and did all the other chores that took precedence over sleep.

After an hour, MacLeod, Dean, and Chapman had one more task to complete. Digging up the previous day's newspaper, they turned to the horoscope section and read the entry for Capricorn: "Today should be a time to relax. Tonight will bring much activity."

Ken MacLeod's service on this and many other similar patrols did not go unrecognized. On 15 April 1966 he was presented with the Bronze Star with Combat "V" and the following citation from the Secretary of the Navy:

For meritorious service from 1 September to 4 November 1965 while serving with friendly foreign forces engaged in armed conflict against the enemy in Viet Nam. As commander of two LCPL river patrol boats attached to Rung Sat Special Zone, Viet Nam, Lieutenant MacLeod participated in over twenty combat night operations in which he came under enemy fire. His exceptional initiative and aggressive action were prime factors in significantly reducing the freedom of movement of the enemy. Although subjected to sniper fire and mining, Lieutenant MacLeod continually ignored the dangers and relentlessly carried out his mission of seeking out and destroying the enemy. His courage, sense of responsibility and dedication to duty were in keeping with the highest traditions of the United States Naval Service.

But this was not the only recognition that MacLeod (and others like him) received. The day after the award ceremony an article appeared in the San Diego papers describing what MacLeod had done to earn the Bronze Star. A few days later he received a letter:

Congratulations on your decoration for cowardly heroism in Viet Nam. The U.S. Christian Crusaders are doing a wonderful job massacring the people and devastating their people with no bombers to bomb back and no warships to fight the mightiest navy in the world.

Killing unarmed people on unarmed fishing junks should be worth the Congressional medal. Fighting a country that can not fight back—must be fun.

Proud—Brave—Reliable

I wish to have no Connection with any Ship that does not sail *fast*, for I intend to go in harm's way.

—JOHN PAUL JONES, November 1778

Willis Slane, president and founder of the Hatteras Yacht Company, leaned over to Jack Hargrave, a naval architect who had been with Slane since the company's start. "I thought the Navy wanted a fifty-foot hull to make into a patrol boat," he whispered. A Navy captain was at the front of the room talking to various pleasure-boat manufacturers about the need for a much smaller, shallow-draft craft.

"So did I," Hargrave whispered back.

Slane lowered his thick silver eyebrows in consternation as he turned to face the speaker again. The two Hatteras men had come to Washington expecting to offer the company's 50-foot hull. But the captain conducting the briefing was describing a boat in the 30-foot range.

"We need to make thirty knots, minimum, gentlemen," the captain droned. ". . . Hundred-and-fifty-mile range, approximately ten thousand pounds, and she needs to be able to chase sampans into exceptionally shallow water."

Hargrave tugged at Slane's sleeve. "Willis," he murmured, "I bet we could put water-jet pumps on our 28-foot hull and meet those specs." He could see a spark in Slane's eyes, a spark he had seen before that meant a roaring fire was not far behind. He was about to suggest that they could go over the details after the meeting when Slane stood up.

"Excuse me, Captain," Slane said. All eyes in the room were on the stocky, rugged man who looked more the fisherman that he was than the president of a rapidly growing, innovative company. "I have just put into production a very fast, broad-beamed hull, twenty-eight feet long, that might do the job." A flicker of interest showed in the captain's face. "If we could drive her with water-jet pumps," Slane continued, "we wouldn't have to contend with shafts, propellers, and rudders. That would allow us high-speed operation in very shallow water."

The captain smiled and said, "Sounds very good, Mr. Slane. When could we expect a formal proposal from Hatteras?"

Hargrave saw a familiar look of tenacity on Slane's handsome features, so he was not entirely surprised when Slane said, "Proposal, hell! I haven't got time for that paperwork stuff. I'll build the damn boat and then you can come down next week and ride in it!"

A polite look of tolerance came over the captain's face as he said, "Well, thank you, Mr. Slane. That sounds very interesting." He turned away and went on with the meeting.

Hargrave was certain that the captain had written Slane off as a madman. That just wasn't the way things were done in the government procurement business, and it certainly was obvious that no one could create a boat to these stringent specifications in a week. But the captain didn't know Willis Slane. Hargrave did.

In 1959 Slane, then a hosiery manufacturer, decided to build yachts out of fiberglass. While fiberglass boats were not unheard of in those days, most boat-builders subscribed to the idea that "fiberglass is for bathtubs—not boats," and such a craft over twenty feet long was rare. But that wasn't going to inhibit Willis Slane. From conception to launching took less than a year with Slane's relentless drive. On 22 March 1960 his wife, Doris, broke a bottle of champagne across the fiberglass bow of *Knit Wits,* and the yachting industry was changed forever.

Now, five years later, Slane was confronted with the "impossible" once again, and he thrived on challenge. Slane returned to High Point, North Carolina, and went to work. Through twenty-hour work days and countless phone calls all over the country, he mobilized the Hatteras plant and its suppliers into an operating mode reminiscent of a World War II shipyard. Components diverted from other destinations arrived within days or hours instead of the usual months or weeks. Indiana Gear Works delivered the all-important water-jet pumps; supercharged diesel engines came from Daytona; and the Morse Control organization provided the unusual steering system necessitated by the unconventional drive system. Slane drove himself like a man possessed, and as always, the Hatteras employees were right there with him, meeting his demands. It was hard to feel overworked when Slane worked harder and longer than everyone else. Sarah Phillips, who had known Slane since childhood and was one of his original Hatteras employees, felt obligated to warn her boss to slow down, although she knew he would not comply. It was no secret that Slane was a diabetic and had a heart in need of a bypass operation. It was also no secret that he chose to ignore these problems.

Work started on a Monday. By the following Sunday the boat was in the water running at 30.5 knots with a 165-mile range and drawing only an astonishing nine inches of water at full speed. Slane called Washington on Monday morning.

The Navy Department wasn't able to get anyone down to North Carolina until Wednesday.

The night before the Navy representatives arrived, Slane headed down the dock for one last check of his new creation. He was not hurrying for the first time in more than a week, and he had stuffed his hands into the pockets of the loose-fitting khaki trousers that he almost always wore when working. The employees at Hatteras had affectionately christened him "Captain Baggy-Ass" because of those pants. He looked older than his forty-four years with his silvered hair and weathered features, but it had been said that was because he crammed more living into a year than most people did.

Slane looked at the prototype patrol craft. He probably knew that the patrol-boat contract was not a promising business venture. Hatteras's recreational boat sales were booming; to shift their building assets away from that to a government patrol-boat contract would probably cost them profits in the long run. And this prototype had been built at Slane's expense without any promise of reimbursement. But during most of World War II Slane had served in the U.S. Army Air Corps as a pilot and had flown vital war supplies over the dangerous route known as "The Hump" from India into China. He was no stranger to patriotic duty.

The next day the demonstrations went well. The Navy agreed to buy the boat as a prototype for further testing and evaluation.

That night Willis Slane died of a heart attack.

Slane never knew what resulted from his efforts. Despite the success of his prototype, Hatteras did not get the contract for the Navy's patrol boats. In fairness to all competitors, the Navy put the contract out for bid. The terms were rigid and not enticing. Eight companies bid on the contract, however, and in November 1965 United Boatbuilders of Bellingham, Washington, landed it, committing themselves to delivering 120 boats by 1 April 1966 at a cost of approximately $75,000 each.

The new craft, designated PBR (for Patrol Boat, River), was built on United's existing 31-foot fiberglass hull. Besides being lightweight, the fiberglass had the advantage of being immune to the teredo worm. She was fitted with General

Motors 220-hp diesel engines and water-jet pumps supplied by Jacuzzi Brothers that shot out a jet of water from nozzles located below the waterline on the stern with sufficient thrust to drive the boat at high speeds. Steering was accomplished by rotating the nozzles right or left with Morse control cables linked to the wheel. For astern propulsion a ''u-gate'' slipped down over the nozzles and rerouted the flow 180 degrees, driving the boat backward.

Weighing in at a combat displacement of 14,600 pounds, this dark-green craft could reverse course in her own length at full speed (not without dousing the crew) and could stop dead in the water from full tilt in three lengths (again with the requisite soapless shower). Ceramic armor designed to stop bullets up to .30-caliber was installed around the coxswain's flat and at the weapons stations. Up forward in an open turret was a twin .50-caliber machine gun. A single machine gun was fixed to a pedestal in the fantail area. Amidships, on each side, a receptacle that looked like a piece of open-ended pipe was ready to receive the pintle mounting of either an M-60 (7.62-mm) machine gun or an MK-18 grenade launcher. A similar mounting arrangement allowed the after machine-gun mount to receive the MK-18 in a piggyback configuration. An assortment of hand-held weapons such as M-16 rifles, M-70 (40-mm) grenade launchers, and shotguns rounded out the arsenal for these potent little craft.

The electronics package for the boats consisted of a Raytheon 1900/N radar and two AN/VRC-46 FM radios. The two radios permitted communications flexibility in a war in which one might have to talk with a U.S. Army helicopter, a Vietnamese Air Force attack aircraft, or an American naval advisor, among others. Having dual radios also improved the odds of maintaining communications in an environment where both climate and enemy could prove hostile to electronics equipment.

Each PBR had a crew of four. Originally the boat captain was to be a first-class petty officer, but because of promotions and battle casualties, boat captains eventually were chief and second-class petty officers as well. They were expected to come from the boatswain's mate, gunner's mate, quartermaster, and radarman ratings, but volunteers emerged from virtually all ratings and so PBRs were skippered by engineers, clerical personnel, and even cooks before the war was over. The rest of the crew consisted of an engineman, a gunner's mate, and a seaman. They all became gunners in combat, and all were thoroughly cross-trained in one another's duties so that any one of them could take over the functions of a fallen shipmate.

The boats usually patrolled in pairs, permitting one to cover the other during searches or other investigations and making enemy ambushes more difficult to effect. A chief petty officer or a junior officer (warrant through lieutenant) usually served as patrol officer. He was responsible for the two boats in a patrol, functioning as a kind of officer in tactical command for the miniformation. He would ride in one of the PBRs in the patrol, and a Vietnamese National policeman, when available, would ride in the other. These policemen were assigned by the Vietnamese government to serve as liaison and interpreter for the patrols.

When asked about their own PBR, boat captains almost always claimed that theirs was the "fastest PBR in Vietnam." This is an indication of the pride in their work that is evident among PBR sailors, but it also reflects the preoccupation with speed as a significant measure of the combat readiness of these little men-of-war. Because the armor was limited, speed became the PBRs' best hope of protection. The Navy had originally hoped for a craft that would exceed 30 knots, but the combined weight of weapons, ammunition, ceramic armor, electronics and engineering components, and crew caused the PBRs to fall short of that ideal.

Conditions in the battle theater also contributed to speed reductions. Wearing of the impeller blades in the Jacuzzi pumps was one of the most serious problems in the early boats. Styrofoam blocks mounted in the bow area to keep the craft partially afloat if flooded became waterlogged by seepage through the hull and weighed the craft down. Poor repair work on damaged areas of the fiberglass hull caused drag on the planing surfaces. Design improvements by engineers and on-scene efforts by the crews corrected these problems.

A new generation of PBRs, the Mark II, were contracted for in March 1967. These craft were similar to their Mark I forerunners but were improved by more powerful jet pumps, relocation of some components, a slightly lower silhouette, and aluminum gunwales to prevent junks and sampans from tearing up the sides of the craft while alongside for inspections. The crews learned better maintenance techniques such as fiberglass repair and sealing the bottoms with gel to prevent seepage. They were always fine-tuning their engines and looking for ways to reduce weight. Some removed part of the ceramic armor. Since firepower was the PBR's other major survival asset, the crews were forever trying to find the right compromise between carrying as much ammunition as possible and reducing the weight. Chief Ed Canby (formerly a Junk Force advisor, later a PBR boat captain) put the PBR's speed in perspective during an interview with free-lance writer Frank Harvey. Quoting what he had heard about the PBRs, Harvey (who described Canby as "the most celebrated Viet Cong fighter in the river war at the time") said, "Those boats go like hell wide open." Canby replied. "They go twenty-five knots wide open. Ever try to outrun a cannon shell at twenty-five knots?"

Because the original 120 boats proved insufficient for their task, in February 1967 the Chief of Naval Operations (CNO) approved a force level of 250 PBRs. This number was achieved by late 1968. More were eventually built for turnover to the Vietnamese. The distribution of the craft varied throughout the war. The original allocation had set the Mekong Delta/Rung Sat ratio at 2–1; by 1968 the ratio was 6–1 as operations in the Rung Sat gradually reduced enemy activity there and the Navy expanded its patrols over more and more of the delta. Eventually a number of PBRs moved into other regions of Vietnam (see Chapter 5, "Task Force Clearwater").

Born in an atmosphere of urgency and tested under actual combat conditions, the PBR could have been a disaster. Instead it proved to be a fierce little combatant that accomplished its mission. Credit is, of course, due to men like Willis Slane and the engineers at United Boatbuilders who brought brains and craftsmanship to the urgent needs of the Navy. But the men who served on the PBRs were the most important factor in the boat's success. From personal contact with these men and from a review of their deeds, it is evident that they would have succeeded with no more than canoes and slingshots. It is a nautical axiom that ships have personalities, and it follows that those personalities are a reflection of the men on them. The smaller the ship, the more this is true. With PBRs, men and craft were inseparable—together they made up an entity about which someone coined the unofficial meaning of the letters PBR: Proud—Brave—Reliable.

Building and Flexing

At the same time that MacLeod's Navy was patrolling the waterways of the Rung Sat, other forces had been set in motion to make U.S. Navy river patrol in Vietnam a reality. The suspicion, backed by convincing evidence, that the North Vietnamese were infiltrating supplies and men into the Mekong Delta from Cambodia, the Viet Cong's strength in both the delta and the Rung Sat (using the many waterways of these regions to move large units and supplies virtually unchallenged and levying taxes on the local people), the threat posed to the Saigon shipping channel by the Viet Cong in the Rung Sat, and the inability of the VNN to handle these problems with their limited resources were compelling reasons for U.S. intervention. In August 1965 the Secretary of Defense authorized the Navy to wage riverine warfare in Vietnam and granted authorization for the procurement of a suitable patrol craft. There weren't enough LCPLs to convert, as MacLeod had done, and in fact they were not ideal for the role. Something faster and with a shallower draft was needed.

The following month, representatives of the Chief of Naval Operations, CINCPAC, CINCPACFLT, MACV, and CHNAVADVGRU met in Saigon to make plans. They decided that the Navy would need 120 boats to patrol the Mekong Delta and Rung Sat Special Zone, with a target date of early 1966. In the months that followed, the problems facing the planned river patrols appeared sufficiently different from those of the coastal forces to warrant the creation of a task force separate from Market Time. On 18 December 1965 the River Patrol Force was created under the code name Operation Game Warden. This new force was designated Task Force 116, and CHNAVADVGRU became its commander.

The mission of Game Warden forces was to enforce curfews, interdict VC infiltration, prevent taxation of water traffic by the Viet Cong, and counter enemy movement and resupply efforts. In addition, the new force was to keep the main shipping channel into Saigon open by patrolling and minesweeping in the Long Tau River.

The plan was for groups of ten river patrol boats to operate from various bases around the delta and the Rung Sat. Some bases would be placed in strategic locations ashore, coinciding wherever practical with already established VNN facilities. The original base sites were Nha Be and Cat Lo for Rung Sat operations and My Tho, Vinh Long, Can Tho, Sa Dec, and Long Xuyen in the delta. Four old LSTs (Landing Ship, Tank) were brought out of mothballs to be fitted out as mobile, floating bases that could anchor near the rivermouths.

In February 1966 the Game Warden operation order took effect, setting up two task groups: Task Group 116.1, assigned the delta and allocated eighty of the forthcoming patrol boats; and Task Group 116.2, designated as the Rung Sat group and promised forty boats. Each task group had a commander in charge who also wore the second hat of senior advisor to the Vietnamese commanders in his area.

In March the first PBRs arrived in Vietnam, and River Squadron 5 was established as the administrative organization for the newly arriving Game Warden units. Four subordinate river divisions, each with three river sections (of ten boats each), were set up within the squadron.

Stateside, the Navy established a training facility for river patrol personnel at the Amphibious Training Center in Coronado, California. A short time later, however, the sloughs of the Sacramento River north of San Francisco were recognized as similar to the geography of the Mekong Delta in many ways, and the training shifted to a new facility at Mare Island called the Naval Inshore Operations Training Center.

As lessons were learned and missions evolved, Game Warden changed in a number of ways. Operating the boats from LSTs at the rivermouths proved impractical because the water there was too rough for the little patrol boats, so the LSTs moved upriver. Mission demands moved them still farther upriver as the war went on, eventually taking them as far up as the Bassac-Mekong crossover, less than twenty nautical miles from the Cambodian border.

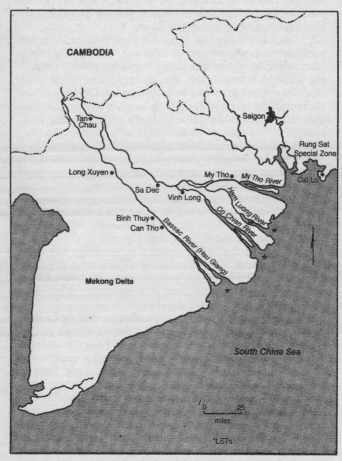

Game Warden Bases

The two original task groups expanded to four in January 1968: Task Group 116.1 on the Bassac, Task Group 116.2 on the Co Chien, Task Group 116.3 on the My Tho, and Task Group 116.4 in the Rung Sat. The Rung Sat commander remained an advisor, but the other three were not given that responsibility. A new advisory billet covering the delta area was created to take up the post formerly held by Commander Task Group 116.1 under the previous organization. In June of that same year, another task group (116.5) was added to cover the upper delta region (the upriver area).

River Squadron 5 headquarters moved from Saigon to Binh Thuy in March 1968. In September the squadron became River Patrol Flotilla 5. Its former divisions were then upgraded to squadrons, and the former sections to divisions. Some squadrons were made up of five divisions and others had only four, with a total by then of twenty-four divisions altogether. Squadron commanders generally served operationally as task group commanders.*

When Game Warden was set up, Rear Admiral Norvell G. Ward, USN, then CHNAVADVGRU and COMNAVFORV, became its commander as Commander Task Force 116. Several months later, on 18 May 1966, Task Force 116 got its own commander, Captain Burton B. Witham, Jr., USN. Commander Kenneth Rucker, USN, became the first Commander River Squadron 5. Later, when the squadron was upgraded to a flotilla, Commander Task Force 116 took on the additional responsibility of Commander River Patrol Flotilla 5, commanding the flotilla as well as the task force.

Because the enemy activity intensified in some areas and fell off in others, and in a few cases for purely logistical or

---

*There are two chains of command within a typical Navy organization. The administrative one consists of squadrons, divisions, etc., and is concerned with such matters as maintenance, personnel administration, and logistics. The operational one has, since World War II, been set up with task forces, groups, units, and elements. This organization is charged with carrying out the mission at hand. In many cases, the two organizations are nearly parallel, with individuals holding positions of responsibility in both; for example, in the January 1968 Game Warden organization, one man was both Commander River Division 51 and Commander Task Group 116.1.

administrative reasons, several of the original seven land bases were moved, some of them more than once. The sections originally at Cat Lo gradually migrated to Nha Be; those at Can Tho moved to Binh Thuy; and those at Long Xuyen moved three times during the war: first to Tan Chau in the upper delta, then to Binh Thuy, and eventually to Ben Tre. Game Warden headquarters also moved several times, from Saigon to Nha Be, then to Tra Noc near Can Tho, and finally to Binh Thuy.

The short history of Game Warden was one of change. The Navy's unpreparedness for river patrol proved to be both a deficit and an advantage. Because of the lack of doctrine and assets, the force had to rely upon trial and error for its development, and sometimes the errors were costly. At the same time, the lack of established doctrine meant that flexibility was inherent in the river force. That flexibility proved to be one of the key factors in Game Warden's success.

Tactics

Established fleet tactical doctrine was of little use in the brown waters of Vietnam's rivers. Game Warden sailors had to write the book as they went along.

Probably the earliest tactical decision was the pairing of patrolling PBRs for mutual protection. The two boats would travel in an open-column formation, about 400 to 600 yards apart, close enough to cover one another adequately but far enough apart to optimize their dual radar surveillance and thwart any hopes Charlie might have of a two-for-one shot in an ambush.

When approaching suspect craft, PBRs were careful to come in at an angle that permitted the most weapons to bear on the potential target. At night, because curfews were in effect, contacts were more likely to be hostile. In that situation a darkened PBR would come in at high speed, illuminate the craft, and, if there was no hostile reaction, order all occupants to show themselves before coming alongside. Searches were conducted as close to midstream as possible to minimize vulnerability to attack from the banks. To ensure quick reaction and maneuvering, the PBRs did not moor themselves to the craft they were searching.

While one PBR searched a suspect craft, the second covered the nearby shore and positioned itself to have a clear line of fire to both sides of the river. The PBR conducting the search always kept one of its .50-calibers trained on the shore opposite the unengaged side of the boat.

Enforcing curfews was a continual problem. If the local villagers had adhered to the rules of curfew, any traffic on the rivers at night could have automatically been identified as hostile. This was not the case, however. Curfew effectiveness depended upon proper promulgation of the rules, and even when this was carried out, many of the villagers ventured onto the rivers at night anyway, for a multitude of reasons. In April 1966 a Game Warden helicopter patrol spotted seven sampans in a restricted zone near Can Gio village in the Rung Sat Special Zone. After requesting and receiving permission from the VNN watch officer at Can Gio district headquarters, the helicopters conducted a successful strike. Tragically, the sampans were those of friendly fishermen who had received permission from their local village chief to fish during the curfew.

PBR unit commanders were assigned portions of the rivers. They divided their zones into patrol areas that did not quite overlap, to prevent interference between adjacent patrols.

The original standard operating procedure for PBRs under fire was to return fire, call for help, and leave the area until help arrived. During the Tet Offensive (February–March 1968) the PBRs proved their ability to hold their own during firefights, so the procedure was modified to allow them to stand and fight at the discretion of the patrol officer.

Another change occurred as the PBRs proved their mettle. The early patrols had kept to the main rivers, but by the end of 1967 they were venturing into the canals and subsidiary waters—again at the discretion of the patrol officer, who had to evaluate possible gains against potential losses.

The early rules of engagement, as defined in the Commander Task Force 116 Operations Order, permitted the PBRs to fire only when fired upon. Consequently, as long as they didn't fire on the PBRs, suspicious junks and sampans could ignore an order to stop for searching and escape. The only actions sanctioned by the Operations Order in this case were for the PBRs to give chase and to fire warning shots. Friendly craft would usually stop for warning shots, but if a Viet Cong craft was able to ignore the shots and outmaneuver a pursuing PBR, the Americans would be helpless to stop it. In October 1966 the orders were changed to permit PBRs to take an escaping craft under fire after all other methods to stop it had failed.

Another aspect of the rules of engagement involved traffic on the Mekong shipping channel. Because the city of Phnom Penh, Cambodia, depended upon the Mekong River as its link to the sea, vessels en route to Phnom Penh were permitted passage through Vietnam by a treaty between the Cambodian and the South Vietnamese governments. Hence, the Operations Order forbade PBRs to stop foreign-flag steel-hull merchant ships or warships on the navigable portions of the Mekong River complex. Merchant vessels of various flags sometimes exploited this immunity by unloading cargo onto small craft in the river or dropping items overboard as they moved up the channel. The Operations Order directed Game Warden patrols to make every effort to apprehend any craft receiving cargo in mid-river from a foreign merchant vessel, but only after it was no longer alongside the merchant. The PBRs were also directed to recover anything dropped overboard from foreign-flag merchants.

Stopping and searching suspicious craft was not the only mission of the Game Warden patrols. They often participated in nighttime ambushes, set up as a result of intelligence information or on the judgment of the patrol officer. PBRs concealed themselves along a riverbank and waited for expected enemy movement through the area, or shut down their engines and drifted silently through a suspect area using starlight scopes to detect enemy movements.

In February 1966, the Navy's SEAL (Sea, Air, Land) teams began operating with Game Warden forces. Best described as "naval commandos," these highly motivated and thoroughly trained individuals are experts in the use of all weapons, hand-to-hand combat, and counterinsurgent warfare techniques. They are SCUBA- and parachute-qualified and are usually multilingual. In Vietnam, they performed counterguerilla operations, reconnaissance patrols, ambushes, listening-post operations, and raids into Viet Cong territory. PBR sailors and SEALS enjoyed a symbiotic relationship: the PBRs often provided the transport and stand-by fire support for the insertions of the SEAL teams, while the SEALS frequently collected intelligence that was useful to PBR operations. SEAL platoons, assigned as integral units in the Task Force 116 organization, operated in both the Mekong Delta and the Rung Sat Special Zone during most of the war.

The search for improved tactics continued throughout the war. Outside help was often proffered by research and development personnel from the scientific community. Remote underwater detection devices, infrared and ultraviolet spotlights, and fluorescent chemical boat-marking systems were just a few of the many projects that research engineers devised to improve the lot of the PBR sailor. At the Naval Postgraduate School in Monterey, California, one completed master's degree thesis was entitled "A Mathematical Analysis of Tactics in a Riverine Ambush," and another was "A Probability Model and Patrol Planning Device for Counter-Insurgency Operations on the Mekong River."

The sailors on the rivers were naturally no less involved in tactics development. Sometimes they fastened small outboard motors to the PBRs to permit them to move more quietly (and slowly) through an area where detection was undesirable. At least one PBR crew mounted an M-60 machine gun on top of the PBR's canopy to allow firing over the elevated canal banks when the tide was low. "Acoustical detection devices" were improvised by using pebble-filled Coke cans attached to trip-wires strung across canals, and a "flame thrower" was created by shooting burning arrows from a standard hunting bow.

Patrol officers and boat captains routinely had to weigh tactical alternatives in a life-and-death environment: how much ammunition to load versus the resultant speed reduction from the added weight, when to require flak jackets and helmets versus the deleterious heat effect of wearing the extra gear, when to shut down to one engine for noise reduction versus the speed-response loss. There were few documents to guide them, very little corporate knowledge existed for them to rely upon, and the margin for error was fatally small.

Not all of the tactics were military. In a *True* magazine

article in February 1968 entitled "America's Strangest Fleet," a young lieutenant in the Game Warden force was quoted as saying:

> I'm still new here and maybe I'll change my mind. But the way I see it, this Vietnamese family is off in a sampan to catch a few fish, and here comes this rugged green boat shooting a shot across the bow. It's carrying a lot of tall, round-eyed white men wearing thick armored vests with all sorts of weapons, who board their boat— which is their home—and search through everything.
>
> Then just when they are most terrified, these huge Americans give the kid a bar of candy and the father a pack of cigarettes, and smile and wave them on. The next time we pass that sampan on the river, the family waves back. I swear to God that means something to me. You can talk all you want about your fire fights, but I think this other kind of thing might add up to more in the end.

The Viet Cong developed their own tactics for dealing with the Game Warden forces. With some notable exceptions, Task Force 116 was mainly attempting to counter logistical movement. Therefore, Charlie usually wanted to avoid confrontation with the American forces. To accomplish this he studied his adversary carefully, looking for exploitable patterns. He frequently operated at night, and liked to hide and wait until an American patrol had just passed and then make his move to cross a river or canal. He often covered his crossings with a contingent of troops armed with rocket launchers, recoilless rifles, and automatic weapons ready to respond should a PBR patrol happen along at the wrong moment. Delta waterways, lined with trees and heavy foliage, provided excellent cover for both the staging of supplies and the positioning of cover troops.

Not all of Charlie's logistics movements occurred at night. It was often advantageous for him to try moving his troops and supplies by mingling with the heavy commercial water traffic during the daylight hours. The simplest method was, of course, simply to hide his contraband under a cargo of bananas or rice or some other common trade item. But as more and more PBRs appeared on the rivers, the odds became greater that he was going to be boarded and searched, so Charlie's methods had to become more sophisticated. False bottoms appeared and contraband was attached to the underside of sampans. Sometimes a boat with legitimate cargo and papers would be positioned as a decoy to lure the PBRs in for the search; a second craft carrying contraband made its move as the PBRs were occupied with the first.

As Charlie got to know his Occidental enemy better, he exploited the weaknesses he observed. He knew that Americans were quick to respond to a medical emergency, so he would use an injured person in a sampan to distract the Americans while his contraband-laden craft slipped by unnoticed. One captured VC smuggler revealed that he had often concealed the raw material for explosives in a false overhead of his junk's deckhouse and carried no other cargo. He had discovered that craft appearing empty were less likely to be searched thoroughly by the Americans than those carrying a full load.

The South Vietnamese government tried to control the flow of contraband and inhibit enemy troop movements by instituting and enforcing a system of cargo manifesting and personal identification. Charlie worked around this paperwork by forgery and by using people with legitimate papers to move his contraband. Various means of "recruiting" were employed, including extortion and hostage-taking as well as playing upon the people's ambivalence to the war or sometimes their outright hostility toward the South Vietnamese government. On occasion Charlie confiscated the papers of innocent civilians, not necessarily for his own use, but merely to confuse and hinder the efforts of the PBR patrols in sorting out legitimate and illegitimate traffic.

Strong testimony to the effectiveness of Game Warden was given by Charlie in the form of ambushes. If it had been possible for him simply to avoid the American patrols, he would most assuredly have done so; whether fighting the French as Viet Minh or fighting the South Vietnamese and Americans as Viet Cong, the Vietnamese Communist had proved himself a soldier of almost infinite patience. Ambushes, however, became a way of life on the waterways of both the delta and the Rung Sat, and Charlie became an expert at them. He used this knowledge of the environment, the habits of his adversary, and the confining waterways to effect carefully orchestrated and, all too often, highly efficient ambushes. He often struck at low tide, when the waterways were constricted and consequently the maneuverability of the PBRs was limited. He frequently hit the Americans when they were returning from patrols because he knew they would be tired and therefore less observant and less efficient. He dug himself into well-fortified bunkers that not only were difficult to penetrate from the river but could withstand the retaliation from above when Seawolf helicopters or fixed-wing Black Ponies (OV-10A Bronco aircraft) were called in. He set up fish traps (which were common and legitimate on the waterways) in a pattern that would cause the PBRs to maneuver (trying to avoid disturbing or becoming fouled in the fish traps) into a predetermined point of ambush. He fired a few shots from one side of a waterway to drive the PBRs closer to the other side where the real firepower waited. He planted command-detonated mines and he waited patiently to make his kill. He set up aiming stakes in the river with just their tops showing and aimed his weapons at them to assure him of a hit when his adversary passed close by. He was, in short, a formidable enemy, and he made the life of the Game Warden sailor tense and hazardous.

In his semiautobiographical novel *River of Death,* James Butler, a former PBR boat captain, described an unusual and harrowing VC tactic:

> Brown suddenly looked ahead and saw the huge tree across the river. . . . He had heard stories about this but had never really believed it could happen to him. If the VC had sprung the trap there would be another fallen tree behind them when they tried to work their way out. . . . He knew that Charlie would often cut one tree, holding it in place with a rope or wire. When a PBR would enter a small river, Charlie would draw the PBR upstream where there was another tree already cut, and then he would spring the trap.

While tactics, both allied and enemy, played a significant role in determining the survivability of the Game Warden sailor, that was not the only factor. Like his counterparts on the Market Time patrols, the Game Warden sailor had to contend with the insidious enemy that haunts all warriors regardless of their nationality or cause. Then Commander, now Rear Admiral (retired), Sayre A. Swarztrauber described this problem in a May 1970 article:

While there is a great deal of adventure and glamour in this work at times, the biggest danger comes not from the enemy, but from boredom and fatigue, which dull alertness and which can catch one unprepared. This is not so hard to understand when it is realized that the PBR sailor endures demanding and long hours, watching, waiting, searching, and inspecting watercraft. The PBR crewman logs a work week of usually more than 80 hours, and half his time on patrol is at night. Each PBR is under way about 40 percent of the time, mainly at low speeds. Normally, PBRs operate at full speed only when in contact with the enemy or when proceeding to and from patrol station. Their endurance is about five and one-half hours at full speed. But the nature of PBR patrols is such that after a normal 12-hour patrol, they return with about 25 percent fuel on board. Searching junks and sampans becomes dull work after the first few hundred. Not at all glamorous. The boats search thousands of craft each week. In a typical month, Game Warden's PBRs will detect 200,000 watercraft, board about one-half of them, or 100,000 for cursory inspection, and carefully search about half of those, or 50,000. Certainly, no one knows for sure how many sampans and junks there are in the area. It is safe to say that many craft are detected and perhaps searched two or more times during a month. In most cases, no irregularities are found. The routine of a standard 12-hour patrol is waiting . . . drifting . . . searching . . . verifying cargo manifests . . . checking ID cards against black lists . . . putting on the rain gear . . . taking off the rain gear. . . .

God Be Here

The lieutenant pulled off his black beret and threw it down on top of the PBR's grenade locker. The black loop of ribbon at the back of the beret had been cut into two pennants—among PBR sailors this signified that he had made his first contact with the enemy—and the ends of each pennant were notched with a V to represent his first enemy kill. Both ceremonial cuts had been made a long time ago. The lieutenant had tallied several hundred patrols since joining River Section 511, and he had engaged the enemy in more than sixty firefights. Back in his locker in Binh Thuy, under a pile of neatly folded olive-drab undershirts, was a Purple Heart he had earned last November when a piece of shrapnel lodged in his jaw. He had had a PBR shot out from under him as well, and he and his crew had been raked by intense small-arms fire at close range while they swam for their lives. (If not for the suppressive fire from their cover boat, it is doubtful that any would have survived.)

Despite all the action that the lieutenant had seen, the enlisted men in River Section 511 liked to have him along as patrol officer on their patrols. He was a "cool head" in combat, and as a "mustang"—an enlisted man who had worked his way up through the ranks—he knew what enlisted men were all about and how to look out for them. There was another reason they liked having him as patrol officer. Sailors are by nature superstitious, and men in combat are often more religious than they were back home. So the sailors liked having the lieutenant along because his name was Dick Godbehere, pronounced exactly as spelled: God-be-here! It was not uncommon to hear someone say, in a play on words that had a measure of seriousness, "I'd rather have Godbehere than anyone else."

The year was 1968, two days before the start of the Vietnamese holiday called Tet. Lieutenant Godbehere's patrol had been assigned a psychological operations mission, one designed to get information to villagers about the government and the war effort. The PBRs were good vehicles for these missions because they could get close to the people in the delta by traveling the rivers and canals. Godbehere's PBR was rigged with a tape recorder and large speakers to broadcast their message, an appeal for the South Vietnamese government's *Chieu Hoi* (open arms) program—the amnesty program that promised protection, money, clothes, and food for any VC who wished to change sides. A sign on each side of the PBR said in Vietnamese, "This is *Chieu Hoi* Rally Point. You will be welcomed here." Godbehere looked at the sign and wondered if any ralliers (called *Hoi Chanhs*) would turn themselves in to him that day. That had happened to other PBRs on patrol, but so far never to Godbehere. He had read a report somewhere that said 28,000 *Hoi Chanhs* had rallied in the previous year. He had also read that the estimated cost of the *Chieu Hoi* program was about $150 per *Hoi Chanh*—compared to the unofficial estimate of $9,000 worth of ammunition expended per enemy killed.

The two-boat patrol got under way and headed down the Bassac River toward the major delta city of Can Tho. Godbehere disliked psychological operations patrols because the PBRs had to move slowly in order to allow the messages to be heard, which made them very vulnerable to attack, and because listening to the tape messages over and over challenged his sanity.

After about twenty minutes, the tape recorder was switched on and the crew settled in for what promised to be a boring patrol. The pre-mission brief had predicted a quiet run. Just a few weeks back, General William Desobry, USA, upon being relieved as U.S. military advisory chief in the delta region, told reporters that the Viet Cong were "poorly motivated, poorly trained" and that the South Vietnamese Army "has the upper hand completely." The area around Can Tho was considered relatively friendly.

But as they plodded along, Godbehere had been scanning the banks, and the hair at the back of his neck was beginning to prickle. He had seen the grass-covered huts along the banks with chickens clucking and strutting in front. Tools rested against thatched walls and fishnets were piled or strewn about. An occasional water buffalo would swing its massive horned head in their direction to detect the source of noise as they passed, and the grunting of pigs could sometimes be heard over the rumble of the engines. Rice baskets swayed on hooks in the breeze and hints of incense tickled the nostrils every now and then. It was a pastoral scene except for one element: not a single human being had been in sight for the last several miles. Godbehere had been around long enough to know that this usually spelled trouble.

"I don't like the looks of this, Boats," he said to the boat captain.

"I know, sir. Too quiet," came the reply. The boat captain had one hand resting lightly on the reined-in throttles. "Gunner, get your helmet on," he called forward to the third-class petty officer lounging in the gun tub.

The rest of the crew began fastening their flak jackets and warily watching the banks.

Godbehere said to no one in particular, "Charlie's out there. I can feel him."

Second crept into minutes as perspiration flowed down tense brows to anxious eyes. The minutes grew into hours that seemed like days as they droned along, the taped Vietnamese voice appealing to unseen ears. Twenty-eight miles passed and nothing happened, yet the tension remained. Something was unquestionably wrong.

As they turned about for the return trip, the boat captain said, "Maybe it's got something to do with this Tet holiday thing. Maybe that's why nobody's around."

"Maybe," Godbehere said, not believing it.

The return trip was more of the same. Everything looked normal in the villages except for the absence of the people. The Americans passed from hamlet to hamlet feeling as if they were the only humans left in the world. Only the infrequent passage of a plane or the distant *whop-whop* of helicopter blades occasionally dispelled this sensation. Godbehere couldn't shake the feeling of being watched, of believing that any moment all hell would break loose.

But it never did. The patrol ended at last, and Godbehere and the others returned to base trying to work the knots of tension out of their muscles. They were exhausted.

That night after Godbehere had filed his patrol report and turned in, he lay under his green mosquito net watching the geckos patrolling the walls of his hootch in search of insect prey. He wondered what the strange day meant. The signs were there for trouble—the situation had "ambush" written all over it. And the PBRs were so vulnerable at the low speed required by the mission—Charlie could have hit them if it had in fact been an ambush. But he didn't. Why? Maybe the boat captain was right: maybe it had something to do with Tet. Maybe the villagers had all gone to their temples or something. . . . No, the animals wouldn't have been left to wander and the tools would have been put away. There were people nearby; he was sure of it. . . . But why were they hiding? If Charlie was there, why hadn't he ambushed the PBRs?. . .

Godbehere mulled over these possibilities for a long time before he was able to go to sleep.

Two days later, Dick Godbehere had his answers. The enemy had chosen the Tet holiday of 1968 to launch a co-ordinated, country-wide offensive within South Vietnam. Thirty-six of the forty-four provincial capitals, five of the six major cities, and many district capitals and hamlets were attacked by Communist forces. In the Mekong Delta, the attacks involved thirteen of the sixteen provincial capitals, including Can Tho, the city near which Godbehere's patrol had been. Four days before Tet, the enemy troops had moved into the hamlets around Can Tho in preparation for the assault. Godbehere had been right: Charlie was there when the PBRs had come through. He had apparently refrained from attacking the small game of two PBRs in order not to reveal his presence before the large-scale attack on Can Tho scheduled to begin in unison with the other attacks throughout the country on the first day of Tet.

The battles of the Tet Offensive raged for seventy-seven days. Game Warden units played a significant role in reversing the tide of battle in the delta. By chance, some units happened to be in the vicinity of the city of Chau Doc, involved in a planned interdiction operation called "Bold Dragon I," when the Tet Offensive began. These few Game Warden sailors and the SEALs on the operation with them played a major role in the defense of the city. The VC battalions assigned to capture Chau Doc, told that they would be met with waving banners and open arms, were quite surprised when met by the resistance led by the Game Warden sailors. PBRs and Seawolf helicopters also provided the firepower that held the enemy at bay in Ben Tre until reinforcing ground troops could arrive to drive the attackers out of the city.

During February, Lieutenant Godbehere was involved in a few skirmishes on the periphery of the major battles, but nothing terribly significant. This proved to be a lull before the storm for Dick Godbehere.

Lieutenant Godbehere's two-PBR patrol left Binh Thuy and headed southeast on the Bassac River en route to its assigned patrol area. The sky was growing dark, and the air was cool for a March night in the Mekong Delta.

Signalman Third Class Jere Beery, the after gunner on the PBR carrying Godbehere, politely looked away as one of the other crew members squatted over the rail of the boat, paying the price for having indulged in a local village's culinary delights. Privacy is one of the casualties of war—particularly on a 31-foot boat with no head.

Beery looked down at his own tailor-made camouflage uniform, but the sky was too dark for him to really see it. He had just bought the outfit from a local Vietnamese seamstress and was wearing it for the first time. His shipmates had teased him about it, saying, "Hey, Jere, where are you? I can't see you with those camis on," or "Look at the walking tree."

The PBRs passed by Can Tho. Most of the city was quiet and dark, but the distant rattle of a machine gun could be heard from the far side. Some weeks back, Can Tho had been enveloped in artillery fire and exploding aircraft ordnance as the allied forces fought to dislodge the Viet Cong from the university there. Beery had heard that the once beautiful Faculty of Science building had been reduced to smoking rubble, but he hadn't seen it.

A reporter who had come along for a story bumped into something in the dark and cursed the offending object and its ancestry. Beery remembered another occasion when a pair of reporters had talked Beery's boat captain into taking them into an infamous area known as the Ti Ti Canal. One of the pair was a large-framed man, wearing brand new fatigues, who had told the section's commanding officer, "We need to show the people back in the States exactly what our boys are going through over here." The other was a man about half his companion's size. They had lugged several cases of camera equipment on board for the patrol. On the way to the canal, the big man was standing on the engine covers with his 16-mm motion-picture camera on top of the boat's awning. As they neared the canal, Bailey, the boat captain, had hollered back to Beery, "Tell that son-of-a-bitch to get down here and put on a flak jacket and helmet." Beery relayed the message (in more polite terms), only to be rebuffed. "I can't maneuver the camera with all that stuff on," the big reporter had said. No sooner had he uttered those words than automatic-weapons fire erupted from both banks. The 16-mm camera flew up into the air as the big reporter dove into the coxswain's flat, landing right at Bailey's feet. The boat captain kicked the reporter and yelled, "You better get up there and get your pictures, you son-of-a-bitch, we ain't comin' through here for you again!" The reporter's camera had been broken, and the only things to show for their efforts were a few still photographs taken by the little reporter and 136 bullet-entry holes in the hull of the PBR.

The two PBRs passed the upriver end of Cu Lao Mae Island. It was totally black on the river now. Only the radar could see.

A sudden flash of light appeared in Beery's peripheral vision over his left shoulder. He turned and realized that it must have been a B-40 rocket, for a second one had just emerged from the darkness of the island. Both rockets were well off target.

Beery could hear Lieutenant Godbehere on the radio—"Red Rose, this is Hand Lash Delta"—checking to make sure there were no friendly units in the area. All gunners were holding their fire, not only because of the possibility of friendly units but because the flashes from their weapons would give Charlie something besides sound to aim at.

Godbehere got the clearance he sought from "Red Rose" and ordered his patrol units to start a firing run. The PBRs swooped in toward the island and hammered the darkness from which the rockets had come. Flames of small-arms fire and machine-gun bursts flickered in the trees on shore as the boats roared in.

Beery squeezed off about a hundred rounds and then leaned down to open another canister of ammunition. Two fireballs burst out of the trees as he bent over. Beery recognized them as B-40 rounds but was certain that they would miss. He was wrong: one of the rockets struck the gunwale on the starboard quarter and exploded.

Lieutenant Godbehere was just aft of the coxswain's flat when the rocket hit. As he saw the reddish-orange rocket explode, he felt a blast of heat and pieces of shrapnel tearing into his legs. A few moments later a second rocket found its mark, this one detonating against the grenade locker on the starboard side. Godbehere, thrown to the deck by the blast, climbed back to his feet and looked about, trying to assess his situation. A gunner named Sherman had been standing near Godbehere before the hits; now he was gone. Godbehere thought he had been blown overboard, but soon he appeared next to the lieutenant, a steel fragment protruding from the back of his arm and another lodged in his foot. Aft, Godbehere saw that Beery was still standing at his gun but wasn't firing. "Go see what's wrong with Beery," Godbehere told Sherman and then turned his attention back to the battle that was still raging.

The other PBR in the patrol had been hit many times, and the damage to both boats was too severe to warrant any further engagement. Godbehere ordered the boat captains to retire to a safe location so that they could evacuate their wounded.

Sherman reappeared and said, "Beery's hurt bad, Mr. Godbehere."

Godbehere moved aft. Every step was painful; clearly, his legs had taken a lot of metal. When he got to Beery, the young gunner was still standing and holding on to his weapon. "Where're you hit?" Godbehere asked.

"In the gut," Beery rasped.

Godbehere looked down. To his dismay and horror, he saw that Beery's abdomen had been sliced open by the exploding rocket: his intestines were trailing down to a grisly heap on the PBR's deck.

Godbehere grasped Beery firmly by the shoulders and, with Sherman's help, laid him down on the deck, then carefully piled the moist entrails onto Beery's abdomen. With a large battle dressing he cautiously covered the hideous mound. Sherman cut away Beery's trousers; the new camis were full of shrapnel holes, and his right leg and hip were a mess. A large piece of shrapnel had penetrated Beery's stomach and was protruding from his back. Godbehere doubted that Beery was going to live.

While Godbehere and Sherman worked, trying to dress Beery's many wounds, Beery tried to speak but didn't have sufficient breath left to be heard above the PBR's engines. He pulled Godbehere down and whispered in his ear. "If I don't make it," he said so softly that Godbehere could barely hear him, "tell my mom and dad what happened."

Godbehere said, "You're going to be all right. Your intestines just fell out. They can put 'em back for you. They do it all the time. You'll be okay."

Beery shook his head slowly.

Godbehere yelled, "Goddammit, Jere, you're going to be all right!"

The two PBRs were out of the firefight by this time, and Godbehere ordered them to head for Tra On village on the east bank of the Bassac River opposite Cu Lao Mae Island. Godbehere had visited several of the eight U.S. Army advisors there, and he knew the village pretty well. It was the nearest place he could think of to effect a safe medical evacuation. As the two boats headed downriver toward Tra On, Godbehere told Bailey to get on the radio and call for "Pedro," the Air Force medical evacuation helicopter. For the rest of the run into Tra On, Godbehere knelt next to Beery in a pool of their mingled blood, ignoring his own wounds and trying to soothe the mangled man's fear and despair.

At the village, the Army advisors loaded Beery onto a stretcher. As they started to carry him off the boat, Beery smiled weakly and said, "I don't know how those guys managed to hit me." He held up a tattered remnant of his brand new camouflage shirt. "I thought I looked like a tree."

Neither Lieutenant Godbehere nor Petty Officer Beery ever fought in Vietnam again. Dick Godbehere's wounds were serious enough to cause his evacuation for recovery and reassignment. He eventually retired from the Navy as a lieutenant commander.

The same spirit that had permitted Jere Beery to make a joke about his camouflage uniform in his hour of crisis got him through a long and trying ordeal of recovery. He lived and went on to become a motion-picture stunt man.

Sweeping Swabs

> The *Avignon*'s bows had begun to swing rap-
> idly through all the points of the compass as
> the river meandered on through the jungle,
> and the tips of the [Saigon] cathedral spires
> seemed to dart around the ship, popping up
> first in one quarter then another like the ears
> of an inquisitive rabbit trying to follow its
> progress. Joseph saw them one minute to
> port, then the next minute to starboard, and
> once they even appeared dead astern as the
> river turned back on itself.
>
> —Anthony Grey, *Saigon*

Because of the maze-like wanderings of the Long Tau River as it passes through the treacherous Rung Sat Special Zone, effectively patrolling Saigon's main shipping channel was extremely difficult. The tight turns of the river hid many segments from the view even of a nearby patrol boat. Consequently, the Viet Cong had ample opportunity to plant mines in the river in hopes of sinking a large vessel in the channel and obstructing traffic. A typical mining evolution required only that the Viet Cong wait until a segment of the river was free of patrols, then emerge from the swamps in a tiny sampan, sow a mine in the channel, and return to the safety of the mangrove forest—low risk with potentially high tactical payoff.

Most of the mines were locally made, using fishnet buoys or metal drums filled with explosives and command-detonated by a wire run from the mine, along the river bottom, to a hidden observation point ashore. This design permitted selective targeting and required little sophistication. In contrast, recovery of Soviet-made mines from the Long Tau during the war proved that not all mines were this simple homemade type.

Since part of Game Warden's mission was to keep the Saigon shipping channel open for traffic, patrolling by gunboats was not enough; sweeping the river for mines was an obvious additional requirement. In June 1966, Mine Squadron Eleven—Detachment Alfa was established at Nha Be, nine miles south of Saigon, to serve as a task unit of the Game Warden force. Earlier, in March, four Minesweeping Boats (MSBs) were sent down to Nha Be from Da Nang, where they had been operating since October 1965, to form the nucleus of the new unit. These original four were joined by eight more MSBs shipped in from the United States. Two officers and 106 enlisted men came in to provide the manpower.

MSBs are 57-foot, wooden-hulled craft with a four-foot draft. They are twin-screwed and diesel-powered, making a maximum nominal speed of 14 knots. For Vietnam service they were configured with a single .50-caliber machine gun mounted in an elevated tub aft and single .30-calibers mounted port and starboard on the forecastle. A chief petty officer or a first-class petty officer with a significant amount of small-craft experience was usually designated as the officer in charge, but sometimes a particularly well-qualified second-class petty officer got the job. A crew of seven (including the officer in charge) was assigned to each boat.

In 1968, after having been awarded a Presidential Unit Citation, Detachment Alfa became Mine Divisions 112 and 113, each with six MSBs and five Minesweepers, Medium (MSMs). The latter were LCM-6s that had been converted to river minesweepers and added to the detachment in July 1967. Several subordinate units of three boats each were broken off and deployed to Da Nang, Qui Nhon, Nha Trang, and Cam Ranh Bay to sweep the harbors there.

The Vietnamese Navy also operated minesweeping launches. By mutual agreement, the VNN units swept the river north of Nha Be up to Saigon, while the USN units swept south of Nha Be, through the Rung Sat, to the sea.

The concern over mining was well founded. In May 1965 a freighter was hit by a mine near Nha Be and forced to beach herself rather than sink in the channel. On 23 August 1966, the SS *Baton Route Victory*, a 10,000-ton freighter, struck a mine twenty miles out of Saigon. Seven crew members were killed in the explosion. Fortunately the ship was able to get out of the channel before she sank. In that month, a VNN minesweeper was sunk by a command-detonated mine in the Rung Sat; Viet Cong soldiers emerged from the jungle and machine-gunned the survivors. The U.S. advisor who had been on board the craft survived, but was seriously wounded.

The Viet Cong considered the MSBs (and later the MSMs) a threat. Sniper fire was commonplace, but when MSB-15 was ambushed and hit by 57-mm recoilless rifle fire in September 1966, the men of Detachment Alfa knew that they were "getting under Charlie's skin." They also surmised that they were in for some rough times. They were right; about a month later MSB-54 swept a mine the hard way and sank, with two crewmen lost and four others wounded.

Danger did not only lurk among the mangroves or beneath the muddy waters. Early in the morning of 14 January 1967, MSB-14 was headed north along the Long Tau, sweeping the channel in a dense fog about thirty miles south-southeast of Saigon. At about 0620, the Norwegian motor ship *Mui Finn* suddenly appeared out of the milky blanket and struck the minesweeper, cutting her in two. Four of the crew were rescued, but three were lost to the dark, muddy waters of the Long Tau.

The American MSB and MSM crews continued their sweeps of the channel throughout the war, until "Vietnamization" caused them to turn their craft over to the VNN in late 1970. They kept the channel open for the average of twenty merchant ships that sailed through to Saigon each day, and they did so at no small personal risk. Death and injury were never far away. In a statement that will never rival the inspirational words of John Paul Jones or Stephen Decatur, yet says a great deal in its own quiet way, a boat captain whose MSB had just been mined out from under him (killing one of his crew) told a journalist, "We know what has to be done and we'll do it."

For the Americans it was the day after Valentine's Day in the Christian calendar year of 1967. For the Vietnamese it was the end of the Lunar New Year holiday known as Tet in the Year of the Goat.

The morning was cool as the Detachment Alfa sailors rolled

out of their mosquito-net-covered beds and shuffled along the raised wooden walkways that led from the hootches to the heads and kept their feet out of the Nha Be mire during the rainy season). The sounds of a waking jungle carried through the barbed-wire perimeter as the men went about their morning ablutions and returned to their hootches to put on their "uniforms." Some donned a full dungaree working uniform; others pulled on fatigue trousers and a flak jacket with only a tee-shirt underneath. A third-class gunner's mate who looked barely beyond puberty gazed at the picture of Joey Heatherton, taped to the inside of his locker door, that he had taken when she had come to Vietnam as part of the Bob Hope show. He gave her a ritualistic pat before heading out for the day's work.

Less than an hour later, at a little past 0600, MSB-49 backed away from the next, her twin screws churning the river water into a chocolate foam. The craft twisted about and headed downriver, taking the left fork into the Long Tau channel; MSB-51, her companion boat, fell in astern. For the next several miles the river was fairly wide and straight. The men of MSB-49 seemed relaxed as they went about their tasks. They had made many sweeps and had been tested under fire. Just two weeks before they had seen their sweep gear take a strain; then an explosion erupted in the wake as a mine detonated. Simultaneously, gunfire had barked from the well-concealed position ashore. The firefight had been brief, no casualties had resulted, and the men had acquitted themselves well.

The crew payed out the 49's sweep-gear, and the 51-boat moved laterally in the channel to cover a different sector but still remained slightly upriver of the 49. Sunlight danced on the water.

As the boats started around the first great bend in the river, recoilless rifle rounds and machine-gun fire engulfed MSB-49. Three of the rifle rounds tore into the port side; one found its way into the fuel tanks and set them ablaze. The firing was coming from both sides of the river out of well-fortified positions. The 51-boat opened up on the firing positions, and several PBRs in the area headed in at full throttle.

The stricken craft had no choice but to beach before she went down. In the midst of a heavy fusillade she headed toward the hostile shore. Boatswain's Mate First Class Hood, boat captain of the 51, brought his craft in close behind her despite the heavy fire. The PBRs streaked into the fray and helped keep the enemy pinned down while the 51's crew evacuated the wounded and stripped the armament off the burning, beached 49.

At 0710 a Navy helicopter fire team arrived and began firing runs along the enemy positions, which stretched for half a mile along each bank of the river. The helicopters were hit five times in the heavy ground fire but were not brought down. At 0750 a fixed-wing airstrike preceded a four-company Regional Force sweep into the area. This reaction force found ten 75-mm recoilless rifle casings, one Claymore mine, and two dead enemy soldiers. A pair of LCMs towed MSB-49 back to Nha Be. MSB-51 resumed sweeping with a new partner, the 32.

Two hours later, MSB-45, in company with MSB-22, was mortally hit by a command-detonated mine fifteen miles southeast of Nha Be. She went down almost immediately after a violent explosion. The 22-boat recovered five survivors from the debris-covered water; four were wounded. A search for Damage Controlman Third Class Gary C. Paddock, USN, was fruitless. Divers stripped the hulk while she lay in the mud beneath the river and then destroyed what was left of her by explosives. Gary Paddock's body was found three days later.

At 1428 on the same day, MSB-51 again came under fire. An unidentified type of heavy weapon scored two direct hits, one in the stack and one in the sweep winch. The 51, her companion boat (MSB-32), and two PBR escorts reversed course and headed north. Two miles upstream a second ambush hit them. Four more PBRs joined the action, followed by helicopter and fixed-wing airstrikes in what one sailor described as "a *hell* of a shootout."

The final count for the day was two Americans killed and sixteen wounded. In the aftermath of that costly day and the next (when MSBs 16 and 52 were attacked only three and one half miles from Nha Be), MSB armament was augmented by the installation of M-18 grenade launchers to give them more "punch in the clinches," another section of PBRs was brought in to operate from the USS *Jennings County* (LST-

846) stationed at the mouth of the Long Tau, and B-52 strikes were called in to pulverize an area of the Rung Sat where it was suspected that the Viet Cong commander had his head-quarters.

In a message sent on 16 February, COMNAVFORV said:

THE COURAGEOUS ACTION, BULLDOG TENACITY AND PER-SONAL HEROISM THAT THE MEN OF DETACHMENT ALFA HAVE DEMONSTRATED UNDER FIRE IS IN KEEPING WITH THE HIGHEST TRADITIONS OF THE NAVY. IT IS SINGU-LARLY SIGNIFICANT THAT IN SPITE OF YESTERDAY'S EF-FORTS BY THE VIET CONG, THE RIVER REMAINS OPEN AND UNBLOCKED. YOUR RESOLUTION IN CONTINUING MAXI-MUM COVERAGE OF THE LONG TAU WITH AVAILABLE AS-SETS IS HIGHLY GRATIFYING.

Operation Monster

In an area due west of Saigon and north of the Mekong River complex lies in a thirty-by-seventy-mile marshland known as the Plain of Reeds. This area is generally flat, perennially inundated (the water depth varying from approximately one foot to six feet depending upon the season), and covered with a dense growth of aquatic grass and reeds ranging in height from three to twelve feet. Even the village areas are dry only half of the year. Adjacent to the waterways (the deeper chan-nels) are stands of trees and vegetation. Occasional clumps of bramble bushes are hidden among the reeds, sometimes growing to heights of ten feet. In short, the area is extraor-dinarily inhospitable: difficult to navigate by boat, impossible to negotiate by other means.

The Viet Cong had long enjoyed hegemony over the region. The difficult terrain made penetration by organized military units next to impossible. Throughout the area the VC had built bunkers that were difficult to detect from the air. And rice (an unusual floating variety with long roots that adapted to the varying water level) grew in plenty. It was a guerrilla's ideal hideout and staging area.

Then in November 1966 the calm of the Plain of Reeds was

shattered by the roar of monsters with gaping mouths that raced across the reeds at phenomenal speeds and crashed through walls of thorns in their search for prey. Operation *Quai Vat* ("monster") was under way. The Navy had loosed the awesome power of its "dragon boats"—the patrol air-cushion vehicles of PACV Division 107—into this Viet Cong sanctuary.

The PACVs had been evaluated in both Market Time and Game Warden operations in the fall of 1966. In both cases, the results were less than spectacular. What advantages these hovercraft did have (high speed, shallow draft, ability to pass over solid objects and dry land) were offset by their noise, poor crew habitability, and cost (compare their price tag of just under a million dollars each to the $90,000 cost of a PBR). But the Plain of Reeds was an environment that seemed made for air-cushion vehicles, so Game Warden was extended into that region to achieve the two-fold purpose of further evaluating the PACVs and challenging Charlie in one of his traditional strongholds.

The PACVs were 39 feet long, 24 feet wide, and driven by a gas-turbine engine that powered both the seven-foot lift fan and the driving propeller. The lift fan created a bubble of air four feet thick under the rubber skirts of the craft, which kept it in a constant hover whenever engaged. The driving propeller provided the thrust necessary for high speed by forcing air aft in a manner similar to that used for air boats in the Florida everglades. The PACVs were armed with grenade launchers and machine guns and were crewed by an officer in charge and three enlisted men.

Three PACVs were stationed at Moc Hoa under the operational control of Commander Task Unit 116.9.1. Their total personnel consisted of four officers and fifteen enlisted. Operations were coordinated with the "Green Beret" soldiers of "B" detachment of the Fifth Special Forces. Eight to twelve troops usually rode outside on the catwalks that ran along the sides of the craft. This was somewhat arduous for the troops because of the high wind, but one soldier probably spoke for most when he said, "It beats sweatin' it out inside an APC [Armored Personnel Carrier]."

Various operations during *Quai Vat* used different combinations of assets. Sampans, Vietnamese air-boats, fixed-wing aircraft, and helicopters were all used with the PACVs, and had varying degrees of success. The PACV-helicopter combination proved the best marriage of assets: the helicopters provided air reconnaissance of the region and vectored the PACVs with their firepower and troops onto targets. The helicopters were able to locate breaks in tree lines through which the PACVs could pass, thereby increasing their efficiency.

At the end of Operation Monster, which lasted sixteen days, the three PACVs were credited with destroying seventy enemy structures and an equal number of enemy sampans, capturing eleven VC, and getting twenty-three confirmed enemy kills. They had proven themselves to be suited to warfare in an unusual environment like the Plain of Reeds and had disrupted Viet Cong hegemony in the area. Despite the treacherous terrain, they had bogged down only once when they had tried a long run through an area thick with fifteen-foot saplings, but were able to free themselves without much difficulty. They were able to cross dikes and embankments as high as four feet and could handle the fields of fifteen-foot elephant grass with nothing more than a reduction in speed.

The PACVs did have some disadvantages. Their communication problems might have caused them some difficult times, had they not had helicopters to help them find their way through the maze of trees. Their noise removed the element of surprise, although their high-speed capability (as much as 70 knots) sometimes compensated by allowing them to move into an enemy area before the VC had time to react.

All in all, it is unlikely that the PACVs ever justified their high cost, but they were a welcome asset in helping U.S. forces to penetrate the forbidding Plain of Reeds. An attempt any other way would have had to be called Operation Nightmare.

Seawolves

While creating the Game Warden operation, Navy strategists were quick to realize the hazards of sending small, lightly armored craft onto hostile waterways. While the speed and heavy firepower of the PBRs were expected to increase their survivability, there were many conceivable situations in which the PBRs might need assistance—fast and potent assistance. The obvious answer was air support. The nature of the environment and the missions pointed to helicopters, but the Navy had no helicopters of its own that were suitable for the attack role envisioned. Helos in the antisubmarine warfare inventory were too large and unsuitable for conversion. A joint service agreement between the Army and the Navy soon remedied the problem. The Army's 197th Aviation Company lent the Navy twenty-two UH-1B Iroquois ("Huey") helicopters for the Game Warden operation. The interservice agreement also specified that the Army would replace any aircraft that were lost.

The first two helicopters arrived in Vietnam even before the first PBRs. These helicopters were initially manned and maintained by Army personnel until Navy crews could be sufficiently trained to assume the mission.

In June 1966, Detachments 25, 27, and 29 of Helicopter Combat Support Squadron One (HC-1) were deployed from Imperial Beach, California, to Tan Son Nhut airbase on the outskirts of Saigon. The eight officers and eight enlisted men in each detachment immediately began training in helicopter gunship warfare under the auspices of the Army's 120th Aviation Company. By the end of the year, the Army personnel had been phased out and Navy crews were flying the Game Warden missions.

In June 1967 the HC-1 detachments were absorbed into a new unit commissioned into service at Vung Tau and christened Helicopter Attack (Light) Squadron Three. This new squadron adopted the nickname "Seawolves"; the name came to refer both to the aircraft and to the men who manned them.

Seawolf helicopters had a crew of four: pilot, co-pilot, crew chief (gunner), and door gunner. They usually operated in pairs (a pair being called a fire team), and the pilot of the lead aircraft was designated as fire team leader, which was analogous to the patrol officer on PBRs.

The UH-1B "Huey" was a Bell Helicopter Company single-engine aircraft that was 53 feet long overall and had a main rotor span of 44 feet. It had a cargo (crew, weapons, ammunition, et cetera) capacity of 4,000 pounds and a maximum speed at combat load of about 90 knots. The Seawolf version of the aircraft was armed with four externally mounted M-60 (7.62-mm) machine guns fired by the co-pilot, fourteen 2.75-inch rockets housed in two externally mounted pods controlled by the pilot, two hand-held M-60 machine guns fired by the crew chief and door gunner, and two hand-held M-79 grenade launchers also fired by the crew chief and door gunner. The externally mounted guns and rockets had to be fired in the direction in which the helo was pointed, but the door weapons were freely trainable. After testing revealed that the aircraft would withstand the stresses created by the firing of a .50-caliber machine gun, one of the door-mounted M-60s on many of the helos was gradually replaced with the more potent and longer-range .50-calibers as they became available.

Because the helicopters had an on-station endurance of only approximately one and a half hours, the Seawolves had to tailor their missions efficiently to complement the PBRs, which conducted twelve-hour patrols on the average. Therefore, Seawolf missions were primarily either preplanned strikes on a known or suspected enemy position designed to coincide with PBR activity in the area, or "scrambles" in response to a PBR call for assistance. In addition, the Seawolves performed Game Warden–related aerial reconnaissance and medical evacuation missions, and sometimes they provided on-station escort support to PBRs venturing into high-risk areas or situations.

When patrolling or going to a mission area, the lead aircraft in the fire team normally flew about one hundred feet higher than his wingman. This gave both helicopters a clear field of fire ahead in the event they made enemy contact. When in actual combat, the most common tactic was to fly a circular pattern over the target with each helicopter alternately engaging the enemy and providing cover.

For the best possible coverage, the Seawolves of Helicopter Attack (Light) Squadron Three were divided up into detachments and placed at bases throughout the delta and the Rung Sat. By September 1968 there were detachments of two helicopters each at Nha Be, Binh Thuy, Dong Tam, Rach Gia, and Vinh Long. Three detachments were also based on the three Game Warden LSTs serving as mobile bases for the PBRs. The remaining helicopters were in a rotating maintenance pool at Vung Tau. Later, in 1969, squadron headquarters and the maintenance pool moved from Vung Tau to Binh Thuy in the central delta.

One would be hard pressed to find a PBR sailor who would offer anything but praise for the Seawolves. PBR crews and Seawolves functioned as a close-knit team who wore their black berets as a symbol of mutual respect and pride. Time and again the Seawolves arrived on station to turn the tide of battle in favor of the Game Warden forces, and many PBR sailors owe their lives to the suppressive firepower or medical evacuation capabilities of this air arm of Game Warden.

Like his counterpart on the rivers and canals, the Seawolf was a sailor out of his normal environment. Even as an aviator he was a long way from the standard operating procedures of naval air, which had until Vietnam been in a blue-water environment. These helicopter pilots and crews found themselves no longer chasing submarines or delivering cargo in a peacetime navy, but instead flying over jungles, rivers, and rice paddies, engaging an insidious and often formidable enemy. They no longer returned to the "three squares and clean sheets" environment of their ships or air stations, but instead lived in a world of tropical discomfort, monsoon weather conditions, and an unseen enemy who was never very far away. They flew day and night missions, rarely letting Mother Nature keep them out of the air, and they often went home wearing Purple Hearts or as cargo on a nonpassenger aircraft.

Black Ponies

Because there never were enough Seawolves to go around, in late 1968 it was decided to supplement the helicopters with a squadron of close-support fixed-wing aircraft. On 3 January 1969 Light Attack Squadron Four was commissioned at North Island, California, for the specific purpose of going to Vietnam.

The newly formed squadron called themselves the "Black Ponies." Their aircraft consisted of fourteen OV-10A Broncos. The OV-10 is a twin-engine, propeller-driven aircraft with a very high twin-boomed tail and a 40-foot wingspan; it usually operated at speeds in the 180–200-knot range with a patrol endurance of two to three hours. The Black Pony version was painted dark green for Vietnam service and had been adapted to its close-support, attack role with a variable weapons configuration of M-60 machine guns, 20-mm gun pods, SUU-11 Gatling-type mini-gun pods, 2.75-inch rockets, 5-inch Zuni rockets, and paraflares for night work. The total ordnance load capability of each aircraft was 2,400 pounds.

Each OV-10A had four M-60 (7.62-mm) machine guns internationally mounted and carried 500 rounds of ball and tracer ammunition per gun. These guns were used primarily for suppression strafing and were accurate enough to work as near as fifty yards to friendly positions. Because the spent brass was jettisoned from the bottom of the aircraft, the pilots avoided flying directly over friendly positions when on a firing run. Being rained upon by empty shell casings was bad for morale.

Mark IV 20-mm gun pods could be mounted externally on the aircraft to provide heavier-caliber firepower. The pods were good for 750 rounds, which were expended at a rate of 400 rounds per minute.

The SUU-11 mini-gun could be mounted to give the Black Ponies a phenomenal amount of firepower. With its six revolving barrels, the SUU-11 spat out 6,000 7.62-mm rounds per minute. This gun not only could fell large numbers of enemy troops quickly, it could be used to make clearings where jungle had previously reigned.

The 2.75-inch rockets, with either a nine- or a sixteen-pound warhead, were similar to those used by the Seawolves. The Black Ponies could carry up to thirty-eight, depending upon the rest of the ordnance load.

The Zuni 5-inch rocket was what the pilots called "the big stick." It packed a 48-pound warhead in any of three configurations: the impact-detonating warhead was a good general service rocket particularly well suited for removing covering foliage and structures; the delayed detonation type permitted the rocket to penetrate the ground before exploding, so it was excellent for dug-in targets like bunkers and tunnel complexes; and the air-detonation warhead exploded about fifty feet in the air, scattering the blast and shrapnel over a large area, which was good for use against personnel in an open area or sampans on the river. The Zuni was a supersonic, unguided rocket that gave off a loud crack when the rocket broke the sound barrier. It was reasonably accurate and could be used as close as one hundred yards from friendly troops if the latter were well dug in. Each aircraft normally carried eight to twelve Zunis on a mission.

The paraflares used during night operations were usually dropped two at a time to illuminate a target area, and the Black Ponies carried four pairs per aircraft. These flares burned for more than three minutes and produced two million candlepower.

Light Attack Squadron Four arrived in Vietnam in April 1969 and set up headquarters at Binh Thuy. They flew from the Vietnamese airbase there to cover the Mekong Delta. A detachment also flew out of the Army airbase at Vung Tau to cover the Rung Sat Special Zone.

The Black Ponies always flew in pairs, or fire teams, for the same reasons that their counterparts on the rivers and in helicopters always traveled in two-boat or two-helo patrols: flexibility and mutual protection. Their weapons were non-trainable, which meant that the pilots had to "aim the aircraft" in order to get their ordnance on target. They developed some very impressive roll tactics (including something called the octa-flugeron) to reduce vulnerability and enhance weapons accuracy during attack runs.

The pilot also invented a hazardous but effective night tactic they called "chumming." One aircraft would fly low over a suspect area with his lights on. The second aircraft would stay above and behind with no lights. If the first aircraft was fired upon, the second would roll in on the perpetrator.

Three basic missions were flown by the Black Ponies. The first type, a normal patrol, was similar to a PBR patrol plan. It was scheduled in advance, and the pair of aircraft would roam the delta or Rung Sat looking for targets. They would also check in with sector advisors, looking for a firefight where air support might be useful. The second type of mission, also scheduled in advance, was the on-station patrol, in which a Black Pony fire team was teamed up with a PBR patrol. These missions were usually scheduled when PBRs were going into new patrol areas or when intelligence reports indicated the need for close air support. On-station patrols could provide instantaneous fire support and could also check out a waterway for both enemy presence and navigation hazards before the PBRs ventured into it. The third type of mission was the "fireman" or scramble alert mission, in which aircraft and crew were kept on call twenty-four hours a day to respond when PBRs got into trouble.

In Al Santoli's *Everything We Had*, Kit Lavell, a VAL-4 pilot in 1971–72, described flying in the Black Ponies:

> Sixty percent of my combat missions were at night, mostly in bad weather, either in monsoon or even worse, in the dry season, when farmers were burning their fields and visibility was a half mile or less. The bad guys never came out until it was bad weather. . . . Many times it was a tremendous problem just to fly the airplane and find the targets because there were no reliable navigational aids in South Viet Nam. We did not have sophisticated navigational equipment in our airplanes. We literally flew seat-of-the-pants and had to fly underneath the clouds. If the ceiling was one hundred feet, which it often was, we flew below one hundred feet.
>
> On more than 80 percent of the missions we took fire. We would take AK-47 rounds all the time through the aircraft. Occasionally we would come up against something a little bit bigger—a .50-caliber would really do the job on us.

He also described the "fireman" missions:

> The duty officer would take the call and sound the horn. . . . We slept in our flight gear. The planes were all set up, all the switches were thrown ready to take off. . . . We would have wheels in the well [be airborne] six minutes from the time we got the call. The furthest place we'd go in the Delta was less than twenty minutes away, so inside twenty-five minutes we would be on station, ready to help out.

The PBR sailors became fond of the Black Ponies. Their quick response time, heavy firepower, and long staying time were significant factors in the survival and mission accomplishment of many Game Warden sailors.

Sticking Out a Big Neck

> . . . no captain can do very wrong if he places
> his ship alongside that of the enemy.
>
> —LORD HORATIO NELSON, *October 1805*

"Those ain't VC," shouted one of the gunners above the diesel roar. "They're goddamned North Vietnamese regulars!"

PBRs 105 and 99 of River Section 531 were closing rapidly on two sampans loaded down with uniformed troops in the middle of the My Tho river. The PBRs were running at full throttle, their American flags stretched taut, great white rooster-tails following close behind.

In October 1966 it was not unusual for American troops to encounter North Vietnamese Army units in the northern provinces and in the Central Highlands, but it was most unusual to find them in the VC-dominated delta, so the men in the PBRs were justifiably startled to see NVA troops on the river.

The two sampans split up; one headed for the north shore, the other toward the south. The soldiers in the sampans fired at the approaching patrol boats and were almost instantaneously answered by the staccato bark of the forward twin fifties of each PBR. The two American craft veered off after the southbound sampan. When they got close enough, they slowed down to stabilize the careening fire of their gunners, and in less than a minute they had destroyed the fleeing enemy craft.

Boatswain's Mate First Class James Elliot Williams, USN, throttled up and banked the 105 in a tight turn that caused the skidding PBR to burrow nose-down into the river before dashing out across the water in hot pursuit of the other sampan. Williams was boat captain for the 105 and patrol officer in charge of both PBRs.

Before the Americans could get to it, the second sampan reached the north bank of the river and disappeared into a channel too small for the PBRs. Williams knew that part of the delta like the back of his hand; he called the 99 on the radio and said in his South Carolina drawl, "Stay with me. I know where he has to come out. We'll get 'im." The two boats raced, prows high, to head off the sampan. A short way down the riverbank they turned into a canal. Some months before, Williams had removed all of the armor from his boat, except that which surrounded the engines, in order to get more speed and to permit the 105 to carry more ammunition. She was a fast boat and was flying through the canal at about 35 knots. The trees lining the banks were a peripheral green blur to those on the craft dashing through.

As they raced around a bend in the canal, Rubin Binder, the 105's forward gunner, shouted something unprintable. Before them were forty or fifty boats scattered over the canal, each carrying fifteen to twenty troops; the sampans were so full of men that they only had about two inches of freeboard remaining. It would be difficult to assess who was more startled, the crews of the PBRs upon suddenly finding the waterway full of an enemy "fleet," or the soldiers of the 261st and 262nd NVA regiments upon seeing these two patrol craft careening around the bend and hurtling down on them.

Binder's shoulders shook violently as he opened up with his fifties. The NVA soldiers stood up in sampans to return fire with their rifles. Williams had only a split second to think: there was little room to turn around, there were no alternative routes to either side, and they were damned near among the enemy craft already. He pressed on.

The banks erupted in heavy fire. The unmistakable *thoonk* of mortar rounds could be heard in the midst of the chattering of automatic weapons and the cracking of rifles. Williams swerved left a little, then right, as much as the narrow canal would permit, trying to give his after gunner's grenade launcher a clear shot. The enemy mortar rounds were not up to the PBRs' speed and missed both boats; the small-arms fire was equally unsuccessful. In another few seconds the 105 had reached the first of the enemy sampans. Williams leaned on the throttles although they were already at full power, and then ran right over the first boat—then another, and another.

The enemy was reduced to chaos as soldiers spilled into the canal from the stricken sampans and still others were rolled into the water by the PBRs' wakes. Soldiers along both banks fired at the boats as they streaked by, not realizing in the confusion that they were hitting their own men opposite. The waterway narrowed even more; still the PBRs roared on. Two 57-mm recoilless rifle rounds lashed out from the right-hand bank, but they hit the 105 in the bow on the starboard side, passed completely through, emerged from the port side, and exploded among the NVA troops on the opposite bank. Throughout, Binder and the other crew members—Castlebury, Alderson, and Spatt—were firing for all their worth. Brass shell-casings rained onto the fiberglass decks as hundreds of rounds spewed out in every direction. The 99 was likewise spraying metal at a phenomenal rate as she followed close behind. The North Vietnamese were suffering staggering losses.

The two PBRs emerged from the gauntlet practically unscathed. The boats were pockmarked and holed, but miraculously no men had been injured, all weapons were still working, and the engines were intact. Williams called on the radio for assistance from the Navy Seawolf helicopters. Among the myriad of troop-carrying sampans behind him, he had spotted several good-sized junks, and he suspected they were carrying ammunition and supplies. Those and the troops remaining would make good hunting for the helicopter gunships.

Out of the havoc, Williams slowed the patrol down. He intended to move on down the canal a safe distance and wait for the Seawolves before taking on that armada again. The PBRs cruised on for about 150 yards. The men on the boats were just beginning to relax when, after a right turn, they found themselves confronted by yet another imposing concentration of junks, sampans, and troops, even larger than the first. Prudence might have dictated that the PBRs should back off and wait for the Seawolves, but Williams never hesitated. He jammed on full power and headed in for an encore.

With the roar of the engines resonating off the banks of the canal, guns hammering relentlessly, and wakes boiling up behind them, the PBRs charged into battle. As in their previous encounter, they caught the NVA unprepared. The canal erupted in shooting, shouting, and explosions. Bullets slapped the water on both sides of the 105, fragments of fiberglass flew in every direction, and everywhere death was poised. But the Americans roared on through, their weapons chewing up sampans and felling enemy soldiers.

The PBRs emerged from the battle area, once again essentially intact, leaving a swath of destruction in their wake. But the battle had not yet ended. The radio came alive, announcing the arrival of the Seawolves. The pilots had made a pass over the two enemy staging areas that Williams' PBRs had passed through, and the lead pilot told Williams that the NVA was still there and that there were plenty of them left.

Williams replied, "I want y'all to go in there and hold a field day on them guys." "Wilco," responded the helo commander, adding, "What are *your* intentions?"

Williams said, "Well, I damn sure ain't goin' to stay here! I'm goin' back through." And once again the 105 and 99 tore through the North Vietnamese regiments, this time with Seawolf support.

The helicopters swooped over the area again and again, 7.62-mm ammunition cascading from their fixed and door-gunner M-60s. Rockets leaped from their side-mounted pods into the troop-infested jungle. Williams took full advantage of the PBRs' extraordinary maneuverability as he ran his craft among the enemy like a skier on an Olympic slalom. He had guessed right about the junks: the secondary explosions that erupted from the four that he and the helicopters nailed sent debris rocketing a thousand feet into the air. Williams pressed the attack relentlessly, undeterred by the maze of bullets and rockets and mortar rounds. As darkness came, the battled raged, and Williams ordered the PBRs' searchlights turned on. When the water was devoid of targets, Williams drove in close to the shore seeking the enemy.

An Army general at a nearby base, unable to believe what he was hearing over the radio during the engagement, flew to the area in an Army helicopter. When he arrived he saw the network of tracers and the smoke in the sky, and the bodies and burning junks and broken sampans in the water, and said, "Well, I'll be damned. Seeing is believing." The general's helicopter circled several times over the area. At one point he said, over the radio, "Get that man in a flak jacket!"

Williams grabbed the radio handset and barked, "Get your damn copter and your ass out of here. We're takin' care of this." The general did not pursue the matter any further.

The battle lasted more than three hours. The final assessment revealed that the NVA had lost well over a thousand men. Sixty-five enemy vessels had been destroyed; many prisoners were taken.

Williams discovered a small piece of shrapnel in his side after the battle was over. Binder had taken a bullet through the wrist, which passed cleanly through the flesh and hadn't broken any bones. These were the only friendly casualties.

On 13 May 1968, in ceremonies held at the Pentagon, President Lyndon Johnson was having difficulty fastening the snaps at the back of the cravat of the Medal of Honor as he attempted to place it around the neck of James Elliot Williams. The struggling president said into Williams's ear, "Damn, Williams, you've got a big neck."

It's a wonder that Williams does not have a big head as well (which he certainly does not), for that Medal of Honor was placed in good company . . . along with his previously earned Navy Cross, two Silver Stars, the Navy and Marine Corps Medal, three Bronze Stars, the Navy Commendation Medal, the Vietnamese Cross of Gallantry (with Palm and Gold Star), and three Purple Hearts.

Postscripts

In March 1968, a *Hoi Chanh*—Viet Cong defector—provided evidence of the effectiveness of Game Warden when he described going without food for two or three days at a time because PBRs had prevented the VC from moving supplies on the river. He also described a two-week period in which the VC had been unable to get their units across one of the rivers because of the Game Warden patrols.

Without more complete testimony from the enemy, which will probably never be forthcoming, it is impossible to assess accurately the effectiveness of Game Warden. A safe assumption is that the operation did not completely stifle enemy movement on the delta waterways, but another reasonable surmise is that Game Warden was largely successful in most of its intended missions. As discussed earlier, the fact that the Viet Cong so frequently engaged the patrols was an indication of their success. Village chiefs reported that once the PBRs were patrolling in significant numbers, the Viet Cong tax-collectors virtually disappeared from the waterways. *Hoi Chanhs* frequently told stories similar to the one above, and they repeatedly confirmed that the Game Warden patrols were a great hindrance to the freedom of movement they had previously enjoyed. And the performance of Game Warden units during the Tet Offensive of 1968 helped save several of the principal capitals from falling into enemy hands.

Some statistics provided by Admiral S. A. Swarztrauber are impressive:

In an average Game Warden month, PBRs will put in about 65,000 to 70,000 patrol hours. Seawolves will fly about 1,500 hours, and Seals will make about 60 missions. There will be about 75 mine-sweeping patrols and about 20 LST gunfire support missions. The PBRs and Seawolves will engage in some 80 fire fights each. Game Warden units will destroy monthly about 80 enemy watercraft and 125 enemy structures, and every month they will log about 75 confirmed enemy killed. Since the beginning of operation Game Warden, more than 100 officers and enlisted men of the Force have lost their lives as a result of enemy fire; but this was very costly to the enemy. The ratio of enemy killed by Game Warden units, to those of Game Warden killed by the enemy, has been something on the order of 40 to 1, one of the highest such ratios of all U.S. forces in Vietnam.

He concluded by observing:

They have racked up their brilliant record from a sleeping, not a running, or even a standing, start. Moreover, they have achieved their record with a force small both in men and equipment. Their manpower represents less than one-half of one percent of the number of Americans in Vietnam. Their principal assets, PBRs and Seawolves, are very cheap, as naval watercraft and aircraft go.

In a luncheon speech given in early 1966, when Task Force 116 was still being put together, Assistant Chief of Naval Operations Rear Admiral Leroy V. Swanson said of the Game Warden plans: "Some observers have ventured the opinion that this force should be labeled 'The Divine Wind Squadron.' However, we do not feel it will be all that bad." The allusion to Japanese kamikazes was not as far from the truth as the admiral indicated. In 1968 alone, Game Warden personnel earned over 500 Purple Hearts—an astounding number when compared to the small size of the Game Warden force. One out of every three PBR sailors was wounded during his tour in Vietnam, many of those more than once. Yet, in spite of this high risk, the Navy never had difficulty filling its Game Warden billets. Volunteers emerged from all rates, ratings, and ranks. Reserves asked to be called into active service for PBR duty. Every man in two succeeding graduating gunnery classes at the Great Lakes Naval Training Center volunteered for duty in the "Divine Wind Squadron" when Game Warden was forming up. One out of every five PBR sailors requested extensions of their tours, and many returned to Vietnam for repeat tours. Admiral Swarztrauber, who commanded an entire task force of PBRs, wrote, "Their morale is the highest of any this writer has ever seen in the service."

Perhaps Petty Officer Jere Beery says it best: "You've got to look at the positive end of things because to think of the negative end of things is a waste of time. That's not valuable or useful information. We were volunteers. Patriots. We were gung-ho as hell. We'd *look* for trouble."

After his tour in Vietnam, Ken MacLeod was transferred to Coronado, California, where he participated in the operational evaluation of the Navy's new patrol craft, the PBR. In 1970 he left the Navy and subsequently spent five years in the dredging business and six years working in the oil fields off Southeast Asia. Today he is senior engineer with M. Rosenblatt & Son, Inc., a naval architecture and marine engineering firm in Annapolis, Maryland.

Paul Dean's Vietnam coverage earned him a Pulitzer Prize

nomination. He continued his career in journalism, traveling the world and covering other hot spots, such as Northern Ireland, and one cold spot known as Antarctica. Today he's a lifestyle writer for the "View" section of the *Los Angeles Times*.

Sarah Phillips is still with Hatteras Yachts.

Dick Godbehere, after retiring from the Navy as a lieutenant commander, worked in business and law enforcement and today is the sheriff of Maricopa County, Arizona. He has also worked closely with Senator (and former prisoner of war) John McCain on veterans' affairs.

Jere Beery, besides working in the movies as a stunt man and actor, is currently writing a screenplay based on his experiences in Vietnam. He is convinced that being saved by a man named Godbehere means that "I have a purpose, and my screenplay is it."

Elliot Williams retired from the Navy and went on to serve a second successful career as a federal marshal. He has been instrumental in organizing several conventions for living Medal of Honor winners.

The spirit exhibited by the Game Warden sailors did not die out at war's end. Today many of them still keep in touch and meet at least once a year as part of an organization called Gamewardens of Vietnam. Few outside their organization know what it is; indeed, it is not uncommon for them to be asked by the curious why we had "forest rangers" in Vietnam. But they maintain a scholarship fund for the coming generation and offer camaraderie and understanding to one another as only former comrades-in-arms can do. And every year they don their black berets and gather around the memorial to their fallen number, which they built with their own money, and salute to the haunting bugle notes of "Taps."

4

THE MOBILE RIVERINE FORCE

(Task Force 117)

Nor must Uncle Sam's web-feet be forgotten. At all the watery margins they have been present. Not only on the deep sea, the broad bay and the rapid river, but also up the narrow muddy bayou and wherever the ground was a little damp, they have been and make their tracks.

—ABRAHAM LINCOLN, on the contribution of the Union Navy during the Civil War

Adhesive Tape and the Padre

Lieutenant Raymond W. Johnson, USN, stepped across the helicopter flight deck of the USS *Benewah* (APB-35), ducking the rotor tie-down strap of a "Huey" as he went. At the rail on the port side he stopped to watch the culmination of the voyage. The *Benewah* was barely making way, and her several overboard discharges were leaving only short trails of white foam to contrast with the coffee-brown of the river. On the ship's only yardarm, the signal flags hung languidly from their halyards in the still afternoon air. The ship's movement during the transit, slow as it was, had kept the air moving across the deck, but now as the *Benewah* crept the last few yards to her anchorage, the lieutenant could feel beads of perspiration gathering on his brow.

The *Benewah* spit her anchor out of the hawsepipe, and the heavy chain followed it to the river's bottom. Whistles blew, signal flags dropped, and the black anchor ball climbed halfway to the gaff's peak. He might have been on any ship in the Navy, thought the young officer, except for all the soldiers on board and that strange green-brown color. The *Benewah*, her sister-ship *Colleton* (APB-36), and the repair ship *Askari* (ARL-30), permanent members of the Mobile Riverine Force, had all been painted this unusual color because of their perpetual presence in the green and brown environment of the Mekong Delta and the nearby Rung Sat Special Zone. Another component of the force, a non-self-propelled barracks ship (APL-26), was similarly hued; since she had no official name, the soldiers and sailors had dubbed her the "green apple." Only the LST that served as part of the force on a rotating basis from the Seventh Fleet retained its Navy-gray color.

The other ships in the force were anchoring now, as evidenced by the sounds of whistles and clattering anchor-chains that drifted across the water. The two YTBs (Large Harbor Tugs) were positioning the "green apple" several hundred yards away off the *Benewah*'s port quarter. Several ATCs (Armored Troop Carriers) were maneuvering flat ammi-pontoon barges into position alongside the *Benewah* to serve as a mooring dock for themselves and the many other small craft of the Mobile Riverine Force.

They're getting pretty good at it, mused Lieutenant Johnson as he watched the activity about him. The force had moved several times since its formation, and its various elements were now functioning like a well-oiled machine.

The ships of the Mobile Riverine Force were anchoring at the confluence of the Soi Rap and Vam Co rivers so that the Army troops they carried, from the U.S. 9th Infantry Division, could conduct search and destroy operations in the nearby mangrove thickets and rice paddies of the Can Giuoc District of Long An Province. The force had just completed the moderately successful Operation Great Bend in the northern region of the Rung Sat and had moved the eight miles from their Nha Be anchorage to this new site. Hoping for surprise, the force would waste no time: the next assault was to take place the following morning.

Lieutenant Johnson watched the many small craft gradually assembling at the ammi-barge alongside the *Benewah*. Similar congregations of the dark green assault craft were forming up alongside the *Colleton* and the LST, the USS *Vernon County,* amid clouds of blue-hued diesel exhaust. One would never guess that these had all been LCM-6 amphibious landing craft at one time, Johnson thought as he watched them maneuver into their nests. Only the ATCs still retained the ramps on their bows; the monitors and the command communications boats (CCBs) had been redesigned with a tapered spoonlike bow that was more like that of a conventional craft. All carried different combinations of weapons and each had cagelike bar-armor strategically located to detonate rockets and recoilless-rifle shells before they could enter the boats's vitals. Just days before, the force had returned the last of the craft borrowed from Vietnamese River Assault Groups. All sixty-eight craft of the force were now American.

Several soldiers were walking along the main deck below Johnson; one with bright red hair looked up and saw him. "Hey, Padre. Good service this morning," the young soldier called, his freckle-peppered face beaming up at Johnson.

"Thanks, Smitty," Johnson replied.

Ray Johnson had been assigned by the Navy to the Mobile

Riverine Force as its chaplain. The Army had not as yet provided its own chaplain, so he had shown his ecumenical spirit by ministering to both Army and Navy alike. He knew every man in the force by name and was popular among the young soldiers and sailors, not only because of his willing ear and helpful advice in times of crisis, but also because he always accompanied the operations, riding in one of the ATCs that had been rigged as a medical aid station. Chaplain Johnson was more than a man of the cloth—he was a man of the battle-dressing, too. He had received formal training as a medical technician and served the force as a field medical officer as well as its chaplain. In the midst of battle it was comforting for a wounded soldier or sailor to see "the Padre" tending both wounds of the body and fears of the soul.

Despite his Lutheran background, Johnson had become an eclectic chaplain, encompassing all faiths and denominations into his flock. Somewhere along the line, the troops had begun affectionately calling him "Padre," and the Catholic-sounding name had stayed with him.

> *Red sky at night,*
> *Sailor's delight.*

Lieutenant Commander Charles L. Horowitz, USN, remembered the words he had learned some years before at the Naval Academy as he watched the crimson western sky. The last vestiges of daylight burned at the horizon like the persistent embers of a dying fire. He turned away from the panorama and paused for a moment to adjust his eyes to the fading images of twilight before heading across the ammi-pontoon barge. Paper cartons of C-rations and ammunition boxes of dark green metal and wood were stacked along the barge next to the inboard boats. Sailors, many stripped to the waist exposing sun-darkened backs that glistened with sweat in the dying light, were passing the boxes out along the nests of boats and stowing them below decks in preparation for the next day's operation. The acrid smell of diesel fuel assaulted Horowitz's nostrils as he maneuvered among the pillars of boxes.

"Evenin', Commodore." A burly first-class gunner's mate spoke around the butt of a well-chewed, unlit cigar. "You ridin' with us or ninety-one tomorrow, sir?'' Horowitz noticed that a red rose with a green stem and the word ''MOM'' were incongruously tattooed on the swell of one of the sailor's mammoth biceps.

''You ninety-two guys get the pleasure of my company,'' Horowitz replied with a wary smile. He knew why the sailor had asked. As squadron commander of River Assault Squadron 9, one of the two squadrons attached to the Mobile Riverine Force, Horowitz always rode with whichever of the two divisions in his squadron he predicted would see more action. He made his pick based on the nature of the operation, the available intelligence, and a dash of intuition. The men in the divisions knew this, and they also knew that he was usually right.

''See you at oh-four-hundred,'' Horowitz said, and moved on to the next nest of boats.

There were about 350 men, two CCBs, five monitors, twenty-six ATCs, and one refueler (an ATC with fuel bladders installed in the well-deck instead of troops) in Horowitz's squadron, evenly distributed between River Assault Divisions 91 and 92. The other squadron in the force, River Assault Squadron 11, commanded by Lieutenant Commander Francis ''Dusty'' Rhodes, Jr., was similarly organized.

Horowitz finished his rounds of the boats and crossed the barge to the accommodation ladder leading up to the *Benewah*'s quarterdeck. A platoon of soldiers passed him carrying an assortment of weapons but very little field equipment. They were headed for a boat that would take them to the riverbank opposite the *Benewah,* where they would set up a defensive ambush site in case the VC decided to pay the Mobile Riverine Force a nocturnal visit. Horowitz reached the ladder and went up. Just aft of the quarterdeck, he paused for a moment, looking out at the mangrove clusters on the near bank of the river, and then headed for his office to take one more look at the charts and operations order.

Padre Johnson leaned back in the gray metal straight-backed chair in his stateroom and opened an envelope with his parents' home address back in Minnesota carefully penned in the corner. He devoured the letter, nostalgic for a world that seemed very far away. Then he carefully unfolded a newspaper article that his father had enclosed and read it.

The U.S. Navy, plunging into river warfare for the first time in 100 years, now can move entire battalions of Army infantry and supporting artillery pieces along Vietnam jungle waterways.

This is the mission of a new river assault force just going into action in an effort to drive Viet Cong guerrillas from their green sanctuaries in the delta country.

Most of the new assault craft were built on the hulls of LCMs that had lain in naval storage for years. All but the troop carriers have had their bows rebuilt to remove the ramps originally used to put men and weapons on a beach.

The task force consists of River Assault Squadrons 9 and 11 and River Support Squadron 7. The latter includes repair ships, self-propelled barracks ships and other craft that will form a "mobile riverine base" (MRB) to support the assault squadrons when they range into the interior.

Operationally, the task force is under the commander of U.S. Naval Forces in Vietnam, but administratively it is part of the Pacific Fleet Amphibious Force, headquartered at Coronado.

This is the first American assault force specifically designed for river operations since the Civil War. The "Mississippi Squadron" wrote many significant chapters in that war, at Vicksburg, Shiloh and elsewhere.

U.S. strategists hope superior numbers, firepower and communications will give the new River Assault Flotilla the edge needed to rid the delta country once and for all of the Viet Cong.

Johnson laid the article flat on his desk and placed a heavy book on top to smooth out the folds. Tomorrow he would pin it up on the mess-deck's bulletin board so everyone could read it.

He looked at his rack and felt the pillow beckon his weary head, but he resisted. Rubbing his tired eyes, he stood up, stretched, and headed down for one more pass through the berthing compartments. On the night before an operation he would find soldiers or sailors wide awake, struggling with their fears. Some tried to hide their uncertainty behind the unconvincing laughter that followed an unnatural barrage of jokes. Some huddled in the semidarkness, staring silently. Others reread letters from home or passages from their Bibles. Johnson would move among them, offering a few welcomed words, listening to them if they wanted to talk, occasionally squeezing a shoulder reassuringly as he passed. His was not an easy job, but he was thankful that he could be there to help these men through their hours of uncertainty and fear.

Lieutenant Commander Horowitz looked over his notes from the briefing in the Tactical Operations Center earlier that evening. He reviewed the boat assignments, call signs, frequencies, and checkpoints once again to ensure that he knew them and that they made sense. As always, his radio call sign was "Adhesive Tape." At the briefing, there had been the usual emphasis on walking the tightrope between blasting the enemy and minimizing the damage to populated areas. There were the standard warnings about keeping the boats out of side streams and canals that were not wide enough to permit the boats to turn around. His notes indicated that the tides would vary within a three-and-a-half-foot range. In handwriting only he could decipher, he had scratched the words "Flood current going in," meaning that their transit time to the drop-off point would be shorter because they were traveling with the current. In the Rung Sat, an eighteen-mile trip might take six hours against the current but only four and a half hours with it.

As usual, the intent of the operation was for the boats to take the troops to the area of operations and unload them after "softening up" the beachhead with their onboard weapons. Then the boats would take up blocking positions to prevent the enemy from escaping and to provide fire-support for the troops should they need it. In this operation, dubbed Concordia I, the troops were to be deployed to three locations in order to form a triangle around a suspect area. Three companies of the 4th Battalion, 47th Infantry, would land on the banks of Van Creek, two and one half miles southeast of the large village of Can Giuoc. Simultaneously, two companies of the 3rd Battalion, 47th Infantry, would land one mile due south of Can Giuoc. The third side of the triangle would be formed by the 2nd Battalion of the Vietnamese Army's 46th Infantry Regiment one mile south of the village of Ap Bac.

The tactic to be used was called a "hammer and anvil," in which units making up the "hammer" drive the enemy toward the waiting and well-dug-in "anvil." The South Vietnamese troops were expected to act as the anvil in this operation.

One platoon had been assigned to each ATC. The boats had large numbers painted on their bows to make them easily identifiable. Barring unforeseen circumstances, each platoon would reembark and return in the same ATC that had delivered it. Besides the painted numbers, each ATC carried a distinctive pennant atop the mast, which the troops could usually see from behind dikes and vegetation. If the troops and the ATC were having difficulty locating each other, which sometimes happened in the more densely foliated areas, the battalion commander, aloft in a helicopter coordinating the operation, would drop colored smoke on the landing site to help the units find each other.

Horowitz smiled when he saw his wife's name on the navigational chart on his desk. En route to the area of operations, the boats always radioed back to the Tactical Operations Center when they passed through predetermined points along the track so the center could plot their progress. For security reasons, these points were always code-named with the names of vegetables, or fruits, or animals, or whatever came to mind. For Concordia, the officers had decided to name the points after their wives.

One of Horowitz's responsibilities, as officer in tactical command of all the boats tomorrow, would be to keep the senior officers back at the Mobile Riverine Base informed of the operation's progress. He always met this responsibility by providing only essential information, believing that if one volunteered too much information, one would receive too much advice in return.

Horowitz looked at his watch. It was time to get some sleep. After looking over the chart one more time, he went out into the red glow of the passageway. On his way to his stateroom, he slipped out through a light locker onto the main deck, where the night air was thick and heavy compared to the air-conditioned interior of the ship. He inhaled deeply and felt as though he were drinking rather than breathing. The bass rumble of a diesel barely above idle was audible as one of the boats patrolling the anchorage passed invisibly along the starboard side of the ship. Horowitz looked down at the nest of boats moored below him. He pictured the sailors lying on folding canvas bunks or air mattresses and wondered how they could sleep amid the heat, humidity, mosquitoes, and periodic thumps of anti-sapper concussion grenades dropped randomly by the sentries. Watch routine required that three men from each boat be on board at all times, but Horowitz knew that because of their dedication, many of the other men chose to sleep aboard their boats rather than the infinitely more comfortable ships.

A faint flicker from somewhere deep in the mangroves on the near shore caught his eye and he stared in that direction for several minutes, feeling a chill between his shoulder-blades as he watched for another flicker. But he saw only darkness, and finally he stepped back from the rail and disappeared into the ship.

Dawn was more than an hour away when the stillness was broken by the cough of diesel engines firing up. With squawks and chatter the local fauna on the riverbanks protested the rude behavior of their new neighbors. More boats joined the diesel chorus and shed their mooring lines to clear the ammipontoons and form up in circles out in the river.

Meanwhile, platoons of soldiers formed up on the ship and moved to the pontoons in a predetermined order for embarkation. The residual smell of bacon emitted from the *Benewah*'s exhaust blowers reminded the troops of the breakfast they had just eaten. For most, it would prove to be the last hot meal they would have for the next three days. For some, it would be the last hot meal they would ever have.

The troops were now fitted out for war, and as they waited their turns to move out, many checked their weapons for the tenth time, or inspected one another's shoulder straps, or reached around to feel for canteens that they already knew were there.

Chaplain Johnson moved along the pontoons among the

soldiers, dispensing smiles, words of encouragement, occasional pats on the shoulder. Like everyone else in the Mobile Riverine Force, soldier and sailor alike, he was dressed in jungle-green fatigues. He encountered the young red-haired soldier who had called to him the day before. "You going with us today, Padre?" the young man asked.

"You bet," Johnson answered.

The freckled face grinned broadly.

Lieutenant Commander Horowitz picked up the webbed belt equipped with a holstered .38-caliber pistol, Lensmatic compass, canteen, battle dressings, extra .38 ammunition, and Kaybar knife and fastened it around his waist. As he made one last check to be sure that he had everything, his eye fell upon the calendar on his desk. "Happy Birthday, Mom," he said quietly to himself.

He picked up the picture of his wife and two children and looked at it longingly. Some time back he had made it a ritual to look at the photograph just before leaving for an operation. In this line of work, one could never be sure that it wasn't for the last time.

A company of soldiers clambered aboard three ATCs at the pontoon dock with a clatter of equipment and periodic curses at struck shins or banged elbows. The sailors already on board extended an occasional helping hand to the heavily laden troops. Expert Navy swimmers were posted nearby in case any of the soldiers fell into the water. After about fifteen minutes the three platoons of the company were aboard their ATCs, which pulled away and rejoined the circle in the river. More groups of three ATCs repeated the process until all troops were on board; then the monitors and CCBs picked up the command personnel. Lieutenant Commander Horowitz was the last to board. As officer in tactical command, he preferred to remain on the pontoon directing the embarkation so that information could be exchanged at the last minute without resorting to radios. This was more efficient and prevented enemy interception.

In the pale blue half-light of early dawn, the armada formed up in a long column and headed for the area of operations. Two ATCs not carrying troops proceeded ahead of the column, one on each flank, streaming their chain-drag gear to sweep any mines that Charlie might have sown. The vanguard of the column was one of the monitors; its heavy weaponry bristled pugnaciously as it led the way up the Rach Cat tributary of the Soi Rap River. Next in line was the River Assault Division 92 CCB carrying Lieutenant Commander Horowitz. Reminiscent of the great World War II task forces, the long column of Navy craft made its way along the twisting, narrowing waterway, American flags taut in the morning breeze, anxious eyes scanning the unfamiliar terrain as it closed in about them. The Navy crews were always alert during the transit phase of an operation, watching for signs of ambush.

In the well-decks of the ATCs, the soldiers found varying ways to deal with the tedium of the transit. Some settled in as best they could to grab some extra "shut-eye." Others struggled to read in the weak but growing light. A few shouted into one another's ears, trying to converse over the diesel din.

From the cockpit of the ATC that had been rigged as a medical aid station, Padre Johnson peered out through the bar armor at the verdant world scrolling by. As the first rays of the morning sun sliced through the gaps in the treelined banks, he could see women already in the rice paddies bending to their work. A tiny man, gnarled and thin with age and a wanting diet, was whipping a huge water buffalo many times his size into line. Had the chaplain not already witnessed the violence of war in the delta and held memorial services for young men, he would have found it impossible to believe that such a pastoral setting could also be the stage for deadly combat. He prayed that he would not have to watch any men die today.

From the River Assault Division 92 CCB, Chuck Horowitz spoke into the radio, detaching the River Assault Division 91 units to continue to their landing point farther north. The River Assault Division 92 units then turned into a creek and proceeded toward their debarkation point.

About fifteen minutes later a radio message came in telling of a sighting of elements of the Viet Cong 5th Nha Be Battalion. River Assault Division 92 was diverted to the new coordinates, to put their troops ashore near the suspected enemy position and drive them northward in a classic hammer-

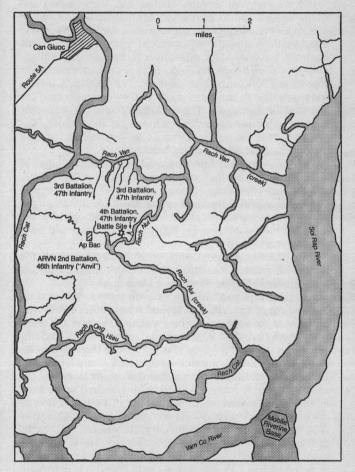

Operation Concordia I

and-anvil manner, sending the VC into the waiting arms of the units already in position to the north.

In the vicinity of the new landing site, the monitors and CCBs opened fire to discourage any unfriendly welcoming committees and to thin out the vegetation for better visibility. They kept firing as the ATCs moved in close to their fields of fire. Then the ATCs themselves picked up the fusillade until they turned into the bank. Each section of three boats was 150 to 300 yards from the next. The boats in a section were only five to ten yards apart as they drove up onto the soft bank of the stream. The individual companies were thus kept intact but had enough room to fan out once ashore. The "heavies," as the monitors and CCBs were called, covered the flanks of the ATCs as they beached.

The firing stopped. Bow ramps fell open across clumps of thick grass fringing the banks. Boots thudded up the ramps, and shouted commands blended with the sounds of engines as the ATCs held themselves against the bank and disgorged their human cargo. A command helicopter swooped by, the turbulent rotor-wash swaying the stands of saplings and palm fronds beneath its track.

Once the troops were ashore, the ATCs backed off the banks and roamed the adjacent waterways ready to deliver fire if needed. For the moment, all was quiet.

Padre Johnson watched as a ten-man reconnaissance team climbed out of the ATC into several rubber boats and shoved off. One of the soldiers saw him watching; he gave the chaplain a toothy grin and a "thumbs up" gesture while he clambered over the side. Johnson kept his eyes on them for several minutes; they fell back in the ATCs wake.

As the lumbering craft negotiated a gentle curve in the narrow tributary, Johnson looked to his right and saw a large number of American troops heading out of a tree line into an open field of rice paddies. He recognized them as Company A of the 4th Battalion, 47th Infantry. He watched their backs as they moved out, trying to recognize individuals from behind. Over the ATC's radio he could hear one of the spotters in the air above. "There's no activity in there," the electronic voice drawled. "We might as well be whistlin' Dixie."

Suddenly several of the soldiers fell backward; Johnson saw droplets of water sparkling in the sunshine as the men splashed into the paddy water. Then the sound reached him—a roar of gunfire greater than any he had heard before. In horror he saw men thrown down before him, lacerated by enemy fire. Falling bullets and bodies turned the usually calm pools of paddy water into miniature storm-wracked seas. The Viet Cong were entrenched in an L-shaped tree line on the far side of the paddies and to the left. They had emerged from well-camouflaged spider holes and bunkers and were spewing out thousands of rounds of machine-gun and recoilless-rifle fire. The Americans were caught in the open, exposed on two sides, and they were being decimated.

Lieutenant Commander Horowitz shouted into the radio handset, trying to be heard. His CCB, the three monitors, and all of the ATCs were pounding out rounds at a furious rate. The Army operations officer for the 4th Battalion, also on board the CCB, was calling into another handset for artillery support from the barge-mounted howitzers beached on a nearby tributary. His calls were heard, and 105-mm rounds screamed in, but instead of finding their way to the VC-infested tree line they fell frighteningly close to the boats commanded by Lieutenant A. C. "Augie" Marano. The Army operations officer called frantically for an adjustment but had lost radio contact with the artillery units. The rounds kept falling short, and geysers of shrapnel-laden mud and water continued to erupt among Marano's boats.

Horowitz called Marano on the tactical net: "Roadrunner, this is Adhesive Tape, you have the option to withdraw, over." Horowitz knew that Marano's boats were desperately trying to suppress the VC fire, but he felt obligated to give them the option to withdraw under the additional hazard of heavy friendly fire. He was not surprised, however, when the radio announced, "Adhesive Tape, this is Roadrunner, we're staying, out."

Finally Horowitz reached the artillery command post through the airborne battalion commander. The 105-mm shells began crashing into the tree line, where they belonged.

Several minutes later, the airborne battalion commander called for support against a .50-caliber machine gun that had already shot down two helicopters and was keeping his own helicopter from getting close enough to the battle to coordi-

nate the action. Horowitz directed the boat captain of his
CCB to push up into a small inlet off the main stream—a
violation of the edict prohibiting craft from entering waterways too narrow in which to turn around, but theory and
practice often diverge in battle. The CCB lurched forward,
came hard about, and slipped into the confines of the inlet.
From overhead, the helicopter directed the CCB's 40-mm
cannon fire first onto a stand of palm trees and then toward
the offending machine gun's position. After a few adjust-
ments, the pilot announced, "You're on him!" The boat's
cannon poured metal and high explosives into the concealing
vegetation. A few moments later, after several clips of ammunition had been expended, the battalion commander reported, "That's it, Adhesive Tape. You just blew the gun in
one direction and the gunner in another."

Carefully, the CCB backed out of the inlet into the wider
stream where the rest of the squadron craft were still hammering at the Viet Cong positions, trying to subdue the fire
chewing up the soldiers in the field.

Padre Johnson watched, agonized, as the men he knew so
well fell before his eyes. A voice inside him screamed in
protest to see them mowed down and hit again and again even
after they had fallen. He could hear their cries amid the gunfire. They were his friends, his congregation. They were so
helpless.

He turned away and looked downstream, but found no sol-
ace there: the reconnaissance team dropped off earlier had
been ambushed, and all ten were floating lifeless in the river.

Looking back to the paddies, his mind reeling, he prayed,
"Make it stop." The confused chatter on the radios told him
that all of the officers in the paddies had been killed, and
most of the ranking enlisted as well. "Make it stop!" his
mind shouted.

A soldier with a radio strapped to his back got up from the
mud of the paddy and headed toward the medical aid boat.
Johnson watched as another bullet found its mark and felled
him. The soldier looked up; his eyes met Johnson's. "Help
me, Padre," Johnson read from his moving lips.

Johnson leaped from the shelter of the boat and dashed out
into the tumult. He raced across the paddy, the mud sucking

at his boots with every stride, the crack and whine of bullets and shrapnel all about him. With adrenaline-powered strength he carried the soldier, equipment and all, back to the medical aid boat.

As Johnson and two medics tended the man's wounds on the deck of the ATC, the soldier panted to him, "Padre, they're bleeding to death. Medics are all dead."

Johnson grabbed a stretcher from the bulkhead and shouted, "There are men out there who are going to die unless we get them out of there." Two sailors from the boat's crew, Boatswain's Mate Third Class C. O. "Swede" Johnson and Engineman Second Class M. W. "Red" Dolezal, grabbed a second stretcher and joined him. He looked at them for a moment and saw in their eyes the combination of terror and determination that he was feeling.

"We're ready, Padre," Dolezal said matter-of-factly. The three men zigzagged across a paddy toward a group of soldiers about 150 yards away. They had seen some movement among the troops just moments before. As they neared one of the dikes that separated the paddies, the chaplain heard an explosion close by on his left and then a jolt and sharp sting in his legs. He toppled into the mud and water and slid into the base of the dike. The two sailors dropped down next to him, all three shielded from the enemy fire by the eighteen-inch-high dike. Johnson checked the shrapnel wounds in his legs, wrapped the bleeding areas tightly, and decided that he could keep going. When he raised himself above the dike to get his bearings, he heard a thud and felt as though he had been hit across the chest by a baseball bat. He fell down behind the dike again. Everything seemed red and blue and he couldn't breathe. Dolezal said, "Jesus, Padre! Are you all right?" Johnson reached into the zipper lining of his flak vest and pulled out a piece of jagged shrapnel.

To see all that was going on, Lieutenant Commander Horowitz climbed out of the armored cockpit and positioned himself atop the CCB. Taking a calculated risk, he ordered the boats to beach themselves in order to stabilize their fire. They were engaged in no small skirmish, and to beat this large VC force would take a lot of well-placed ordnance. Besides, in many cases the boats were firing over their own soldiers to get at the enemy entrenchments, so accuracy was paramount.

The boats poured out their 20- and 40-mm, .30- and .50-caliber rounds. The monitor's mortars thumped out 81-mm projectiles in a continuous barrage, and hand-held weapons sounded from all quarters. Army artillery thundered and various aircraft dropped ordnance. Arms ached and sweat flowed as the Army-Navy team fought on, slowly turning the tide.

Horowitz stayed on top of the CCB despite the danger and the warnings from his staff. He directed the fire of his boats, gradually sweeping away the confusion and organizing a team effort. Smoke billowed about him, concussion buffeted him, metal flew about. Occasionally he heard rounds striking the boat's armor, but he held his position, coordinating the actions of his boats with the Army movements ashore. While delivering close gunfire support, he maneuvered the boats into new positions when necessary and sent ATCs to bring soldiers from other areas as reinforcements.

The chaplain and the two sailors crouched low behind the dike. Machine-gun bullets thumped into it from the other side, throwing clods of mud over them. They huddled there until the enemy gunner seemed to lose interest. Johnson peered over the dike and saw a group of soldiers clustered down behind a mound of mud about thirty yards away. He told Swede Johnson to join them. The young boatswain's mate stared at him wide-eyed and said, "You want me to go alone?"

Replied the chaplain, "You'll make it, Swede." The sailor jumped up and headed for soldiers; the chaplain prayed that he was right.

Padre Johnson and Red Dolezal likewise sprinted seventy-five yards through open terrain toward a wounded soldier. As they ran, clumps of mud leaped up in their path and to their left as many enemy gunners tried to connect. When they reached the man and placed him on the stretcher, the soldier looked at them through a veil of pain and said, "Thank God," and the chaplain knew why he had come.

Lifting the stretcher, Johnson and Dolezal headed back across the three-hundred-yard stretch toward the medical-aid ATC. The added weight made them sink deeper into the mud, which frequently oozed over the tops of their boots and made their progress agonizingly slow. Johnson knew that the nearby boats were pouring a hail of fire into the VC positions, keeping the enemy heads down and giving the stretcher-bearers a hope of survival. But although the enemy fire was impeded, it was not eliminated. Bullets and fragments still whipped about them. Dolezal hollered above the noise of battle, "Damn it, Chaplain, I hope you're praying!"

When they were about a hundred yards from the ATC, Johnson saw another soldier off to the right lift his head and call for help. Johnson shouted to him, "Play dead. We'll be back in a minute."

Johnson and Dolezal reached the ATC, unloaded their man, and headed back out as promised. When they returned with the second soldier, they collapsed and lay for several minutes, gasping for breath. To the chaplain's relief, Swede Johnson soon joined them. After a moment the chaplain rolled onto one elbow and vomited; then he waved off a medic who was trying to see to his wounds. "Go take care of those soldiers," he said. "They need you more than I." He checked his wounds himself.

The battle raged on. By this time, four helicopters had been shot down; casualties on both sides mounted. The soldiers and sailors fought on and on, and at last the tide of battle turned. With the arrival of more American soldiers, with the Mobile Riverine Force boats blocking the escape routes, and with the relentless pounding of air strikes and artillery, the Viet Cong had lost the initiative. Now they were fighting a battle of desperation.

Following the example set by Chaplain Johnson and the two sailors, other rescue parties ventured out to bring in more of the wounded.

When he had recovered his strength, Padre Johnson gathered up his medical aid kit, helmet, and punctured flak jacket and went back out into the blood-soaked rice paddy. He crawled from man to man, tending wounds and offering spiritual comfort. Twice men were hit while he was helping them. Too many times he helped the soldiers face oncoming death. He would forever describe this 19 June as the "longest day of my life."

Lieutenant Commander Horowitz, still perched above the cockpit of the CCB, felt the craft shudder repeatedly as the 40-mm fired into the tree line about seventy yards away. To his left he saw muzzle flashes in the nearby reeds; the rattle of small-arms fire competed with the sound of heavy ordnance falling from the sky. His staff had given up trying to get Horowitz to take cover, and he remained in position coordinating the operation until his luck at last ran out. An enemy AK-47 round found its mark.

The battle continued into the night, and Operation Concordia I lasted another two days. The final casualty counts listed 46 Americans killed and approximately 150 wounded. The Viet Cong left 255 dead on the battlefield; how many dead and wounded were carried away by those who managed to escape is unknown. As a result of that engagement, the Viet Cong were rendered ineffective in Long An Province for more than a year. The boats fared better than the helicopters involved in the operation. Only one boat, ATC 112-4, received major damage when she was hit below the waterline by an enemy rocket and was forced to beach for repairs. Other boats and crewmen were hit by shrapnel. The operation was a success, but a costly one.

The Mobile Riverine Force remained anchored at the junction of the Vam Co and Soi Rap rivers, conducting operations in the southeastern districts of Long An Province until the end of June. No other major contact with the enemy occurred during this period.

Padre Johnson walked down the corridor of the Army field hospital at Long Binh, limping slightly. He pushed open the double doors to one of the wards and entered.

"Wouldn't it have been simpler just to put in leave papers if you wanted a vacation?" he asked as he strode into the large room.

Chuck Horowitz looked up from the magazine he had been reading. "Oh no. Not you, Padre!" he said with a grin. He turned toward an orderly who had just entered the room from another door. "Did you ever hear of a chaplain who's a jinx?" he asked the orderly.

The startled orderly shrugged but said nothing.

"Every time this man goes out on an op with me, something happens," Horowitz said in mock seriousness. "We either hit heavy action or one of my boats gets a line fouled in the screws or something else goes wrong. It's always something. This time he gets me *this!*" He pointed to his bandage-wrapped foot, then smiled at the chaplain. "Seriously, Padre, it's good to see you."

Johnson pulled up a chair next to the bed and sat down. "I hear they tried to shoot your foot off."

"Oh, it's not all that bad," Horowitz answered.

"Well, that's good news, because the men in the squadron are asking when they're getting their skipper back," Johnson said.

"I'll *bet* they are." Horowitz looked over at the orderly, who was still standing nearby. "Isn't it about time for chow?" he asked. "I'm famished."

"That's what I came to tell you, sir." The orderly spoke for the first time. "They just ran out of food. It's going to be a while before they can get some more."

"What did I tell you?" Horowitz boomed. His large frame rose up as if he were going to come right out of the bed. "I knew it! The man's a jinx! Meals have been right on schedule since I got here. The Padre shows up and now I have to starve!"

In recognition of their courage under fire during Operation Concordia I, Lieutenant Raymond "Padre" Johnson and Lieutenant Commander Charles Horowitz were each awarded the Silver Star for valor and the Purple Heart for wounds received.

Upon his return home, Johnson was recognized by the United States Junior Chamber of Commerce as one of "America's Ten Outstanding Young Men for 1968," an honor which in years past had been given to such notables as Henry Ford and John F. Kennedy.

Horowitz, after being hit, had insisted upon staying at his battle station; despite his profuse bleeding, he refused to leave until he was able to brief Lieutenant Commander Rhodes on the situation. Although he lost consciousness once, he remained until he was confident that Rhodes had all the information he needed to continue the battle. Refusing to acknowledge the seriousness of his wound and retaining his sense of humor despite this pain, Horowitz told his staff member who was encoding the message reporting that he was wounded, "Maybe we should just say that Adhesive Tape needs a Band-Aid."

Origins

In *A Soldier Reports,* General Westmoreland wrote, "Having long followed a policy of committing no American troops in the Mekong Delta (IV Corps Zone) other than support and advisory forces, I had begun in 1966 to consider how relatively small American numbers might bolster the ARVN effort there." The general was considering this move because by that point in the war it was evident that the Viet Cong strategy included dominating Dinh Tuong and Kien Hoa Provinces in the delta. This would give them control of Route 4, which was the only real link between Saigon and the southernmost portion of the country, the Ca Mau Peninsula. In addition, Dinh Tuong Province was the most populated province, with more than half a million people. Loss of control in the delta, the so-called "rice bowl" of South Vietnam, would have far-reaching derogating effects on the war effort. Game Warden forces were operating there with notable success, but their mission was to disrupt the enemy's movements and logistics, not to clear him from the delta. Ground forces on the offensive would have to do that.

The South Vietnamese Army had three infantry divisions (containing approximately 7500 men) in the delta, which operated chiefly in the heavily populated areas along the four main branches of the Mekong. Two problems impaired their mobility.

First, the delta terrain, with all of its waterways, rice paddies, and mud, resisted any conventional movement of troops. Roads were few and primitive except for Route 4, making wheeled vehicles all but useless, and the soft, spongy soil was unable to support the weight of artillery in most areas. Troops on foot quickly bogged down in the mire, found the crossing of waterways both time-consuming and tactically vulnerable, and were easily fatigued in the oppressive climate. Helicopters were not available in sufficient numbers to take up the entire burden, and their efficiency was substantially impaired by the high temperature and humidity, which reduced their lift. This meant, for example, that a CH-46 that could lift a complete 105-mm howitzer only under optimum conditions would have to move artillery in pieces rather than as a whole weapon in the delta.

Second, ARVN, the senior of the two services, had relegated the VNN River Assault Groups to a logistic support role, using the boats for supply runs rather than employing them tactically for the movement of troops. To some degree this happened because of parochial views and interservice rivalries, but the situation also had its roots in a more pragmatic consideration: previous experience had shown the River Assault Groups to be notably vulnerable when attacked by the increasingly better-armed Viet Cong forces. Rocket and recoilless-rifle rounds had a high rate of success against the inadequately armored craft of the River Assault Groups.

There was a significant obstacle to the introduction of U.S. infantry troops into the Mekong Delta. The dense population and agricultural emphasis of the region meant that there was no land available for basing a sizable force. The necessary land would have to be taken from the farmer peasants; this would provide invaluable propaganda "ammunition" to the Viet Cong, who were continually preaching to the villagers that the Americans were imperialists and that the South Vietnamese government did not have the best interests of the people at heart. General Westmoreland solved the problems by adopting "an idea advanced originally by a U.S. Navy officer, Captain David F. Welch. In much the same way that U.S. forces in, for example, the Seminole War and the Civil War had used waterways to facilitate military operations, why could we not create special units equipped to utilize the extensive waterways of the Delta to get at the Viet Cong?"

So the Mobile Riverine Force was born; in the planning stages it was dubbed the Mekong Delta Mobile Afloat Force. The Navy part of the force was called the Riverine Assault Force and was designated Task Force 117. It was made up of a large fleet of converted landing craft supported by several converted LST hulls that were redesigned as barracks and repair vessels. The small craft were equally divided into River Assault Squadrons; the support vessels constituted their own administrative unit, known as River Support Squadron 7. The redesigning of the landing craft was similar to what had been done previously for the VNN River Assault Group units, but improvements in armor and weapons assignment were incorporated. The new craft were more potent and less vulnerable than their VNN and French *Dinassaut* counterparts had been.

The infantry part of the newly conceived force would ideally have been elements of the U.S. Marine Corps, because of their capabilities in amphibious warfare and their familiarity with working alongside the Navy. But the Marines had been committed in force to the northernmost military region early in the war, and they did not have the resources to commit to the delta as well. To meet this new requirement, the Army reactivated the Ninth Infantry Division (coincidentally General Westmoreland's old outfit during World War II). The Second Brigade of the Ninth was to operate with the Mobile Riverine Force.

As an adjunct to the force, an unusual base was established near My Tho (the capital of Dinh Tuong Province, in the central delta). The base was named Dong Tam by General Westmoreland, meaning in Vietnamese "united hearts and minds." He chose the name because of its meaning and because it was easy for Americans to pronounce. Dong Tam was unusual in having been created by Navy Seabees and the Army Corps of Engineers, who had dredged up sand from the bottom of the My Tho River and made land where there had previously been none. (This dredging operation proved to be hazardous: three dredges were damaged or destroyed by VC sapper-swimmers, and still another was sunk when it sucked up and detonated some live ordnance from the river bottom.) General Westmoreland describes Dong Tam as "an island of sand that in the dry season was one of the dustiest places on earth," adding, "but it served the purpose"—to provide a home base for the force and space for additional Army troops that could not be taken along. The dredged basin and six-ammi-pontoon pier could accommodate one entire river assault squadron. Army battalions and Navy squadrons would rotate between Dong Tam and the force to provide a change of pace and prevent operational stagnation.

In September 1966, representatives from the Army, Navy, and Office of the Secretary of Defense met in Coronado, California, to discuss the anticipated joint operations of the Mobile Riverine Force. At this "Coronado Conference," as it came to be called, the framework and many of the specifics were laid out. Captain Wade C. Wells, USN, prospective commander of the Navy component, and Colonel William B. Fulton, USA, prospective commander of the Army component, met at this conference and began what was to prove to be an amazingly cooperative relationship, considering the circumstances. In another parallel to the Civil War, neither officer was designated as overall commander of the force, and each followed his own service's command structure up through several levels until reaching General Westmoreland himself, the first common element. It is interesting to note that in various publications that followed the formation of the Mobile Riverine Force, "who was in charge" depends upon the viewpoint of the author. Navy authors tend to describe the force as a logical extension of amphibious warfare, seeing the Army as involved only because the Marine Corps was not available. They sometimes refer to Captain Wells as "Commander of the Mobile Riverine Force." Army authors, on the other hand, view the force as an expedient for getting infantry forces into the delta, seeing the Navy as a means of supporting that end and often indicating that the Army was in command. These inconsistencies are essentially irrelevant, however, since Captain Wells and Colonel Fulton functioned as a team; they had some differences but always resolved them for the sake of the mission. In his debriefing report for the period from June 1967 to February 1968, Major General George G. O'Connor, commanding general of the Ninth Infantry Division, wrote: "These two elements have operated in close coordination and cooperation. Harmony prevails as neither element controls, and no joint headquarters has been superimposed. They have functioned well together because they wanted to."

The chain of command below the captain (by Navy tradition called "commodore" because of his multi-ship command) and the colonel had its own difficulties. The Navy's river assault organization did not correspond directly to the Army's battalion organization, and there were, at the lower levels in particular, some substantial rank differences involved. The Army's platoon leaders, for example, were officers, but the Navy's boat commanders were senior enlisted men, yet they were required to work together as organizational equivalents. Staff equivalencies varied too, but as at the top, both sides adapted well for the most part and cooperation superseded differences.

The original plan for the force called for the support of five self-propelled barracks ships (APBs), four light repair ships (ARLs), two support ships (LSTs), and two tugs (YTBs). The Office of the Secretary of Defense deleted three of the APBs and two of the ARLs with the provision that they could be restored if the force proved as successful as anticipated. The Navy offset this setback by providing an APL (non-self-propelled barracks ship), but instead of supporting all three battalions of the Second Brigade afloat, only two could be accommodated. This initially negative aspect proved in the end to have a positive result: the reduced number of U.S. troops available caused the Americans to rely on VNMC (Vietnamese Marine Corps) and ARVN units to make up the shortcoming, which was ultimately in line with the long-term goal of turning the war back over to the Vietnamese.

The Ninth Infantry Division was activated on 1 February 1966 at Fort Riley, Kansas. Its 2nd Brigade was modified for the planned Mobile Riverine Force role: the usual complement of heavy wheeled vehicles was dropped, and because of the anticipated firepower of the boats, some of the heavy weapons were deleted as well. Personnel who would normally have been assigned to these vehicles and weapons were trained as riflemen instead. There were nine rifle companies in the brigade—three each in three battalions—and three artillery batteries were also assigned. A significant amount of the usual equipment for a modern infantry brigade was deleted because of the unique operations planned: tents, mess facilities, and other camp paraphernalia were unnecessary because the troops would be berthing aboard the Mobile Riverine Base ships, and antitank missiles were deleted because of the nature of the enemy.

After accelerated training and organization, the first combat increments arrived in Vietnam in December 1966, and the entire division was in place by January 1967. The force immediately began training in the Rung Sat area using borrowed Vietnamese River Assault Group boats until the U.S. boats started to arrive in March 1967. The USS *Benewah* arrived to assume the role of force flagship in late April; her sister, the USS *Colleton,* arrived in early May. By mid-June 1967 flotilla strength had been achieved, and the force had become a viable entity in the delta and Rung Sat regions of Vietnam.

The Flotilla

The Navy part of the force, the River Assault Force (administratively organized into River Assault Flotilla I), officially came into being in September 1966. When it first began operations in Vietnam, it consisted of two River Assault Squadrons (consisting of assault craft) and one River Support Squadron (the ships that served as the Mobile Riverine Base).

River Assault Squadron 9 was the first to arrive in Vietnam, followed shortly by River Assault Squadron 11. Each squadron had two divisions, one consisting of thirteen ATCs, one CCB, and three monitors, the other containing a refueler in place of one of the monitors. Later, as they were built, eight ASPBs were added to each division.

Of all the Mobile Riverine Force assault craft, the ATC looked the most like the amphibious landing craft it had been before its riverine metamorphosis. Unlike the other LCM-6 conversions, the ATC had retained its bow-ramp door. These "Tango boats," as they were popularly called, were 56 feet long, displaced 66 tons, and had a draft of about three and a half feet. Their diesel-powered twin screws could drive them at a maximum speed of 8.5 knots, and they had a range of 110 miles at a more economical 6 knots. Armed with one 20-mm cannon, two .50-caliber machine guns, two Mark 18 grenade-launchers, and an assortment of hand-held weapons, the ATCs with their seven-man crews not only could land a platoon of troops (approximately forty men), but also could provide close-in fire support and keep the soldiers resupplied as well. They carried a load of food, ammunition, and various other supplies on board, and could also ferry additional supplies from the Mobile Riverine Base to the battle area during extended operations. Besides their armor plating and the stand-off bar armor used to predetonate incoming rounds, the ATC's well deck was covered by a canvas awning that prevented grenades from being lobbed in (as well as providing shade).

Yankee ingenuity soon stepped in. On 4 July 1967 a helicopter successfully landed on an ATC that had been modified by welding a steel platform in place of the awning. Others soon followed suit, and these ''flight-deck''-modified ATCs were used to evacuate casualties and allowed command personnel to become airborne or return to the scene of battle. The craft were touted by the force as the ''world's smallest aircraft carriers.''

The ''world's smallest hospital ships,'' designated ATC(H), were created by converting the interior of selected ATCs into medical aid stations; some were equipped with operating tables, refrigerated blood, and surgeons to handle critical cases. During one battle in September 1967, one of these ATC(H)s treated fifty-six battle casualties.

The riverine counterpart to the fleet oiler was created by inserting fuel bladders into the well-decks of certain ATCs. This version, called simply a refueler, could carry ten thousand gallons of fuel and keep other Mobile Riverine Force units on station for longer periods by refueling them and ferrying still more fuel from the base if necessary.

The monitors were the ''battleships'' of the riverine armada; their function could also be likened to that of the tank on land. They had a faired bow to increase their maneuverability and speed, and were armored like the ATCs. They carried the same weapons as the ATC, but were further endowed with a potent 81-mm naval mortar amidships and a 40-mm cannon mounted in a turret forward. The machine guns and the 40-mm were limited in range because they were ''line-of-sight'' weapons and were often inhibited by the obstruction of shoreline foliage, but the 81-mm mortar could either be employed as a line-of-sight weapon or could be called in by artillery observers from as far away as 4,000 yards. The monitors were 60 feet long, had a beam of 17.5 feet, displaced 75 tons (fully loaded), and drew three and a half feet of water. They were crewed by eleven men and were limited in speed to 8 knots.

Flamethrowers were added to some monitors as the force matured. These were used to burn away heavy vegetation to allow troop landings, and sometimes were employed to eliminate heavily fortified VC bunkers along the banks of the waterways. The use of flamethrowers was first tested by placing an Army armored personnel carrier equipped with an M-132-A1 flamethrower in the well-deck of an ATC. After the concept had been proven using this jury-rig, flamethrowers were permanently installed in some monitors. Thereafter, a monitor so equipped was called a ''Zippo'' by members of the force. Several ATCs were later called a ''Zippo'' by members of the force. Several ATCs were later equipped with flamethrowers as well and were given the designation ATC(F).

The CCBs were similar to the monitors except that they contained a command and control console amidships instead of the 81-mm mortar. The console contained a bank of HF, VHF, and UHF radios used to coordinate operations. These craft served as flagships for the Navy squadron and division commanders as well as command posts for the Army battalion commanders.

Both the monitors and the CCBs were equipped with radar and with navigation read-out systems that enhanced their ability to operate during periods of reduced visibility and darkness. The ATCs were not so equipped, but because they rarely traveled without monitors or CCBs, this was not a major drawback.

Late in 1967, a new craft, the assault support patrol boat (ASPB), joined the force. Unlike all the other craft, which were LCM-6 conversions, this 50-foot long, 28-ton boat was the only craft specifically built from scratch for the Mobile Riverine Force. It had a strengthened hull designed to resist underwater concussion damage from mines and was equipped with the same chain-drag mine-countermeasures rig that the other boats in the force had been using. These factors, combined with a speed capability of 16 knots and a weapons package that included an 81-mm mortar on the stern, a 20-mm cannon mounted forward, and an array of heavy machine guns and grenade launchers, made the ASPB a minesweeper/destroyer for the force. The designed versatility of this craft suited it for escort, reconnaissance, patrol, and counter-ambush operations. It required a crew of seven.

One of the more unusual aspects of the "Alpha boats" as the troops called the ASPBs, was the exhaust system. Instead of discharging directly to the atmosphere like most marine diesel engines, the ASPB's exhaust was expelled into the water. This reduced engine noise considerably and gave the enemy much less warning of its approach than did normal diesel craft. This innovation was not without its cost, however. Because of its complexity, the system proved to be more difficult than conventional systems to maintain and gave many an engineman headaches.

The construction of the ASPB was tested soon after its arrival in Vietnam, as evidenced by this COMNAVFORV report:

In the early morning hours of 21 December [1967] an ASPB, A-111-4, the lead minesweeper of several riverine craft transitting the Xang Canal in the Long Dinh district of Dinh Tuong province, two miles northwest of Dong Tam, was mined. As a result of the explosion one U.S. sailor . . . was killed and three others were wounded. The boat's hull was dished in, but not holed, and the damaged ASPB returned to the MRB under its own power. Considering the accuracy of the 75-pound command-detonated mine, which exploded 3–4 feet to starboard of the keel, the ASPB suffered only moderate hull damage. Although the keel was bent upward, and several frames and transverse and longitudinal stringers were bent inward and deformed, the rugged craft could have continued the mission if the tactical situation had dictated and replacement personnel were placed on-board.

Pride of "ownership" was characteristic of the boat crews. An early letter sent home to the families of the Mobile Riverine Force sailors by Commodore Wells said: "Most of the boat crews are naming their boats. Just a few of the names they have chosen so far are: Delta Dragon, Little Mo, Poison Ivy, 8-Ball Express, The Boat, Swamp Fox, Green Grabber, Granny Goose, The Fugitive." That same letter also pointed out the new argot created for the force by including a glossary and a cartoon showing a sailor writing home with the caption reading ". . . And so, Mom, the OOD told me to stop by RIVFLOT ONE on the APB before reporting to COMRIV-RON 9 for duty on an ATC in RAD 92. . . ."

The original plan for the Army's artillery was to carry the 105-mm howitzers in ATCs, unload them near the area of operations, and set up small fire-bases ashore. Colonel Fulton toured the delta in advance of his brigade's arrival, however, and became convinced that this plan would not work. The steep banks and great tidal range would make unloading the heavy guns nearly impossible, and there was a paucity of ground firm enough to support the 105s once they were unloaded. Each of the three artillery batteries attached to the brigade had six howitzers, capable of delivering effective fire support to a maximum range of approximately seven miles, and the Army was not prepared to give them up. The solution was found in creating barges large enough to hold two howitzers each and towing them to the desired location, where they could be secured to the shore and provide a stable platform for the guns. Because their greater capacity would enable them to carry the large amounts of ammunition that would be required, LCM-8s were chosen to tow the barges, rather than the smaller LCM-6s that had made up the rest of the force. As the Navy had no available LCM-8s, the Army had to supply the necessary craft and their crews. Men and boats of the 1097th Transportation Company were assigned to the force for this purpose.

The LCM-8s, or "Mike boats," would run the barges up onto the banks. Grappling hooks attached to winched lines were fastened to nearby trees; the winches would snug the boats up tight to the shore for maximum stability, and could subsequently be tightened or eased off as the tide changed.

Some of the force's twenty-seven LCM-8s were configured as fire-support direction centers. One was made into a forward command post for the brigade commander. An "aqua-jail" was prepared by configuring one of the "Mike boats" as an interrogation and holding center where captured Viet Cong or suspects could be processed. A "damage control" version was also created to handle on-scene maintenance and repair.

Even though the APBs were equipped with flight decks, some means of landing helicopters closer to the area of operations was needed. The mini-flight decks mounted on some of the ATCs helped somewhat, but they were only good for a quick landing and were not suitable for stowing the helicopters for extended periods. For this purpose, pontoon barges were created, capable of handling three helicopters at a time and carrying 1,500 gallons of aviation fuel each. They were also towed to the area of operations by LCM-8s.

The ships of River Support Squadron 7 made up the Mobile Riverine Base of the Mobile Riverine Force. The flagship of the force was the *Benewah*. She and her sister ship, the *Colleton*, were World War II–vintage LSTs from the inactive ("mothball") fleet that had undergone major conversions at Philadelphia Naval Shipyard, where each received a coat of jungle-green paint, a helicopter platform, an air-conditioned interior, and an upgrading in equipment and facilities, including the installation of a Tactical Operations Center with extensive communications capability. Each ship's armament consisted of an array of two 3-inch/.50-caliber slow-fire guns, eight 40-mm guns mounted in two quad mounts, and eight .50-caliber machine guns.

The non-self-propelled barracks ship, APL-26, had a berthing capacity of approximately 650 men; about 175 extra berths above the original design had been gained by building bunks topside under a canvas canopy that became known as "the Penthouse." To provide mobility for the APL, two YTBs were attached to the force. The APL's modest armament package consisted of several .30- and .50-caliber machine guns.

To give repair and maintenance support to the force, the USS *Askari* (ARL-30) was activated. She was a reconfigured LST that housed the various repair shops necessary to fix the engines, weapons, and electronics of the assault craft. In addition, a non-self-propelled barge (YFNB) was converted to a repair and maintenance barge (YRBM) and attached to the force. Rather than travel with the Mobile Riverine Base, the YRBM remained at Dong Tam, where assault craft could come for overhauls.

LSTs were assigned to the force from the Seventh Fleet. One, an 1156-class (chosen for its large capacity and acceptable draft), stayed as part of the Mobile Riverine Base, stowing a ten-day supply of ammunition and C-rations, a ten-day emergency store of food, and extra Army equipment that could not be stowed in the APBs. It also accommodated the brigade's helicopter detachment and the personnel from one infantry company and one river assault division. A second LST, this one a smaller 542-class, shuttled from Vung Tau to the force weekly, bringing food, ammunition, and fuel.

To provide docking facilities for the assault craft once the ships anchored, two 30-by-90-foot pontoons called "ammi-pontoons" were moored alongside each anchored ship. These not only provided docking space for the boats, they served as embarkation facilities for the soldiers, obviating the necessity for embarkation nets draped over the side and allowing the troops to step aboard the boats with relative ease and little energy consumption. When the base moved to a new anchorage, the pontoons were towed alongside if the water was not too choppy or behind if conditions warranted.

Security for the Mobile Riverine Base was provided by both the Navy and the Army. One division was assigned security duty on a rotating basis and would conduct patrols around the base, sweeping for mines, dropping percussion grenades, inspecting hulls and anchor chains, and keeping local traffic at a safe distance from the force. One Army rifle company was also assigned on a rotating basis. The usual procedure was for one platoon to cover each bank of the river opposite the base, with the third platoon held in reserve. Because the base, when anchored, stretched out for more than a mile, it was impossible for a mere platoon to tightly cover the expanse, so ambush sites were often used at night and moving patrols during the day to discourage enemy movement in the area and provide early warning of an attack.

In June 1968 the force was expanded by the addition of another River Assault Squadron; in September of the same year, a fourth squadron arrived. With the addition of squadrons 13 and 15 to the original squadrons 9 and 11, the force was subdivided into two groups: divisions 91, 92, 111, 112, and 151 to Mobile Riverine Group Alfa, and divisions 131, 132, and 152 to Mobile Riverine Group Bravo. The two groups conducted separate operations in different parts of the delta and Rung Sat.

The new craft arriving in 1968 were improved versions of earlier designs. All the new ATCs were equipped with armor-plated helicopter flight decks, and the weapons complement was enhanced by the addition of two 20-mm aircraft cannon and a Mark 19 long-range, 40-mm grenade launcher. To improve the punch of the new monitors, a 105-mm howitzer replaced the 40-mm cannon; this new weapon not only increased the range and power of the monitor, it enhanced its flexibility as well by being able to fire nine different types of rounds. Increased communications, navigation, and encryption capabilities were included in the new CCBs, and air-conditioning to protect the sensitive electronic equipment was also added.

The support squadron for the force was also expanded with two more self-propelled barracks ships, the USS *Mercer* (APB-39) and USS *Nueces* (APB-40); three more repair ships, the USS *Satyr* (ARL-23), USS *Sphinx* (ARL-24), and USS *Indra* (ARL-37); and two additional LSTs.

The force continued to operate at this strength until February 1969, when the River Assault Division 91 boats were turned over to the Vietnamese Navy in the first of a succession of turnovers that would eventually dissolve the force. In March the two groups were once again combined into a single Mobile Riverine Force, and remained this way until their disestablishment.

Operations

In early 1967, while Mobile Riverine Force assets were gradually materializing in Vietnam, those elements which had arrived began training together. At the same time, the Viet Cong stepped up the frequency and the effectiveness of their attacks in the Rung Sat Special Zone. On 15 February an American minesweeper was sunk by a mine on the Long Tau River.

The very next day a makeshift force made up of troops of the 3rd Battalion, 47th Infantry, and sailors from River Assault Squadron 9 embarked in seven LCM-6s and one *commandement* borrowed from the Vietnamese Navy and began Operation River Raider I, penetrating the Rung Sat and conducting search-and-destroy missions. They made no contact with large enemy units, but in several skirmishes they killed a confirmed twelve Viet Cong with seventeen probables. There were no U.S. fatalities; only eight American soldiers were wounded. Numerous enemy camps, bunkers, supply caches, and munitions factories were discovered and destroyed during the month-long operation. For example, on 21 February a large enemy installation containing seventeen sleeping-huts, two workshops, and a galley was found, and on 7 March one of the companies uncovered a large cache of mines, mortar rounds, small arms ammunition, and rice in the lower Rung Sat. Three days later the same company found a camp containing several sampans, seventy-five TNT blocks, two water mines, and a significant quantity of documents. On the last day of the operation, two newly arrived ATCs joined in—the first time that American Mobile Riverine Force assault craft had participated in combat operations.

River Raider I was only moderately successful in statistical terms, but it was invaluable as experience. Its various lessons included the realization that troops should not wear underwear while operating in this moist environment; underwear did not dry as rapidly as fatigues, so the troops were better off without it. Soon every squad was equipped with a hundred-foot nylon line and a grappling hook, and every man carried a ten-foot piece of line with a snap-link attached; these items were helpful in making water crossings and in detonating booby traps.

Rust and corrosion proved to be nearly as insidious an enemy as the Viet Cong. Weapons had to be broken down and scrubbed in a mixture of cleaning solvent and oil at least every third day. Metal link-belt ammunition frequently corroded so badly that it had to be discarded, and compass components froze up with regularity. Radios performed well, but their handsets and antennas were often damaged by the moisture and rust.

Optimum boat capacity was forty men for the troop carriers, but during the operation they could accommodate sixty if necessary. This meant that if an ATC was disabled by enemy action or by simple breakdown, then its forty-man platoon, divided into two groups, could board two of the other boats.

Placing mortars in the Rung Sat was difficult because of the soft ground. To compensate, one of the LCMs was rigged with a pair of 81-mm mortars mounted just aft of the bow ramp. The mortar's base-plates were placed on 2½-ton truck tires filled with sandbags to absorb the shock of firing and covered by another layer of sandbags to dampen the bounce after recoil. This "mortar boat" was nosed ashore and secured by lines running from the stern quarters to the bank at about a 30-degree angle. It provided not only a stable platform for the mortars but also good mobility with a large supply of ammunition at hand. The rig was used day and night during the operation.

Tactics were tried and proven. On one occasion a feint was accomplished by firing artillery and running continuous radio chatter as though the troops were making a landing, when in actuality they had remained in the boats. The boats patrolled as they would when empty until it was completely dark; then they quietly inserted the troops to set up ambush positions. Several contacts with the enemy during the night proved that the deception had been successful.

Operation River Raider I was deemed a success. In an Army after-action report the boats were described as having "provided great flexibility as well as reliability throughout the operation." The most significant success was the capture of substantial stores of water-mines and the destruction of VC facilities for constructing these mines, resulting in a notable curtailment of VC mining incidents in the Long Tau shipping channel.

Operation Spearhead I followed River Raider I in the Rung Sat, beginning in mid-March. River Assault Squadron 11 arrived during this operation and took over for River Assault Squadron 9 so that the latter could move to Dong Tam in preparation for Mobile Riverine Force operations in the Mekong Delta.

Some minor operations were conducted in mid- and late April using U.S. assault craft in the delta for the first time, but the force conducted its first major delta operation in May 1967. An area called the Cam Son Secret Zone, located upriver from Dong Tam between the Rach Ba Rai and Rach Tra Tan tributaries of the My Tho River, was one of four known major base areas of the Viet Cong in Dinh Tuong Province. Two of the force's three infantry battalions, twenty-two ATCs, two monitors, and two CCBs combined to launch a strike into the southern sector of the Cam Son area. The operation, called Hop Tac XVIII, brought the force face to face with the Viet Cong's 514th Battalion. The VC proved no match for the Americans and were driven off after losing more than a hundred troops. The river assault craft proved their tactical utility by standing up to several fierce attacks and by blocking one of the enemy's escape routes. They also revealed their limitations when, at a critical point, a combination of low tides and enemy antitank rounds prevented the ATCs from moving troops upstream where they were needed to outflank the fleeing Viet Cong soldiers. American wounded included eight assault-craft sailors (one of them the river division commander), but overall casualties were light and damage minor.

In early June, the Mobile Riverine Force began the first in a long series of operations bearing the name Coronado, after Coronado, California, where the force had been born. A Coronado operation was renumbered whenever the base changed locations; therefore, the length of each Coronado operation could range from a few days to several months.

The purpose of Coronado I, which began on 1 June, was the securing of the Dong Tam area while refining doctrine and tactics. On 6 June, ATC 112-3 was damaged by a mine that blew the port .50-caliber gun and its gunner over the side and caused extensive damage to the boat's hull and engines, underscoring the need for the ASPBs that were being built to sweep mines and to endure them when they went off. On 7 and 8 June, the heaviest enemy contact of Coronado I occurred in Dinh Tuong Province, twelve miles west of Dong Tam. Casualties were not severe, but four naval personnel were wounded when elements of Task Unit 117.1.1 were hit by a reinforced enemy platoon near the Rach Ba Rai tributary.

On 11 June, the Mobile Riverine Force made its first major movement, sailing down the My Tho River from Dong Tam and crossing a twenty-five-mile stretch of the South China Sea to Vung Tau, where it anchored temporarily to pick up boats newly arrived from the United States before going to a

Rung Sat anchorage at Nha Be. There the last of the borrowed craft were returned to the Vietnamese. By this time, River Assault Flotilla 1 had grown to a total inventory of fifty-two ATCs, ten monitors, four CCBs, and two refuelers.

From 13 through 17 June, the force participated in the Ninth Infantry Division's Operation Great Bend, but made no direct contact with enemy forces. On the 18th the force moved to the junction of the Soi Rap and Vam Co rivers and the following day started Operation Concordia I, which proved to be both costly and highly successful. At its conclusion, Rear Admiral Veth, then COMNAVFORV, sent a message to Commander Task Force 117 (Commodore Wells) and the commanding officer of the Second Brigade, Ninth Infantry Division (Colonel Fulton):

THE PERFORMANCE AND GALLANTRY OF YOUR MEN DURING OPERATION CONCORDIA I WERE A SOURCE OF PRIDE AND GRATIFICATION TO ALL OF US. . . . THE MOBILE RIVERINE FORCE HAS PROVED TO BE THE POTENT FLEXIBLE FIGHTING TEAM SO VITAL TO THE SUCCESS OF THE CAMPAIGN IN THE DELTA. . . . MAY YOU HAVE CONTINUED GOOD HUNTING.

During a follow-on operation, dubbed Concordia II, the Mobile Riverine Force suffered its first naval fatality. On 11 July the force encountered stiff resistance from the Viet Cong while leap-frogging along one of the creeks in Long An Province. At one point, the VC detonated a Claymore mine just as ATC 112-4 dropped its ramp, wounding seven sailors and four soldiers. The engagement that followed grew in intensity; throughout the day, blows were traded by the adversaries with varying success. At 1800 a rocket slammed into the conning station of one of the monitors, instantly killing the boat captain, Chief Boatswain's Mate Howard W. Bannister, and wounding six others, including the river division commander. The fighting continued into the night, and the operation itself ended on the 14th. During the four-day period, known enemy losses were fifty-nine killed, six captured, and three defected.

Later in July, a series of minings along Route 4 in the delta and a number of mortar attacks on the U.S. base at Dong

Tam indicated that the Viet Cong were marshaling their forces in that area. In response, the force moved back into the heart of the delta to commence Operation Coronado II. Throughout July, the force operated in Dinh Tuong Province and yielded seventy-three enemy killed in action and sixty-eight captured. Nine U.S. soldiers were killed and thirty-three were wounded, while the Navy's tally was thirty-one wounded. During one engagement an ATC was retiring from the scene to have the wounded evacuated after a hit by a B-40 rocket when it was hit a second time, causing further serious injuries. During the later part of the operation many of the soldiers suffered debilitating fungus infections and cases of immersion foot as a result of operating in flooded areas for five successive days. Experience proved that three days of continuous operations without rotation was about the maximum the men could tolerate in that environment. But this phase, conducted jointly with South Vietnamese forces, did serious damage to the Viet Cong's 263rd Main Force Battalion and probably thwarted a major attack on either Dong Tam or the city of My Tho. Game Warden PBRs joined in the operation to help seal off the area and prevent enemy movement along or across the waterways. Later intelligence reports corroborated their success in this mission.

At the beginning of August, the force went back to the Rung Sat and began Operation Great Bend IV, later renamed Coronado III. A series of search-and-destroy missions in Gia Dinh Province followed, which yielded only light contact with the enemy but uncovered some weapons and explosives caches.

Coronado IV began on 18 August, with the Mobile Riverine Force anchored once again at the junction of the Vam Co and Soi Rap Rivers in the Rung Sat Special Zone. Suffering only six wounded, the force killed thirty-four enemy soldiers in one skirmish, when their landing flushed out an element of the 506th Local Force Battalion and forced them into the open, where helicopter gunships could take them under fire. Total enemy killed in action for Coronado IV was forty-nine. This operation was unusual in that the actual area of operations was a significant distance from the base (approximately forty miles). To handle the demanding logistics of this situation, six ATCs took supplies to a position six miles from the area of operations to serve as forward supply posts. Another problem was solved in an unnautical but efficient manner: on the second day of the operation, boats assigned to the forward area were refueled from a tanker-truck. Positioned on a bridge near Ben Luc, the truck lowered its hose over the side of the bridge and the thirsty boats below drank their fill. A crusty chief petty officer, a veteran of more than two decades of service, muttered, "I've refueled from oilers, aircraft carriers, destroyers, and even merchantmen, but never in all my years did I ever think I'd be doing an unrep [underway replenishment] with a goddamned Army truck!"

In September 1967 the force inflicted the heaviest losses to date on the Viet Cong, killing nearly four hundred enemy soldiers and capturing or destroying tons of supplies and munitions. For the Navy component of the force, September also proved to be the costliest month so far; six Navy men were killed in action and eighty-four more were wounded. The Viet Cong, finding in their early contacts with the force that their RPG-2 (B-40) rockets had been largely unsuccessful against the armor-clad boats, had ordered something more potent from their Russian and Chinese suppliers. By September the RPG-7s were arriving. This weapon has an effective range of more than 500 yards (as compared to the RPG-2's range of about 150 yards) and is capable of penetrating up to a foot of armor. The bar armor of the assault boats dissipated the explosive power of those rockets by predetonation (otherwise, the casualty figures would have been much higher), but the success of VC ambushes was markedly improved by the introduction of this weapon.

Coronado V began on 11 September in the vicinity of Dong Tam. Four days later, river assault units designated as Task Group 117.2 headed up the Ba Rai Creek forty-seven miles southeast of Saigon, conducting reconnaissance by fire en route to a troop insertion point. An ambush erupted along a two-mile stretch of dense foliage that had been well prepared with enemy fortifications. During the four-hour battle that ensued, the river assault craft came under the heaviest fire they had yet experienced. In all, eighteen boats received damage. COMNAVFORV's monthly historical supplement summed up the battle:

Three U.S. Navymen were killed and 77 were wounded in this action. Viet Cong casualties consisted of 213 killed with 66 probably killed. Individual acts of heroism were abundant with wounded sailors refusing to be sent back to the ships of the Mobile Riverine Base so that they could stay with their boats and continue to fight. As a result of this battle, CTF 117 has recommended that the following awards be given to the brave sailors of the River Assault Force: three Navy Crosses, 23 Silver Stars (three posthumously), 34 Bronze Stars, and 10 Navy Commendation Medals.

The report also singled out "Dusty" Rhodes:

Lieutenant Commander Francis E. Rhodes, COMRIV-RON 11 and CTG 117.2 was in command of the 23 riverine assault craft, which had elements of the 2nd Brigade, Ninth Infantry Division embarked. LCDR Rhodes was on board CCB-111-1 when the command boat was hit by two rockets, knocking him and his crew to the deck. Although stunned from momentary unconsciousness, he stationed himself in an exposed position on his command boat and in the face of direct enemy fire from close range, quickly noted the condition and disposition of his units. Taking personal command of all his units by radio, he ordered them out of the enemy fortified area. He then regrouped his forces, transferred his dead, evacuated his seriously wounded men and reassigned personnel so that all of his boats were properly manned. Then he reentered the melee with his task group, suppressed the heavy enemy rocket and recoilless-rifle fire and successfully landed his assault troops.

Operation Coronado V continued through the end of the month, racking up impressive statistics. On 27 September, Mobile Riverine Force units were again ambushed, this time in Ben Tre Creek forty miles southwest of Saigon. Three more Navy men died in that engagement, and six others were wounded.

A significant aspect of Coronado V was the first employment of the newly arrived ASPBs. These fast, heavily armored, multipurpose craft were a welcome addition to the force, particularly for minesweeping. The two boats hit hardest in the 27 September ambush had been the lead ATCs functioning as minesweepers. The first two ASPBs had arrived in Vietnam at Vung Tau on 20 September, and saw their first combat action eight days later in the twilight of Coronado V.

On 10 October the force made a night transit from Dong Tam to Vung Tau in preparation for Operation Coronado VI in the Rung Sat—the first time that the big ships of the Mobile Riverine Base had made a major move under the cover of darkness. The operation lasted eight days and yielded a significant amount of enemy supplies, but direct contact with the enemy was never established.

The day after Coronado VII ended, the force moved to Vung Tau and Coronado VIII began. Elements of the force worked in conjunction with the Royal Thai Volunteer Regiment for the first time. Enemy contact was light during the three-day operation. Three Viet Cong were killed, several tons of supplies were captured, and seventy-eight bunkers and nineteen sampans were destroyed.

On 1 November the Mobile Riverine Force headed back to the delta, where it would operate in the vicinity of Dong Tam for the next several months. The trip across the stretch of the South China Sea from Vung Tau to the mouth of the My Tho River was slow because of high winds and heavy seas, and towing the ammi-pontoons was particularly difficult under these circumstances. But all units arrived safely, and Coronado IX began on 2 November. The operation, lasting until mid-January 1968, involved a variety of probes and reactions in the provinces surrounding Dong Tam. The cumulative results were 434 enemy killed in action and several hundred captured at a cost of 76 friendly dead and 374 wounded.

While this operation was in progress, Commodore Wells was relieved as Commander River Assault Force (and Commander Task Force 117) by Captain Robert S. Salzer, USN. After participating in his first action, the new commodore was quoted in the COMNAVFORV Monthly Historical Supplement: "To a newcomer in one of these actions, the battle of the boats is incredible. The crossfire between the Viet Cong and our rugged craft at 25 yards is like nothing in naval warfare since the days of the great frigates.''

Shortly after assuming command, Commodore Salzer introduced a new tactical element into the force. He observed through analysis of after-action reports that nearly every major enemy contact had been triggered by the assault boats. To fully exploit this potential to generate enemy contact and to provide greater protection for those ATCs actually carrying troops, the commodore created the Riverine Armored Reconnaissance Element, made up of two ATCs equipped with flame-throwing APCs, two ASPBs, and two monitors. It would precede the main formation into the area of operations in order to provoke enemy contact before the troop-carrying ATCs arrived. The heavy and varied firepower was deemed sufficient to effectively counter most threats that might be waiting for the oncoming force.

Coronado X, which had been running through the latter part of January, was abruptly interrupted on 30 January, when reports came flowing in of massive attacks on cities in the delta. My Tho, Ben Tre, Vinh Long, and Can Tho were all under siege. The Tet Offensive had begun.

The Mobile Riverine Base was anchored near the city of Vinh Long when the offensive began. Initially, a company of Mobile Riverine Force troops joined ARVN units, VNN River Assault Group craft, and U.S. Navy Game Warden PBRs in defending the airfield west of Vinh Long against a 1,200-man Viet Cong force. Other Mobile Riverine Force troops were airlifted back to the Dong Tam area to bolster defenses there.

At a little past midnight on 1 February, units of River Assault Division 91 and a contingent of artillery barges moved southward along the Rach Ruong tributary to rendezvous with the base. They approached the area where, in early December, a large VC force had ambushed riverine units along a three-mile stretch of the waterway. Not willing to be burned twice, the U.S. forces were ready for a repeat performance should the enemy be foolhardy enough to attempt one. The artillerymen had leveled their 105-mm howitzers and loaded them with deadly ''Beehive'' antipersonnel rounds. At 0020, the unsuspecting Viet Cong opened up with machine-gun, rocket, and recoilless-rifle fire from both banks of the thirty-yard-wide waterway. The artillery barges, monitors, ASPBs, and ATCs retaliated with a barrage that stirred images of broadsides in the days of close-quarters sailing battles. The battle lasted less than a half hour. The riverine units continued downstream, leaving an unknown but doubtless large number of enemy dead and wounded. One U.S. Navy man, a monitor boat captain, was killed in the battle.

The reassembled force weighed anchor on the morning of 1 February. Troop-laden assault craft preceded the base and at approximately 1515 landed at the waterfront of My Tho city, where they immediately engaged enemy forces. The base made the twenty-five-mile transit following the assault craft and anchored off Dong Tam at about the same time the assault craft were landing at My Tho. A twenty-one-hour pitched battle ensued as the troops pushed the VC back while the boats provided blocking and fire support along the waterfront area. At the end of the engagement 115 enemy lay dead in the city streets; friendly losses were 3 dead and 67 wounded.

For the next two days, the force conducted operations in Dinh Tuong Province, moving once to the Cai Lay area. The enemy thrust there was blunted, and the VC withdrew. Then on 4 February, responding to a rapidly deteriorating situation in Vinh Long, the force rapidly returned to that city, arriving at 1630. Intelligence reports indicated that two or three VC battalions were going to strike at Vinh Long that night. Together with the ARVN troops in and around the city, the force battled with the intruding VC for the next two days, driving them back out of and away from the city. On 6 February the exhausted soldiers and sailors returned to the base for their first rest in eight days of continuous operations.

In the weeks that followed, the Mobile Riverine Force played a decisive role against Viet Cong forces. In his seminal work on the 1968 offensive, *Tet!*, Don Oberdorfer wrote: "A total of 5,200 Viet Cong are reported to have been killed in the Mekong delta and 560 captured. Whatever the accuracy of this estimate, it is clear that large numbers of the most dedicated and most experienced guerillas and local force troops met their death inside the unfamiliar cities." The force is credited with having saved the major cities of the delta during the Tet Offensive. There can be no question that the presence and mobility of this force was critical to the ultimate defeat of large Viet Cong forces at this pivotal time. Had the force not been created and introduced into the delta a year earlier, the Tet Offensive would more than likely have had a much different outcome in this southern "rice bowl" region of South Vietnam.

Operations continued in the months following Tet. Both sides suffered losses and several assault craft were sunk, but the ratio unquestionably favored the U.S. forces. The force continued to hammer away at the Viet Cong until, in May and June, the enemy chose to elude the Americans rather than take any more beatings. Their elusiveness continued until the last two days in July, when the force caught the enemy in Chuong Thien Province and struck him a devastating blow. Operations continued in this region and on into Kien Giang Province in August—the first allied major ground operation into this traditional enemy stronghold in more than a decade.

Not all the events were victories, however. A series of VC ambushes in the Can Tho area during August drew an over-zealous response from the riverine units: in their eagerness to strike at the enemy, artillery and gunboat strikes accidentally killed and injured a considerable number of Vietnamese civilians and soldiers. Then, in November, the Navy suffered its greatest loss of life as a result of enemy action in a single incident, when Viet Cong sappers successfully attached several limpet mines to the hull of one of the Mobile Riverine Base ships, the USS *Westchester County* (LST-1167). The explosions ripped into the starboard side, amidships, causing severe damage in a number of berthing, stowage, and fuel compartments. Eighteen American sailors died in the explosion, as well as five American soldiers, one VNN sailor, and one ARVN soldier. Twenty-seven other men were also wounded, seven requiring medical evacuation.

As 1968 drew to a close, some of the force's assets were incorporated into a new strategy known as SEA LORDS (see Chapter 6), and a new policy called ACTOV (Accelerated Turnover to the Vietnamese—see Chapter 7) was being talked about with the coming of a new administration in Washington. Some additional Mobile Riverine Force operations were conducted in the early months of 1969, but summer marked the closing days of the force. In June sixty-four craft were turned over to the VNN, and by August the remaining craft had been either transferred to the SEA LORDS operation or turned over to the Vietnamese, and the 2nd Brigade of the Ninth Infantry Division had returned to the United States. It was the end of a brief but uniquely successful era.

Postscripts

General Westmoreland wrote:

> In the first year—1967—the Riverine Force engaged in five major actions and destroyed over a thousand VC. As operations began, ambushes from shore with the enemy using rockets and recoilless rifles were common, and the enemy was often encountered in battalion strength. As time passed, a sharp decrease both in the number of ambushes and the size of enemy forces attested to the success achieved. Sections of the Delta long given over to the VC were by the end of 1968 readily accessible.

There can be little doubt that the presence of the Mobile Riverine Force in both the Rung Sat Special Zone and the northern portion of the Mekong Delta shifted the balance of power in those regions in favor of the allies. The force inflicted significant casualties on the enemy and disrupted his logistics. It laid the groundwork for the forthcoming SEA LORDS operation. The establishment of the base at Dong Tam provided security to the nearby important city of My Tho, and the force's presence was responsible for the reopening of Route 4, which permitted produce to flow to market and reestablished communications in the area.

The question of whether the South Vietnamese were ready to carry on the role of the force when it departed was strenuously debated at the time. The finale to the Vietnam War makes the question ever more debatable and not likely to find universally acceptable resolution in the near future. This grand-strategy question notwithstanding, it is safe to assert that the concept and the actual execution of the Mobile Riverine Force were innovative, appropriate to the prevailing situation, and tactically sound. Moreover, the soldiers and sailors who manned this mini-armada and took it ''in harm's way" deserve more than the few accolades they have received. They struggled with an inhospitable environment and faced a deadly enemy at point-blank range. Their courage is indisputable.

Lieutenant Commander Charles L. Horowitz remained in the Navy, becoming a weapons engineering specialist and working with the Polaris ballistic missile system, a far cry from the primitive weaponry of his tour in Vietnam. He retired a captain after twenty-eight years of service. Today he works for the Sperry Corporation as program manager for the Spanish Navy Frigate and Carrier Program.

Lieutenant Raymond W. Johnson wrote a book entitled *Postmark Mekong Delta* after his return from Vietnam. He remained in the Naval Reserve and is today a commander in the Chaplain Corps. An exceptionally talented artist, he has traveled extensively, painting a variety of subjects, including a thematic collection he calls "The Faces and Horsemen of the World." In 1984 he was awarded the prestigious Gold Medal Award for "Creative Excellence as an Artist-Painter" by the International Art Honor Society in Paris.

5

TASK FORCE CLEARWATER

River Security Groups— I Corps Tactical Zone

The passage of great rivers in the presence of the enemy is one of the most delicate operations in war.

—FREDERICK THE GREAT, c. 1785

Northern Frontier

The commander climbed up the wooden rungs of the tower that stood near the northern perimeter of the base. A Marine sentry saluted him as he entered the observation box that sat atop the tower. "Quiet today, sir," the sentry said, and resumed his position gazing out over the sand dunes.

"So far," the commander replied. He picked up a pair of binoculars and looked northward. The day was particularly clear, with a sharp blue sky, and in the distance he could make out the form of a guard tower similar to the one in which he was standing. A spot of motionless khaki just below the roof of the tower told him that a North Vietnamese soldier was probably staring back at him across the DMZ that separated North from South Vietnam. He knew the distance between the two towers to be just about ten miles.

The commander put down the binoculars and turned to look at the base that had been incongruously inserted into the expanse of sand marking the mouth of the Cua Viet River. The South China Sea sparkled along the base's eastern perimeter, and the jade green of the Annamite Mountains loomed in the distant west. Coils of barbed wire defined the perimeter of the base; sandbagged outcroppings marked its functional structures.

Commander Sayre Swarztrauber had assumed command of Task Force Clearwater the previous fall. It was now the middle of January 1969. He had served in Operation Game Warden for nearly half a year as Commander River Squadron Five before moving to I Corps to become Commander Task Force Clearwater. From his lofty perch, Commander Swarztrauber's attention was drawn to the Cua Viet River below by the sound of diesel engines. An LCU (Landing Craft, Utility) and two LCMs were arriving from Da Nang, ninety miles down the coast. The three craft, laden with food and ammunition, would proceed upriver after a stopover at the Cua Viet base. A PBR and an LCM-6 minesweeper from the Clearwater task force would escort the convoy upstream to Dong Ha, where the cargo would be transferred to trucks for distribution to combat units at Cam Lo, Quang Tri, and various other inland sites. Swarztrauber had made periodic trips up the river himself and had been amazed at how different the Cua Viet was from the Mekong. Just a half mile up the river, the white sand dunes yielded to the shimmering green of overgrown rice paddies. The rusting hulks of armored vehicles and empty, pockmarked huts flanked the river in silent testimony to the earlier clash of armies and the flight of civilians.

Earlier, the PBRs had played a vital role as escorts because ambushes along the river were frequent. Now, with Task Force Clearwater nearly a year old, the minesweepers had become the most important part of the convoys. Ambushes had become infrequent but minings were a constant threat. Since Swarztrauber had taken command, Clearwater personnel were still being killed in action, but none had been lost in firefights along the river. Minings and artillery attacks on the base had been responsible for the deaths. Most of the mines were primitive in construction—often made with such unsophisticated items as inner tubes, clothespins, or toy balloons—but they were deadly nonetheless.

The upstream leg of the trip was the most dangerous because the majority of the mines were free-floating, and moving counter to the current increased the danger of hitting one. It was not uncommon for patrols to open fire on floating hibiscus plants because they closely resembled some of the mines used by the enemy. The downstream leg of the journey was usually accomplished by drifting with the current, which meant that boats and mines would drift along at approximately the same speed, thereby minimizing the chances for contact.

Swarztrauber climbed down from the observation tower and crossed the compound toward the mess hall. He paused for a moment, looking at the base command post, which had been built by placing a standard metal quonset hut in a pit about four feet below ground level, piling sand up around the sides all the way to the roof, and placing multiple layers of sandbags on the roof itself. The building had little in common with the command post in which he had stood watches at the Pentagon during a previous duty assignment.

He entered the mess hall—it too was a semi-buried quonset

enshrouded in sand—and headed for the coffeepot. Over the radio in the galley he recognized the voice of Hanoi Hannah, this war's rough equivalent to Tokyo Rose. She was, as usual, predicting the "inevitable defeat of American forces and their Saigon puppets." Some months before, a North Vietnamese artillery round had scored a direct hit on the mess hall, destroying it and killing the solitary cook inside. Shortly afterward, Hannah had broadcast, "You Americans who burrow in the sand like moles, we have destroyed your mess hall. There is no point in building a new one because our gunners will knock it out too." Swarztrauber knew that it had been an empty threat: the NVA gunners were firing their weapons at maximum range and therefore had little or no accuracy. Any hits that occurred were pure luck. By the sheer number of rounds that they expended on the Cua Viet facility, it was inevitable that some would find their mark. The Americans had built a new mess hall despite Hannah's warnings and had named it after the cook who had been killed. The most disconcerting element of the incident was the fact that Hannah knew about the mess hall hit. This meant that the enemy had contacts inside the compound.

As he sipped his coffee, Swarztrauber watched several sailors at the far end of the mess hall eating an early lunch. They sat at the metal tables wearing helmets and flak jackets while they ate. Such was life at Cua Viet. One never knew when incoming rounds would suddenly hit. Since its inception, the Cua Viet base had been subjected to frequent shellings and occasional attempted intrusions by sappers. The prudent man was never very far from his helmet, flak jacket, or personal weapon.

Just after 1700 the shelling resumed. There was a brief hiss followed by a deafening explosion as the first round detonated near the north perimeter. Then, as the warning siren told Cua Viet what it already knew, the rounds fell in random bursts that caused the earth to tremble and sand to rain down in the quonsets. It was both routine and terrifying for the men of Clearwater. All they could do was wait helplessly, praying that the North Vietnamese gunners wouldn't get lucky.

The incoming rounds continued for nearly fifteen minutes. Most of the rounds fell short, dropping into the river or along the north bank, but two hit inside the compound. One detonated harmlessly near the defensive bunkers along the western perimeter; the other struck dangerously close to the ramp, showering sand and light shrapnel over several of the PBRs moored nearby.

At last silence returned, and only hammering hearts could be heard.

Green Wave

In the summer of 1967, the Navy began looking into the feasibility of conducting river patrol operations in the I Corps Tactical Zone, and decided to deploy a section of PBRs there as a test. On 18 September, the USS *Hunterdon County* (LST-838), pregnant with ten PBRs, arrived at the mouth of Cau Hai Bay some seventeen miles northwest of Da Nang. The mission, named Operation Green Wave, was to conduct patrols in the I Corps rivers and lagoons.

Things did not proceed smoothly at the start. Because the LST could not safely enter the bay, the PBRs had to be unloaded from a position offshore. Heavy swells made the process difficult and frequently dangerous. Once the PBRs got inshore, their lack of familiarity with the area resulted in a number of groundings. Recovering the PBRs after their patrols was equally difficult in the uncooperative surf.

For the first ten days enemy contact was light. Then on the 28th the *Hunterdon County* and her brood moved south to the mouth of the Cua Dai River, approximately eighteen miles southeast of Da Nang. This portion of the operations did not start off well, either. Within three hours of their arrival, four PBRs went to the headquarters of Coastal Group 14 for a briefing before their patrol. At the start of their patrol, while still within 1,000 yards of the coastal group base, a heavy barrage of automatic-weapons fire opened up on the four craft. While withdrawing at high speed, PBR-118 received five hits on the starboard side, which perforated the lube oil filters and caused all of the oil to be lost. Both engines seized up and the craft was put out of commission for a while. One VNN junk sailor who had joined them for the patrol was shot through the buttocks and groin in the engagement.

The next day, at a little before noon, PBRs 54 and 79 were operating about five miles up the river near Hoi An when they received twenty rounds of rifle-grenade and about two hundred rounds of automatic-weapons fire. One of the soldiers was killed when a bullet passed through his flak jacket and struck him behind the left ear; another sailor was wounded. Enemy casualties were unknown.

Three hours later, PBRs 53 and 84, patrolling in the same vicinity, were attacked. Calling in a pair of Army helicopters for support, the PBRs counterattacked and destroyed fifteen huts and bunkers. Again enemy casualties were unknown. Later, however, the same two PBRs and their helicopter support engaged a group of enemy sampans and this time confirmed seven VC killed as well as three sampans sunk and one bunker destroyed. No U.S. casualties resulted on this occasion.

On the 29th, fifteen incidents occurred. Commander Task Unit 116.1.3, the on-scene commander, described the day as a "running gun-battle." The next day, patrols of the area ceased. All of the engagements had involved relatively light enemy weaponry. If the enemy were to bring in heavier armament, which was a distinct possibility, severe losses were almost certain to occur.

On 7 October Operation Green Wave was terminated; the *Hunterdon County* packed up her PBRs and went "home" to the Mekong Delta. A COMNAVFORV report said:

An immediate analysis of the operation revealed that navigational hazards restricted the PBR speed and maneuverability; intense enemy ground threat precludes proper waterway traffic control by the PBRs; and the grounding and battle damage to 50 percent of the 10-boat task unit precludes sustained operations. Therefore, it was recommended that I Corps PBR deployment be terminated due to unproductive traffic control and heavy enemy weapons and fortifications against which the PBR was not designed to stand.

Perfume and Cua Viet

After the less than spectacular results of Operation Green Wave, it appeared that I Corps had seen the last of the PBRs. But subsequent events were to dictate otherwise.

All U.S. forces in the two northernmost provinces of South Vietnam, Quang Tri and Thua Thien, were supported logistically by the Commander Naval Support Activity, Da Nang. The vast majority of supplies destined for the forces in these two provinces traveled by water from Da Nang up the coast and then inland by river. In Thua Thien Province the supplies were transported up the Perfume River (Huong Giang in Vietnamese—so called because of the fragrance of lotus blossoms that pervades the air there); in Quang Tri it was the Cua Viet River that served as the inland supply route. The enemy did not fail to recognize the military significance of these routes and took advantage of the narrowness of the rivers by planting mines in them and setting up frequent ambushes along their banks.

In response to this threat, General Lewis W. Walt, commanding general of the III Marine Amphibious Force, asked MACV early in 1967 to assign Navy patrol craft to these two rivers to provide protection for the vital logistics traffic. The Navy was reluctant to meet this request because it would mean drawing sorely needed craft away from the Mekong Delta, but they recognized its importance and made plans to accommodate the request. A PBR Mobile Support Base was created by nesting a number of ammi-pontoon barges together and building makeshift repair, berthing, messing, and communications facilities on them. PBR Division 55 was formed and sent north, including the same section of PBRs that had earlier ventured into I Corps during Operation Green Wave.

The units gathered at Tan My on the Perfume and commenced patrols on the river and nearby lagoons on 9 January 1968. Initially, contact was light, but when the Tet Offensive began on 31 January, the PBRs got into the thick of things. A call from personnel at the supply off-loading ramp in Hue said an attack was under way. Eight PBRs charged up the river in response and met heavy rocket, mortar, and small-arms fire when they arrived. They made repeated firing runs on the enemy positions on the north bank of the river opposite the ramp until they suppressed the hostile fire. They held the VC at bay until that evening, when Marines were able to move in and secure the area. The PBRs continued security patrols around Hue for the next several days.

Meanwhile, the overall situation in I Corps had been worsening. As 1967 drew to a close, General Westmoreland had sent his deputy, General Creighton Abrams, to Phu Bai, a military base near Hue, where he could monitor and react to developments more efficiently. When the now-famous siege at Khe Sanh began in the latter part of January, General Abrams reemphasized the need for naval support on the rivers, particularly the Cua Viet. Essential supplies bound for Khe Sanh were traveling up the river to Dong Ha, where they were then airlifted the rest of the way into Khe Sanh. With the eyes of the world focused on this highland outpost, security on the Cua Viet became more important than ever.

In response to General Abrams's request, COMNAVFORV established Task Force Clearwater as a formal command under Captain G. W. Smith on 24 February, incorporating elements already on the scene at Tan My and initiating plans for more units to be sent north for the Cua Viet contingent. Since the VNN base at the mouth of the Cua Viet was frequently under North Vietnamese artillery attack from across the nearby DMZ, and heavy ambushes on the Cua Viet were becoming more and more frequent, COMNAVFORV decided to detach the armored craft of River Assault Division 112 from the Mobile Riverine Force and send them north instead of an additional contingent of the more vulnerable PBRs. The ASPBs from River Assault Division 112 were left behind in the delta, but the ATCs, monitors, and CCB all went and were on station by March.

Commander Task Force Clearwater issued an operation order setting up his organization. He divided the force into two task groups. One, responsible for providing security along the Cua Viet River from its mouth to the supply terminus at Dong Ha, was named the Dong Ha River Security Group. The other, whose area of responsibility was the Perfume River and surrounding waterways as far upriver as the City of Hue, was named the Hue River Security Group. (Unlike other Navy task organizations, Clearwater was never assigned a numerical designation. For its entire existence it remained simply Task Force Clearwater, and its two subordinate task groups retained their unorthodox names as well.) The Dong Ha River Security Group consisted of the ten ATCs, three monitors, and one CCB of River Assault Division 112, while the River Security Group was made up of Mobile Base 1, ten PBRs, and five LCM-6s that had been locally converted into minesweepers.

For administrative purposes the chain of command went from Commander Task Force Clearwater to COMNAVFORV, but operationally Commander Task Force Clearwater reported directly to COMUSMACV (Forward), the post created by General Abrams's move to Phu Bai in late 1967. (In March 1968, COMUSMACV (Forward) changed its name to Provisional Corps Vietnam and, in the summer of that same year, changed again to XXIV Corps. Commander Task Force Clearwater moved his primary headquarters on 29 February from Tan My to Cua Viet, where it remained until Clearwater was disbanded. The assembled staff of Clearwater consisted of Navy, Army, and Marine Corps personnel. The force itself was augmented by Army helicopter support, an Army signal (communications) detachment, and Marines from a searchlight battery, assigned to man 24-inch xenon gas infrared searchlights that had been mounted on seven LCPLs subsequently assigned to the Dong Ha River Security Group for surveillance patrols at night.

Once established, the task groups patrolled and escorted convoys. On the Cua Viet, the action was heavy right from the start. A large ambush hit one of the early convoys two miles northeast of Dong Ha, killing the convoy commander, a Navy lieutenant, and wounding four other Navy men. A few days later, an ATC hit a sizable mine that flipped the 66-ton craft upside down, causing extensive damage, severely wounding one crew member, and killing six others. And so it went for the Dong Ha River Security Group convoys. Rocket, mortar, and artillery attacks against the base at Cua Viet and against Dong Ha were also frequent.

Once the fury of the Tet Offensive had subsided, the presence of large numbers of American forces in the area kept the situation on the Perfume River quiet for a while. Occa-

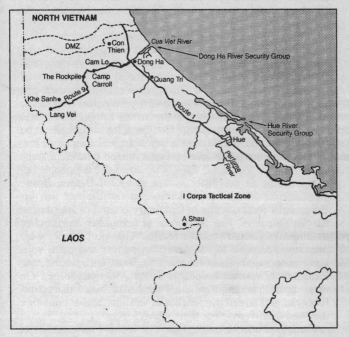

Task Force Clearwater

sional attacks on the river and at the ramp in Hue kept the river security group from ever letting down their guard, however. By June the area around Hue and along the Perfume River proper was largely pacified, so Commander Task Force Clearwater obtained permission from his Army boss to expand the mission of his forces into a wider and more diversified patrol effort similar to the Game Warden mission in the delta.

The Hue River Security Group forces began to conduct a variety of operations in the waterways and lagoons that connected with the Perfume River, including troop insertion and coordinated operations with elements of the Army's 101st Airborne Division, cordon and search scenarios, medical and dental aid visits to the villages, and psychological operations. In line with the latter category, an astute intelligence officer recognized that the people of Hue consider the dragon to be powerful and honorable, so the psychological operations material passed out in the area carried a dragon symbol, and the PBRs flew dragon's-head flags. Consequently, the people began referring to the PBRs as *Tau Rong,* or Dragon Boats. This, combined with the aid missions and the fact that the Communist forces, while in temporary control of Hue during the Tet Offensive, had massacred at least three thousand of its citizens, yielded positive results. The local people were primarily receptive to the American patrols and often willingly cooperated. Even on the Cua Viet farther north, the local people seemed hospitable to the American forces. On many occasions, children along the banks hailed the patrolling craft and turned over caches of weapons and ammunition they had discovered near their villages.

Continued attacks on the Cua Viet led to a reevaluation of Clearwater's response capability. The analysts decided that the speed of PBRs was more important in responding to attacks than was the armor of the Mobile Riverine Force craft in protecting the boats from damage. Consequently, they requested more PBRs. Ten PBRs taken from the Rung Sat Special Zone arrived to join the Dong Ha River Security Group, five in May and five in June. With the arrival of these additional craft, most of the River Assault Division 112 craft were detached to return to operations in the delta. Six ATCs temporarily remained with the group to serve as minesweepers until five LCM-6s could be locally transfigured for the mine-sweeping role.

Also in June, an earlier request for more assets for Clearwater was answered by the arrival of the Navy's three PACVs. Having proven themselves to be of little real value in Game Warden and Market Time because of their limitation on narrow waterways or in the open sea, and having had the most success in the open environment of the Plain of Reeds during Operation Monster, the PACVs had the potential to fare well in the lagoons of the Hue River Security Group's operational area. Indeed, the strange craft worked well as part of Clearwater. The environment of lagoons, rice paddies, and salt flats in the Hue area was ideal for the PACVs. They worked exceptionally well in conjunction with ground forces, able to pursue fleeing enemy troops no matter what combination of land-water escape route they tried. They also performed well for medical evacuation and emergency troop extraction. The Navy's PACVs continued to function as part of Clearwater until mid-1969, when they were slated for retirement. So well had they performed that the Army replaced them with air-cushion vehicles of their own.

As time went on, the efforts of Clearwater, coupled with sweeps by the Army and Marine ground forces in the region, virtually eliminated the ambush threat from the banks of either river. But enemy mining continued, so minesweeping assets in addition to the LCM-6s were incorporated into Clearwater, including MSMs, an LCM-6 conversion that had previously served in the Rung Sat as part of Mine Division 113, and MSBs. In late 1969, two of the MSMs were outfitted with a mine-hunting sonar, called Shadowgraph, that was capable of locating mines in the rivers.

Task Force Clearwater remained in service for several years, fighting to keep the vital I Corps rivers open. The enemy continued to mine, and Clearwater forces continued to sweep, patrol, and escort. Then in June 1970, in a relieving ceremony, the Vietnamese Navy assumed the mission of Clearwater and the Americans were reassigned in Vietnam or went home.

In a 1971 article, Commander R. L. Schreadley wrote a fitting tribute to the men who served in Clearwater:

During the long months of the northeast monsoon the climate is probably the country's worst, with cold, grey and rainy days following each other in seemingly endless succession. Outside the river mouth[s], there are restless shoals and a pounding surf. Some of the unsung heroes of this war are the captains who guided low-powered and frequently age-weakened ships and craft through the treacherous white water of the . . . hazardous channels in northern I Corps. . . .

The men at Cua Viet lived little better than moles in heavily bunkered huts burrowed down among the sand dunes. When the rain stopped falling, the sand, fine-grained and gritty, began to blow, accumulating in drifts before the huts, sifting through screens and under doors, finding its way into lockers and between sheets and even into the food the men ate.

In October 1968, a program was initiated to gradually rotate all Cua Viet personnel back to Da Nang or Tan My, to ensure that no one would be required to spend more than six months at the advanced base. It is a tribute to the splendid morale of our sailors, and their sense of sharing in what was in many ways a unique drama, that many volunteered to stay on and finish their tours at Cua Viet.

Postscripts

The mission of Task Force Clearwater never did go away. American forces continued the patrols, sweeps, troop insertions and withdrawals, and escort duties until June 1970, when they turned the assets and the mission over to the VNN. Throughout their tenure, the American sailors, Marines, and soldiers carried out their unheralded task in the face of sudden death or maiming by the lurking mines, frequent artillery barrages, and ever-present sapper units. Their existence as an operational unit is rarely acknowledged in the Vietnam War literature, but their mission was an important one and their conduct under fire was above reproach. The names of those who died are carved in black granite, yet they, like so many whose deeds or passing do not catch the myopic eye of their countrymen, are relegated to the obscurity of collective sacrifice.

Commander Swarztrauber went on to command the USS *Decatur* (DDG-31) and ultimately retired from the Navy as a rear admiral. He received his Ph.D. in international studies from American University, has written extensively, and is currently the superintendent of the Maine Maritime Academy.

6
SEA LORDS

The New Strategy
(Task Force 194)

Come not between the dragon and his wrath.

—SHAKESPEARE, *King Lear*

ZWI

The Navy Seawolf helicopter descended toward the waiting deck of the USS *Benewah,* its whirling rotor blades sending shimmering ripples across the brown surface of the river in a pattern that seemed to emanate from the dark green hull of the ship. As the helicopter touched down, Captain Robert S. Salzer, Commander Task Force 117, led the greeting party toward the still shuddering aircraft. The helicopter's side sliding-door was already open, and from it emerged a young-looking vice admiral, the three silver stars on each of his collar points glinting. On this day in September 1968, Vice Admiral Elmo R. Zumwalt, Jr., was about to take the helm as COMNAVFORV and had come to the Mobile Riverine Force flagship for an orientation visit.

Captain Salzer led the admiral into the *Benewah*'s cool interior. After an exchange of pleasantries the briefing began—not merely a summary of operations but an appeal from Captain Salzer for a change in strategy. He felt that the "search and destroy" concept that had been employed by the force was losing its effectiveness. Other Navy assets around the delta seemed effective in their assigned missions, but those missions were too limited in scope. He urged an interdiction campaign that would hurt the enemy more.

Captain Salzer had correctly guessed that his appeal would not fall upon deaf ears. Admiral Zumwalt was known for his innovativeness and his willingness to take a calculated risk. He himself recognized his unusual approach and often sent some of his unorthodox proposals to his staff members flagged with the large capital letters "ZWI," which stood for "Zumwalt's Wild Idea."

Even before arriving in Vietnam, the admiral had been contemplating a number of strategic changes, so Captain Salzer's briefing added fuel to the fire. The briefings Zumwalt had received at CINCPAC and CINCPACFLT headquarters in Hawaii had described what seemed to him to be an under-utilized force. The Navy was some 38,000 strong in South

Vietnam, yet did not seem to be playing a proportionate role in the overall war effort.

Captain Rex Rectanus, the COMNAVFORV assistant chief of staff for intelligence, had kindled the fire. He had been analyzing the enemy's logistics system. Confirming what the Bucklew Report had predicted back in 1964, he concluded that Cambodia had become a major enemy supply depot. He had also briefed the admiral that supplies were coming in across the Cambodian border and traveling along a network of tributary waterways deep into the delta. Market Time had effectively inhibited major infiltration from the sea and Game Warden had pretty well denied the enemy free use of the major rivers, but there were still many small waterways through every region of the delta that the enemy could use.

When Captain Salzer's briefing was over, Admiral Zumwalt climbed back into the helicopter. He sat on his flak jacket, which was lying on the seat where he had left it, and strapped himself in. His flag secretary, Lieutenant Howard Kerr, smiled at his boss: the admiral, like many of the GIs in Vietnam, felt that sitting on a flak jacket in a helicopter made more sense than wearing one in the normal fashion.

The helicopter lifted off. Zumwalt, characteristically, pulled out paper and pen and began to write, despite the vibration of the aircraft. As he flew back to Saigon, his mind was made up. The input from his staff and subordinates, such as Rectanus and Salzer, had confirmed what he had believed for some time. It was time for a change, time for a "ZWI."

Shortly after returning to Saigon, Admiral Zumwalt called his senior commanders and staff members together to work out the details of the new strategy, which he had named SEA LORDS, for South-East Asia Lake, Ocean, River, and Delta Strategy. The admiral began by pointing out that brown-water warfare was unsupported and likewise unencumbered by established doctrine. It was necessary, he said, to use ingenuity and improvisation. "You have to make up riverine warfare as you go along," he told them. He also described his belief that the best way to keep the enemy off balance was to "keep changing the game plan," adding that "you can get away with almost anything once or even twice, but you must change strategies frequently in order to keep the enemy from exploiting you.''

Admiral Zumwalt was aware that the U.S. Navy at this time was at peak strength in South Vietnam. The Coastal Surveillance Force numbered 81 Swift Boats, 24 Coast Guard WPBs, and 39 assorted other vessels; the River Patrol Force had 258 craft and 25 helicopters; and the Mobile Riverine Force consisted of 184 assault craft. Captain Rectanus's briefers had pointed out that the Tet Offensive earlier that year had proven that the enemy was still getting significant logistics support in the delta despite the efforts of Market Time, Game Warden, and the Mobile Riverine Force. There was little question that the enemy's activities had been greatly restricted by the efforts of these three task forces, but until the routes from Cambodia could be closed off, the Navy's effectiveness would not be complete. Evidence had accumulated that enemy supplies were entering South Vietnam west of Chau Phu (where the Bassac crosses into Vietnam from Cambodia), across the Plain of Reeds, and in the Parrot's Beak region (an area west of Saigon where the Cambodian border makes a deep penetration into what is otherwise South Vietnamese territory).

Another problem was that there were a number of regions in the delta where there was little or no allied presence and, consequently, the Viet Cong were in virtual control. The U Minh Forest along the southern part of the western coast and the Nam Can area of the Ca Mau Peninsula were such areas.

During his indoctrination tour around Vietnam, Zumwalt had come to realize that morale was ebbing among many of the Navy people there because they were no longer playing the active role they once had. The enemy had been driven from the major rivers and infiltration attempts through the Market Time barrier were infrequent, so these men who had once been in direct contact with the enemy now found themselves in a holding operation. Yet it was clear that the war was not won, so their frustration was growing. The only way to remedy this problem, and to simultaneously achieve the strategic objective of cutting off the flow of men and supplies from North Vietnam, was to once again carry the fight to the enemy. Just as Game Warden, Market Time, and the Mobile Riverine Force had once challenged the enemy in his previously uncontested domain, it was time again to take the initiative, to go "in harm's way."

The new strategy that evolved included a consolidation of a number of elements from each of the three existing task forces to create a new task force, which would be used to form an interdiction barrier across the upper reaches of the Mekong Delta extending eastward as far as the Parrot's Beak region. This barrier would be intensive and would close off, or at least seriously hamper, the flow of supplies from Cambodia. Game Warden and Market Time would continue their respective operations, but Market Time would be reduced somewhat in order to permit some of its craft to come up into the rivers for patrols, which would in turn release a sizable number of PBRs for the new operations being planned. Because the Mobile Riverine Force had been gradually winding down its operations in preparation for turnover to the Vietnamese, significant portions of its assets could be peeled off for use in SEA LORDS operations.

Another new task for the Market Time PCFs and WPBs was to be hit-and-run raids into rivers and canals in VC-held territory. Captain Roy Hoffman, then Commander Task Force 115, had already set the precedent for this by sending some of his craft on missions of this nature. Earlier that month, in the Ca Mau Peninsula, three PCFs had gone seven miles up the Ong Doc River and then four miles down a connecting canal into an enemy stronghold known as "VC Lake." The Swifts had roared into the enemy base, creating havoc among the enemy forces, as well as destroying more than a hundred base structures and dozens of sampans. This aggressiveness typified the Zumwalt posture of keeping the enemy off balance and not allowing him the security of certain regions that he had traditionally enjoyed. It was decided to incorporate such raids into the SEA LORDS concept and to conduct them wherever there was enough water to float the American craft.

Admiral Zumwalt had been so impressed with Captain Salzer's grasp of the situation in the delta and his suggested changes in strategy that he assigned the captain the task of developing the details of SEA LORDS and gave him overall command of the operation, designating him "First Sea Lord." (Zumwalt had deliberately picked his title, recognizing that the Royal Navy's equivalent to Chief of Naval Operations had long been called First Sea Lord. What he had not anticipated, however, was that the crossovers in allied communication circuits somehow permitted Mekong Delta message traffic to be routed to England, where the "First Sea Lord" title apparently caused some temporary confusion.)

When the concept was fully developed and Salzer had composed an operation plan delineating the strategy and its various responsibilities, he and Zumwalt took it on a Sunday morning to General Creighton Abrams, then COMUSMACV and Admiral Zumwalt's immediate superior. The general approved with the one requirement that it be acceptable to the senior advisor of IV Corps Tactical Zone. The two naval officers then flew down to see Major General George S. Eckhardt to get his concurrence, and once that was accomplished, SEA LORDS was officially set into motion with the issuance of Operation Plan 111-69 on 5 November 1968.

"Bernique's Creek"

The barrier that the planners of SEA LORDS had envisioned would ideally have been placed right along the Cambodian border, but as Commander Richard L. Schreadley, COMNAVFORV special assistant (1969-70), wrote in 1970:

> . . . the expected heavy risk of real or contrived border incidents dictated against the positioning of a SEA LORDS barrier there until the concept was tested and proved in a less sensitive area. It was decided, therefore, that two parallel canals some thirty-five and forty miles removed from the border to the southeast—the Rach Gia di Long Xuyen and the Cai San—would be used to form a double barrier and inaugurate the SEA LORDS interdiction campaign.

This initial operation was named "Search Turn" and commenced on 2 November 1968. The canal system Commander Schreadley described connects the city of Rach Gia, on the Gulf of Thailand coast, with the inland delta city of Long

Xuyen, on the west bank of the Bassac River. Salzer later described his intentions as "First Sea Lord":

> . . . as near as we could see . . . supplies were coming into what used to be called Sihanoukville [now Kompong Som] and coming down the Gulf of Siam [Thailand] coast about 10-20 miles inland through a canal network. We had a foothold in the town of Rach Gia and no control above that at all. What I wanted to do was to make a probe or a strike down the canal network . . . to establish a series of outposts along that river-canal network first, then spread it up to the north.

The operation began with a five-day assault on enemy positions along the waterway using Mobile Riverine Force craft and ground troops. Sizable quantities of arms and ammunition were captured, lending credibility to the assumption that this area was being used for infiltration, and twenty-one enemy soldiers were killed. After the assault phase, naval patrols were established along the main canals and were extended into many of the adjoining smaller waterways.

While encouraging, the early returns on Search Turn were not spectacular. Supplies were in fact running through the area, but to be successful the interdiction would have to be extended across the delta to the Parrot's Beak region. While plans were being formulated for that extension, a spontaneous occurrence caused a shift in strategy.

On 14 October, Lieutenant (j.g.) Michael Bernique, officer in charge of one of the Market Time PCFs, had his craft in Ha Tien (on the Gulf of Thailand very near the Cambodian border) to give his crew a rest from the rigors of patrol. While he was there, some friendly Vietnamese told him that the Viet Cong had established a tax-collecting station a few miles up the Rach Giang Thanh, a small river that had been declared off limits to U.S. Navy patrol craft because of its proximity to the politically sensitive Cambodian border. Bernique reasoned that these were extenuating circumstances and chose to violate the prohibition. He got under way and headed up the forbidden waterway.

A short time later, Bernique's PCF rounded a bend and saw a group of complacent VC openly running the tax collection station. The enemy soldiers were so startled to see an American patrol craft on the prohibited river that they were at first unable to react. Bernique immediately took the initiative. He opened fire, killing three and scattering the others in a panic. The fleeing VC left behind weapons, ammunition, supplies, and documents, which Bernique's men confiscated. Meanwhile, the VC had regrouped and returned to renew the contest. In a brief but vicious firefight, two more enemy died while the Americans stood their ground. Eventually, Bernique retired from the scene with his captured equipment and documents, only to be headed into a different kind of battle.

A furor erupted over Bernique's violation of the ban on the Rach Giang Thanh, and it appeared that he was facing a court-martial for his actions. Called to Saigon for questioning, he was ordered upon his arrival to appear before COMNAVFORV himself. Admiral Zumwalt and several of his staff listened to the young lieutenant's explanation of his actions and his colorful description of the battle. During the interrogation one of the officers told Bernique that Prince Sihanouk of Cambodia had accused him of firing into Cambodia and killing innocent civilians. Bernique turned to the officer and said, "Well, you tell Sihanouk he's a lying son-of-a-bitch." At the end of the interrogation, the admiral decided that Bernique was "the kind of captain we need more of" and chose to award him the Silver Star rather than a court-martial. From then on, the Rach Giang Thanh became known as "Bernique's Creek" among Navy men in Vietnam.

Adhering to his principle that "you can get away with almost anything once or twice," Admiral Zumwalt decided to follow up on Bernique's incursion into the Rach Giang Thanh by making a second incursion. This time it would be a planned operation and would test the feasibility of American naval forces transiting the entire length of "Bernique's Creek" and the adjoining Vinh Te Canal. If this operation succeeded, it would permit the establishment of a second barrier from Ha Tien to Chao Duc parallel to and northward of the one created by Operation Search Turn. This second barrier would extend allied control and interdict enemy logistics operations much closer to the border with Cambodia.

On the morning of 16 November, three PCFs and a Seawolf fire team of two helicopters began the operation. Their orders were to enter "Bernique's Creek" at Ha Tien, then proceed upstream (roughly northeast) to the junction of the Vinh Te Canal and follow it (east, then northeast) to the city of Chau Duc, on the west bank of the Bassac River. The journey would keep them within a mile of the Cambodian border throughout (at several points, much closer) and would take them through marshes, swamps, dense forests, and a rugged area known as the Seven Mountains. They would pass scattered hamlets of questionable allegiance and would cross several known and many suspected enemy supply routes. Their mission was to engage enemy forces in the area, disrupt enemy supply lines, board and search suspicious vessels, and reconnoiter the area. The lead Swift in the three-boat task group was none other than Lieutenant (j.g.) Michael Bernique's.

Early in the journey, the group was told by local villagers that the VC had established two tax-collection stations at points farther upstream. Less than half an hour later, Bernique's craft approached the first point described by the villagers. As promised, a group of armed men was sighted and a firefight followed. At the second location, the same thing occurred. In both cases, the enemy soldiers were driven off. The rest of the journey was uneventful, but in the aftermath Bernique found himself once again in the midst of a political tempest. The International Control Commission had received a formal protest from the Cambodian government stating that the armed men Bernique had engaged had not been Viet Cong but were members of a Cambodian paramilitary group known as the Khmer Kampuchea Kron (KKK). The protest charged that ten of these bandits had been killed and that ten "South Vietnamese women of Cambodian origin" in a large sampan had also been killed by the Americans.

A subsequent investigation, however, revealed that the charges had been false: the local KKK leader was found and he denied that his men had been slain, insisting instead that they were in fact VC; film taken during the firefights did not support the charges; and no bodies or other evidence of the slain women could be produced. It was deduced that the incident had been concocted by the Communists to try to prevent the establishment of the new barrier—a measure of the enemy's concern about this new strategic move. Despite the political sensitivity of the operation, COMUSMACV agreed with COMNAVFORV that the barrier should be established and maintained. To do otherwise would not only have given up a newly discovered strategic advantage, it would have meant a serious loss of credibility for the allies in this already touchy region of South Vietnam.

Named at first Operation Foul Deck and later renamed Tran Hung Dao (after a thirteenth-century Vietnamese hero similar in stature to the American Navy's John Paul Jones) when VNN participation became more significant, the barrier became the second most active (in terms of enemy contact) of the four established as part of SEA LORDS. Maintained by a combination of PCFs, PBRs, and ASPBs, the operation kept a naval presence on the waterways for all but the two months of the year when the water level dropped below that necessary to sustain the craft. Large captures of enemy contraband; high enemy casualties, defections, and captures; and increased mining and ambush attempts by enemy forces were strong indicators of the success of the barrier operation. Intelligence gathered from defectors and prisoners supported the analysis that the operation never completely shut off the infiltration, but it very seriously hampered it. Foul Deck/Tran Hung Dao I continued for several years, eventually being assimilated by the VNN as part of the Vietnamization process. "Bernique's Creek" eventually became the Rach Giang Thanh once again as the American presence faded away, but one man's boldness had had its effect.

Giant Slingshot and Barrier Reef

Since enemy supplies were entering South Vietnam from many points along the Cambodian border, any attempt at establishing an effective barrier was going to have to extend across the entire upper region of the delta, from the Gulf of Thailand to the region west of Saigon known as the "Parrot's Beak." Because this latter geographic feature projects deeply into Vietnam and comes within twenty-five miles of the capital city of Saigon, the Parrot's Beak was an ideal area for infiltration by enemy forces. Navy planners noted, however, that they had their own geographical asset in the region. The

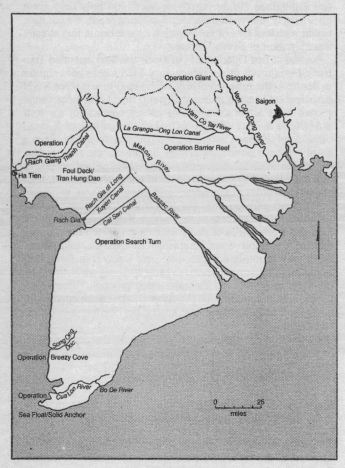

Sea Lords

Vam Co River, which flows south of Saigon, joining the Soi Rap in the Rung Sat Special Zone, is fed by two tributaries, the Vam Co Tay (west) and Vam Co Dong (east). These two tributaries, both navigable by patrol craft, form a V that surrounds the Parrot's Beak. So it was natural to set up a barrier using the Vam Co Tay and Vam Co Dong to contain the Parrot's Beak. Because, when viewed on a map, the two tributaries and the main river together look very much like a slingshot, this barrier operation was named Giant Slingshot.

By early December 1968, Captain Salzer had been relieved as First Sea Lord by Rear Admiral W. H. House. The SEA LORDS organization was formally designated as Task Force 194 and Giant Slingshot as Task Group 194.9. Captain Arthur W. Price, Jr., then commander of the River Patrol Forces (Commander Task Force 116), was also Commander Task Group 194.9 in charge of the Giant Slingshot operation. In order to make the operation a joint one, Captain Price asked the VNN to provide an officer to serve as his assistant; the VNN complied.

Captain Price broke off three PBR divisions (of ten boats each) from his Game Warden forces to serve in the Giant Slingshot campaign. He was given a River Assault Division, a YRBM, and an ARL from the Mobile Riverine Force; an LST was promised as well. He decided to set up his base of operations at Tan An, near the junction of the two tributaries and also the headquarters of the Third Brigade of the U.S. Ninth Infantry Division, which Captain Price hoped to incorporate into some of the Giant Slingshot operations. Realizing that his boats would be moving more than fifty miles up each tributary, he decided to establish small base camps upriver, dubbed ATSBs for Advanced Tactical Support Bases. These were originally at Tra Cu and Hiep Hoa on the Vam Co Dong River and at Tuyen Nhon and Moc Hoa on the Vam Co Tay. ATSBs were later established at Go Dau Ha and Ben Keo, further north on the Vam Co Dong. In a December 1970 article, Lieutenant Commander Robert C. Powers described the ATSB at Go Dau Ha:

It was here that the "ammi" pontoon proved its worth. Six of these giant pontoons were towed upriver, through Blood Alley to Go Dau Ha, laden with supplies and tents.

These pontoons were moored on the east bank of the river, and a temporary base was erected on them. The standard of living began to go up as generators, reefers [refrigerators], electric stoves, and a liberal supply of steaks were brought in by truck, helicopter, and also boats. . . .

ATSB Go Dau Ha suffered rocket and mortar attacks, ground probes, sniper fire, and minings, but each attack was repulsed by the fire of the base and the boats stationed there. . . . Stand-off rocket fences were built beyond the perimeter to pre-detonate incoming rounds. A large chain link fence was erected along the north side of the bridge to prevent a Honda-mounted sapper from dropping a satchel charge on the base as he crossed the bridge. Trip flares and claymore mines were also installed. And, the Viet Cong found that the Navy had come to stay.

The YRBM and *Askari* were situated near Tan An; the *Harnett County* was brought upriver to Ben Luc. These vessels provided support facilities for the boats operating on the Vam Co Tay and Vam Co Dong, respectively. The *Harnett County*'s vulnerability to attack while in the narrow river was a matter of great concern to CINCPACFLT. To reduce the risk, Admiral Zumwalt directed all available personnel in the area to chop down the foliage within a two-thousand-yard radius of the ship.

On 5 December 1968, Captain Price sent a message to First Sea Lord and COMNAVFORV:

YRBM-18 ARRIVED TAN AN 051700 H DECEMBER 1968, CTG 194.9 EMBARKED. . . . MOVEMENT OF BOAT ASSETS A THING OF BEAUTY WITH ALL UNITS ARRIVING WITHIN MINUTES OF YRBM AT TAN AN. RON [remain overnight] FOR ALL BOAT UNITS AT TAN AN WITH MOVEMENT TO SECONDARY SITES AND COMMENCEMENT OF PATROL OPERATIONS SCHEDULED FOR 060800 H.

Giant Slingshot was under way.

The next evening an Army helicopter was flying a surveillance mission along the Vam Co Dong River when it was fired upon from the ground. The pilot called in two PBRs of the newly deployed Giant Slingshot force to investigate. The two boats received heavy machine-gun fire from the riverbanks. They returned the fire and, in a second pass at the firing positions, silenced them. There were no friendly casualties. The next day, 7 December, two more enemy-initiated firefights erupted. Three firefights in two days was a higher rate of combat activity than was normally experienced by the PBRs on Game Warden. It was a portent of things to come.

By the 14th of the month, the first members of Giant Slingshot had been killed in action. Two PBRs from River Division 534 were ambushed that afternoon about eight miles north of Tra Cu on the Vam Co Dong. Intense rocket and machine-gun fire engulfed the two craft, wounding six of the crewmen; one of them, a second class boatswain's mate, later died of his wounds. At the end of the month, the first naval officer was killed in Giant Slingshot.

Firefights became so frequent in Giant Slingshot that a new argot emerged to speed up the report-writing process. An ENIFF was an enemy-initiated firefight and a FRIFF was a friendly-initiated firefight, while an ENENG represented a contact with the enemy in which fire had been initiated by the enemy but had not been returned by friendly forces and a FRENG was the converse.

ENIFFs on the Vam Co Dong between Tra Cu and Go Dau Ha were so frequent that this stretch of the river became known as "Blood Alley." Some of the heaviest fighting and consequently the highest casualty rates of the war for the Navy occurred during Giant Slingshot. The total number of ENIFFs and FRIFFs for this one operation was more than double that of all the other operations combined. Over a thousand firefights occurred during the 515 days of the operation, an average of two per day.

This heavy combat activity proved that the enemy was in the area and that he considered the naval interdiction a threat to his activities. Any doubts that might have been harbored concerning the enemy's use of Cambodia as a logistics staging area and the Parrot's Beak as an entry point were shattered by this operation, which uncovered 266 supply caches totaling nearly 150 tons of ammunition and approximately 400 tons of other war supplies.

With the operation less than a month old, two more PBR River Divisions were added, bringing the total to five. As other assets became available to the VNN through Vietnamization, more VNN craft and personnel joined Giant Slingshot. This high ratio of craft to area of operations led to the use and further development of a nighttime tactic that had been used to a lesser extent by Game Warden forces. It began as the "waterborne ambush" and, as the posture of the war took on a more defensive look, eventually was euphemistically changed to the "waterborne guard post." The tactic relied on stealth rather than speed and was remarkably effective. It also effectively turned the tables on the enemy, using what had long been his primary tactic in the water war. Instead of noisily patrolling up and down the waterways, as the Game Warden forces had done because of their low craft-to-area-of-operations ratio, the boats would conceal themselves along the riverbank and wait for the enemy to come to them. The Vam Co tributaries were well suited to this tactic because of the heavy foliage along their banks. The large number of craft permitted a fairly dense distribution of waterborne guard posts along the waterways, and the high level of enemy activity ensured frequent contact.

Various tactics were employed to secretly deploy these waterborne guard posts. Sometimes one craft would tow a second, cutting it loose along the way to drift quietly into the bank, thereby not alerting the enemy to the sudden reduction in engine noise. Another method, requiring a little more finesse, was called the "sync." This was accomplished by one of two boats gradually increasing the throttle on one engine and easing back on the other. This put the two engine sounds out of synchronization; if the other craft cut its engines off at the right moment, the sounds from the first would simulate those of two different craft. The quieted craft could then drift silently into the foliage and wait to spring the trap. The waterborne guard posts yielded excellent results. Intelligence sources indicated not only that they cost the enemy when contact was made, but that even when the posts were not around, fear of them caused him to be more cautious, which slowed him down considerably.

An extrapolation of the waterborne guard posts was a tactic called "Bushwhack Ops," which began in May 1969. A platoon of U.S. Army soldiers would be divided in two and carried in two boats to the assigned area, where they would debark and move two hundred yards inland. There they would set up an ambush for enemy troops passing by. This deployment enhanced the probability of contact, increased the overall firepower and flexibility of the ambush, gave the boats some warning of the approaching enemy, and provided the soldiers with a means of quick extraction or redeployment if necessary. It was a symbiotic relationship for the Army and the Navy personnel involved, and resulted in a substantial increase in contacts and subsequent kills.

"Bushwhack" was not the only interaction between Army and Navy during Giant Slingshot. In January 1969 the Army's First Air Cavalry division conducted operations in the Slingshot area and coordinated with the Navy on numerous occasions. In early February the Army provided troops for a four-day joint operation called "Keel Haul" that yielded little enemy contact. The operation concentrated a large number of boats in the "Blood Alley" sector, with soldiers on board to respond to contacts. Later in the same month, Operation Keel Haul II had slightly better results by dedicating thirty-five air-mobile troops to stand ready for a quick response if the boats made contact, but the Army did not feel that the results justified the troop commitment, so the effort was short-lived. In March, Navy craft began working with Long Range Reconnaissance Patrol personnel, inserting them for patrols and retrieving them days later at a predetermined rendezvous. In mid-April, Eagle Flat Ops began. These were similar to Mobile Riverine Force tactics in that Army troops were inserted in company strength and the boats would serve as a blocking force for the subsequent sweep. Again, the results did not justify the expenditure. In May, River Assault Squadron 13 and the VNN River Assault and Interdiction Division 70 worked in conjunction with the U.S. 199th Light Infantry Brigade and elements of the South Vietnamese Army in Operation Caesar II. Lasting eight days, it was a cordon-and-search operation that netted enemy dead whose number (depending upon the source reviewed) ranged between fourteen and forty.

All of these mediocre joint operations were at last vindicated in July, when the Army and Navy again teamed up in an operation named Double Shift. Intelligence reports had warned that the Viet Cong were gathering forces for an attack on Tay Ninh, the third largest city in South Vietnam. They were apparently planning to seize control of the city and hold it long enough to declare the establishment of a Communist Provisional Revolutionary Government with its capital at Tay Ninh, hoping that many nations, weary of the conflict in Southeast Asia, would recognize the newly formed government. This would, of course, be a major blow to the integrity of the South Vietnamese government and a propaganda victory for the Viet Cong.

Soldiers of the 25th Infantry Division dug in, and the Navy executed its Double Shift plan. The Giant Slingshot forces at two of the ATSBs in the Tay Ninh vicinity were tripled within twenty-four hours by shifting River Division 513 and 574 from Binh Thuy to Go Dau Ha and River Divisions 532 and 533 from My Tho to Ben Keo. River Assault Division 151 also moved to Ben Keo, and the VNN shifted its River Assault and Interdiction Division 71 to Go Dau Ha. This boosted the total strength at each ATSB to thirty PBRs and approximately twenty assault craft. Reporting the completion of this rapid move, Commander Task Group 194.9 sent the following message to First Sea Lord: "Double Shift completed in double time with doubled units ready to give double trouble."

For the next fifteen days the Double Shift forces conducted roving patrols and established waterborne ambushes on a twenty-four-hour basis with the heaviest concentration at night. This resulted in seventeen ENIFFs, seventy FRIFFs, forty-nine ENENGs and FRENGs, thirty-four enemy killed (confirmed), and ninety enemy structures and craft destroyed. Friendly personnel casualties amounted to eleven wounded; eight friendly craft were damaged. The concentration of craft was able to prevent large numbers of VC forces from crossing the waterways in the area. On the night of 13 July, significant contact was made with the enemy on twelve occasions; on 14 July, eight contacts were made; on 15 July, eleven; and on the 16th, seven. The result was that the enemy was unable to mount the forces needed to launch a coordinated attack on Tay Ninh. The VC plan was aborted and the city spared from attack.

One other Army-Navy operation during Giant Slingshot

bears mention. In one week in November, a long tradition of battle was upheld when Army and Navy helicopters flew over the various Army and Navy bases in the region dropping leaflets that said "Beat Army" or "Beat Navy" as appropriate.

Besides the various Army units that worked with Navy Slingshot elements, Navy SEAL teams frequently gathered intelligence and conducted covert operations. In April 1969 a SEAL platoon was based at Moc Hoa for integrated operations.

Throughout the Vietnam War, research and development played a significant role: such inventions as the starlight scope, the M-79 grenade launcher, and the flight-deck-equipped armored troop carriers were all innovations that were important for combat operations. Operation Giant Slingshot was the scene of testing and implementation of a number of these continuing innovations.

Remote electronic detection devices developed in 1968 were made operational in the Slingshot area. Placed in areas where enemy concentrations or movements were suspected, they would detect movement with a certain radius and permit alerted forces to respond appropriately (often with an artillery barrage, but sometimes by sending in reaction teams of boats, helicopters, troops, et cetera). In March 1970, a *Hoi Chanh* told interrogators that the enemy had great respect for these detectors.

A portable hydrophone with a mile-long wire, the Remote Underwater Detection Device, was used during Slingshot. A squeeze-bore machine gun was also tested: it squeezed .50-caliber ammunition to .30-caliber size as it passed through the weapon, thereby increasing the coverage while reducing the range—an important consideration where enemy forces are operating close to friendly villages. Another device used a special radar signal to detect metal contraband being transported in watercraft, and the "Duval Detector" was designed to detect false bottoms in boats.

"Project Douche" introduced the "Douche Boat," an ATC with two high-pressure pumps installed in the well deck. These supplied water cannons capable of directing 3,000-psi water streams into enemy bunkers to destroy them. They were capable of disintegrating cement.

Operation Giant Slingshot was formally turned over to the

Vietnamese Navy in May 1970 and renamed Operation Tran Hung Dao II. By that time 38 American Navy men had been killed in action and 518 had been wounded. Considering the low number of participants, this casualty rate was extraordinarily high. The total number of wounds received was greater than the number of personnel involved.

The final link in the upper Mekong Delta barrier was forged in January 1969 with the commencement of Operation Barrier Reef. This last barrier ran from Tuyen Nhon on the Vam Co Tay to An Long on the upper Mekong via the La Grange, Ong Lon, and Dong Tien canals. Cutting through the infamous Plain of Reeds, it connected the twin barriers in the west, Foul Deck and Search Turn, with the Parrot's Beak barrier in the east, Giant Slingshot, completing a continuous waterway barrier that extended from Tay Ninh City, northwest of Saigon, to Ha Tien and Rach Gia on the Gulf of Thailand.

The enemy's reaction to this new operation was at first intense; an example appears in the prologue. Four U.S. Navy men were killed and sixteen wounded in the first few weeks of the operation. Ambushes and mining were frequent at first but tapered off markedly as the naval presence took hold. The open terrain of the Plain of Reeds made infiltrations through this area risky for the enemy. Once detected, he had difficulty in withdrawing because of the lack of cover and the long stretch (from six to twenty-one miles) between the barrier and the Cambodian border. So after the initial forays, the enemy backed off somewhat; contacts were less frequent here than on the other barriers.

Despite the lighter activity, Barrier Reef had to be maintained in order to ensure the integrity of the entire barrier. The operation continued into the summer of 1970 and was then gradually taken over by the VNN. Like the other operations, this one was also renamed once under Vietnamese direction. Barrier Reef became Tran Hung Dao IX in August 1970.

Evenings in Vietnam

Heavy black clouds had enshrouded the sky most of the afternoon. As dusk approached, the clouds absorbed the failing light like a sponge. Two PBRs from River Division 593 crawled along close to one bank of the upper Saigon River, their throttled-back engines muttering as they barely made way. Palm fronds drooped in their path as they eased in closer to the muddy bank.

A single raindrop thumped on the awning over the coxswain's flat of the lead boat, soon followed by more as the black clouds released their burden. Their engines cut, the two boats drifted the last few yards into the tangle of vines and fronds along the banks. They were assuming position for a waterborne guard post—a night of waiting that promised to mix boredom and tension in the proportions hardest on the nerves. Like chameleons, the dark green hulls blended into the foliage, and the crews donned their rain gear as the tempo of the storm increased.

Shower became downpour became deluge, and the heavy drops pounded upon the jungle's verdant canopy. The PBR sailors huddled in their ponchos trying to escape the driving rain while perspiration ran down their bodies beneath the plastic. The forward gunner of the cover boat peered miserably through the gloom, wondering if the rain would fall all night or if it would stop later so that the mosquitoes might have a turn at inflicting their own special brand of torture. Suddenly, in the strobing flashes of lightning, his eye caught a movement; his heart slammed in his chest as he realized that it was a North Vietnamese soldier less than thirty yards away. Before he could pass the word he saw a second, and a third, and then he realized that it was a continuous column of soldiers snaking through the vegetation. It seemed impossible that they hadn't seen the PBRs, but their heads were lowered against the rain and they were truly oblivious to the presence of the Americans.

The gunner passed the word to the patrol officer, a chief petty officer, who could see, through the torrents of falling rain, that several columns were moving by, the soldiers' backs bowed under the weight of packs, rocket launchers, and machine guns. The patrol officer estimated their number to be at least eighty.

In response to the chief's orders, the two PBRs simultaneously ignited their engines and backed away from the bank, opening fire at the point-blank targets as they went. Their weapons were soon answered by confused but rapidly increasing fire from both banks of the river. The PBRs dashed into the middle of the stream trying to replace surprise with speed as their tactical advantage. They were evidently in the midst of a major enemy movement. As the North Vietnamese soldiers recovered from the suddenness of the attack, their combined firepower promised to become lethal if the Americans did not do something to keep the odds in their favor.

The patrol officer called for assistance, and as his boats raced along the banks, pouring heavy gunfire into the rain- and blood-spattered foliage, a team of Seawolf helicopters emerged from the curtains of rain and joined the battle. They swooped in low like birds of prey on the hunt, the bright flashes of their machine guns contrasting sharply with the darkness of dusk and storm. Moments later, the battle was joined by Navy OV-10 Black Ponies, and Army artillery rounds were dropping into the enemy positions whenever the aircraft were clear. More PBRs raced to the scene from downriver posts and joined in.

The battle raged for more than two hours. Then, when all return fire seemed to have ceased, the air assets went home and the PBRs remained in the area to watch for more enemy activity; or, as one of the sailors (a damage controlman by rate) put it, "We set a reflash watch."

The next morning, ground troops swept the area and found forty-one enemy soldiers dead in the jungle. The PBRs recovered eight others from the river. There were no friendly casualties.

During the late afternoon of 12 April 1969, eight PCFs carrying 6th Battalion Vietnamese Marines sailed the Duong Keo River en route to a sweep operation as part of Operation Silver Mace II. At 1734, the PCFs in column formation had reached a position four miles upstream from the rivermouth when a large-scale enemy-initiated firefight was unleashed by two Viet Cong companies. The VC detonated two Claymore mines from the northwest bank and followed with intensive B-40 rocket, recoilless rifle, .30- and .50-caliber machine-gun, rifle-grenade, and small-arms fire. PCF-43 was hit by recoilless rifle and B-40 rounds, which disabled her steering gear and fatally wounded the boat's officer in charge. The boat beached at high speed in the center of the ambush, as B-40 rockets continued to smash into her.

Uninjured crewmen and underwater demolition team personnel aboard set up a hasty perimeter around the boat as PCFs 5 and 31 came alongside to assist the stricken PCF while maintaining heavy fire. Seawolf helicopters reacted within five minutes and suppressed the enemy fire with machine-gun fire. All personnel were removed from PCF-43, and PCFs 5 and 31 cleared the area. Shortly after, a fire in PCF-43 reached ammunition stored on board for underwater demolition teams and caused an explosion that destroyed the craft. The final results were three U.S. Navy men killed and thirty-three wounded, and two Vietnamese Marines killed and thirteen wounded. PCF-43 was destroyed, two others were badly damaged, and two more received moderate damage. Enemy losses were eighteen Viet Cong killed.

In the early evening of 6 August 1969, a forward air controller in an Army observation aircraft spotted a number of Viet Cong soldiers running along a small canal off the west bank of the Vam Co Dong River two miles south of Hip Hoa. The controller called in a nearby team of patrolling Seawolves; as they were being vectored to the site, a PBR patrol from River Division 552 headed in as well. After several minor firefights, the Seawolves left to refuel and rearm at a nearby base. Artillery was called in and two more PBR patrols came looking for contact, one carrying an Army Long Range Reconnaissance Patrol team on board.

The team debarked and crept into the tangled green, maintaining silence, communicating by hand signal. Their camouflaged uniforms, mottled faces, stealthy movements, and carefully strapped and taped equipment made them almost impossible to detect. The artillery had been called off for their insertion, so the only sound they could hear was that of the PBRs' engines back in the canal, and that was growing fainter as they went deeper into the vegetation, their trained eyes scanning for clues, their ears selectively tuned for telltale sounds.

Then they heard whispering nearby and saw the telltale swish of moving vegetation, signaling movement in several directions about them. The team placed Claymore mines in a peripheral pattern and then, on signal, opened up on the enemy with the mines and their automatic weapons. The response was more than they had anticipated. The early phase of the battle, with its light contact, had indicated a small enemy force, but now in the thick of things the team found that they had encountered a more potent force. They called the PBRs and began an ordered withdrawal as the PBRs delivered heavy covering fire to their flanks. The explosion of the booby trap shattered their hopes; several men were injured, and the enemy gunfire was intense and building. The reconnaissance team was pinned down.

When apprised of the situation by radio, a number of PBR sailors grabbed their M-16s, M-79s, and first-aid kits and left their boats, charging into the jungle, firing as they went, until they reached the soldiers. Some administered first aid while others fired into the enemy-infested surroundings. The sailors were out of their traditional environment but acquitted themselves well, holding on until the Seawolves came back and turned the tide of battle. Two soldiers were killed and four wounded in the action, but if not for the courage of those PBR sailors, the casualty count would have been far more grim.

The USS *Harnett County,* the nerve-center of Giant Slingshot, rode at anchor near Ben Luc. The night was sultry. Patrols moved cautiously along the banks of the Vam Co Dong; the thump of concussion grenades sown randomly into the furrows of the river seemed muffled and detached like the harassment and interdiction fire of distant artillery.

At a little after midnight a 107-mm rocket emerged from the dark ridge of a paddy dike on the west bank of the river and streaked toward the motionless LST. The round pierced the ship's skin and entered the wardroom, where it struck a reefer in the galley and exploded, spreading shrapnel through the vulnerable interior. The blast and resultant flooding from ruptured piping caused extensive damage. Three Navy men and one civilian were wounded; fortunately no one died.

Two ASPBs settled in for all-night waterborne guard post duty on the Ong Doc River on the evening of 22 November 1969. Only the buzz of mosquitoes and the gentle lap of the river varied the hours of monotony. The sailors sat at their guns fighting off sleep.

When a faint light emerged from the darkness of the nearby Cui Canal, the sailors were flooded with relief and anxiety. The light went out almost immediately, and the patrol officer, using a starlight scope, watched a tiny sampan enter the river from the canal. In the surreal green of the scope the sampan appeared to be crudely camouflaged. In any case, it was out on the water after curfew and had to be presumed an enemy. The two ASPBs got under way, opening fire and illuminating the target. The sampan veered for the opposite bank and beached. One of the occupants scrambled up the bank but was cut off by the heavy fire from the patrol boats. The ASPBs moved in to capture the sampan and its occupants. To the horror of the sailors, the searchlights trained on the tiny craft revealed two children, a teenage girl, and a fifty-year-old woman. All were wounded.

One of the ASPBs rushed the group to a nearby town for treatment by American and Vietnamese medics and evacuation by helicopter to Can Tho. A three-year-old boy and a nineteen-year-old girl had received only minor shrapnel wounds of the head, but an eleven-year-old girl had a compound fracture of the left leg where shrapnel had struck her, and the old woman had lost her left hand.

After dark on 7 June 1970, a VNN patrol craft, PBR-708, was on waterborne guard post duty in the Kin Moi Canal ten miles southeast of Moc Hoa as part of the Barrier Reef operation. A young third-class petty officer, who had been assigned to the VNN River Patrol Group 59 as an advisor, was lying on the PBR's canopy, taking advantage of the comfort it provided.

Two Viet Cong appeared unexpectedly on the east bank of the canal. The VNN patrol officer immediately opened fire and set out in hot pursuit. As the PBR roared out of its lair among the reeds, the sudden movement caught the American petty officer off guard; he rolled off the canopy and fell into the canal. He was never seen again.

Penetrations

Admiral Zumwalt's aggressive SEA LORDS concept called for "keeping the enemy off balance." Besides conducting the barrier operations, the SEA LORDS planners had decided to penetrate areas long dominated by the enemy. One such area was the Ca Mau Peninsula. Admiral Zumwalt described this region:

> . . . a place of streams and mangrove swamps, hard to get to and even harder to get into, at the extreme southern tip of Vietnam. For years the Viet Cong had been using the peninsula as a sort of surge tank, taking sanctuary there when our forces in the neighboring areas of the delta had the upper hand and sallying forth when the fortunes of war shifted. The U.S. command had regarded the peninsula as so irremediably enemy country that it had evacuated as many of the inhabitants as possible and then bombed it with B-52s.

Initially the Navy's approach to the area was similar to that of the B-52s: Market Time craft surged up the rivers for hit-and-run raids on the enemy base camps. In the early months of 1969 these Market Time Raiders were augmented by raids and strikes by U.S. Navy SEAL Teams, Vietnamese RF/PF troops, and various Army, Navy and Air Force aircraft. Between 7 and 18 April, an extensive, coordinated strike operation called Silver Mace II was conducted in the Nam Can Forest area of the Ca Mau Peninsula. Twenty-nine river assault craft of River Assault Squadron 13, three battalions of Vietnamese Marines (approximately 2,400 men), twenty-five VNN River Assault Group boats, thirteen U.S. Navy PCFs, and a number of support vessels participated. The troops were carried into the various waterways of the Nam Can District, conducting more than sixty assault landings (six by PCFs) during the campaign. The results of the operation showed thirty-eight VC killed, forty-seven sampans and 209 structures destroyed, and more than 4,400 rounds of ammunition and 380 weapons captured. These raids were deemed successful and were certainly consistent with the SEA LORDS mission of keeping the enemy off balance, but Admiral Zumwalt had more constructive ideas:

> It occurred to me that if the Navy could gain control of a section of the principal river in the area [Song Cua Lon], it might be possible for a resettlement effort to begin on the river banks and gradually spread up and downstream and inland as the foothold expanded. The local Army judged a riverside base in that part of the country to be foolishly risky so I hit upon the expedient of setting a base up on pontoons anchored in midstream. The local Army people judged that to be even more foolishly risky but General Abrams, overruling the IV Corps Senior Advisor, approved it. From Sea Float, as we called it, swift boats and PBRs could range up and down the river and it had a pad for helos as well. We supported it with three-inch gunboats so it had sufficient fire power to dominate the river banks on both sides to a distance of several miles. It was protected from mines floated downstream or swimmers carrying demolition charges by nets and various warning devices.

Lessons learned from the ATSBs in Giant Slingshot were brought to Sea Float. Nine ammi-pontoons were gathered and joined at the naval support base in Saigon, and living facilities for 150 men were built onto them. Some of the pontoons were provided with overhead steel girders supporting steel matting, which was covered with layers of sandbags; these were designed to provide protection against incoming mortar rounds and were nicknamed "turtle ammis." Diesel generators were added for power, and the hollow compartments of the ammis were used for fuel and water stowage. Weapons mounts, a sick bay, and an operations center were provided, and messing facilities capable of feeding seven hundred men were also included.

In June 1969 the entire complex, along with most of its

crew, was loaded into three LSDs and transported to the mouth of the Bo De River. From there, tugs towed the ammis up the Bo De, then into the Cua Lon River, and ultimately anchored the complex adjacent to what had once been Nam Can City. This site was deliberately chosen for psychological and political reasons. Nam Can had been a thriving city with a population of four thousand people before the 1968 Tet Offensive. At that time the Viet Cong had taken over the city, and most of its residents had fled. Subsequent battles had destroyed the city; continued enemy domination of the area prevented rebuilding. Sea Float was meant to change that by wresting tactical control from the enemy and by demonstrating to the local people that the Viet Cong were no longer in charge. The site was also ideal because it was accessible from both the Gulf of Thailand and the South China Sea via the Cua Lon and Bo De rivers, respectively, which meant that patrol craft from both areas could reach Sea Float to provide support. If successful, it also meant that water traffic could move from the gulf to the sea via this waterway rather than having to make the longer, more arduous passage around the Ca Mau Peninsula.

Because by this stage, America was looking more and more at ways to "Vietnamize" the war, Sea Float was designed from the outset as a joint USN/VNN effort. The commander of Sea Float was a U.S. Navy commander; his deputy commander was Vietnamese. All of the cooks, radio operators, medical personnel, boatswain's mates, and gunner's mates were American, but most of the psychological warfare and intelligence personnel were Vietnamese. Both American and Vietnamese naval craft provided the mobility and tactical punch of the operation. The mixed command structure, coupled with the varied interests of U.S. Navy and Army advisors and Vietnamese Army commanders with responsibilities in the region, caused some difficulties in coordination, but the exigency of Vietnamization made the attempt necessary. Considering its experimental, nontraditional nature, the organization functioned amazingly well.

Defense of Sea Float was provided by the firepower of four 81-mm mortars, six .50-caliber machine guns, ten M-60 machine guns, and numerous small arms. In addition, the USN and VNN craft present wielded various armaments, and Seawolves and Black Ponies were available as well. A current in the area (sometimes as strong as eight knots) served as a natural defense against would-be swimmer sappers; electronic sensors placed along the adjacent banks warned of approaching enemy soldiers.

That same current which served to deter enemy swimmers also complicated the Sea Float set-up. A six-point mooring using 9,000-pound anchors and huge deposits of concrete was required to keep the nine-pontoon complex in place.

The various craft initially based at Sea Float were eight PCFs, a PG (Patrol Gunboat), and an LST, all American; an LSM (Landing Ship, Medium) fitted with medical and dental care vans and an LSIL (Landing Ship, Infantry, Large) made up the early VNN complement. Two Seawolf helicopters were also attached.

Besides the American and Vietnamese sailors who manned the Sea Float base and assorted craft, the Americans provided a platoon of SEALs, several underwater demolition teams, and some explosive ordnance disposal personnel, while the Vietnamese added ten Kit Carson scouts (former VC who had changed sides) to the enterprise.

Once established, Sea Float began operations. Patrols, organized sorties, emergency response actions, ambushes, and searches combined to apply "randomized pressure," a strategy that used available assets in constantly changing ways. These military actions were complemented by extensive psychological operations such as broadcasting messages from naval craft and helicopters, sending out teams to provide medical and dental assistance to villagers, setting up a sampan repair shop and an ax-sharpening facility (woodcutting was a primary occupation) aboard the Sea Float complex, and building and outfitting schools in several nearby hamlets.

Mining and ambushes soon told of VC sentiments toward Sea Float. Banners threatening in various terms to eliminate the "intruders" appeared along waterways. Little wooden rafts sailed on the current carrying leaflets with similar messages.

But as time went on, other indications told of the apparent success of the combined military and psychological operations of Sea Float. South Vietnamese flags began appearing on watercraft and in the villages and hamlets. More and more local people dared to visit the complex to use the facilities there and volunteered warnings of impending VC movements, attacks, and ambushes. Water traffic increased and trade with other regions was restored. New hamlets were spawned and grew rapidly.

More U.S. and Vietnamese forces joined the effort, including American ATCs, ASPBs, and a "Zippo" monitor, and VNN Yabuta junks and *Biet Hai* troops (VNN sailors with infantry training). Eventually the complex was moved ashore. On 24 October 1969 Operation Solid Anchor was born, calling for the establishment of a permanent Vietnamese naval base on the site of what had been Nam Can City.

Ultimately, the Sea Float/Solid Anchor project was turned over completely to the Vietnamese and became known as Tran Hung Dao III. The Mobile Advanced Tactical Support Base, as Sea Float had originally been called, had evolved into a permanent base facility and had ended enemy domination in an area once deemed suitable only for strategic bombing.

Another area long dominated by the Viet Cong was the infamous U Minh Forest. Lying to the north of the Ca Mau peninsula along the Gulf of Thailand coast, the forest was bordered on the south by the Ong Doc River. COMNAVFORV decided to set up an operation on the river. The original plan called for it to be a joint USN/VNN operation right from the start, but the Vietnamese Navy postponed its participation until more PBRs had been turned over, so the operation began as a strictly American venture.

A COMNAVFORV message transmitted on 18 September 1969 prescribed the operation:

SITUATION: THE SONG [river] ONG DOC IS ONE OF THE PRINCIPAL WATER LOCS [lines of communication] LEADING TO THE CITY OF CA MAU. AS SUCH, ITS FREEDOM OF USE AS A TRADE ROUTE IS IMPORTANT TO THE GROWTH AND GVN [government of Viet Nam] CONTROL OF THE CITY OF CA MAU AND AN XUYEN PROVINCE. ENEMY UNITS OPERATING ALONG THIS WATERWAY IMPEDE THE FLOW OF WATERBORNE TRAFFIC BY HARASSMENT AND TAX EXTORTION OPERATIONS. . . .

MISSION: CONDUCT PATROLS, NIGHT WATERBORNE GUARDPOST, MINE COUNTERMEASURES, AND BANK SWEEPS (UTILIZING RF/PF OR 21ST ARVN DIV TROOPS AS AVAILABLE). . . . CONDUCT ACTIVE PSYOP [psychological operations] PROGRAMS . . . IN ORDER TO STIMULATE THE RESETTLEMENT OF THE AREAS ALONG THE WATERWAY AND TO PROMOTE THE GVN IMAGE. . . .

In late September, River Division 572, three ATCs, two ASPBs, and a Seawolf detachment began patrolling the Ong Doc River in an operation called "Breezy Cove." They operated from an ATSB near the mouth of the river that had been created from seven ammi-pontoons and was supported by the USS *Garrett County,* anchored offshore. The weather was bad in the Gulf of Thailand, and unloading the pontoons from the LSDs that had brought them from Nha Be was difficult. Two towing craft were damaged while trying to get the ammis into the river. The choppy seas required the Seawolves to be securely tied down to the deck of the *Garrett County* offshore, which caused some concern because more time would be needed to get them airborne for scrambles in support of the river forces. But the operation commenced as planned. In October, several monitors joined the force, including one equipped with a 105-mm howitzer for artillery support, and a SEAL Team detachment was added to gather intelligence.

Enemy troops and supplies frequently crossed the Ong Doc on their way south to the Ca Mau Peninsula area, so the patrols often encountered them. The first friendly troop was killed in action just days after the beginning of the operation.

More units were added to Breezy Cove as the operation continued. The monthly statistics were impressive throughout the operation's existence, averaging about forty enemy killed per month. February 1970 proved to be the most significant month when enemy killed soared to the unprecedented number of 230. The number of engagements for that month had been no higher than in previous months, but the size of the enemy forces engaged was markedly greater.

Breezy Cove continued as a U.S. Navy operation until December 1970, when it became Tran Hung Dao X under the control of the Vietnamese Navy.

In mid-February 1969 First Coastal Zone PCFs extended the aggressive posture then typical of SEA LORDS into the rivers of the I Corps Tactical Zone. PCFs penetrated the Cua Dai River near Hoi An, fifteen miles southeast of Da Nang. These patrols were extended into the Truong Giang and various other waterways in the zone. Given the code name Operation Sea Tiger, these penetrations became routine and included troop insertions and gunfire support missions. In November the PCFs were augmented by PBRs from Task Force Clearwater to allow penetration into areas too shallow for the Swifts.

Sea Tiger continued until the end of May 1970, when it became Operation Tran Hung Dao VII. During the sixteen-month span of this U.S. operation, frequent enemy contact was made. Hostile fire sank several American boats, and casualties ran equivalent to other operations in the SEA LORDS era. Like Operation Sea Float, Sea Tiger carried a Task Force 115 designator rather than a SEA LORDS (Task Force 194) number and was, therefore, technically part of the Coastal Surveillance Force. This stemmed primarily from its origins as an inland penetration of Task Force 115 PCFs. When the penetration grew, with PBRs added to its inventory and troop insertions added to its mission, it took on the complexion of a SEA LORDS operation, and most sources written since the war refer to it as such.

One of the more unusual penetrations of an enemy-dominated area occurred in May 1969. Wanting to move a number of PBRs into a region on the upper Saigon River not previously included in the Navy's area of operations, planners called upon Army aviation for help. Huge CH-54 Sky Crane helicopters lifted six PBRs of River Division 574 clear out of the water, dangling them beneath like prey in the clutches of an eagle, and flew them and their crews from Go Dau Ha on the Vam Co Dong River to a point sixteen miles away on the upper Saigon. The entire airlift took only three hours; on the water it would have taken four days. The unexpected appearance of the PBRs caught the Viet Cong by surprise as had been hoped.

The same tactic was again employed the following month.

This time the Sky Cranes deposited the PBRs in the Rach Cai Cai, a north-south waterway in the Plain of Reeds that the Viet Cong were believed to be using as a major infiltration route. Interdiction on this waterway was to serve as a strategic enhancement of the Barrier Reef operation.

On 20 June 1969, six PBRs and thirty-five personnel were flown to the U.S. Special Forces camp at Cai Cai. This tiny outpost had been designed to accommodate only fourteen men, so conditions there were a bit crowded, to say the least. Nevertheless, Army and Navy personnel peacefully coexisted for the duration of the operation.

After thirty days, COMNAVFORV decided to terminate the operation because light contact had indicated that the enemy was probably no longer using the canal as an infiltration route, perhaps because of Operation Barrier Reef or maybe because of the presence of the PBRs. In any case, logistic support of the operation was very difficult because of the remoteness of the location, and the light contact convinced COMNAVFORV that the end did not justify the means. On 21 July the PBRs were again lifted into the sky and taken back to the Mekong.

The following month, Admiral John S. McCain, CINC-PAC, while being briefed at COMNAVFORV headquarters in Saigon, was told of the "flying PBR" operations. He looked thoughtfully at Admiral Zumwalt for a moment, then with a wry smile asked how it would have been reported had a U.S. Navy river patrol boat been shot down over dry land by enemy antiaircraft fire.

The airlift of PBRs to the upper Saigon River in May 1969 had been fruitful, so in June River Division 554 arrived at Phu Cuong and began northwestward patrols to the vicinity of Dau Tieng. In July River Division 593 relieved 554 at the austere ATSB established at Phu Cuong, and in August River Division 571 was added. VNN River Assault Group 24 also joined the operation in July. It was apparent that the success of the Giant Slingshot campaign was causing the enemy to run his infiltration around the northeast side of Tay Ninh City to avoid the barrier; the stretch of the Saigon River between Phu Cuong and Dau Tieng was a major artery in this new route.

Coordinated sweeps were conducted with the river forces

by local RF/PF forces, the 5th ARVN Division, and the U.S. 82nd Airborne Division. While enemy contact was light, the sweeps uncovered numerous booby-trapped bunkers in the area. Tellingly, the older bunkers had faced away from the river, but freshly made ones now faced the waterways.

On 10 October the operation was officially dubbed Ready Deck. Five days later it was incorporated as part of the SEA LORDS campaign and given the designator Task Group 194.6. Its USN commander was called Interdiction Commander, Upper Saigon River.

Ready Deck continued until May 1970, when it came under VNN command as Tran Hung Dao V. Six U.S. Navy men had died by that time, and thirty-three had been wounded. A total of 123 firefights had taken place, which was low compared to the other SEA LORDS or SEA LORDS–related operations, but the kill ratio, at sixty enemy to every one U.S. Navy man, was one of the highest of all the American naval campaigns.

FM CTF ONE ONE FIVE
TO PCF 37/PCF 35/PCF 100/PCF 102
UNCLAS

1. THE EXTENSIVE GDA [Gun Damage Assessment] IN THE SONG GANH HAO OPERATION WHICH TOTALLED 28 SAMPANS DESTROYED, 24 SAMPANS DAMAGED, 19 STRUCTURES DESTROYED, 49 STRUCTURES DAMAGED, PLUS 10 BUNKERS DAMAGED CERTAINLY DEALT A HEAVY BLOW TO THE ENEMY IN THIS REGION.

2. SUCCESSFUL MARKET TIME FORAYS SUCH AS THIS ONE ARE CONTINUING TO DRIVE THE ENEMY FROM HIS MOST TREASURED SANCTUARIES.

3. WELL DONE TO ALL GUNCREWS FOR THEIR DEVASTATING GUNFIRE.

The above message followed one of hundreds of Swift boat and WPB operations conducted in the rivers of South Vietnam between October 1968 and May 1970. The "Market Time Raider" campaign, although retaining its Coastal Surveillance Force task designation, was a part of the Zumwalt concept presented at the early SEA LORDS meetings and was recognized as part of the overall SEA LORDS operation. Once used exclusively for coastal patrols, the PCFs and WPBs penetrated deep into the various river complexes on hit-and-run raids, troop insertions, and patrols. Coordinating with various air assets, both American and Vietnamese, and using innovative means such as 13-foot skimmer craft (Boston Whalers) to penetrate the smaller waterways, these former coastal sailors were rapidly initiated into the brown-water world.

At one point Admiral Zumwalt discovered that Captain Roy Hoffman, Commander Task Force 115, had been riding on the lead craft during many of these forays. Zumwalt gave Hoffman a direct order to stop riding the boats because he didn't want him to be killed. Hoffman replied that he couldn't order his men to go on hazardous missions without going himself, and he continued to ride in the lead boat on many of the raids.

At one point the enemy provided an indication of the raids' apparent success. In response to a raid in the Ca Mau Peninsula, the Viet Cong crisscrossed logs about the size of telephone poles on the river to create several barriers, apparently to stop or at least hamper the Market Time Raiders.

In May 1970, the Market Time Raiders campaign was officially ended. A new operation, similar in scope and intent, immediately began under the name Blue Shark. The new operation was concentrated in the delta and was a combined USN/VNN effort. The commander of Blue Shark was American, with a VNN officer as his deputy. The results were comparable to those of the Raider campaign. SEAL and Kit Carson Scout teams were frequently inserted, covered, and extracted during these operations.

In November 1970, Blue Shark ended, leaving only a few U.S. Navy commands still active in South Vietnam.

Contrasts

Radarman Third Class Virgil Chambers sat on the deck forward of the pilothouse of PCF-60. His legs stretched into the boat's chain locker, one boot resting lightly on one of the uneven piles of rusty anchor chain. The Swift was cruising up the river with three others at about 15 knots, its snubbed bow tossing a light brown froth along both sides of the gray hull. It was late afternoon. The boats were still nearly a quarter of an hour away from their turn-point into the canal, so Chambers lay back on the deck and covered his eyes with the front lip of his helmet. He tried to picture the rolling green mountains where he had hunted as a boy, but it was hard to bring them into focus. Pennsylvania was a long way away. The hint of a sarcastic smile pulled at the corners of his mouth as he recalled how he had gotten here to this inhospitable river bound for a hostile canal.

Less than a year earlier, Petty Officer Chambers had been serving as a radarman in the USS *Bayfield* (APA-33). He was eighteen years old then, and the Navy was not one of his high priorities in life. He was patriotic and willing to do his duty; he just was not fond of being at sea. He had called his detailer about the possibility of a shore tour somewhere, but he had been told that the only shore duty available was in Vietnam. Chambers had pictured a billet in Saigon or at some other facility where life might not be comparable to the way it was in Pennsylvania, but at least he wouldn't be under way most of the time as he had been on the *Bayfield*. When he agreed to the transfer, he found that the detailer's idea of "shore duty" was different from his own, and he found himself with orders to a Market Time PCF out of Qui Nhon.

He remembered the training he had undergone in California before being sent to Vietnam. It had all been organized and logical, and he had been impressed. He came away feeling motivated, ready to undertake his new assignment with fervor.

The first night in Qui Nhon he learned the difference between training and war. The base came under attack, and as mortar rounds and grenades exploded all around him, he saw that men at blackboards and men in firing-pits had very little in common. Amid his own terror, he saw people dashing about, heard shouting and cursing that only added to the confusion. He assumed that the officers knew what was happening, but it all seemed so disorganized.

It had quieted down for a while after that first night. Chambers's PCF patrolled as part of Market Time, and things went pretty much as he had been told they would in training. Market Time operations were by and large routine and quiet at this point in the war. As he got to know the other men in his boat, Chambers realized that they seemed thirsty for action. They continually talked about the war and how they wanted to do more. The officer in charge was particularly aggressive and was forever lamenting the quiet of their patrols. Chambers, though liking the other men in his boat and feeling a natural curiosity about combat operations, did not share the eagerness for action that he saw in his shipmates. He had a girlfriend back in Pennsylvania whom he wanted to see again.

Then one day Chambers left his quiet corner of the war. A message from COMNAVFORV asked for volunteers for a new operation called SEA LORDS, in which PCFs were going to be sent into the rivers to conduct raids on enemy strongholds. Chambers's officer in charge didn't hesitate a second; he immediately volunteered his craft, and within a few days PCF-60 was under way from Qui Nhon, headed south.

Chambers recalled the voyage south to Cat Lo. He had been awed by the changes that took place as they made their trek; the farther south they moved, the more evidence of hostilities they saw. He remembered acutely the sense of foreboding he had felt upon seeing the sunken hulk of a helicopter in the water. The wreckage was badly mutilated and lay in silent testimony to the proximity of violence and death. He remembered seeing the sailors at Cat Lo returning from missions. They had a different look about them than those at Qui Nhon; it was hard to define but unmistakably there. And they didn't bother to put their shirts back on! In Qui Nhon, regulations were pretty tight, and even though he and his shipmates had often removed their shirts while on patrol, they were always careful to don them before returning to port. In Cat Lo there was more of a wartime atmosphere. Shirts were insignificant in an environment where flak jackets were the norm.

Chambers felt the Swift heel over as she turned. He knew they must be heading toward the canal's entrance, so he sat up and adjusted his helmet. He eased himself partway down into the chain locker, then positioned the bipod-mounted M-60 machine gun in front of him. He checked the bolt of ammunition for a clean lead from the ammo-box to the receiver, then rested his finger lightly on the trigger so that he could feel the grooves in it.

As the craft steadied, its bow pointed toward a narrow opening in the nipa palms on the bank, he saw one of the other PCFs off the port side, maneuvering to fall in astern. His friend Richard was on the other boat's forecastle—like Chambers, in his boat's chain locker, looking along the barrel of an M-60. Chambers wanted to exchange a smile or a nod with his friend, but he knew that Richard would be too intense at this point to look anywhere but toward the approaching enemy shore.

Radarman Third Class Richard O'Mara had also served in the *Bayfield,* and there he had met Virgil Chambers. Now the two men found themselves serving as forward gunners on two different PCFs. Occasionally their boats conducted SEA LORDS raids together.

O'Mara, unlike Chambers, did not yearn for the life he had left behind—in O'Mara's case, in the Bronx. He had thrust himself into the war with almost complete abandon, yet he had been sorely disappointed. Like Chambers, he saw the confusion during combat, but unlike his friend, he did not believe that the officers were in control. He saw most of the officers as "ticket-punchers"—men whose interest in accomplishing their mission was subordinate to getting combat service onto their records. He particularly disliked his officer in charge and saw him as dangerously incompetent. O'Mara believed in fighting the Communists in Vietnam, but he was convinced that the tactics used were wrong and wasteful.

These feelings had started less than two weeks after his arrival in Vietnam. His boat had been called into one of the rivers to rescue several American advisors operating with a Vietnamese provincial force and had come under heavy fire near the river. As the Swift roared up the river, O'Mara had seen figures running along the banks, wearing clothing that looked like black pajamas and carrying weapons. He had instinctively whirled around to open fire and nearly did, until he realized that no one else was firing and no orders had been given. These were friendly soldiers of the provincial force.

O'Mara had been under the impression that only the VC dressed this way, and no one had warned him to the contrary. He had nearly killed some of them!

As time wore on, he saw his negative feelings ratified when more and more sailors, some of them good friends, were killed or severely wounded. He was convinced that their regular raids were inadequately planned and poorly coordinated. On occasion the boats farther back in a column would begin firing without due regard for the friendly units ahead, and O'Mara cursed the poor leadership that was permitting friendly bullets to pass dangerously close to him. He could remember night operations when his boat had gone aground in a dead-end waterway and had been vulnerable while the crew worked themselves free.

O'Mara's boat entered the canal fifty yards astern of Chambers's. The PCFs dropped their speed to 7 knots as they entered. For the first several hundred yards the canal was very narrow. Palm Fronds along the banks brushed both sides of the boats, issuing a complaining hiss at the boats as they glided past. O'Mara had to duck several times to avoid being struck in the face by low-hanging vines. The smell of wild-flowers occasionally broke through the musk of rotting leaves. O'Mara's eyes scanned the tangled vegetation, watching for shapes or colors that didn't fit. After several minutes a second canal joined the one they were in and created a new waterway twice as wide as the original. The lead PCF accelerated, and the others followed suit. O'Mara tore his eyes from the banks long enough to doublecheck his arms inventory. Besides the M-60 in front of him, he had an M-16 rifle in case accurate fire was needed, a hand-held grenade-launcher in the event some extra punch was called for, and a .38 revolver for good measure.

Less than half a mile up the waterway, the lead Swift throttled back, her hull settling quickly into the brown canal water as she lost momentum. Must be a wire, thought O'Mara.

Chambers had spotted the wire stretched taut across the canal at the same instant as his officer in charge. As the boat slowed, Chambers reached down into the chain locker and found a large pair of bolt-cutters where he had left them. As forward gunner on the lead boat, he had the job of cutting the wire so that the raiding party could pass. He knew that the wire had been placed across the canal by the enemy. Feeling vulnerable, he pulled upward on his flak jacket's zipper as though trying to squeeze out an extra millimeter of protection from it. Despite his efforts not to, he considered the possibilities as the Swift crept slowly forward toward the wire. It could have been left there just to slow them down. The wire was almost to the craft's prow. Or it could be a warning system that would signal the raiding party's approach. The wire was over the bullnose, and Chambers opened the jaws of the bolt-cutters. Or it could be a trip wire for explosives. He lifted the cutters toward the wire. Or . . . A rocket burst out of the palm fronds and across the canal, detonating on the opposite bank with a blast of heat and concussion that rocked the Swift. Several more followed. Before Chambers could react, the boat leaped forward as the officer in charge slammed the throttles ahead against their stops. Chambers was caught off balance and fell backward with the lurch. Then he felt the wire seize him across the chest and pin him to the pilothouse. For a brief, panic-stricken moment, feeling the wire tighten across his body, he was certain that he was going to be cut in half, but then one end pulled free from its tether on the bank. Chambers barely had time to be thankful before he realized that there were more wires stretched across the canal ahead. The Swift charged ahead at full bore amidst gunfire, explosions, shouts, and engine roar. Chambers threw himself face down on the deck just as a second wire passed above him; it too pulled free with a snap. A third and then a fourth wire passed over Chambers, each torn free by the charging craft. With all the noise, it was impossible to tell if the wires were tripping explosive charges. Chambers thought not, but he couldn't be sure.

As soon as the canal ahead appeared clear of wires, Chambers scrambled to his M-60 and joined the firing. Everyone was pouring rounds into the surrounding jungle at a furious rate. Leaves and fronds were shredded and branches and trunks were shattered and tossed in the hurricane of metal as thousands of rounds came from the Swift boats. Chambers, his finger tight against the trigger, swept his machine gun back and forth. He felt safe as long as he was firing; he knew that the enemy would be blown away or would have to keep their heads down. As in all his firefights, Chambers never wanted to stop firing once he had started. He felt instinctively that the moment he let go of that trigger, he would become a target.

From somewhere in the distance, it seemed, he became aware of a voice saying, "Cease fire." All the Swift's guns continued. The voice again called, "Cease fire," but the crew was still caught up in their surrealistic world of violence and survival, and the explosive chattering continued. "Cease fire!" The voice seemed louder now, and the rest of the world came back into focus as the gunfire died away. Chambers looked down and saw the last of his spent shell-casings dance across the deck in a brass ballet. Then all was silent except the continuous growl of the straining diesel engines, which seemed mellow in contrast to the chaos that had just ended.

For several minutes a blurred paisley of greens and browns rushed by. The speeding boats threw their wakes against the banks in an angry slap as they raced through the narrow waterway. Then the trees on the right bank vanished, revealing a village teeming with people and livestock. O'Mara knew that the presence of people and animals meant that the village was either friendly or had not been warned in advance of the boats' coming. Frequently, the raiding Swift boats would encounter deserted villages, which meant that the villagers had known of the coming raid and had left with their animals and any contraband they might have. O'Mara doubted that they were friendly, but the raiding PCFs continued up the canal without even slowing down. Either this village was not their target, or they were making a first pass to reconnoiter. The jungled banks closed in about them once again.

The four boats entered a wide stream about ten minutes later, and O'Mara could see Chambers's PCF ahead beginning to come about. As his boat followed, O'Mara realized that they were looping around and heading back into the canal from which they had just come. The village they had just passed was being held by VC regulars, and they were going in for a firing run. O'Mara checked his M-60 even though he knew it was ready to fire.

* * *

The Swifts roared down the canal at full throttle. The village came into view again, and Chambers heard his officer in charge order, "Open fire." At what? thought Chambers. All he could see was villagers, chickens, a few pigs, and a water buffalo. Chambers had learned very young that a hunter never fires his weapon until he can see his target. As the firing erupted from the other guns on his boat and the people began to run wildly, he honestly didn't know what he was supposed to be shooting. He saw no threat from the fleeing villagers and he was not aware of any return fire. He was in turmoil. All of the villages they had raided before had been deserted, or at least had appeared so. He was beginning to wonder if maybe they were committing some kind of war crime when he heard shattering glass. He looked behind him and saw that the pilothouse windows were no longer there. Seeing the blood-spattered face of the quartermaster on the helm, in a rush of horror he knew that they were receiving fire from the village. Chambers tried to bring his weapon to bear on the village huts, but it was too late; they were already past.

O'Mara saw muzzle flashes coming from a stand of bamboo near the village perimeter. He knew from experience that when muzzle flashes were brightly visible they were aiming somewhere else, and when they were barely visible they were coming at the observer. He opened up with his M-60 and walked the rounds up to this target. With his back braced against the pilothouse, he poured rounds into the bamboo. He felt the frustration of confused firefights, missed opportunities, and tactics he didn't understand flowing out of him through the machine gun. Images of war movies flashed through his mind, and he imagined himself to be the greatest warrior since Audie Murphy. He fired round after round, venting hostility. He had no idea if he was hitting any enemy soldiers and he really didn't care. He wanted to go on shooting forever, to feel the cathartic quaking of his weapon until his anger had been drained away.

A moment later the boat swerved, and the village was no longer in his field of fire. He ceased firing.

* * *

Chambers didn't move for several minutes as the Swifts continued down the narrow waterway, leaving the village astern. He sat stone-still, pondering what had just happened. He knew he had been wrong not to fire. He could hear the reports in the pilothouse behind him and learned that, besides the helmsman, his officer in charge and the twin-.50 gunner on top of the pilothouse had been wounded. The raid on the village had been based on good intelligence, yet it had seemed so wrong at the time to open fire without a specific target. He felt confused. The whole war was confusing. People back home were marching in the streets, saying that he shouldn't even be there; the government and his sense of duty demanded that he do what he was told; his homesickness and will to live caused him to yearn desperately for home. Sometimes it was almost too much to bear.

He remembered an earlier incident that had caused him pain and confusion not unlike what he felt now. His boat had stopped a sampan on one of the larger tributaries, and Chambers had been standing on the forecastle, looking down at a thin Vietnamese man who was lifting up a wooden plank for inspection when someone shouted, "He's got a gun!" Chambers instinctively fired his shotgun into the bottom of the boat near the man. Some of the shot struck the Vietnamese man in the legs and feet, and he fell to the deck, yelling in pain and losing the weapon over the side. The wounded man was brought aboard to be turned over to the South Vietnamese authorities. Chambers had not felt any sense of victory at having shot the enemy. On the trip back to the base he watched the curled-up form lying on the deck near the pilothouse and felt nothing but pity. He got one of the first-aid kits from below and knelt beside the wounded man with a battle-dressing in his hand. The man's large brown eyes rolled upward to meet Chambers's for a moment. Then the Vietnamese spat on Chambers and slapped the battle-dressing away.

Chambers had been confused by this incident, not so much by the Vietnamese prisoner's actions as by the fact that the Vietnamese man's feelings seemed so clear-cut but his own were not. Why was his enemy able to hate so freely when he, Chambers, was not?

It was all so confusing sometimes.

* * *

O'Mara put on an asbestos glove and quickly replaced the hot barrel of his M-60 with the spare he kept nearby. He wanted to be ready on the way out.

He wiped the sweat from his upper lip and cursed under his breath. The firefight had felt good, but it was not enough. He was still frustrated and angry. He could hear his officer in charge talking on the radio and felt a surge of rage at the sound of his voice, thinking of all the times that this officer had put his boat into needless danger. He was convinced that sooner or later the man would get them all killed. Yet O'Mara did not want to run from the fight. It was not in his nature.

It was all so confusing sometimes.

Postscripts

In June 1970, a major reorganization occurred in the American and Vietnamese navies in South Vietnam. Among the many changes, Task Force 194 was deactivated and placed in reserve for contingency use. The SEA LORDS operations that were still under American command (Sea Float/Solid Anchor, Breezy Cove, Search Turn, Barrier Reef, and Blue Shark) were reassigned under Task Force 116 designators, but the rest of SEA LORDS was absorbed by the VNN. By year's end only Solid Anchor remained under American command, and that was turned over to the VNN on 1 April 1971, marking the end of U.S. Navy operations in South Vietnam.

SEA LORDS had been unique to the U.S. Navy's involvement in Vietnam because of its innovativeness, but the barrier portion was also unique to the war as a whole because it provided a "front" of sorts in a war that was characterized as having no fronts. It gave to those involved some geography they could relate to, and therefore was more tangible than any of the other operations. Only Market Time had done anything similar. The River Patrol Force and the Mobile Riverine Force had worked a probing, seeking, largely random type of warfare, in which the participants were rarely able to see their objectives clearly and often felt as though they were hunting for shadows on a moonless night.

But the psychological advantages that might have been realized by the mission clarity of SEA LORDS were canceled out by the changing times. Petty Officers Chambers's and O'Mara's attitudes about the war were not atypical for the period in which SEA LORDS came into being. These men were no less patriotic than Lieutenant Meyerkord or Petty Officer Williams had been in 1965 and 1966. But times had changed: the war was being protested by antiwar activists, press coverage had been less and less favorable since Tet in 1968, and U.S. policy had obviously turned from one of victory to one of extrication. The very issue of why they were there had been clouded, and the man serving in Vietnam from 1969 on were often confused by conflicting feelings of duty and survival and by growing questions of the value or even the morality of the cause.

Howard Kerr, Admiral Zumwalt's flag secretary, discussed some problems that combatants in Vietnam had to face:

> Throughout the year, I used to have some of the young lieutenants come to town. I say some of the young lieutenants, hell at that time, that's what I was. And they'd sit down and talk to me about some of the conflicts they were having over the war, some of the orders they were given, and the problems they had in executing those orders. . . . [There] was a dimension that probably pervaded this war. . . . it was the political dimension, and we couldn't expect all the officers to understand that, and certainly it shouldn't take priority when you're getting shot at if you're the guy that's on the scene. There were also instances where the officers were caught in this enormous dilemma of whether or not to fire on something that was moving at night in the water. . . . I remember one lieutenant getting me aside one evening and in a very emotional, tearful way telling me that he had been told that he was to waste anything that moved on the water after midnight. He said he just couldn't do it, because he knew that a lot of these movements on the water were just locals who were out at night for very routine, peaceful, domestic reasons, and if we started

opening fire at everything that moved we were going to end up by killing a lot of innocent people. Yet he was under direct orders from his immediate superior to do that, and he found himself in a very difficult situation where he didn't want to disobey his orders, yet on the other hand, his conscience wouldn't let him do what he had been directed to do.

One might argue that the dilemma described above is no different from the one faced in all wars. Certainly the bombardier in World War II knew that innocent people could die by his hand. The difference is that the bombardier had the support of his countrymen, and only the tiniest minorities back home questioned his actions. The sailors, soldiers, and Marines of the late sixties and early seventies did not have that overwhelming support. They delivered death in a world that no longer saw things in clear-cut terms. The young lieutenant on the waterways of Vietnam did not have the luxury of rationalizing that "this is war" and anyone out on the water violating curfew would be a legitimate target just as children had been in 1945 because they happened to live in Dresden.

The potency of these inner conflicts is particularly manifested in the case of one young lieutenant, John Kerry. After proving his mettle in combat on Swift boats in the Mekong Delta (earning a Silver Star, a Bronze Star, and three Purple Hearts), he returned home to become an organizer of Vietnam Veterans Against the War (VVAW).

Not every man who served in Vietnam was troubled by these matters. The other men in Virgil Chambers's boat did not seem to share his circumspection. While one can never be certain why Quincy Truett (see the prologue) went back to Vietnam for a second tour, his motivations were not terribly confused when he said to his wife, "That's where the war is; that's where I belong." Some men see things that simply, others do not.

Quincy Truett died on the waterways of Vietnam, and so did many others. Truett was not the only SEA LORDS participant to have a ship named in his honor. Two *Spruance*-class destroyers, the USS *Elliot* (DD-967) and USS *Peterson* (DD-969), were named after lieutenant commanders who were both killed in separate incidents on the Vam Co Dong River during Giant Slingshot. (In his subsequent assignment as Chief of Naval Operations, Admiral Zumwalt made it his mission to have ships named for these two officers. He considered both to be superb leaders and had been with each just minutes before they were killed.) The casualty rates for the SEA LORDS operations were the highest for the Navy in Vietnam. Interviews with members of Admiral Zumwalt's staff reveal that he was deeply concerned about the American and South Vietnamese casualties that his changes in strategy had brought about, but he also knew that few things worthwhile are gained in war if one is not willing to take risks.

If friendly casualties were high, so were the enemy's. Vietnam in many ways was a statistician's war, so such grisly figures as kill-ratios were kept. While the value of these statistics is questionable, the figures for this operation reveal that the enemy paid a high price once SEA LORDS was created. Ratios averaged about 30 to 1, sometimes reaching the staggering heights of over 100 to 1. While the accuracy of these figures is subject to question because of the known inflation of body counts that occurred in other arenas of the war, the Navy's figures appear to have been fairly accurate because the counting methods prescribed by COMNAVFORV emphasized the low side of the probability curve. Even assuming some inflation, the kill figures still reflect a severe penalty on Viet Cong forces in areas where these SEA LORDS ventures occurred.

Captures of enemy personnel and matériel also produced impressive figures. These coupled with the number of enemy-initiated firefights make credible the intelligence assessments of enemy presence and infiltration in the SEA LORDS areas of operations.

One possible indication of the enemy's feeling about the SEA LORDS campaign was manifested in an incident that occurred one day several months into Admiral Zumwalt's tour. He and some of his staff and a number of the Vietnamese who worked at the admiral's quarters would meet regularly for a volleyball game at noon. On this particular day a would-be assassin heaved a satchel charge over the wall and onto the volleyball court. It went off, but fortunately this day Zumwalt had gone on a longer than usual trip into the field and the volleyball game had not formed up as it usually did. No one was injured.

It was apparent that the enemy had been watching the compound and, observing this daily volleyball ritual, had decided to cash in on it. Whether the assassination attempt was in response to anything specific, such as SEA LORDS, or was simply a random terrorist attack will probably never be known, but it is not far-fetched to imagine that the admiral who had instigated these barriers and penetrations was being targeted.

A proper assessment of SEA LORDS is not possible without considering the significance of the man behind it. When Admiral Zumwalt came to Vietnam, the Navy had become static in its "in-country" role. By that time it had also come to be common knowledge that a tour in Vietnam was not career-enhancing for naval personnel. These factors, added to the growing antiwar sentiment back home, presented Zumwalt with a force whose morale was suffering and whose importance in the war effort had become a matter of debate. Zumwalt could not control the sentiment back home, but he didn't hesitate to meet the other problems head on.

Besides resuscitating the Navy's role in the war with his bold strategy changes, he personally fought the morale problem by frequently visiting the troops in the field. Every morning he had his staff go through the message traffic relating to the previous day's events and pick out the two areas that had seen the heaviest enemy action. He would then fly to those areas to visit with the men and personally debrief them. So it was not at all unusual for sailors to be in a firefight in the middle of the night and be discussing it the next morning with COMNAVFORV himself. During these debriefings he would also talk with them about their problems to find out what he could do to improve their situations.

Besides offering encouragement and showing the men his personal interest, he would decorate deserving men right on the spot, bypassing the required paperwork. This caused some consternation in bureaucratic circles, but he felt the effect on the men made it worthwhile.

He tackled the career-enhancement problem by continuous liaison with the Bureau of Personnel, trying to ensure that his people received meaningful, career-enhancing assignments after their tours in Vietnam. Admiral Zumwalt was unquestionably people-oriented, and this orientation, coupled with the changes in strategy, raised both the Navy's image and its morale.

Admiral Salzer shared his thoughts on the SEA LORDS campaign:

The concept behind the SEA LORDS interdiction tactic stemmed from over appreciation of the VC/NV situation at that time. They had made an all-out effort in the February-June 1968 period ("Tet Offensive"), and their urgent need was to reorganize, regroup and resupply. Consequently, apart from the normal small-unit rocket ambushes, the VC were set on *avoiding* contact; and that was a fairly easy task against "search and destroy" tactics with multi-battalion units complete with artillery support plowing through the paddy. It appeared to us that the best chance of bringing the enemy into the open was to imperil his primary objective of resupply and reinforcement by multiple interdiction barriers athwart his lines of communications to the Delta. No single interdiction barrier had much chance of imposing significant attrition in view of the availability of alternate rivers and streams. But a series of such barriers maintained by combined river, ground and air forces might have brought the VC to the point where they had to use sizable units to break through. Then with ready reaction (air-mobile battalions) the enemy could be engaged on our terms—a "bait and destroy" tactic.

Despite SEA LORDS' successes, the sporadic and frequently inadequate nature of ground force participation in the interdiction effort precluded full realization of its potential in my opinion. Significantly, after Vietnamization of the barriers, ground force participation in these operations virtually ceased.

The lack of enthusiasm for providing ground forces to riverine interdiction operations stemmed from two factors in my judgment. Most importantly, it was a secondary priority (by a wide margin) of the Divisional Commanders and Provincial Chiefs in each area. They were preoccupied—by directive—with search and destroy tactics and pacification of their particular areas. Participation in riverine interdiction operations had to be on a "not-to-interfere basis"; and too often it was. The other inhibiting element was the frequently undramatic nature of the results. Waiting for the enemy to come to you is frustrating and almost guaranteed to wreck the "body count" and "battalion days in the field" statistics on which ground force effectiveness was too often judged.

No matter how one evaluates the strategic soundness or the tactical success of the SEA LORDS campaign, one fact is irrefutable: as in the other in-country naval operations in Vietnam, the vast majority of the men who participated in SEA LORDS did so with courage and tenacity that has long characterized the American sea services. They carried out their missions in the face of controversy and in a milieu of doubt and domestic strife. They did so with few rewards and at great risk. No nation could expect more of its citizens.

Vice Admiral Zumwalt so impressed President Nixon and several of his cabinet members that at age forty-nine he became the youngest four-star admiral in U.S. Navy history, and was catapulted over many officers senior to him to become the youngest Chief of Naval Operations.

Captains Salzer and Price were promoted to rear admiral subsequent to their SEA LORDS service, and both later served as COMNAVFORV (Rear Admiral Salzer from April 1971 to June 1972 and Rear Admiral Price from June to August 1972). Salzer was later promoted to vice admiral and served as Commander Amphibious Forces Pacific before retiring.

After the war, Virgil Chambers left the Navy and used his "G.I. Bill" benefits to graduate from college. Today he is chief of Boating Safety Education for the Commonwealth of Pennsylvania.

Richard O'Mara lives in Pacific Grove, California. He

graduated with a degree in political science from UCLA, is active in various veterans' affairs, and is a self-employed entrepreneur. He and Virgil Chambers are still close friends.

G. H. Childress remained in the Navy after Vietnam, earning a commission and ultimately retiring as a lieutenant. Today he teaches high school and community college mathematics in the Summerville, South Carolina, area.

Today John Kerry is the junior senator from Massachusetts.

7
EXODUS

Vietnamization

That no life lives forever;
That dead men rise up never;
That even the weariest river
Winds somewhere safe to sea.

—ALGERNON CHARLES SWINBURNE,
"The Garden of Prosperpine," 1866

Advisors Again

The naval advisor had never gone away. Even though the U.S. Navy and Coast Guard had taken over a major portion of the coastal and riverine operations starting in 1965 and continuing for the better part of five years, Americans were still assigned continuously as advisors to the VNN. During these years theirs was perhaps the most difficult task in one respect: the little acclaim from the home front given to forces in Vietnam was almost exclusively granted to those conducting operations under the American flag. Advisors were generally living under more difficult conditions, getting wounded and dying in about the same proportions as their operational counterparts, and struggling with a program that was temporarily subordinated in importance and attention.

Sometimes advisors had to contend with extraordinary circumstances. Stewart M. Harris, a naval officer who had participated in the early barrier patrols near the DMZ that presaged Market Time and then found himself involved in the war during two subsequent tours, wrote:

> My last trip to Vietnam was as senior advisor to Coastal Group 16. I believe I am the only person ever to survive a full year tour. I know that my three predecessors were killed. Coastal Group 16 was considered a very "low rent" district. Ten days after my departure, my assistant was killed. One village across the river I remember as being very hostile. Walking through the area, small children would spit at me. I didn't really understand until six months after my return from Viet Nam. The village was My Lai.* I was "visiting" after LT Calley and before the press made it famous.

---

* My Lai was the scene of the slaughter of several hundred unarmed villagers by a U.S. Army platoon in March 1968. The incident did not become public knowledge until the end of 1969, when charges were brought against Lieutenant William F. Calley, the platoon leader.

By 1969 a decade had passed since CINCPAC had authorized American advisors to go "in harm's way" with their Vietnamese counterparts. Yet little had changed. An article appearing in *Our Navy* magazine in November 1970 could just as well have been written about Lieutenant Jim Vincent in the pre–Market Time days of 1964: "Junk force advisors are probably the most isolated sailors in Vietnam. Some 100 advisors serve with 20 Vietnamese Navy coastal groups located along 1,000 miles of coastline in South Vietnam. Many of these bases are accessible only by air or water."

But changes were in the wind. Talk of victory in Vietnam had all but vanished in America. More and more the subject of withdrawal from the war dominated discussions. The question became not *whether* to withdraw but *how* to withdraw from the war in Vietnam. The advisors were about to be called to the forefront once again.

ACTOV

On 2 November 1968, General Creighton Abrams, COMUS-MACV, looking tired from his trip to Washington, walked into the MACV conference room and sat down. "All right, let's get on with the briefing," he said. An Air Force colonel stepped to the front of the room and spoke while colored slides appeared on the screen beside him.

The chief advisors from each of the services had been summoned with their briefing officers to present their plans for turning the war over to the Vietnamese. Vice Admiral Zumwalt, as chief of the Naval Advisory Group as well as Commander Naval Forces Vietnam, waited for the Air Force briefer to finish so that he could present the Navy's plan. It was to be the first official briefing Zumwalt would present to Abrams since recently taking the helm in Vietnam.

General Abrams watched the Air Force colonel through weary, reddened eyes as the briefing progressed. A slide was on the screen showing projected turnovers of aircraft to the Vietnamese Air Force, and the blue bars of the graph reached across the grid to the year 1976.

Suddenly General Abrams slammed his fist down on the

table so hard that an ashtray near him flipped over. "Bullshit!" he barked.

The color drained out of the colonel's face, and the others in the room froze.

"Don't you people realize what's happening?" the general said, looking around the room. "There is no longer a consensus of support for the war back in the United States. I have a letter in my pocket from the president that tells me to turn the war over to the Vietnamese." He pointed his large cigar at the colonel still standing by the screen. "You tell me that we'll be all turned over by 1976. That's out of the question! The country will not sit still for that kind of commitment. The president wants to get the war turned over as soon as possible. We have to make that happen!" The general rose from his chair and angrily left the room.

For a moment total silence hung in the room. Then General Abrams's chief of staff, Major General Corcoran, walked quietly over to Admiral Zumwalt. "Bud," he said, "the general's tired. It might be better if we rescheduled your briefing for another time. He'll probably eat you alive if you try to brief him now."

Without hesitation, Admiral Zumwalt replied, "I'd like to go ahead and make my presentation."

General Corcoran looked at the admiral disbelievingly and then went to check with his boss. While General Abrams was still out of the room, Admiral Zumwalt and Lieutenant Kerr hurriedly made some changes in the presentation, scratching out the words "maybe" and "possibly" wherever they appeared and writing "will" in their stead.

General Abrams returned and sat down. Admiral Zumwalt made his presentation, promising an accelerated Navy turnover throughout. He projected a complete turnover of all U.S. Navy operational responsibilities by 30 June 1970. It was exactly what Abrams had wanted to hear. When the presentation was over, General Abrams rose, put his arm around Zumwalt's shoulder, and led the young vice admiral into his office.

Zumwalt had read the home-front situation correctly and had already foreseen the need for a rapid turnover; when he saw Abrams's reaction to the Air Force presentation, he simply strengthened the language of his own. In one move he had gained General Abrams's respect and support and had successfully kicked off the program that he would later call "the one closest to my heart." The Navy turnover program was under way.

His turnover plan, like all good military programs, soon was called by an acronym. Zumwalt liked ACTOV, for Accelerated Turnover to the Vietnamese, because it sounded like "active," and he was determined that this program was going to be just that. Besides the obvious concern of an ever-lengthening list of casualties and the fact that the war in Vietnam had become a political liability, Zumwalt knew that the Navy's shipbuilding and weapons procurement plans were suffering massively from the continued expenditures required to finance the war. The U.S. Navy was already sliding into a growth depression at a time when the Soviet Navy was expanding. The sooner the Navy could divest itself of the financial (and manpower) drain of Vietnam, the sooner it could get back to concentrating on its blue-water commitments.

The planners decided that the best method for turning over assets and missions to the Vietnamese was to rely on graduated "on-the-job" training. This was accomplished by first bringing a VNN sailor aboard an American craft as a member of the crew. He would be trained in the duties of his American counterpart until he was ready to take over the job. Once he took over, the American sailor would leave the boat. Then a second Vietnamese sailor would come aboard and start training in the duties of a different USN sailor. The process would continue until the entire crew had been replaced by VNN personnel. The last to leave was the American officer in charge, and once he had been replaced, the craft would be formally turned over to the Vietnamese Navy. Americans would remain with Vietnamese units as advisors, some at the squadron or division level and some on board the larger individual ships, until they were no longer necessary. Training facilities, logistics support functions, and bases would also be turned over as quickly as possible.

The language barrier was a problem that had to be overcome. Remembering William J. Lederer and Eugene Burdick's book *The Ugly American*, which had attacked American diplomats for not learning the language of host countries, some of the idealists among Navy planners insisted that it was the Americans who must learn Vietnamese in order to overcome the language problem. But Vietnamese was an agrarian language with little technical vocabulary suitable to the modern boats and equipment that were to be turned over. If Vietnamese was to be used, terms would have to be invented and learned. In addition, many of the Vietnamese already had at least a rudimentary knowledge of English, and a fair number were fluent. Few Americans spoke Vietnamese effectively, and their one-year tours of duty meant that it was far more cost-effective to train the Vietnamese. So, with Vietnamese concurrence, English became the common language of the two navies.

Admiral Zumwalt's promise of an operational turnover by mid-1970 was ambitious, to say the least. VNN readiness to accept both the American craft and the operational mission was mixed at best. Like any large organization, the Vietnamese Navy had its strengths and weaknesses, and conditions varied from unit to unit, but a review of reports from American advisors about the VNN units they were with reveals a significant number of problems that had to be overcome in a hurry if ACTOV were to succeed. Among these were varying degrees of discipline, low morale, inefficient employment of assets, supply problems, weaknesses in the training system, and maintenance practices that varied from good on guns to poor on electronics. The VNN had long suffered from a "second-class citizen" status, being dominated first by the more politically important Vietnamese Army and then overshadowed by the intervention of the U.S. Navy. Its officers and men had had little opportunity to prove themselves, and consequently had very little experience and self-confidence.

To those who were faint-hearted, the goals set by ACTOV seemed impossible. In more than a decade of advising, the Americans had not been able to transform the VNN into a viable force, so it seemed unlikely that this could be done in less than two years. But there were some significant differences. Previously, advising had been relegated to a lower priority than operations. Few people, American or Vietnamese, had seen any great need for turnover as long as the U.S. Navy was accomplishing the naval mission. Now ACTOV was going to take a more aggressive approach. The Americans were being told in no uncertain terms that turnover—

"Vietnamization," as President Nixon called it in his 31 December 1969 speech—was their foremost priority. The Vietnamese realized that they were not going to be able to rely on the Americans forever, so they began viewing the turnover process in a different light. Some of them may have been anxious to have the Americans out of the way so that they might do things their own way for a change, while others may not have wanted to lose their powerful ally; but in either case, the reality of the coming American exodus could not be ignored. Whether out of pride or self-preservation, the Vietnamese began to take ACTOV seriously.

The vast cultural gap between the Americans and Vietnamese was a crucial concern. Many Americans brought their racial prejudices with them to Vietnam. This was a serious problem when the Americans were dealing with the Vietnamese only infrequently, but now that the order of the day was practically cohabitation, the matter became critical. Even Americans without notable prejudices were often unprepared for Vietnamese ways. For example, it was not uncommon for a Vietnamese man to place his hand on his American counterpart's leg while sitting and talking with him. Americans who had not been warned in advance that this is a normal gesture in Vietnamese society and is not an indication of sexual preference often reacted with anything from quiet uneasiness to throwing a punch.

To overcome these problems, the Personal Response Program was developed. It amounted to a training program designed to help Americans understand the Vietnamese better and to recognize and control their own prejudices.

The Personal Response Program continued beyond ACTOV and became an integral part of the training package that would-be advisors received before going to Vietnam. It evolved into an extensive program toward the latter part of the war, including many unconventional training methods that were a reflection of the times, such as having the men feel one another's faces and listen to one another's stomachs gurgle. It met with varying degrees of success and receptivity among the trainees. One burly "mustang" lieutenant, when told by his enlisted "facilitator" (instructor) that "we're all on a first-name basis in this class," replied with a growl, "Mine's Lieutenant!"

There were several other unusual aspects of the ACTOV program. One involved the building of ferrocement boats, which was a relatively inexpensive way to increase the VNN's inventory of patrol craft. These unusual craft were built of steel framework, wire mesh, and cement. They required very little hull maintenance and were not susceptible to the teredo worms. Two designs, the Coastal Raider and the Viper (designed for river interdiction), were created.

Another priority of the ACTOV program was spelled out by Admiral Zumwalt in a January 1970 message summarizing some of the past year's accomplishments and the coming year's goals:

A SAIGON TAXI DRIVER MAKES ABOUT THREE TIMES AS MUCH AS A MARRIED VNN LIEUTENANT. ALTHOUGH RVNAF [Republic of Vietnam Armed Forces] PAY HAS INCREASED BY 30% IN THE LAST THREE YEARS, THE COST OF LIVING HAS INCREASED BY NEARLY 300%. THUS, WE INTRODUCED THE DEPENDENT SHELTER AND ANIMAL HUSBANDRY PROGRAM TO GIVE THE VNN SAILOR A HOUSE AND FOOD SOURCE ESSENTIALLY INDEPENDENT OF HIS PAY. THE INABILITY OF THE SAILOR TO PROVIDE HIMSELF AND HIS FAMILY WITH THE BASIC ESSENTIALS COULD CAUSE US TO LOSE EVERYTHING FASTER THAN ANY MAJOR COMMUNIST OFFENSIVE. THE LOW VNN STANDARD OF LIVING IS, IN MY OPINION, A WORSE LONG TERM THREAT THAN THE VC.

The Dependent Shelter and Animal Husbandry Program that he mentions in the message was another of the unconventional ways that the U.S. Navy fought the war in Vietnam. Homes were built for VNN families (some of them with ferrocement); the "animal husbandry" portion of the program consisted of importing small livestock into Vietnam for distribution to the families. This program, known as "pigs and chickens" among American Navy men, added protein to the poor Vietnamese diet and had the advantage of being self-perpetuating through breeding. Only the long-term investment of feed for the animals was required once the animals were introduced.

ACTOV began immediately after the Abrams briefing in

late 1968. The detail planning was hammered out very rapidly during many late-night sessions, and actual implementation was under way shortly thereafter. The Navy was consistently out in front of the other services in Vietnamization.

In February 1969 River Assault Division 91 of the Mobile Riverine Force became River Assault and Interdiction Divisions 70 and 71 of the VNN, which were assigned to the Giant Slingshot operation and performed well. By the end of June, four more divisions (a total of sixty-four additional craft) were turned over to the Vietnamese and combined with the first two to become Task Force 211 in the new VNN organization. The Mobile Riverine Force was officially disestablished on 25 August 1969, and the assault craft that had not yet been turned over to the Vietnamese were organized into the Riverine Strike Group (Task Group 194.7) as part of SEA LORDS while awaiting turnover.

The first PBRs were turned over in August, when River Division 574 became VNN River Patrol Group 52 in the Rung Sat Special Zone. These were followed in October by River Divisions 533, 534, and 591 plus ten craft taken piecemeal from other divisions. Forty additional PBRs were shipped over from the United States and added to the VNN inventory at this time.

The turnover package for Market Time included the PCFs, WPBs, and a number of WHECs and DERs, but did not include the aircraft that had augmented the ship and boat patrols with expanded visual and radar coverage. To fill this gap, a chain of coastal radar stations was created. Sixteen stations, placed at regular intervals along the coast, were constructed or modernized. One station was a U.S. Coast Guard lightship that was converted for the purpose.

In November the operational base at My Tho became the first to be turned over. Within a year six more bases had followed.

Simultaneous to the turnover of assets, the number of VNN personnel grew rapidly as well. In only one year, the number increased from 8,000 to 26,500. The planned growth was for the VNN to reach a total of 30,000; as such it would stand as the fourteenth largest Navy in the world.

In the beginning of 1970, Admiral Zumwalt made the following appeal to his forces: "Progress to date has exceeded my fondest expectations, but we must accelerate still more to stay ahead of the power curve. Go team go."

Admiral Zumwalt was relieved as COMNAVFORV on 15 May 1970 by Vice Admiral Jerome H. King, Jr., in a ceremony aboard the USS *Page County* (LST-1096) moored in the Saigon River near Vietnamese Navy Headquarters. Admiral Zumwalt left Vietnam to become Chief of Naval Operations, but in his change-of-command address he promised to "continue to provide priority to this Vietnamization process." ACTOV continued in full swing under Admiral King and his successors.

In less than a year, the last U.S. Navy operation, Solid Anchor, was given to the Vietnamese, and the only American Navy men remaining in Vietnam were advisors. By mid-year 1971 the total number of in-country Navy personnel was one third what it had been at its 38,000 peak in 1968–69. When the last vessel was turned over to the Vietnamese by the U.S. Navy and Coast Guard, the totals were:

2 DERs	84 ASPBs
7 WHECs	22 monitors
9 LSTs*	10 CCBs
26 WPBs	100 ATCs
107 PCFs	25 LCPLs
293 PBRs	123 LCMs

(Other patrol, mine-sweeping, and auxiliary vessels beyond the scope of this book were also turned over.)

The Incursion

A November 1980 article in *Surface Warfare* magazine included the following account, provided by Master Chief Henry C. Farrior:

> We went into a heavily fortified bunker area. You could tell that it had been used for a long time by enemy

---

* Several LSTs had been converted to other vessel types (e.g., ARL).

forces. We went in there—started drawing fire—shot our way in.

We knew that it was a free fire zone. Anything that moved was fair game. The Vietnamese were running the operation. I spoke some Vietnamese. They spoke some English. I guess we could make ourselves understood about 50% of the time. . . .

Two or three sampans passed us. They cut right by us and the Vietnamese called for them to halt. Of course nobody was halting. Then the crew would fire at them. When it quieted down about one or two o'clock in the morning, I just laid down in the bow of the boat by the gun turret and went to sleep.

We were up at daybreak and we could see the sampans that we had machine-gunned during the late evening and early morning. They were loaded with weapons and rice.

The boat covering our movement took a direct hit . . . the explosion blew the boat up onto the beach. It was right up on the bank—half in and half out of the water.

. . . and just as I stepped up on the engine covers, the boat took a hit from an antitank round. I was behind a splinter shield. . . . The antitank round came through that, creating its own shrapnel. It got my left side, all the way from my little toe up to my armpit. I must have been hit in 15–20 places.

. . . I looked down and saw the blood. We were still under fire.

There was nothing unusual in the above account compared with the countless other firefights experienced by Americans in Vietnam. Even the fact that Farrior, then a first-class petty officer, was awarded the Silver Star for directing and delivering fire from an exposed position on the boat for some thirty minutes after he was wounded was not unusual. The fact that he was an advisor during this action was also not unusual. What was different about his account was that it did not take place in Vietnam.

At 0730 on 9 May 1970, a joint American and Vietnamese task force had crossed the national boundary of South Vietnam and swept up the Mekong River into Cambodia. Numbering about 140 vessels, it was the largest task force ever formed in the history of the war. Simultaneously, Vietnamese and American ships set up a blockade along the Cambodian coast to prevent enemy infiltration by sea.

These naval operations were a part of the larger incursion by the American and Vietnamese armies into Cambodia to strike at the longstanding North Vietnamese sanctuaries there. The naval aspect of the operation, dubbed Tran Hung Dao XI, had as one of its primary objectives the securing of the strategically important Highway 1 ferry crossing at Neak Luong. The Viet Cong were holding the town, and the armada, carrying Vietnamese Marines, was to take control of the crossing away from the enemy. Once Neak Luong had been secured, a portion of the task force was to continue up the Mekong to Phnom Penh to deliver food and supplies and to evacuate refugees. The American advisors were to go only as far as Neak Luong. After that the operation was to become a VNN solo.

The force took Neak Luong without much difficulty. The two ferries that had previously serviced the crossing were missing, presumably sunk by retreating enemy forces to prevent their use by the allies, so the joint American/Vietnamese force began searching for them. Numerous reconnaissance flights failed to locate the missing ferries, but then on 12 May, Rear Admiral Matthews (Deputy COMNAVFORV) spotted one of them while inspecting the area by air. The ferry had been sunk near the east bank of the river some distance north of the crossing. In a message to his boss later that day, Rear Admiral Matthews said, "CTG 194.0 [HIMSELF] CONTEMPLATING WILLING HIS AGED EYEBALLS TO SOME NEEDY YOUNG AIR OBSERVER."

Salvage operations were begun on the two ferries (the second had been subsequently discovered sunk near the one Rear Admiral Matthews had spotted), and they were eventually raised and repaired.

On 11 May the VNN solo operation began as two LSTs, three LSMs (Landing Ships, Medium; formerly French), fifteen PCFs, and ten LCM-8s proceeded upriver after unloading their USN advisors. The mission was not the easiest; the Vietnamese were unfamiliar with the Cambodian Mekong, and some of their navigation had to be done at night. But they performed well, meeting all schedules and successfully evacuating many more refugees than had originally been planned. The most significant aspect of the operation was that the VNN did it without American involvement, an indication that ACTOV was working.

Despite the military soundness of an operation that took away an enemy sanctuary, political pressures brought about the order for all Americans to withdraw from Cambodia on 30 June. VNN forces remained in Cambodia to keep the river open between Phnom Penh and the Vietnam border.

The incursion had a noticeable effect on conditions in the delta. As controversial as the incursion may have been politically (causing massive protest demonstrations back in the United States), there can be little doubt that militarily it was a strategic move that was long overdue. The COMNAVFORV Monthly Historical Summary for May 1970 supports this in its "Operations SEA LORDS Summary" by noting the immediate effect of the incursion along the barrier close to Cambodia:

With . . . penetration into the Cambodian Parrot's Beak area on 30 April 1970, enemy infiltration into the Republic of Viet Nam seems to have at least temporarily abated. As North Vietnamese and Viet Cong pulled back to the north and west as the Allies advanced, both in the Parrot's Beak area and along the Mekong River, enemy pressure was relieved in most SEA LORDS AOs [areas of operation]. Units in operations Ready Deck, Barrier Reef, and Search Turn saw very little hostile action during the month and Giant Slingshot assets were turned over to the Vietnamese Navy by 5 May. In the southernmost regions of South Viet Nam, however, the Cambodian involvement was apparently of little consequence as units of Operation Breezy Cove reported a number of actions along the Song Ong Doc and its tributaries.

SCATTOR

On 16 May 1969 the U.S. Coast Guard cutters *Point Garnet* (WPB-82310) and *Point League* (WPB-82304) hauled down their American flags for the last time in a ceremony at Saigon. The craft from that day forward were to be known as the *Le Phuoc Duc* and *Le Van Nga,* respectively. They were the first of twenty-six WPBs eventually turned over to the Vietnamese Navy by the U.S. Coast Guard.

The process had begun on 3 February 1969, when two VNN lieutenants reported for duty as prospective commanding officers of the two vessels. The Coast Guard turnover program, named Small Craft Assets, Training, and Turnover of Resources (SCATTOR), differed from the Navy's ACTOV program in that the prospective commanding officer was the first to report aboard rather than the last. The VNN prospective commanding officers immediately assumed the role of executive officers under the American commanding officers. They remained in this role throughout the sequenced relieving of personnel on the craft to assist in the training of the VNN personnel. (The Navy had not incorporated this method into the ACTOV program because there were not as many qualified VNN officers as there were vessels to be turned over. The prospective commanding officers were being trained to assume their roles while turnover was gradually taking place.) When the entire crew had been replaced by Vietnamese sailors and the only Americans remaining on board were the commanding officers, the two craft and the VNN crews were given an operational readiness inspection, conducted by a team of USN, USCG, and VNN personnel, similar to the ones American ships periodically receive in the United States. After successful completion of the inspection, the craft were ready for transfer to the Vietnamese Navy. The integrity of the Market Time patrols was maintained throughout this process.

This procedure was repeated again and again until, on 15 August 1970, the last two cutters of the twenty-six, the *Point Marone* (WPB-82331) and *Point Cypress* (WPB-82326), were turned over.

Postscripts

A letter dated 13 April 1973 from COMNAVFORV to CINC-PACFLT, the subject of which was "Status of Vietnamization Upon Withdrawal of U.S. Naval Forces" (originally classified Secret), appraised the VNN as follows:

> In conclusion, this appraisal of the VNN and VNMC [Vietnamese Marine Corps] finds that both services are capable of successfully meeting the demands that are likely to be placed upon them in the immediate and near term future. In the case of the VNN, current combat capabilities are adequate but if current progress toward self-sufficiency is to be sustained, certain critical deficiencies must be remedied.

These "critical deficiencies" were listed as enclosures to the letter:

> Commanding officers and executive officers are not thoroughly prepared to assume their responsibilities. . . . Properly trained and qualified petty officers and officers are not always assigned to the key billets. . . . With the exception of Harbor Entrance Control Post (HECP) Da Nang, the HECPs are not performing their mission. . . . The VNN is not capable of neutralizing a concentrated countrywide enemy mining effort. . . . The VNN lacks a permanent work force of trained specialists in positions of responsibility who can provide organizational continuity within the logistics system. . . . There is insufficient command interest and monitoring of the units' performance of the Planned Maintenance System. . . . The revised VNN supply system is deficient in formalized VNN officer and supply training. . . .

The American exodus was complete, ACTOV had run its course, and the Vietnamese Navy was on its own. Yet there were serious deficiencies, as described in the preceding letter. Were the deficiencies serious enough to prevent the VNN from succeeding? Or were the problems surmountable given the right circumstances? These questions can never be definitively answered because Vietnamization was not permitted to run its course as originally planned.

American logistic support and the promise of American reintervention should the North invade the South were essential components of the Vietnamization plan. But in the months following the American withdrawal, interest in funding the logistical support dwindled. The money so slated in 1973–74 was seriously reduced. The request for funding for South Vietnam that was included in the military procurement bill for fiscal year 1975 (beginning 1 July 1974) was cut by more than 30 percent. This, coupled with the subordinate role of the VNN in South Vietnamese politics (the Army had always overshadowed the Navy in the Saigon hierarchy), took much of the wind out of the sails of the Vietnamese Navy. Operational readiness in the VNN steadily declined. Eventually a number of its riverine units were deactivated, and more and more boats and associated equipment went out of commission with no hope of repair.

President Richard M. Nixon had promised to take retaliatory action if the North Vietnamese did not live up to the terms of the peace treaty, but problems with the Watergate crisis and a national reluctance to get embroiled in Vietnam again changed that from a commitment to an empty threat. On 1 July 1973 the president was compelled to sign into law a bill that included the following restriction:

> None of the funds herein appropriated under this Act may be expended to support directly or indirectly combat activities in or over Cambodia, Laos, North Vietnam and South Vietnam or off the shores of Cambodia, Laos, North Vietnam and South Vietnam by United States forces, and after August 15, 1973, no other funds heretofore appropriated under any other Act may be expended for such purpose.

Then, on 7 November 1973, Congress overrode the president's veto and created Public Law 93-148, the War Powers Resolution, which limited the president's ability to introduce (or, in the case of Vietnam, reintroduce) American forces into hostilities.

The death knell had been sounded for South Vietnam. Hanoi did not require any extraordinary acumen to realize that America was no longer going to stand behind its former ally. The violations of the Paris Peace Accords, which had been going on since the signing, became more flagrant. North Vietnamese troops backed by Soviet logistics poured into South Vietnam.

On 30 April 1975, it was all over. Saigon fell to North Vietnamese forces, and America had lost a war for the first time in its nearly two-century-long history.

So it was that the success of ACTOV and SCATTOR, and Vietnamization in general, were never really given a fair test. The ground rules upon which the programs had been built were changed, so an appraisal is impossible and, sadly, irrelevant.

The accelerating pace of the turnover and the recognized shortcomings of the VNN at the time of withdrawal suggests that perhaps the process was too hasty. Certainly the target dates were driven more by political pressures than by military assessments.

Yet there can be little doubt that the South Vietnamese armed forces improved markedly during the Vietnamization period. When the North launched its Easter Offensive of 1972, in which virtually all of the North Vietnamese Army invaded the South, the performance of the South Vietnamese was impressive. They repulsed the invasion on all fronts. But again a clear assessment is impossible because American air power was still involved in full force and U.S. advisors were still present.

Because the VNN was faced with few significant challenges during the years between turnover and collapse, it is difficult to focus on that part of Vietnamization. All indications are that the VNN lost no ground in the delta after turnover until the final days in April 1975. Market Time apparently still maintained an effective barrier, picking up contraband and sinking an occasional trawler. The only VNN base lost during the 1972 invasion was Cua Viet at the DMZ, and this author remembers well the dispatches that came into Naval Advisory Unit 1 during the early hours of the offensive, telling of the heroic stand made by the sailors there before they succumbed to the weight of the NVA armored thrust.

Successful or not, Vietnamization was the order of the day. And the Navy and Coast Guard met this challenge with their ACTOV and SCATTOR programs. Given the conditions that prevailed at the time, it seems that these programs were the best that could have been devised and carried out. For some, the administrators who arrived late in the war, the task was no more difficult than any of the other challenges their naval careers had offered. But some of those called upon to carry out these tasks were the same ones who had taken their craft into the narrow, jungle-covered canals where they knew the enemy lay in wait; who had seen tracers piercing the night in search of them; who had screamed into a radio calling for the medical help they knew could not save a wounded friend. These men found yielding victory for the political expedient of extrication a most difficult task. It is to their credit especially that ACTOV and SCATTOR were carried out.

EPILOGUE

. . . selecting and combining as he pleases, each man reads his own peculiar lesson according to his own peculiar mind and mood.

—HERMAN MELVILLE, *Pierre*

He had come at dawn because he knew that then, before the world had awakened, he would find the silence he knew was essential. He had come early because he also knew that he must be alone.

The eastern sky glowed with the pink that heralds the coming of the sun on clear mornings, and he stopped for a moment to gaze at it, basking in the warmth that it evoked within him. There was a chill in the air, and he had been fighting back the urge to shiver.

He moved on, wishing his footsteps were not audible in the morning stillness. Looking ahead through the bud-laden boughs of the young trees, he could see them: the three men.

They stood motionless, maintaining the silence he had felt so important. He drew nearer and felt his stomach muscles tighten as he saw that one of the men held an M-60 machine gun on his right shoulder. And a wash of nostalgia swept through him as he recognized the flak jacket worn by the man in the middle.

The three men didn't move when he stepped up to them and pulled the black beret from his head. Their bronze eyes looked beyond him, filled with conviction and a trace of ironic despair. They were eyes that had seen the power and the glory of America, yet had witnessed the agony of shattered ideals and the sorrow of purposeless death. Their vigilance, which had once scanned bamboo thickets in search of Viet Cong, now centered upon a long black wall covered with names that bore poignant testimony to days and people gone but not forgotten.

He looked at these three men for a long time and saw something of himself in them. Then the rays of the rising sun began to glint off their metallic features. He turned, and the four of them together watched the etched names on the granite wall grow brighter in the morning sunlight.

GLOSSARY

ACTOV
Accelerated Turnover to the Vietnamese

APB
Self-propelled Barracks Ship

APC
Armored Personnel Carrier

APL
Non-self-propelled Barracks Ship

ARL
Light Repair Ship

ARVN
Army of (South) Vietnam

ASPB
Assault Support Patrol Boat

ATC
Armored Troop Carrier

ATSB
Advanced Tactical Support Base

CCB
Command Communications Boat

CHNAVADVGRU
Chief, Naval Advisory Group

CINCPAC
Commander in Chief, Pacific

CINCPACFLT
Commander in Chief, Pacific Fleet

CNO
Chief of Naval Operations

COMIUWGRU1
Commander Inshore Undersea Warfare Group 1

COMNAVFORV
Commander Naval Forces Vietnam

COMUSMACV
Commander U.S. Military Assistance Command Vietnam

DD
Destroyer

DE
Destroyer Escort

GLOSSARY

DER
Destroyer Escort (Radar Picket)

Dinassaut
Divisions navales d'assaut (naval assault divisions)

DMZ
Demilitarized Zone

ENENG
Enemy Engagement (Fire Not Returned by Friendly Forces)

ENIFF
Enemy-Initiated Firefight

FOM
France Outre Mer (French Patrol Craft Used by VNN)

FRENG
Friendly-Initiated Engagement (Fire Not Returned by Enemy Forces)

FRIFF
Friendly- (Forces) Initiated Firefight

HC-1
Helicopter Combat Support Squadron 1

Hoi Chanh
Former Viet Cong who has rallied to the South Vietnamese side

IUWU
Inshore Undersea Warfare Units

KIA
Killed in Action

KKK
Khmer Kampuchea Kron

LCI
Landing Craft, Infantry

LCM
Landing Craft, Mechanized

LCPL
Landing Craft, Personnel, Large

LCT
Landing Craft, Tank

LCU
Landing Craft, Utility

LCVP
Landing Craft, Vehicle, Personnel

LSD
Landing Ship, Dock

LSIL
Landing Ship, Infantry, Large

LSM
Landing Ship, Medium

LSSL
Landing Support Ship, Large

LST
Landing Ship, Tank

MAAG
Military Assistance Advisory Group

MACV
Military Assistance Command Vietnam

MSB
Minesweeping Boat

MSC
Minesweeper, Coastal

324

MSL
Minesweeper, Light

MSM
Minesweeper, Medium

MSO
Minesweeper, Ocean

NVA
North Vietnamese Army

PACV
Patrol Air Cushion Vehicle

PBR
Patrol Boat, River

PCF
Patrol Craft, Fast

PG
Patrol Gunboat

PGH
Patrol Gunboat, Hydrofoil

reefer
refrigerator

RF/PF
Regional Forces/Popular Forces ("Ruff Puff")

RPC
River Patrol Craft

SCATTOR
Small Craft Assets, Training, and Turnover of Resources

SEAL
Sea, Air, Land (USN Special Warfare Personnel)

SEA LORDS
Southeast Asia Lake, Ocean, River, Delta Strategy

STCAN
Services Techniques des Constructions et Armes Navales (French Patrol Craft used by VNN)

USA
United States Army

USCG
United States Coast Guard

USCGC
United States Coast Guard Cutter

USN
United States Navy

USS
United States Ship

VC
Viet Cong

VNMC
Vietnamese Marine Corps

VNN
Vietnamese Navy

WHEC
High-Endurance Cutter (USCG)

WPB
Patrol Boat (USCG)

YFNB
Non-self-propelled Barge

YRBM
Repair and Maintenance Barge

YTB
Large Harbor Tug

CHRONOLOGY

1964

January
Captain Bucklew writes his report.
Captain and Mrs. Hardcastle arrive in Saigon.

June
Lieutenant Dale Meyerkord arrives in Vietnam.

November
Dickey Chapelle visits Lieutenant Jim Vincent to do a story on the Junk Force.

1965

February
President Johnson orders all American dependents to leave Vietnam.

March
Lieutenant Dale Meyerkord is killed in an ambush.

A North Vietnamese trawler is sighted and subsequently captured in Vung Ro Bay, South Vietnam, in what comes to be known as the "Vung Ro Incident."

Operation Market Time begins.

May
Crewmen from the USS *Buck* (DD-761) board a junk near the 17th parallel and make the first capture of infiltrators.

CHRONOLOGY

July

Operational control of Market Time shifts from Commander Seventh Fleet to the Chief of the Naval Advisory Group as Task Force 115.

The first Coast Guard WPBs arrive in Vietnam.

September

"MacLeod's Navy" begins the first river patrols in South Vietnam under the American flag.

United Boatbuilders lands the PBR contract and promises delivery of the first 120 boats by April 1966.

PACVs commence operations as part of Task Force 115 (Market Time).

October

The first "Swift boats" (PCFs) arrive in Vietnam.

The PACVs complete operations with Task Force 115.

November

Dickey Chapelle is killed while on patrol with Marines near Chu Lai. She is the first American woman correspondent to die in action.

December

Operation Game Warden officially begins.

1966

January

MACV orders CHNAVADVGRU to develop plans for defense of Vietnam's harbors. (This later becomes Operation Stable Door.)

February

The U.S. Army Ninth Infantry Division is activated at Fort Riley, Kansas, in anticipation of its use in the Mekong Delta. The Second Brigade is modified for its role in the Mobile Riverine Force.

U.S. Navy SEALS begin operations with Task Force 116 (Operation Game Warden).

The first Swift boat is lost: PCF-4 sinks after a mine is detonated as her crew attempts to take a Viet Cong flag as a souvenir.

March

U.S. Army helicopter pilots report to Task Force 116 to begin turnover of their helicopters to the Navy for what will become the "Seawolves" of Operation Game Warden.

The first minesweeping craft arrive in Vietnam to sweep the Long Tau River as part of the assigned mission of Operation Game Warden.

The first PBRs arrive in Vietnam.

April

The Chief of the Naval Advisory Group assumes the new, additional title of Commander Naval Forces Vietnam.

June

Navy pilots take over the helicopter role in Operation Game Warden. They become known as the "Seawolves."

Mine Squadron 11—Detachment Alfa is established at Nha Be to carry out the minesweeping role of Game Warden on the Long Tau River.

August

The USCGC *Point Welcome* is accidentally sunk by U.S. Air Force planes.

September

"Coronado Conference" meets to plan operations for the Mobile Riverine Force.

River Assault Flotilla 1 (the Navy element of the Mobile Riverine Force) is commissioned into service and begins operations in Vietnam.

October

Boatswain's Mate First Class James Elliott Williams's PBR patrol, with Seawolf support, destroys sixty-five enemy vessels and kills and captures well over a thousand enemy soldiers. (He is later awarded the Medal of Honor for his actions.)

CHRONOLOGY

November
Operation Monster, using PACVs, is conducted in the enemy-controlled region known as the Plain of Reeds.

The first MSB is lost on the Long Tau River to a Viet Cong mine.

1967

January
The Mobile Riverine Force begins training as an integrated Army-Navy task force in the Rung Sat region.

February
The Mobile Riverine Force conducts its first major operation (River Raider I) in the Rung Sat Special Zone.

March
United Boatbuilders gets the contract for the new, improved Mark II PBR.

April
Coast Guard WHECs begin patrols along the coast of South Vietnam as part of Operation Market Time.

The first patrol gunboat arrives in Vietnamese waters. These PGs and, later, PGHs make up the newly created Coastal Squadron 3 component of Task Force 115.

May
The Mobile Riverine Force conducts its first major operation (Hop Tac XVIII) in the Mekong Delta.

June
The Mobile Riverine Force begins a long series of operations dubbed "Coronado."

Lieutenant "Padre" Johnson and Lieutenant Commander Chuck Horowitz participate in Operation Concordia I as members of the Mobile Riverine Force.

September
Operation Green Wave tests the feasibility of conducting river patrol operations in the I Corps Tactical Zone.

1968

January

The "Tet Offensive" begins on the last day of the month. PBR Division 55 is formed and sent north to patrol the river and lagoons of the Hue area as a forerunner to Task Force Clearwater.

February

Four North Vietnamese trawlers attempt to infiltrate South Vietnam. Three are destroyed and one is turned back by Market Time forces.

Task Force Clearwater is officially established.

March

The Godbehere patrol is ambushed on the Bassac River.

May

In ceremonies at the Pentagon, James Elliott Williams receives the Medal of Honor from President Johnson.

June

PCF-19 is sunk by "friendly fire."

The VNN assumes a minesweeping role on the Long Tau River.

September

Vice Admiral Elmo Zumwalt III assumes command as COMNAVFORV.

October

Lieutenant (j.g.) Michael Bernique engages the enemy in an off-limits waterway near the Cambodian border.

November

Operation SEA LORDS begins, combining assets of Task Force 115, Task Force 116, and Task Force 117 into new Task Force 194.

Operation Search Turn begins.

Operation Foul Deck begins.

December
Operation Giant Slingshot begins.

The U.S. Navy begins its ACTOV program.

1969

January
Light Attack Squadron 4 is commissioned at North Island, California, to deploy to Vietnam as additional air support for Game Warden forces. This unusual Navy squadron flies OV-10A aircraft and becomes known as the ''Black Ponies.''

Operation Barrier Reef begins.

Quincy Truett dies in the Kinh Dong Tien Canal.

February
Operation Sea Tiger begins, conducting raids into I Corps Tactical Zone rivers.

The Coast Guard's SCATTOR program begins.

April
The Black Ponies begin operations in Vietnam.

May
The first two Coast Guard WPBs are turned over to the VNN.

The Sea Float complex is established near Nam Can in the Ca Mau Peninsula.

August
The Mobile Riverine Force is disbanded, and its craft are either turned over to the VNN or are committed to the new SEA LORDS strategy.

The first PBRs are turned over to the VNN.

September
Operation Breezy Cove is established on the Ong Doc River near the U Minh Forest.

CHRONOLOGY

October

Sea Float moves ashore and is renamed Solid Anchor.

Operation Ready Deck conducts interdiction operations into the upper Saigon River region.

November

The U.S. Navy base at My Tho is turned over to the VNN. This is the first operational base to be transferred to the Vietnamese.

1970

May

A joint American and South Vietnamese incursion into Cambodia takes place.

Operation Blue Shark replaces the Market Time Raider campaign.

Admiral Zumwalt is relieved as COMNAVFORV to become Chief of Naval Operations.

June

Task Force Clearwater is officially turned over to the VNN.

Task Force 194 (SEA LORDS) is deactivated.

August

The last of the Coast Guard WPBs are turned over to the VNN.

November

Operation Blue Shark ends.

December

All U.S. craft programmed for transfer to the VNN are turned over.

1971

December

The U.S. Coast Guard cutter *Cook Inlet* makes the last WHEC combat patrol in Vietnamese waters.

CHRONOLOGY

1972

April
The last American naval bases at Nha Be, Binh Thuy, Cam Ranh Bay, and Da Nang are turned over to the Vietnamese.

The North Vietnamese launch a major invasion of South Vietnam.

1973

January
The Paris Peace Accords are signed.

March
The last U.S. troops leave South Vietnam.

1975

April
Saigon falls to the North Vietnamese Army.

SOURCE NOTES

The works used in writing particular sections of the book are discussed here with enough information to identify them. Complete information on each work is provided in the bibliography immediately following these source notes.

Since my work focuses upon the military rather than the political aspects of the war, many of the works I have read about Vietnam do not appear here or in the bibliography. But some general works that helped lay the background for *Brown Water, Black Berets* are noteworthy. Stanley Karnow's *Vietnam: A History* surveys the historical background of the American involvement in Vietnam by reviewing in fair detail the significant events from early Vietnamese history to 1975. An excellent summary of American military operations in the war is found in Dave Richard Palmer's *Summons of the Trumpet;* a more detailed account is provided by *America in Vietnam* by Guenter Lewy. More critical analyses are available in Cecil B. Currey's *Self-Destruction: The Disintegration and Decay of the United States Army During the Vietnam Era,* U. S. G. Sharp's *Strategy for Defeat: Vietnam in Retrospect,* and *On Strategy: A Critical Analysis of the Vietnam War,* by Harry G. Summers, Jr. In 1979 the BDM Corporation, under government contract, produced a massive (nine-volume) study of the war, which provides good background material and some interesting insights. This work, entitled *A Study of Strategic Lessons Learned in Vietnam,* has not been published, but is available at the Nimitz Library of the U.S. Naval Academy, in Annapolis, Maryland.

Sources dealing specifically with the Navy's roles in Vietnam are scant. A planned three-volume work by the Naval

Historical Center entitled *The United States Navy and the Vietnam Conflict* is under way, but at this writing only Volume 1, *The Setting of the Stage to 1959,* is in print. As an interim measure the division has produced *A Short History of the United States Navy and the Southeast Asian Conflict 1950–1975,* by Edward J. Marolda and G. Wesley Price III, which briefly covers not only the "in-country" roles of the Navy but the air and fleet operations conducted in support of the war. Another useful summary document, produced by the Naval Historical Center while the war was still going on, is *Riverine Warfare: The U.S. Navy's Operations on Inland Waters.* It includes such operations throughout American history, but the treatment of the Vietnam War is an excellent introduction to the subject (particularly in the revised edition, which appeared in 1969).

While serving on the staff of COMNAVFORV, Richard L. Schreadley wrote a fairly extensive document entitled "The Naval War in Vietnam," which was never published but can be viewed in the Naval Historical Center's Operational Archives in Washington, D.C. Schreadley subsequently pared down and revised that work into an article entitled "The Naval War in Vietnam 1950–1970," which appeared in the 1971 *Naval Review.* Both the original document and the resultant article are useful sources.

Early in the war, CHNAVADVGRU implemented the "Monthly Historical Summary" as a means of recording the events occurring within his purview. These summaries continued for the duration (although the last fifteen months of the war were covered by quarterly, not monthly, summaries) and were joined by additional "Monthly Historical Supplements" between January 1967 and July 1968, for a total of more than one hundred documents. After April 1966, these reports became the COMNAVFORV (not CHNAVADVGRU) Monthly Historical Summaries, reflecting the new title of the Navy's Vietnam commander. While they are not without bias, these documents, now fully declassified and available at the Naval Historical Center in Washington, D.C., are useful in gathering specifics and in correlating and certifying information from other sources.

Another group of documents available at the Naval Historical Center is the "end-of-tour reports" submitted by advisors and operational commanders at the completion of their tours of duty in Vietnam. Although some of these reports appear to reflect only what superiors wanted to hear (or, more likely, what the individual thought that his superiors wanted to hear), most provide insight on the challenges, frustrations, and remedies perceived by the participants. I have not directly employed many of these reports, however, because they are rarely conclusive. For every one that stands on one side of an issue, there is another that opposes it with equal conviction. These varied viewpoints are a mine of virtually virgin material that awaits excavation by an enterprising analytical historian but are unfortunately beyond the scope of *Brown Water, Black Berets*.

Two other sources that have recently appeared are Victor Croizat's *The Brown Water Navy: The River and Coastal War in Indo-China and Vietnam, 1948–1972*, and Jim Mesko's *Riverine: A Pictorial History of the Brown Water War in Vietnam*. The former is a particularly valuable source for the early advisory years but is somewhat weak in its treatment of the American operational role. Mesko's work is good as a summary document if carefully employed, but contains a significant number of errors that detract from its overall credibility.

Several additional works served throughout the writing of *Brown Water, Black Berets* for reference and background material. Harvey H. Smith and Donald W. Bernier's *Area Handbook for South Vietnam* was published by the Department of the Army in 1967 (it is no longer in print) and was helpful for geographic and demographic material. The U.S. Naval Institute's *Naval and Maritime Chronology 1961–1971* and Jack Sweetman's *American Naval History: An Illustrated Chronology of the U.S. Navy and Marine Corps 1775–Present* were valuable not only for maintaining the chronology but for providing clues that stimulated further research. Richard T. Miller's "Fighting Boats of the United States," which appeared in the 1968 *Naval Review*, is an excellent compilation of data on the various craft that play a central role in *Brown Water, Black Berets*.

Prologue

The account of events in the prologue was based almost entirely upon interviews conducted with G. H. Childress and Geri Truett, and corroborated by reference to COM-NAVFORV's Monthly Historical Summary for January 1969, Quincy Truett's Navy Cross citation, and the *Dictionary of American Fighting Ships*.

1. Genesis

Mary Hardcastle

This section was based upon a series of interviews I conducted with both Captain and Mrs. William Hardcastle. During those interviews, the Hardcastles were kind enough to let me peruse their family photograph albums, which also helped to solidify some of the images portrayed in this section.

"Support Any Friend, Oppose Any Foe"

Much of the material was derived from readings in *Vietnam: History, Documents, and Opinions*, by Marvin E. Gettleman; President Lyndon Johnson's memoir, entitled *The Vantage Point; Vietnam: A History in Documents*, edited by Gareth Porter; Ronald H. Spector's *Advice and Support: The Early Years, 1941–1960* (part of the *U.S. Army in Vietnam* series issued by the U.S. Army Center of Military History); the Naval Historical Center's *The United States Navy and the Vietnam Conflict* (Volume 1: *The Setting of the Stage to 1959); Vietnam: A History*, by Stanley Karnow; *The Pentagon Papers* (Neil Sheehan *et al.*, editors); and the BDM Corporation's *A Study of Strategic Lessons Learned in Vietnam* (Volume 5: *Planning the War*).

Figures concerning the numbers of personnel in the Military Assistance Advisory Group, the Naval Advisory Group, and the Vietnamese Navy were taken from Spector's *Advice and Support* and the Naval Historical Center's *The United States Navy and the Vietnam Conflict*.

The John Foster Dulles quote was taken from page 182 of

John Emmet Hughes's *The Ordeal of Power*. The quote referring to a "slight but notable increase" in Communist-inspired violence came from the so-called "Pentagon Papers" (actually titled *United States—Vietnam Relations: 1945–1967*) and is included (with a detailed citation) on page 371 of the Naval Historical Center's *The United States Navy and the Vietnam Conflict* (Volume 1). The Viet Cong document referring to 1957–58 is quoted on page 330 of Spector's *Advice and Support* and refers to "The Situation in Nam Bo Since the Restoration of Peace to the Present," apparently written in 1961 and seized by American forces in April 1969; a copy of the document is held by the Army's Center of Military History in Washington, D.C. President Kennedy's inaugural address is, of course, available from many sources, but was in this instance taken from *John F. Kennedy: 1917–1963* by Urs Schwarz.

General Maxwell Taylor's message to President Kennedy recommending expansion of the U.S. commitment was quoted from page 145 of *The Pentagon Papers* by Neil Sheehan. The Vice President Johnson quote is from page 57 of his published memoirs entitled *The Vantage Point*.

CHNAVADVGRU

This section was based almost entirely upon the interviews conducted with Captain Hardcastle. The historical background was drawn from Karnow's *Vietnam: A History;* Allan R. Millett and Peter Maslowski's *For the Common Defense; Combined Operations in the Civil War,* by Rowena Reed; *Viet Nam: The Unheard Voices,* by Don Luce and John Sommer; and the Naval Historical Center's *Riverine Warfare: The U.S. Navy's Operations on Inland Waters.*

Sat Cong

"Sat Cong" was primarily the result of several interviews with Jim Vincent and material in an article entitled "Water War in Viet Nam" by Dickey Chapelle. Also quite useful in this chapter were W. E. Garrett's article "What Was a Woman Doing There?"; Richard F. Brown's "Role of the Junk Fleet

Advisor in Base Defense''; ''Vietnam Junk Force on Patrol'' by John E. Jones; and Richard Tregaskis's *Vietnam Diary*.

The dialogue was re-created from the memories of Jim Vincent; the descriptions of Ms. Chapelle, the base, and the various craft were drawn from photographs and recollections provided by Vincent and by W. E. Garrett.

River Assault Groups

This section was the result of readings in the Naval Historical Center's *The United States Navy and the Vietnam Conflict* (Volume 1) and *Riverine Warfare: The U.S. Navy's Operations on Inland Waters;* Victor Croizat's *The Brown Water Navy;* and *Street Without Joy* by Bernard Fall.

Hornblower

Interviews with Eugene Barney, Captain and Mrs. Hardcastle, Louise Meyerkord (mother of Lieutenant Meyerkord), and Jane Bonfanti (his widow) were supplemented by the CHNAVADVGRU Monthly Historical Summaries, Dickey Chapelle's ''Water War in Viet Nam,'' and Loudon Wainwright's ''In Search of a Vietnam Hero.'' Also very useful were the personal logs kept by Dale Meyerkord and Eugene Barney of their own volition. The Meyerkord log is held by the Operational Archives section of the Naval Historical Center; Barney has maintained possession of his but was kind enough to permit me to use it.

Details of Dale's early life were provided by his mother; the quote concerning his aggressiveness is taken from the Wainwright article. The 13 August and 22 September entries from Meyerkord's log were taken verbatim from the original. The ''sketching with words'' quote attributed to Ms. Chapelle was derived from her *National Geographic* article (page 295) and Eugene Barney's observations. The exchange between Major Padgett and Lieutenant Meyerkord was derived from quotes included in the Wainwright article and re-created with the assistance of Eugene Barney. The 16 March log entries were quoted verbatim from Barney's log. The MACV Monthly Evaluation Report for the month of March 1965 quoted in the last section of "Hornblower" is available through the Defense Technical Information Center.

Postscripts

The paragraph describing Dickey Chapelle's death was derived from W. E. Garrett's "What Was a Woman Doing There?"

2. Operation Market Time

"On Mission in Distant Areas"

Article 14 of the Geneva Accords was quoted from page 168 of Gettleman's *Vietnam: History, Documents, and Opinions*. Statistics concerning the "Passage to Freedom" were taken from the chapter of the same name in the Naval Historical Center's *The United States Navy and the Vietnam Conflict* (Volume 1).

The International Control Commission quote was from page 13 of Edwin Bickford Hooper's *Mobility, Support, Endurance*. The Hardcastle interviews provided Captain Chung Tan Cang's paraphrased opinions regarding infiltration.

The section concerning the Bucklew Report is a product of the report itself (copy available at the Naval Historical Center) and the U.S. Naval Institute's Oral History Program interview with Captain Bucklew. The quote was taken directly from the report.

The shift in Communist strategy in 1964–65 is covered in Palmer's *Summons of the Trumpet*, Robert J. O'Neill's *General Giap: Politician and Strategist*, and Richard L. Schreadley's "The Naval War in Vietnam 1950–70."

The Vung Ro Incident was re-created from information in *A Short History of the United States Navy and the Southeast Asian Conflict 1950–1975*, by Edward J. Marolda and G. Wesley Price III; a Commander Task Force 115 press release (see L.L. Champlin in the bibliography); the CHNA-VADVGRU Monthly Historical Summary for March 1965; "Duty: Coastal Surveillance," by Thomas L. Moore and Jean C. Cote; and an oral history interview with Commodore Ho

Van Ky Thoai, Vietnamese Navy. Specific figures for this chapter were taken from the U.S. Department of State's *Aggression from the North: The Record of North Viet-Nam's Campaign to Conquer South Viet-Nam*.

Nascent Market Time

Useful sources for this chapter were Schreadley's "The Naval War in Vietnam," Keith R. Tidman's *The Operations Evaluation Group*, General William C. Westmoreland's *A Soldier Reports*, Karnow's *Vietnam: A History*, and the CHNAVADVGRU Monthly Historical Summaries.

The advisors' comments were derived from the Ho Van Ky Thoai oral history interview. Material concerning the Westmoreland-convened meeting of March 1965 was taken from Tidman's *The Operations Evaluation Group* and Schreadley's "The Naval War in Vietnam." The quote concerning authorization from the South Vietnamese government for American units to "stop, board, search" was taken from page 265 of *The Operations Evaluation Group*.

The MACV quote came from page 188 of Schreadley's "The Naval War in Vietnam."

The dates and figures concerning the introduction of Coast Guard assets were extracted from Chapter 2 of Eugene N. Tulich's monograph *The United States Coast Guard in South East Asia During the Vietnam Conflict* (available from the Coast Guard's Public Affairs Division).

The quote near the end of the chapter granting approval for U.S. boarding operations and establishing the zones of control off the coast were taken from the BDM Corporation's *A Study of Strategic Lessons Learned in Vietnam* (page 7–17 of Book 1: "Operational Analyses," Volume VI: *Conduct of the War*).

Hardware

The John F. Kennedy quote came from page 398 of the article "Navy Small Craft in Market Time" by Captain Phil H. Bucklew. The Voltaire quote is included in the preface to Barbara Tuchman's *A Distant Mirror*.

For the Coast Guard portion of Market Time "hardware,"

details of vessel configurations and deployment numbers and dates were drawn from James A. Hodgman's "Market Time in the Gulf of Thailand," Dennis L. Noble's "Cutters and Sampans," and Tulich's *The United States Coast Guard in South East Asia*. Information regarding acquisition and deployment of the Navy's PCFs was gleaned from Bucklew's "Navy Small Craft in Market Time," Croizat's *The Brown Water Navy*, and the transcript of a speech by Leroy V. Swanson (then Assistant Chief of Naval Operations for Fleet Operations) entitled "Market Time—Game Warden: The Navy in Vietnam." Peter B. Mersky and Norman Polmar's *The Naval Air War in Vietnam* provided specifics on the air portion of Market Time, "Skimmer Ops" by J.F. Ebersole explained the use of Boston Whalers, W. J. Moredock's "The DER in Market Time" described the radar picket destroyer escort's role in the operation, and D. F. Wright's "Those 'Innocent Looking' Vietnamese Junks" was the source of information for minesweeper patrols.

Specific data on the various craft are also available in Richards T. Miller's "Fighting Boats of the United States." Where contradictions existed in specific data, such as speed capabilities or weapons configurations, I attempted to resolve them by consulting with interviewees and by comparing data in other standard reference works, such as Blackman's *Jane's Fighting Ships 1968–69* and Rowe and Morison's *Ships and Aircraft of the U.S. Fleet*.

Nonspecific background came from H. R. Kaplan's "The Coast Guard in Viet Nam" and his later article "Coast Guard Played Vital Role in Viet War," and from Thomas L. Moore's "U.S.—Viet Nam Anti-Smuggling Patrol."

The oversight of leaving the cutters white on their first patrol was described on page 51 of Noble's "Cutters and Sampans."

Details concerning the establishment of Boat Squadron 1 were taken from an oral history interview with Commander Arthur Ismay.

Besides the Moredock article "The DER in Market Time," some of the details concerning radar picket destroyer escort patrols were taken from a taped interview with then-Lieutenant Ross McElroy.

The details of PACV use in Market Time patrols were taken

from the COMNAVFORV Monthly Historical Summaries for September and October 1966. Operational characteristics of the craft were formed from Miller's "Fighting Boats of the United States."

Details of PG operations in Vietnam were drawn from Marolda and Price's *A Short History of the United States Navy and the Southeast Asian Conflict.*

The Market Time pilot describing the nighttime scene was quoted from page 30 of Mersky and Polmar's *The Naval Air War in Vietnam.* The description of the attack on Market Time aircraft at Tan Son Nhut airbase was derived from the COMNAVFORV Monthly Historical Summary for December 1966.

Souvenirs

The quote concerning the frustration of Market Time personnel was taken directly from the CHNAVADVGRU Monthly Historical Summary of January 1966.

The "Souvenirs" incident was re-created by piecing together the details found in the CHNAVADVGRU Monthly Historical Summary of February 1966, Phil Bucklew's "Navy Small Craft in Market Time," and interviews I conducted with Gil Dunn. The name of the officer in charge has been changed to preclude any potential embarrassment.

Tedium and Terror

This section is a composite of descriptions of Market Time operations found in Hanson W. Baldwin's " 'Spitkits' in Tropic Seas"; Leroy Swanson's "Market Time-Game Warden"; "Market Time in the Gulf of Thailand" by Hodgman; "Duty: Coastal Surveillance" by Thomas L. Moore and Jean C. Cote; Noble's "Cutters and Sampans"; "Skimmer Ops" by Ebersole; "Trawler!" by Charles R. Stephan; "Market Time Mother Ship" by William R. Harris; Moredock's "The DER in Market Time"; Tidman's *The Operations Evaluation Group; Mobility, Support, Endurance* by Hooper; the appropriate COMNAVFORV Monthly Historical Summaries; the Ismay oral history; and an interview with Richard O'Mara.

The veteran who is quoted concerning vessel cleanliness

and the roaches wishes to remain anonymous. The Bowler "Sherwood Forest" quote was taken directly from a letter he sent to me in response to an advertisement I ran in the U.S. Naval Academy Alumni Association's *Shipmate* magazine. The Swift boat veteran with the "thick Brooklyn accent" quoted near the end of the chapter is Dennis O'Mara. The quote concerning the officers in charge of PCFs was taken from page 10 of Hanson Baldwin's article " 'Spitkits' in Tropic Seas."

Fragments

The *Point Glover* incident was re-created from Hodgman's "Market Time in the Gulf of Thailand" and Kaplan's "The Coast Guard in Viet Nam."

The *Point Marone* incident was taken from the CHNAVADVGRU Monthly Historical Summary for September 1965, Kaplan's "The Coast Guard in Viet Nam," and Tulich's *The United States Coast Guard in South East Asia During the Vietnam Conflict.*

The *Point White* engagement was also derived from Kaplan's article and from the March 1966 CHNAVADVGRU Monthly Historical Summary.

The *Point Welcome* tragedy was re-created from the August 1966 COMNAVFORV Monthly Historical Summary and *Tim Page's Nam.* Page's quotes (the longer one describing the attack and the shorter one concerning his reasons for being out on the patrol) came from page 10 of that work.

The North Vietnamese helicopter incident was derived from the June 1968 COMNAVFORV Monthly Historical Summary.

The three incidents in the fall of 1966 were all taken from Kaplan's article and from the March 1966 CHNAVADVGRU Monthly Historical Summary.

The account of the rescue of Chinese fishermen came from the December 1966 COMNAVFORV Monthly Historical Summary.

The explosion of the landing craft at Duc Pho was recounted from the June 1967 COMNAVFORV Monthly Historical Summary.

The attempted infiltration by a North Vietnamese trawler

on 15 July 1967 was re-created from the appropriate COM-NAVFORV Monthly Historical Summary and from Stephan's "Trawler!" The quote at the end of the section concerning the MSO *Pledge* and nearby Swift boats was taken from page 71 of the Stephan article.

The August 1967 frontal assault on Coast Group 16 was taken from that month's COMNAVFORV Monthly Historical Summary.

Stable Door

The COMNAVFORV Monthly Historical Summary and Richard G. Bachmann's "Harbor Defense in Vietnam" were the sources for this chapter. The George Young quotes were taken from a 1968 COMNAVFORV press release (see J. D. Sheets in the bibliography).

"Bait a Trap and Clobber the Catch"

The opening quote came from the March 1968 COM-NAVFORV Monthly Historical Summary, where it was re-printed from a message that had been sent to all naval forces in Vietnam by Rear Admiral Kenneth L. Veth (then COM-NAVFORV).

The *Androscoggin* material in this chapter came from the transcript of W. H. Stewart's oral history. Confirmation of facts and the details of the three other simultaneous infiltration attempts were drawn from the appropriate COM-NAVFORV Monthly Historical Summary.

Postscripts

The statistics quoted were drawn from the L. L. Champlin press release and from the COMNAVFORV Monthly Historical Summary as indicated. The BDM quote is from page 7–18 of Book 1, volume VI, of that study. The first Westmoreland quote was taken from page 240 of his book *A Soldier Reports* and the second was included in the L. L. Champlin press release. The Palmer quote was taken from page 52 of his book *The 25-Year War;* Admiral Zumwalt's words on Market Time were drawn from page 36 of his book *On Watch.*

3. Operation Game Warden

S. A. Swarztrauber's "River Patrol Relearned" is the single best document on Game Warden, and was the basis for much of this chapter. The Operations Evaluation Group of the Center for Naval Analyses did a study of Game Warden in 1976 that covers the period from the operation's inception to the beginning of SEA LORDS in October 1968. This study has not been published, but is available through the Defense Technical Information Center in Alexandria, Virginia, and the Naval History Division at the Washington Navy Yard. Tidman's *The Operations Evaluations Group* (previously mentioned) was helpful in some areas, particularly in assessing various aspects of the operation, and the COMNAVFORV Monthly Historical Summaries were used throughout.

Nine Dragons

This section was derived from the U.S. Army's *Area Handbook for South Vietnam* (see Harvey H. Smith *et al.* in the bibliography) and an article by Peter T. White entitled "The Mekong: River of Terror and Hope." The American embassy official quote is taken from page 778 of the *National Geographic* article, where the official is not identified.

MacLeod's Navy

"MacLeod's Navy" resulted primarily from interviews with Kenneth L. MacLeod and access to his personal papers. Some of the Saigon details were based upon my own experiences, but have been put into proper historical context by referring to a book published there in 1965 as a guide for Americans, entitled *Saigon in the Flesh* by Doan Bich and Le Trang. Two of Paul Dean's articles written for syndication in 1965 were used in conjunction with telephone conversations with Dean and the MacLeod interviews to hone in on the details of the nights they were together in the Rung Sat. The bibliography lists Dean's articles as appearing in the *Indianapolis Star* even though he was working for the *Arizona Republic* on this assignment; the copies I was able to obtain had been picked up in syndication by the *Star*.

The quoted horoscope was included in Dean's article "MacLeod's Navy Has Tough Patrol." The Bronze Star citation was quoted directly from the original document. The letter of "congratulations" was quoted from the actual document, which Ken MacLeod has retained among his personal papers.

"Proud—Brave—Reliable"

The idea for "Proud—Brave—Reliable" came initially from an article in *Yachting* by Boughton Cobb, entitled "River Patrol Boat for Vietnam." Through Hatteras Yachts I was able to contact Sarah Phillips, Fred Joest, and Jack Hargrave, who all provided background and specifics for the Willis Slane story.

The dialogue between Willis Slane and Jack Hargrave, as well as Slane's words at the Navy meeting, were re-created from recollections provided by Mr. Hargrave and from an account of the meeting in the Cobb article.

Dollar amounts and contract specifications were taken from the Cobb article, interviews with Sea McGowen, and Swarztrauber's "River Patrol Relearned" article. The latter also provided much of the information concerning the PBR crews and patrols, while the McGowen interviews and an interview with Fred Joest were particularly helpful in explaining the modifications to the Mark II version of the PBR. The numbers of PBRs arriving in Vietnam at various times and their distribution in-country were taken from the Swarztrauber article and the study entitled *Game Warden* conducted by the Navy's Operations Evaluation Group. All figures were compared to the appropriate COMNAVFORV Monthly Historical Summaries.

The Canby quote (as well as the quote about Canby) was taken from page 88 of Frank Harvey's book *Air War—Vietnam*.

The unofficial meaning (Proud—Brave—Reliable) ascribed to the PBR acronym appeared commonly throughout the war; the words are on the division logo of River Division 543.

SOURCE NOTES
Building and Flexing

The primary sources for this chapter were the COM-
NAVFORV Monthly Historical Summary, Swarztrauber's
"River Patrol Relearned," and the Operations Evaluation
Group's *Game Warden* study. Specific numbers, dates, and
task organizations were found and cross-verified in these
sources. Occasional telephone calls to some of my interview
sources clarified my understanding of the many changes during *Game Warden*'s evolution.

Tactics

The Operations Evaluation Group's *Game Warden* study was
a principal source of the tactics described in this section.
Verification and some additional information was drawn from
Swarztrauber's "River Patrol Relearned" and from many of
the COMNAVFORV Monthly Historical Summaries.

Rules of engagement were found in the Commander Task
Force 116 Operation Order dated 1 February 1967; a copy of
this document can be found at the Operational Archives section of the Naval Historical Center.

The titles of the master's degree theses were taken from a
Defense Technical Information Center report bibliography
provided to me by Nimitz Library as a result of a computer
search request.

The quote from *True* magazine was taken from page 71 of
the February 1968 issue.

The fallen-tree tactic quote appears on page 68 of James
Butler's book, *River of Death*.

The concluding quote was taken from Swarztrauber's
"River Patrol Relearned," pages 135–137.

God Be Here

The God Be Here story was re-created by combining the information provided during a series of interviews with Richard
Godbehere and Jere Beery. The dialogue was re-created from
the memories of these two men and is probably quite accurate, since the two men's recollections in independent inter-

views were amazingly compatible considering the number of intervening years.

The details about the *Chieu Hoi* rallying program and the specific statistics on numbers of *Hoi Chanhs* were drawn from "Psychological Operations in Vietnam" by Victor G. Reiling and G. W. Scott.

The description of the Tet Offensive was derived from Don Oberdorfer's *Tet!*, Palmer's *Summons of the Trumpet,* and the January, February, and March COMNAVFORV Monthly Historical Summaries.

The incident with the reporters was written as Jere Beery recalls it. Neither of the reporters nor the boat captain, Bailey, could be located for confirmation or rebuttal.

Sweeping Swabs

Most useful in writing this section were George R. Kolbenschlag's "Minesweeping on the Long Tau River," "U.S. Minesweeping Boats Keep Clear the River to Saigon" by Jerry Riggs, and Swarztrauber's "River Patrol Relearned."

The opening description of the Long Tau River is quoted from pages 17–18 of Anthony Grey's *Saigon.*

The descriptions of the MSB craft were gleaned from Miller's "Fighting Boats of the United States" and from the Kolbenschlag and Riggs articles mentioned above. Some discrepancy exists among these sources as to the maximum speed of the MSB. I used the 14-knot speed found in Miller's article because his piece proved accurate in other verifiable instances and because his was the highest speed listed. I qualified the term, however, with the word "nominal," since some of the veterans I interviewed assured me that 14 knots were certainly "in name only."

Incidents involving the minesweepers were culled from the COMNAVFORV Monthly Historical Summaries.

The incidents involving MSBs 22, 32, 45, 49, and 51 were re-created from details provided in the after-action summaries included in the February 1967 COMNAVFORV Monthly Historical Summary. The concluding quote is also from that source.

Operation Monster

The principal source of information for this section was pages 141–142 of Swarztrauber's "River Patrol Relearned." Operational characteristics of the PACV were cross-checked with Miller's "Fighting Boats of the United States," and details of chronology and summary statistics were confirmed with the November COMNAVFORV Monthly Historical Summary.

Seawolves

The Swarztrauber article and two other *Proceedings* articles, "Navy Gunship Helicopters in the Mekong" by Dan Dodd and "The 'Seawolf' Helo Pilots of Vietnam" by A. E. Weseleskey, were the chief sources of material for the "Seawolves" chapter.

Black Ponies

The primary source for the "Black Ponies" chapter was a booklet put out by Light Attack Squadron Four (VAL-4) to explain the squadron's capabilities and functions to other allied forces in the Mekong Delta. All operational capabilities, tactics, and the squadron history were taken from this source. The Gamewardens of Vietnam organization (headquartered in Virginia Beach, Virginia) provided me with a copy.

The Kit Lavell quote was taken from Al Santoli's *Everything We Had*. Lavell's account, which appears on pages 134–141 of Santoli's work, was also helpful in understanding some of the tactics and flying conditions of the Black Ponies.

Sticking Out a Big Neck

I was privileged to interview James Eliott Williams for this chapter. Most of what appears in this chapter is derived from those interviews, as well as his Medal of Honor citation (available from several sources, including pages 228–230 of *The Congressional Medal of Honor Library)*, the October 1966 COMNAVFORV Monthly Historical Summary, and the Naval History Division's booklet *Riverine Warfare: The U.S. Navy's Operations on Inland Waters.*

Postscripts

The March 1968 *Hoi Chanh*'s observations were taken from page 35 of the Operations Evaluation Group's study *Game Warden.* The other *Hoi Chanh* information alluded to is found scattered throughout the COMNAVFORV Monthly Historical Summaries and is also discussed in Swarztrauber's "River Patrol Relearned." The first Swarztrauber quote was taken from page 151 of the article; the second quote was drawn from page 157.

The Swanson quote appears on page 394 of the transcript of his speech appearing in the June 1966 *Naval Engineers Journal.*

The quote from Godbehere's letter was taken directly from a letter he sent to Jere Beery, and which Beery was kind enough to let me use. Jere Beery's "philosophy" was quoted from a tape-recorded interview I conducted.

4. The Mobile Riverine Force

The Mobile Riverine Force has been written about more than the other coastal and riverine aspects of the war because of the joint service participation. Most useful of all the sources were William B. Fulton's monograph *Vietnam Studies: Riverine Operations 1966–1969* and W. C. Wells's article "The Riverine Force in Action, 1966–1967." These two sources did not always correspond, so some additional research was necessary to clarify the conflicts. Useful for this purpose were "Army Forces in Riverine Operations," by John W. Baker and Lee C. Dickson; Dan Dagle's "The Mobile Riverine Force, Vietnam"; Scott MacDonald's "Riverine Warfare: How Services Are Meeting the Delta Test"; Cecil B. Smyth's "United States Coastal and River Forces in Vietnam"; John B. Spore's "Floating Assault Force: Scourge of the Mekong Delta"; and Robert A. Weaver's "The Second Mobile Riverine Force: A Page from History." Three unpublished Department of the Army documents provided important details on specific operations as well as useful background material: they are Combat After Action Report—Operation River Raider I; Senior Officer Debriefing Report, IV Corps, August 1965–January 1968; and Senior Officer Debriefing Report, Commanding General, 9th Infantry Division, 1 June 1967–25 February 1968. An oral history interview of Julian J. Ewell was valuable along these same lines. Three pictorial works lent perspective: Robert D. Moeser's photographic essay *U.S. Navy: Vietnam; Riverine Assault Force TF-117* (a "cruise book" put together as a souvenir for the soldiers and sailors participating—similar to a high school yearbook); and Dan Dodd's "The Mobile Riverine Force." Information regarding the base at Dong Tam came from Edwin B. Hooper's *Mobility, Support, Endurance,* Edward J. Marolda's article on Dong Tam that appeared in Paolo Coletta's *United States Navy and Marine Corps Bases, Overseas,* and Richard Tregaskis's *Southeast Asia: Building the Bases.*

Adhesive Tape and the Padre

This chapter was based upon a series of interviews conducted with Charles L. Horowitz and Raymond W. Johnson; *Postmark: Mekong Delta,* by Johnson; a "Comment and Discussion" article by Horowitz; Johnson's and Horowitz's Navy Cross citations; and the COMNAVFORV Monthly Historical Summary.

The newspaper article read by Johnson is an excerpt of Robert Zimmerman's "Navy Out to Win New 'Seas.' "

The end-of-battle statistics were gathered from and cross-referenced with the June 1967 COMNAVFORV Monthly Historical Summary, Fulton's *Vietnam Studies: Riverine Operations 1966–69,* and Wells's "The Riverine Force in Action, 1966–1967."

Origins

This section is primarily a product of the Fulton monograph and the Wells article with (as previously mentioned) the discrepancies eliminated by consulting the other sources listed at the beginning of this discussion on Mobile Riverine Force sources.

The opening Westmoreland quote was taken from page 217 of his *A Soldier Reports*.

The details of the pre–Mobile Riverine Force situation in the Mekong Delta were taken from the sources already mentioned and also from Robert E. Mumford's "Jackstay: New Dimensions in Amphibious Warfare."

The Westmoreland quote attributing Captain Welch with the idea of using the delta waterways was taken from page 271 of General Westmoreland's *A Soldier Reports*.

The naming of Dong Tam and General Westmoreland's description of the base were taken from page 273 of his book.

The Major General O'Connor quote was found on page 7 of the Department of the Army's Senior Officer Debriefing Report for the 1 June 1967–25 February 1968 period.

The Flotilla

Dates, quantities, and operational characteristics for "The Flotilla" were gleaned from the Fulton monograph, the Wells article, Miller's "Fighting Boats of the United States," Robert R. Yohanan's "Joint Training for Inshore Naval Operations," "Fire Support in Riverine Operations" by Thomas H. Simpson and David La Boissiere, John B. Spore's "Floating Assault Force: Scourge of the Mekong Delta," and a Trip Report: Second Brigade, Ninth Infantry Division, dated 4 January 1968 (trip taken by Colonel George F. Hoge; report signed by Lieutenant Colonel Theodore S. Riggs, Jr., of the U.S. Army Combat Developments Command). The latter report is unpublished but available through the Defense Technical Information Center, Alexandria, Virginia.

The quote concerning the ASPB was taken from the December 1967 COMNAVFORV Monthly Historical Summary.

The quotes concerning the naming of the boats by their crews and the demonstration of Mobile Riverine Force argot were both taken from a newsletter dated 31 May 1967 sent home to the families of the Mobile Riverine Force sailors (a "family gram" in Navy jargon) by Commodore Wells. A copy was provided to me by Captain Horowitz.

The details of improved versions of Mobile Riverine Force craft arriving in 1968 were found on pages 115–116 of a "Comment and Discussion" article by Melville L. Stephens.

Operations

This section is a composite of information gained from COMNAVFORV Monthly Historical Summaries, Fulton's monograph, *Vietnam Studies: Riverine Operations 1966–1969,* and Wells's article, "The Riverine Force in Action." Also useful in sorting out ambiguities were *Riverine: A Pictorial History of the Brown Water War in Vietnam,* by Jim Mesko, and "United States Coastal and River Forces in Vietnam," by Cecil B. Smyth, Jr.

The details of Operation River Raider I, particularly the lessons learned from that operation, were obtained from the Army's combat after-action report dated 5 April 1968. This report is unpublished but is available from the Defense Technical Information Center.

Rear Admiral Veth's message sent at the conclusion of Operation Concordia I is quoted from the June 1967 COMNAVFORV Monthly Historical Summary.

The chief petty officer's comment about refueling from Army trucks was gleaned from my interviews with Captain Horowitz.

The quotation summarizing the battle in the Ba Rai Creek during Operation Coronado V was taken from the COMNAVFORV Monthly Historical Summary of September 1967. The "Dusty" Rhodes quotation is from the same source.

The Captain Salzer quote is from the supplement to the January 1968 COMNAVFORV Monthly Historical Summary.

The quote concerning the number of Viet Cong killed and captured during the Tet Offensive is from page 154 of *Tet!* by Don Oberdorfer.

Nearly everything written about the Mobile Riverine Force maintains that General Westmoreland credited the Mobile Riverine Force with having saved the major cities of the delta, yet I have been unable to find the primary source of this statement. I alluded to this attribution but did not quote Westmoreland directly because of the lack of confirmation.

Postscripts

The Westmoreland quote is from page 274 of the general's *A Soldier Reports.*

5. Task Force Clearwater

Interviews with Admiral Swarztrauber supplemented the material in his "River Patrol Relearned" article to make up the bulk of "Task Force Clearwater." "Psychological Operations in Vietnam" by Reiling and Scott, and "Behind the Headlines in Viet Nam" by Peter T. White, supplied details on psychological operations and I Corps geography, respectively. The COMNAVFORV Monthly Historical Summaries were also useful in reconstructing the complete history of this task force.

The October 1967 COMNAVFORV Monthly Historical Summary supplied the quoted analysis of Operation Green Wave.

The Schreadley quote that ends the "Perfume and Cua Viet" section is from page 197 of his "The Naval War in Vietnam."

6. SEA LORDS

Interviews with Admirals Zumwalt, Salzer, and Price; Naval Institute oral history interviews with Admirals Felt, Price, and Salzer and Captains Kerr and Glenn; and the articles "SEA LORDS," "Nothing to Report': A Day on the Vam Co Tay," and "Swift Raiders," all by R. L. Schreadley, were the principal sources for "SEA LORDS." In addition to their consenting to be interviewed, Admirals Zumwalt, Salzer, and Price were kind enough to read and correct applicable portions of this part of the book.

ZWI

The aforementioned sources were useful in preparing this chapter. The Salzer, Kerr, and Glenn oral histories were particularly helpful, as were Admiral Zumwalt's *On Watch* (pages 35–42), Tidman's *Operations Evaluation Group,* and Marolda and Price's *A Short History of the United STates Navy and the Southeast Asian Conflict 1950–1975.*

Human interest details, such as Admiral Zumwalt's sitting

upon his flak jacket, were drawn from the oral histories and interviews.

The specific numbers of craft in the naval forces were extracted from the COMNAVFORV Monthly Historical Summaries, which provide statistical summaries of this nature each month.

"Bernique's Creek"

All attempts to locate Michael Bernique failed, so the "Bernique's Creek" chapter is based upon accounts included in Schreadley's "SEA LORDS" article, the COMNAVFORV summaries, the interviews with Admirals Zumwalt and Salzer, and Captain Kerr's oral history.

The early Schreadley quote is from page 25 of his "SEA LORDS" article, and the early Salzer quote was taken from pages 485–486 of the transcript of the Salzer oral history conducted and held by the Naval Institute.

The quote attributed to Bernique (referring to Sihanouk as a "lying son-of-a-bitch") is from page 101 of the transcript of Captain Kerr's oral history interview number one, held by the Naval Institute. Admiral Zumwalt's description of Bernique as "the kind of captain we need more of" and his quoted principle of "getting away with almost anything once or twice" were provided by the admiral himself during an interview with me.

Giant Slingshot and Barrier Reef

An unpublished but very useful source of information for the Giant Slingshot and Barrier Reef operations was a historical paper put together by Arie C. A. Sigmond and his staff, presumably while serving on the COMNAVFORV staff. This document is available at the Naval Historical Center in Washington, D.C.

Details of the advanced tactical support bases were found in Robert C. Powers's "Beans and Bullets for Sea Lords," and the quoted description of the Go Dau Ha ATSB was taken from pages 96 and 97 of that article.

The message sent by Captain Price is quoted from the December 1968 COMNAVFORV Monthly Historical Summary.

The details of actions, captured materials, and casualties were also drawn and compiled from this and other COM-NAVFORV summaries. Tactics were taken from the oral histories previously mentioned, the Sigmond document, various COMNAVFORV Monthly Historical Summaries, and Butler's *River of Death*.

The terms ENIFF, FRIFF, ENENG, and FRENG are explained on pages 11 and 12 of the Sigmond document.

Evenings in Vietnam

"Evenings in Vietnam" was taken almost entirely from the COMNAVFORV summaries. Some details of the first incident were obtained from Schreadley's "The Naval War in Vietnam" (both the published and the unpublished versions).

Penetrations

The published and unpublished versions of Schreadley's "The Naval War in Vietnam" provided a great deal of information cornering the penetrations into VC territory by Sea Float/Solid Anchor and Breezy Cove. The descriptions of Sea Tiger and Blue Shark were taken from the COMNAVFORV Monthly Historical Summaries. The "flying RBR" incidents are described in the unpublished version of Schreadley's "The Naval War in Vietnam."

The two Zumwalt quotes are both taken from page 39 of his book *On Watch*.

The COMNAVFORV message prescribing the Breezy Cove operation is quoted from the September 1969 COM-NAVFORV Monthly Historical Summary.

A copy of the message from "CTF ONE ONE FIVE" was provided to me by Dennis O'Mara, who has kept it among his personal memorabilia.

Contrasts

The "Contrasts" section was the result of numerous interviews with Virgil Chambers and Richard O'Mara, with some supplementary information provided by Schreadley's "Swift Raiders" article.

Postscripts

The Felt, Kerr, and Glenn oral histories were used significantly for the "Postscripts" section. The information on John Kerry came from Thomas D. Boettcher's *Vietnam: The Valor and the Sorrow,* Christopher Lydon's "Here We Come: The Kerry Charge," and a corroborative telephone call to the senator's Washington office. Dates and reorganization information were drawn from the COMNAVFORV Monthly Historical Summaries.

The Kerr quote is from page 77 of the oral history he provided to the Naval Institute.

The Quincy Truett quote was given to me during an interview with his widow, Geri Truett.

The note concerning Admiral Zumwalt's efforts at having ships named for Lieutenant Commanders Elliott and Peterson was supplied by Admiral Zumwalt himself.

The Admiral Salzer quote is taken from a letter that he very kindly took the time to write to me to help in the preparation of this book.

7. Exodus

Advisors Again

"Advisors Again" drew upon portions of *Changing Interpretations and New Sources in Naval History,* edited by Robert William Love, Jr.; Tom Rainwater's "Coastal Group Advisor"; Allan P. Slaff's "Naval Advisor Vietnam"; and an article (no author credited) appearing in *Our Navy* entitled "Junk Advisors—Men of Many Talents."

The Harris quote was taken directly from a letter he sent to me, dated 12 September 1984. The quote concerning Junk Force advisors is from page 22 of the uncredited *Our Navy* article entitled "Junk Advisors—Men of Many Talents."

ACTOV

The account of the briefing for General Abrams was re-created from the Glenn and Kerr oral histories and from interviews with Admiral Zumwalt. The closing quote about the ACTOV program being closest to Zumwalt's heart is taken from page 40 of his book *On Watch*.

The details of the ACTOV program were compiled through research into the various COMNAVFORV Monthly Historical Summaries for the period, Schreadley's published and unpublished versions of "The Naval War in Vietnam," Tidman's *Operations Evaluation Group*, Jack M. White's article "ACTOV—The U.S. Navy's Accelerated Turnover Program," and an article (no author credited) entitled "Navy's ACTOV Plan Nearing Completion" that appeared in a naval advisors' newspaper published in Saigon.

The incident involving the burly lieutenant in the Personal Response Program was taken from my own experience.

The Zumwalt message concerning the standard of living of Vietnamese armed forces personnel appeared in the COMNAVFORV Monthly Historical Summary for January 1970. The later Zumwalt quote appealing to his force for program acceleration was taken from the same message.

The statistics concerning base and vessel turnovers were compiled from the COMNAVFORV Monthly Historical Summaries.

The Incursion

The extensive quote that opens this section is drawn from pages 4 and 5 of the "Forged Under Fire" article by Bill Green.

The rest of the material for this chapter was derived from the COMNAVFORV Monthly Historical Summaries for May and June 1970 and from George W. Ashworth's "South Vietnamese Navy Wins Its Spurs in Cambodia." The Rear Admiral Matthews quote appeared in the May 1970 COMNAVFORV Monthly Historical Summary, as did the closing quote.

SCATTOR

The two sources for "SCATTOR" were Schreadley's unpublished "The Naval War in Vietnam" and Tulich's monograph "The United States Coast Guard in South East Asia During the Vietnam Conflict."

SOURCE NOTES
Postscripts

The acknowledged quote in the beginning of the "Postscripts" section is from a COMNAVFORV letter held in the Operational Archives section of the Naval Historical Center.

The Real War by Richard Nixon and *Strategy for Defeat* by U. S. G. Sharp were useful in reconstructing the events leading to the demise of South Vietnam. The quoted section of the law concerning the cut-off of funds was taken from page 263 of Sharp's book.

Epilogue

The epilogue, while based on the experience of one particular veteran, is not attributed to any individual because it represents the feelings of countless military men who served in the rivers and coastal waters of Vietnam.

BIBLIOGRAPHY

Books

Blackman, Raymond V. B., ed. *Jane's Fighting Ships 1968–69.* London: B.P.C. Publishing, 1969.

Boettcher, Thomas D. *Vietnam: The Valor and the Sorrow.* Boston: Little, Brown, 1985.

Butler, James. *River of Death: Song Vam Sat.* Reseda, CA: Mojave Books, 1979.

Coletta, Paolo E. *United States Navy and Marine Corps Bases, Overseas.* Westport, CT: Greenwood Press, 1985.

The Congressional Medal of Honor Library: Vietnam, the Names, the Deeds. New York: Dell, 1986.

Croizat, Victor. *The Brown Water Navy: The River and Coastal War in Indo-China and Vietnam, 1948–1972.* Dorset, England: Blandford Press, 1984.

Currey, Cecil B. ("Cincinnatus"). *Self-Destruction: The Disintegration and Decay of the United States Army During the Vietnam Era.* New York: W. W. Norton, 1981.

Dictionary of American Naval Fighting Ships. Washington, DC: Naval Historical Center, Department of the Navy, 1976.

Doan Bich and Le Trang. *Saigon in the Flesh.* Saigon: Le Trang Publishing House, 1965.

Fall, Bernard B. *Street Without Joy.* New York: Schocken Books, 1972.

Fulton, William B. *Vietnam Studies: Riverine Operations 1966–1969.* Washington, DC: Department of the Army, 1973.

Gettleman, Marvin E. *Vietnam: History, Documents, and Opinions.* New York: New American Library, 1970.

Grey, Anthony. *Saigon.* Boston: Little, Brown, 1982.

BIBLIOGRAPHY

Harvey, Frank. *Air War—Vietnam*. New York: Bantam, 1967.

Hickey, Gerald Cannon. *Village in Vietnam*. New Haven, CT: Yale University Press, 1964.

Hooper, Edwin Bickford. *Mobility, Support, Endurance: A Story of Naval Operational Logistics in the Vietnam War, 1965–1968*. Washington, DC: Naval Historical Center, Department of the Navy, 1972.

———, Dean C. Allard, and Oscar P. Fitzgerald. *The United States Navy and the Vietnam Conflict*. Vol. 1, *The Setting of the Stage to 1959*. Washington, DC: Naval Historical Center, Department of the Navy, 1976.

Hughes, John Emmet. *The Ordeal of Power*. New York: Dell, 1962.

Johnson, Lyndon Baines. *The Vantage Point: Perspectives of the Presidency, 1963–1969*. New York: Popular Library, 1971.

Johnson, Raymond W. *Postmark: Mekong Delta*. Westwood, NJ: Fleming H. Revell, 1968.

Karnow, Stanley. *Vietnam: A History*. New York: Viking Press, 1983.

Lewy, Guenter. *America in Vietnam*. New York: Oxford University Press, 1978.

Love, Robert William, Jr., ed. *Changing Interpretations and New Sources in Naval History*. New York: Garland Publishing, 1980.

Luce, Don and John Sommer. *Viet Nam: The Unheard Voices*. Ithaca, NY: Cornell University Press, 1969.

Marolda, Edward J., and G. Wesley Price III. *A Short History of the United States Navy and the Southeast Asian Conflict 1950–1975*. Washington, DC: Naval Historical Center, Department of the Navy, 1984.

Mersky, Peter B., and Norman Polmar. *The Naval Air War in Vietnam*. Baltimore, MD: Nautical and Aviation Publishing Company of America, 1981.

Mesko, Jim. *Riverine: A Pictorial History of the Brown Water War in Vietnam*. Carrollton, TX: Squadron/Signal Publications, 1985.

Millett, Allan R., and Peter Maslowski. *For the Common Defense: A Military History of the United States of America*. New York: Free Press, 1984.

Moeser, Robert D. *U.S. Navy: Vietnam*. Annapolis, MD: U.S. Naval Institute, 1969.

Naval and Maritime Chronology 1961–1971. Annapolis, MD: Naval Institute Press, 1973.

BIBLIOGRAPHY

Nixon, Richard. *The Real War*. New York: Warner, 1981.

Oberdorfer, Don. *Tet!: The Turning Point in the Vietnam War*. Garden City, NY: Doubleday, 1971.

O'Neill, Robert J. *General Giap: Politician and Strategist*. New York: Praeger, 1969.

Page, Tim. *Tim Page's Nam*. New York: Alfred A. Knopf, 1983.

Palmer, Bruce, Jr. *The 25-Year War: America's Military Role in Vietnam*. Lexington, KY: The University Press of Kentucky, 1984.

Palmer, Dave Richard. *Summons of the Trumpet: U.S.—Vietnam in Perspective*. Novato, CA: Presidio Press, 1978.

Porter, Gareth, ed. *Vietnam: A History in Documents*. New York: New American Library, 1979.

Reed, Rowena. *Combined Operations in the Civil War*. Annapolis, MD: Naval Institute Press, 1978.

Riverine Assault Force TF-117 ("Cruise Book"). Tokyo: Daito Art Printing Company, November 1967.

Riverine Warfare: The U.S. Navy's Operations on Inland Waters. Rev. ed. Washington, DC: Naval Historical Center, Navy Department, 1969.

Rowe, John S., and Samuel L. Morison. *The Ships and Aircraft of the U.S. Fleet*. Annapolis, MD: Naval Institute Press, 1972.

Santoli, Al. *Everything We Had: An Oral History of the Vietnam War by Thirty-Three American Soldiers Who Fought It*. New York: Ballantine Books, 1982.

Schwarz, Urs. *John F. Kennedy: 1917–1963*. London: Paul Hamlyn, 1964.

Sharp, U. S. G. *Strategy for Defeat: Vietnam in Retrospect*. Novato, CA: Presidio Press, 1978.

Sheehan, Neil, *et al. The Pentagon Papers*. New York: Bantam, 1971.

Smith, Harvey H., Donald W. Bernier, Frederica M. Bunge, Frances Chadwick Rintz, Rinn-Sup Shinn, and Suzanne Teleki. *Area Handbook for South Vietnam*. Department of the Army Pamphlet No. 550-55. Washington, DC: Department of the Army, 1967.

Spector, Ronald H. *The U.S. Army in Vietnam*. Vol. 1, *Advice and Support: The Early Years, 1941-60*. Washington, DC: U.S. Army Center of Military History, 1983.

Summers, Harry G., Jr. *On Strategy: A Critical Analysis of the Vietnam War*. Novato, CA: Presidio Press, 1982.

BIBLIOGRAPHY

Sweetman, Jack. *American Naval History: An Illustrated Chronology of the U.S. Navy and Marine Corps 1775–Present*. Annapolis, MD: Naval Institute Press, 1984.

Tidman, Keith R. *The Operations Evaluation Group: A History of Naval Operations Analysis*. Annapolis, MD: Naval Institute Press, 1984.

Tregaskis, Richard. *Vietnam Diary*. New York: Popular Library, 1963.

Tregaskis, Richard. *Southeast Asia: Building the Bases*. Department of the Navy. Washington, DC: 1975.

Tuchman, Barbara W. *A Distant Mirror: The Calamitous Fourteenth Century*. New York: Alfred A. Knopf, 1978.

U.S. Department of State, Office of Media Services. *Aggression from the North: The Record of North Viet-Nam's Campaign to Conquer South Viet-Nam*. Washington, DC: U.S. Government Printing Office, 1965.

Westmoreland, William C. *A Soldier Reports*. New York: Doubleday, 1976.

Zumwalt, Elmo R., Jr. *On Watch*. New York: Quadrangle/The New York Times Book Company, 1976.

Articles

Ashworth, George W. "South Vietnamese Navy Wins Its Spurs in Cambodia." *Navy Magazine*, July–August 1970, 33–37.

Bachmann, Richard G. "Harbor Defense in Vietnam." *U.S. Naval Institute Proceedings*, September 1968, 136–137.

Baker, John W., and Lee C. Dickson. "Army Forces in Riverine Operations." *Military Review*, August 1967, 64–74.

Baldwin, Hanson W. " 'Spitkits' in Tropic Seas." *Shipmate*, August–September 1966, 8–12.

Brown, Richard F. "Role of the Junk Fleet Advisor in Base Defense." *U.S. Naval Institute Proceedings*, October 1968, 128–131.

Bucklew, Phil H. "Navy Small Craft in Market Time." *Naval Engineers Journal*, June 1966, 395–402.

Chapelle, Dickey. "Water War in Viet Nam." *National Geographic*, February 1966, 270–296.

Cobb, Boughton. "River Patrol Boat for Vietnam." *Yachting*, December 1966, 65, 99–102.

BIBLIOGRAPHY

Dagle, Dan. "The Mobile Riverine Force, Vietnam." *U.S. Naval Institute Proceedings*, January 1969, 126–128.

Dean, Paul. "MacLeod's Navy Has Tough Patrol." *Indianapolis Star*, 14 October 1965.

———. "Average Guy Dies Thousand Deaths While with MacLeod's Navy." *Indianapolis Star*, 15 October 1965.

———. "Navy Gunship Helicopters in the Mekong." (Pictorial.) *U.S. Naval Institute Proceedings*, May 1968, 91–104.

Dodd, Dan. "The Mobile Riverine Force." (Pictorial.) *U.S. Naval Institute Proceedings*, June 1969, 80–95.

Ebersole, J.F. "Skimmer Ops." *U.S. Naval Institute Proceedings*, July 1974, 40–46.

Emery, Thomas R. M. "River Power," *U.S. Naval Institute Proceedings*, August 1970, 117–121.

Garrett, W. E. "What Was a Woman Doing There?" *National Geographic*, February 1966, 270–271.

Green, Bill. "Forged Under Fire." *Surface Warfare*, November 1980, 2–7.

Harris, William R. "Market Time Mother Ship." *U.S. Naval Institute Proceedings*, December 1966, 148–151.

Hodgman, James A. "Market Time in the Gulf of Thailand." *Naval Review*, 1968, 36–67.

Horowitz, C. L. "Comment and Discussion." *U.S. Naval Institute Proceedings*, November 1969, 116–189.

Jones, John E. "Vietnam Junk Force on Patrol." *All Hands*, September 1964, 6–8.

"Junk Advisors—Men of Many Talents." *Our Navy*, November 1970, 22–23.

Kaplan, H. R. "The Coast Guard in Viet Nam." *Navy Magazine*, June 1966, 24–27.

———. "Coast Guard Played Vital Role in Viet War." *Navy Magazine*, November 1970, 31–34.

Kolbenschlag, George R. "Minesweeping on the Long Tau River." *U.S. Naval Institute Proceedings*, June 1967, 88–102.

Lydon, Christopher. "Here We Come: The Kerry Charge." *VVA Veteran*, January 1985, 12–14.

MacDonald, Scott. "Riverine Warfare: How Services Are Meeting the Delta Test." *Armed Forces Management*, July 1968, 42–46.

Miller, Richards T. "Fighting Boats of the United States." *Naval Review*, 1968, 297–329.

BIBLIOGRAPHY

Moore, Thomas L. "U.S.—Viet Nam Anti-Smuggling Patrol." *Navy Magazine*, August 1965, 22–25.

———, and Jean C. Cote. "Duty: Coastal Surveillance." *All Hands*, September 1965, 20–22.

Moredock, W. J. "The DER in Market Time." *U.S. Naval Institute Proceedings*, February 1967, 136–138.

Mumford, Robert E., Jr. "Jackstay: New Dimensions in Amphibious Warfare." *Naval Review*, 1968, 68–87.

"Navy's ACTOV Plan Nearing Completion." *Hai Quan* (Naval Forces Vietnam Newspaper), 24 November 1971, 4.

Noble, Dennis L. "Cutters and Sampans." *U.S. Naval Institute Proceedings*, June 1984, 46–53.

Powers, Robert C. "Beans and Bullets for Sea Lords." *U.S. Naval Institute Proceedings*, December 1970, 95–97.

Rainwater, Tom. "Coastal Group Advisor." *Navy Magazine*, December 1971, 39–40.

Reiling, Victor G., and G. W. Scott. "Psychological Operations in Vietnam." *U.S. Naval Institute Proceedings*, July 1968, 122–126.

Riggs, Jerry. "U.S. Minesweeping Boats Keep Clear the River to Saigon." *Navy Magazine*, May 1967, 15–18.

Schreadley, Richard L. "SEA LORDS." *U.S. Naval Institute Proceedings*, August 1970, 22–31.

———. " 'Nothing to Report': A Day on the Vam Co Tay." *U.S. Naval Institute Proceedings*, December 1970, 23–27.

———. "The Naval War in Vietnam 1950–1970." *Naval Review*, 1971, 180–209.

———. "Swift Raiders." *U.S. Naval Institute Proceedings*, June 1984, 53–56.

Simpson, Thomas H., and David La Boissiere. "Fire Support in Riverine Operations." *Marine Corps Gazette*, August 1969, 43–47.

Slaff, Allan P. "Naval Advisor Vietnam." *U.S. Naval Institute Proceedings*, April 1969, 38–44.

Smith, Albert C. "Rung Sat Special Zone, Vietnam's Mekong Delta." *U.S. Naval Institute Proceedings*, April 1968, 116–121.

Smyth, Cecil B., Jr. "United States Coastal and River Forces in Vietnam." *Trading Post*, October–December 1983, 2–16.

Spore, John B. "Floating Assault Force: Scourge of the Mekong Delta." *Army*, February 1968, 28–32.

BIBLIOGRAPHY

Stephan, Charles R. "Trawler!" *U.S. Naval Institute Proceedings*, September 1968, 60–71.

Stephens, Melville L. "Comment and Discussion." *U.S. Naval Institute Proceedings*, November 1969, 115–116.

Storck, T. S. "PBRs Thwart Viet Cong on Delta Waterways." *Our Navy*, April 1968, 38–39.

Swanson, Leroy V. "Market Time-Game Warden: The Navy in Vietnam." *Naval Engineers Journal*, June 1966, 391–394.

Swarztrauber, S. A. "River Patrol Relearned." *Naval Review*, 1970, 120–157.

Tuohy, William. "America's Strangest Fleet." *True*, February 1966, 38–40, 69–71.

Wainwright, Loudon. "In Search of a Vietnam Hero." *Life*, 26 May 1965.

Weaver, Robert A. "The Second Mobile Riverine Force: A Page from History." *Journal of the Council on Abandoned Military Posts*, January 1981, 3–10.

Wells, W. C. "The Riverine Force in Action, 1966–1967." *Naval Review*, 1969, 46–83.

Weseleskey, A. E. "The 'Seawolf' Helo Pilots of Vietnam." *U.S. Naval Institute Proceedings*, May 1968, 128–130.

White, Jack M. "ACTOV—The U.S. Navy's Accelerated Turnover Program." *U.S. Naval Institute Proceedings*, February 1970, 112–113.

White, Peter T. "Behind the Headlines in Viet Nam." *National Geographic*, February 1967, 149–193.

———. "The Mekong: River of Terror and Hope." *National Geographic*, December 1968, 737–787.

Wright, D. F. "Those 'Innocent Looking' Vietnamese Junks." *Navy Magazine*, September 1966, 14–17.

Yohanan, Robert R. "Joint Training for Inshore Naval Operations." *U.S. Naval Institute Proceedings*, March 1968, 130–132.

Zimmerman, Robert. "Navy Out to Win New 'Seas.'" *San Diego Union*, 30 May 1967.

BIBLIOGRAPHY

Unpublished Documents

Barney, Eugene. Personal log, 13 January–16 March 1965.

The BDM Corporation. *A Study of Strategic Lessons Learned in Vietnam*. 9 vols. McLean, VA: BDM Corporation, 1979.

Bowler, Daniel R. Letter to author, 30 August 1984.

Champlin, L. L. "Operation Market Time: A Unique Mission for an Unusual Organization." A Commander Task Force 115 Press Release, Serial 09-65, dated 1 November 1968.

Commander Task Force 116 Operation Order (COMRIVPATFOR No. 201-YR), Can Tho, Vietnam, 1 February 1967.

Defense Technical Information Center. "DTIC Report Bibliography" (Search Control No. BQM44E). Alexandria, VA, October 1984.

Department of the Army. Combat After Action Report—Operation River Raider I. 5 April 1968.

———. Senior Officer Debriefing Report, Commanding General, 9th Infantry Division, USARV, 1 June 1967–25 February 1968.

———. Senior Officer Debriefing Report, IV Corps, Republic of Vietnam, August 1965–January 1968.

———. Trip Report: Second Brigade, Ninth Infantry Division. U.S. Army Combat Developments Group, 4 January 1968.

Harris, Stewart M. Letter to author, 12 September 1984.

Light Attack Squadron Four (VAL-4). "OV-10A 'Bronco' Fact Sheet." August 1969.

Meyerkord, Harold Dale. Personal log, 4 July 1964–16 March 1965. Washington, DC: Naval Historical Center.

Naval Historical Center, Department of the Navy, Washington, DC. Chief of the Naval Advisory Group: Monthly Historical Summaries, 1964–65.

———. Commander Naval Forces Vietnam letter 5000, serial 0039: Status of Vietnamization Upon Withdrawal of U.S. Naval Forces, 13 April 1973.

———. Commander Naval Forces Vietnam: Monthly Historical Summaries and Supplements, 1966–1973.

———. Report of Recommendations Pertaining to Infiltration into South Vietnam of Viet Cong Personnel, Supporting Materials, Weapons, and Ammunition ("The Bucklew Report"). Phil H. Bucklew, 15 February 1964.

———. Personal log of Lieutenant Harold Dale Meyerkord, USN, 1964–1965.

BIBLIOGRAPHY

The Operations Evaluation Group of the Center for Naval Analyses. *Game Warden.* Arlington, VA: Center for Naval Analyses, 1976.

Schreadley, Richard L. "The Naval War in Vietnam." Saigon: Commander Naval Forces Vietnam, 1 May 1970.

Sheets, J. D. "My Job Is Sorting Out Sampans—and It's Tough." A Commander Naval Forces Vietnam News Release dated 12 September 1968.

Sigmond, Arie C. A. "Operation 'Giant Slingshot.' " Prepared by Sigmond and members of his staff while serving with Commander Naval Forces, Vietnam. No date provided.

Tulich, Eugene N. "The United States Coast Guard in South East Asia During the Vietnam Conflict." Washington, DC: U.S. Coast Guard Historical Monograph Program, 1975.

Wells, Wade C. Newsletter sent to families of River Assault Flotilla One. Commander River Assault Flotilla One, 31 May 1967.

Oral Histories

Bucklew, Phil H. (Captain, USN, Retired). Interview by John T. Mason, 29 May 1980. Tape recording and transcript. U.S. Naval Institute Oral History Program, Annapolis, MD.

Ewell, Julian J. (Lieutenant General, USA). Interview conducted by Robert Crowley and Norman M. Bissel, 10 April 1979. Tape recording and transcript. U.S. Army Military History Institute, Carlisle Barracks, PA.

Felt, Harry D. (Admiral, USN, Retired). Interview by John T. Mason, 12 March 1972. Tape recording and transcript. U.S. Naval Institute Oral History Program, Annapolis, MD.

Glenn, W. Lewis, Jr. (Captain, USN, Retired). Interview by Paul Stillwell, 16 May 1984. Tape recording and transcript. U.S. Naval Institute Oral History Program, Annapolis, MD.

Ismay, Arthur (Commander, USN). Interview by D. C. Allard *et al.*, 6 June 1967. Tape recording and transcript. Naval Historical Center, Washington, DC.

Kerr, Howard J. (Captain, USN, Retired). Interview by Paul Stillwell, 22 September 1982. Tape recording and transcript. U.S. Naval Institute Oral History Program, Annapolis, MD.

McElroy, Ross (Lieutenant, USN). Interview by staff of Naval Historical Center, date uncertain. Tape recording only. Naval Historical Center, Washington, DC.

Price, Arthur W., Jr. (Rear Admiral, USN, Retired). Interview by Etta Belle Kitchen, 15 May 1970. Tape recording and transcript. U.S. Naval Institute Oral History Program, Annapolis, MD.

Salzer, Robert S. (Vice Admiral, USN, Retired). Interview by John T. Mason, 19 July 1977. Tape recording and transcript. U.S. Naval Institure Oral History Program, Annapolis, MD.

Stewart, W. H. (Commander, USCG, at time of interview; current status unknown). Narrative transcribed from tape included in Coast Guard Vietnam files borrowed by Naval Historical Center for duplication in March 1969.

Thoai, Ho Van Ky (Commodore, Vietnamese Navy). Interview by Oscar P. Fitzgerald, 20 September 1975. Tape recording and transcript. Naval Historical Center, Washington, DC.

Interviews by Author

Barney, Eugene (Master Chief Petty Officer, U.S. Navy, Retired)
Beery, Jere (Former Petty Officer, U.S. Navy)
Bonfanti, Jane (Formerly Mrs. Harold D. Meyerkord)
Chambers, Virgil (Former Petty Officer, U.S. Navy)
Childress, G. H. (Lieutenant, U.S. Navy, Retired)
Dean, Paul (*Los Angeles Times*)
Dunn, Gillam (Lieutenant, U.S. Navy, Retired)
Godbehere, Richard G. (Lieutenant Commander, U.S. Navy, Retired)
Hardcastle, Mary (Wife of Captain W. H. Hardcastle)
Hardcastle, William H. (Captain, U.S. Navy, Retired)
Hargrave, J. B. (J. B. Hargrave, Naval Architects, Inc.)
Horowitz, Charles L. (Captain, U.S. Navy, Retired)
Joest, Fred (Naval Sea Systems Command)
Johnson, Raymond (Commander, Chaplain Corps, U.S. Naval Reserve)
McGowen, Sea (Naval Sea Systems Command)
MacLeod, Kenneth L. (Former Lieutenant, U.S. Navy)
Meyerkord, Louise (Mother of Dale Meyerkord)
O'Mara, Richard (Former Petty Officer, U.S. Navy)
Phillips, Sarah (Hatteras Yachts)

BIBLIOGRAPHY

Price, Arthur W., Jr. (Rear Admiral, U.S. Navy, Retired)
Salzer, Robert S. (Vice Admiral, U.S. Navy, Retired)
Swarztrauber, S. A. (Rear Admiral, U.S. Navy, Retired)
Truett, Geri (Widow of Quincy Truett)
Vincent, James Monroe (Lieutenant Commander, U.S. Navy, Retired)
Williams, James Elliott (Chief Petty Officer, U.S. Navy, Retired)
Zumwalt, Elmo R., Jr. (Admiral, U.S. Navy, Retired)

Index

Abrams, Creighton, 239, 240, 253, 273, 302, 303, 304, 307

Accelerated Turnover to the Vietnamese. *See* ACTOV

ACTOV, 227, 302–09, 312, 313, 314, 316, 317

Advisors, 302, 305, 307, 308; number of, 11, 16, 21; early commitment of, 17; number allowed by Geneva Accords, 17; on combat operations, 18–19; recommended by Taylor, Rusk, and McNamara, 20–21; missions of, 23–24; difficulties encountered by, 24–26; living conditions of, 26; methods used, 26–27; to VNN Junk Force, 28; recognize value of *Dinassaut*, 41; to VNN RAGs, 42; U.S. Army, 49, 55, 159, 274; number increased, 67; Coastal Zone senior, 68; perception of VNN, 70; at Rach Gia, 86; defend base, 105; communications with, 137; senior, 141; on VNN minesweeper, 162; as part of Vietnamization, 301–17; in Cambodian incursions, 310–11; during Easter Offensive, 316; mention, 65, 127, 139, 172

Aircraft: A-1 Skyraider, 71; P-3 Orion, 71, 82; P-5 Marlin, 82; P-2 Neptune, 82–83, 104; squadrons in Market Time Patrol, 82; SP2H Neptune, 83; B-57 bomber, 99, 100; F-4C fighter, 99; Phantom, 100; Vulcan, 100; friendly attack, 101; search for lost PCF, 102; C-47, 106; flare ship, 112, 115; AC-47, 115; Black Ponies, 150, 170–74, 268, 275; Seawolf, 5, 7, 150, 155, 167–170, 171, 176, 177, 179, 180, 249, 255, 268–70, 274–75, 277; B-52, 165, 272; HC-1 detachments, 168; Helicopter Attack (Light) Squadron Three, 168–169; Helicopter Combat Support Squadron One, 168–69; UH-1B "Huey," 168; Light Attack Squadron Four, 170, 172; ordnance support, 199–200; CH-54 Sky Crane helicopters, 278

Air-cushioned vehicle. *See* Ships and craft (PACV)

375

ABOUT THE AUTHOR:
THOMAS J. CUTLER, a lieutenant commander in the U.S. Navy, teaches history at the Naval Academy, and serves as an associate editor of the U.S. Naval Institute's <u>Proceedings</u> magazine. Cutler served in Vietnam from January to December of 1972 as an in-country naval advisor to South Vietnamese forces. He also served on the staff of the chief of the U.S. Naval Advisory Group in Saigon. He earned the Navy Commendation and Achievement Medals, a Combat Action Ribbon, and campaign, service, and unit awards.